POLICING ISSUES

CHALLENGES AND CONTROVERSIES

Jeffrey Ian Ross, PhD

Associate Professor
School of Criminal Justice
College of Public Affairs
Research Fellow, Center for Comparative and International Law
2003 Distinguished Chair in Research
University of Baltimore
Baltimore, Maryland

D1599508

JONES & BARTLETT
LEARNING

World Headquarters

Jones & Bartlett Learning
40 Tall Pine Drive
Sudbury, MA 01776
978-443-5000
info@jblearning.com
www.jblearning.com

Jones & Bartlett Learning Canada
6339 Ormindale Way
Mississauga, Ontario L5V 1J2
Canada

Jones & Bartlett Learning International
Barb House, Barb Mews
London W6 7PA
United Kingdom

Jones & Bartlett Learning books and products are available through most bookstores and online booksellers. To contact Jones & Bartlett Learning directly, call 800-832-0034, fax 978-443-8000, or visit our website, www.jblearning.com.

Substantial discounts on bulk quantities of Jones & Bartlett Learning publications are available to corporations, professional associations, and other qualified organizations. For details and specific discount information, contact the special sales department at Jones & Bartlett Learning via the above contact information or send an email to specialsales@jblearning.com.

Production Credits
Publisher, Higher Education: Cathleen Sether
Acquisitions Editor: Sean Connelly
Editorial Assistant: Caitlin Murphy
Production Manager: Jenny L. Corriveau
Associate Marketing Manager: Lindsay White
Manufacturing and Inventory Control Supervisor: Amy Bacus
Cover Design: Scott Moden
Composition: Shepherd, Inc.
Cover Image: © Lane V. Erickson/ShutterStock, Inc.
Printing and Binding: Malloy, Inc.
Cover Printing: Malloy, Inc.

Library of Congress Cataloging-in-Publication Data
Ross, Jeffrey Ian.
  Policing issues : challenges and controversies / Jeffrey Ian Ross.
     p. cm.
  Includes bibliographical references and index.
  ISBN-13: 978-0-7637-7138-6 (pbk.)
  ISBN-10: 0-7637-7138-4 (pbk.)
  1. Police. 2. Police misconduct. 3. Police administration. I. Title.
  HV7921.R67 2012
  363.2—dc22
          2010038304

6048
Printed in the United States of America
15 14 13 12 11   10 9 8 7 6 5 4 3 2 1

Dedication

Dedicated to Roger Riendeau, mentor and friend

Contents

Preface   *vii*

Acknowledgments   *xvii*

About the Author   *xix*

Foreword   *xxi*

PART I: Introduction to Policing   1

1 Introduction to Policing   3

2 The History of Municipal Policing in the United States   23

3 The Mythology of Municipal Policing   41

PART II: Problems for Citizens and the Community   55

4 Emphasizing Public Relations over Crime Reduction   57

5 Failure to Properly Investigate Crime: Problems with the Detective Function   75

6 Improper Discretion   91

7 Inability to Significantly Reduce Crime: Problems with Patrol and Domestic Violence Arrests   105

8 Poor Police–Community Relations   115

9 Deviance and Corruption   131

10 Police Violence/Excessive Force   149

PART III: Problems for Police Officers and Administrators   177

11 Failure to Adopt and/or Properly Use New Technology   179

12 Inability to Properly Manage, Supervise, and Lead
    Police Organizations   193

13 Cooperation/Collaboration with Other Police Departments
    and Criminal Justice Agencies   209

14 Underfunding   221

15 Inadequate Wages and Compensation   231

16 Ineffective/Insufficient Recruitment, Education, and Training   243

17 Working Conditions   263

18 The Future of Municipal Policing   275

Answer Key for Multiple Choice Questions   *285*

Bibliography   *289*

Subject Index   *313*

Author Index   *331*

Preface

Reflective Statement

The average person is not likely to be too concerned about policing, but I am. The challenges of policing and law enforcement have intrigued me since adolescence. My interest in this topic led me to write my dissertation on the problem of police violence in New York City and Toronto (Ross, 1993). Shortly after this research, I went to work for the National Institute of Justice (NIJ, a division of the U.S. Department of Justice), where I worked for three years as a social science analyst, managing research grants connected to policing issues. I started in 1995, after Congress passed the Violent Crime Control and Law Enforcement Act (a.k.a. the "Crime Bill"). This legislation not only authorized funds for the employment of 100,000 officers to provide community policing services to U.S. jurisdictions, but also set aside money for policing research. As a social science analyst, I contributed to and coordinated the writing of requests for proposals, managed and monitored the peer review process, directed a team that conducted strategic planning around NIJ's policing research, and managed as many as 35 research grants. Almost all of them dealt with issues connected to community policing and police violence (Ross, 2000a).

Nevertheless, now that I have been teaching classes on policing for over 15 years, I have become increasingly motivated to identify the most important problems within this field as well as their solutions.

I am under the belief, misguided as it may seem, that this information will help us focus our efforts on meaningful reform. I am not alone. A veritable army of law enforcement experts who work in university settings, police colleges, and nonprofit organizations conduct research on policing. At any given time, police consultants, whether alone or as part of a team, are crisscrossing the country and sometimes traveling the world to provide all sorts of technical assistance and evaluations of police policies and practices. I'm also aware of the politically-charged atmosphere in which police reform exists, which can significantly affect meaningful efforts for change. Suggestions for change, even those based on sound empirical research methods, may be ignored because they rub politicians, practitioners, and the public the wrong way. Additionally, poorly researched programs may be funded and implemented simply because they have temporary political cache.

Why I Wrote This Book

I wrote this book because of the limitations I found within standard nuts-and-bolts texts on policing. Although most policing books used for introductory college and university courses provide an overview of the history and practices of policing and may make some effort to review the problems of policing in the United States, too often this field of study and practice is approached in an uncritical (i.e., politically conservative) fashion. This is understandable. Why?

Most research and writing on policing tend to reflect the language and special interests of the policing bureaucracy. After all, the government typically funds the studies. Therefore it sets the agenda, limits the parameters, and often decides if the final report will be widely distributed, used to inform policies and procedures, or be buried in a locked file cabinet.

One of the difficulties I found with most introductory textbooks is that they are too anecdotal either in the context of the book, and/or with numerous distracting exhibit boxes and photographs. Although their authors and editors might believe this approach enlivens and/or adds to the discussion or better holds students' attention, I think that it can equally give readers the impression that policing research is simply a collection of stories.

Regardless of whether the research is state-sponsored, foundation-sponsored, or self-funded, the methodology that many researchers use can often be faulted because it consists disproportionately of complicated statistical analyses. This typically means that investigators do not have to "get their hands dirty" by interacting with citizens, criminals, ex-cons, or police professionals to have a better contextual understanding of their subject matter and findings.

It must be noted that this book is not an anti-policing text, per se. Many police officers and administrators might consider some of my points within this book to be disturbing or objectionable. My prose might seem overly opinionated, ideological, and political. Some might think that I editorialize too much. I attribute these impressions to a number of factors, including a poor understanding of what constitutes an opinion in academic and pedagogical discourse, what the terms *ideology* and *politics* exactly mean, and what relationship ideology and politics have to policy and practice. I also point the finger at the socialization process imposed upon most policing professionals, as I believe it fosters a kind of tunnel vision, an us-versus-them mentality, and the view that anyone who criticizes policing simply has an axe to grind. Indeed, there are often large perceptual gaps among practitioners and scholars that make it seem as though they are operating in separate worlds.

On the other hand, many of my critical criminology colleagues may fault me for not taking a more radical stance. For example, this book does not advocate the abolishment of police.

Overview of the Book

When examining the profession and practice of policing, one is almost immediately struck and perhaps overwhelmed by the countless problems to be addressed. They are identified in numerous ways by different individuals and constituencies (e.g., experts, citizen groups, national policing organizations, the media).

This book systematically examines the problems associated with municipal policing in America. In an attempt to accomplish this goal, each chapter addresses a major difficulty identified by experts, observers, or consumers of policing services. It briefly reviews the history of these problems and, to the extent possible, the solutions that have been introduced and/or promoted to minimize or lessen its effects. These solutions are then objectively critiqued. There are 18 chapters in total, covering everything from the myths of policing to issues of recruitment and training.

Before introducing this material, it might be helpful to talk a little about how we might go about identifying the problems of policing.

How to Identify the Problems

In any given field, several different methods can be used to identify and judge the severity of a problem. Caution, however, must be exerted in this task. One must take into consideration who is doing the research, who is the audience (i.e., for what ends is the research conducted), and how the investigators are doing the research.

Who is doing the research? Investigators need to acknowledge who is conducting the evaluation as well as any biases that person(s) or organization(s) might bring to the research. For example, is the investigator an insider or an outsider? Insiders, those who work for the organization, may have considerable knowledge about the functioning of the agency, but they can suffer from undue bias. Outsiders, on the other hand, may not be sensitive to the internal dynamics of organizations and may end up missing important cues. Needless to say, it is very difficult for outsiders to gain access to organizations—and for good reason (Manning, 1985). These individuals could be anyone from suspicious reporters to researchers. It is possible that these people have an axe to grind and wish nothing more than to expose the underbelly of an organization. The goal here is to determine who has the appropriate knowledge, skills, and objectivity to best evaluate or analyze a program or organization.

Who is the audience? One must also take into account one's audience (i.e., who will read the information and who might make use of this information).

Depending on the end users, certain issues may be examined in greater detail than others, while other elements may be analyzed superficially. Readers and users vary considerably in their ability to understand the subject matter and attention spans.

What method(s) should be employed? The method investigators use to identify problems will naturally impact the findings (Welsh and Harris, 2004). Regardless, before any data is gathered, researchers need to perform a thorough review of the scholarly work (i.e., articles and books) in the field of policing. This method provides investigators with an idea of academics' perceptions of the most dominant problems and editors' and reviewers' judgments of which papers are the most worthy of journal publication. However, just because journal editors decide to publish an article on a specific topic does not mean that this issue is the most important for practitioners, citizens, or criminals; it could simply be a reflection of the kinds of manuscripts that have been submitted, the availability of space, or the current editor's (or editorial board's) predilections.

Additionally, in the social sciences, difficulties can typically be determined and examined at the micro or macro level—and at several levels of analysis in between, as well. Embedded within each level of analysis are a number of appropriate questions and data that can be collected, each with its own advantages and disadvantages.

Micro Level

The micro level typically examines problems at the individual or interactional level. Here we are typically talking about police officers. There are numerous ways that one can go about understanding and gathering data about the special challenges of policing at the micro level.

1. Conduct a survey of police officers and administrators. As simple as it sounds, this approach presents a whole host of problems, including the method through which it is achieved as well as access to the appropriate amount of resources necessary to properly and successfully complete one of these efforts. A modification of this approach is to conduct a Delphi Study (e.g., Tafoya, 1996). This involves a systematic procedure for using experts to inform us about the challenges that face policing and what solutions should be pursued. Since the team may not agree on the most important issues, a generally accepted protocol should be developed in order to resolve differences among the participants.

2. Examine complaints made by officers to their superiors or to their police associations. Keep in mind, however, that police officers are reluctant to complain through official channels. Likewise, this type of situation may contribute to learned helplessness or increased feelings of powerlessness. In turn, after numerous rejections, officers simply do not try to address their grievances. Additionally, officers' performances can be assessed

through activity reports or periodic personnel evaluations. In most organizations, this process is conducted at the very least on an annual basis. But this sort of bureaucratic information is typically superficial and sanitized. It generally does not go into enough detail for investigators to draw meaningful conclusions.

3. Gather anecdotal evidence or confirm evidence by interviewing sources, experts, or "key informants" such as citizens and criminals, police officers, administrators, and police scholars. The police officers and their direct administrators are probably the best sources to provide this kind of information because they are on the front lines every day. Preferred by journalists and ethnographic researchers, this method provides information that is typically current and rich in detail, but also potentially biased because it is difficult to judge the veracity of the information.

Nonetheless, sources have a human factor; they may lie, embellish, or forget critical material. Thus it is essential that several individuals from the same agency be consulted and observed over a sufficient period of time, because workers are often initially on their best behavior but have difficulty sustaining this demeanor. Alternatively, key personnel may be on vacation, on a leave of absence, or out sick. In addition, it is difficult for outsiders (i.e., researchers) to gain access to most police departments, and if access is granted, it is often limited and censored.

Meso Level

The meso level emphasizes the power of the organization (i.e., police agency), community, or specific region. Under this category we have the following types of studies:

1. Thoroughly review organizational performance indicators. One such example is the occurrence report. This document lists the various incidents that have occurred in a police jurisdiction over a period of time. These numbers include arrests, chases, firearm discharges, complaints, and personnel statistics. Additionally these statistics can be compared with those from previous days, weeks, months, or years to determine if things are improving, remaining the same, or worsening. Unfortunately, it is difficult for outsiders to gain access to this information. We also know how this type of reporting can be tainted, redirected, and/or biased. Thus, in the long run, these efforts may not be that useful in improving policing. Collecting data from this source is important, but it must be interpreted in an unbiased fashion.

2. Administer a survey of the public to determine such things as satisfaction with police services. This sample should include a broad constituency of individuals who have a strong interest and/or expertise in the field of incarceration (i.e., officers, administrators, citizens, and criminals). A popular method involving experts in the field is commonly referred to as a Delphi study and has been perfected in several branches of the criminal justice

system (e.g., Tafoya, 1986). Unfortunately, this method is like a snapshot in time and may not be useful for long-term planning.

3. Organize a series of community forums on policing and use this to gather information on police problems. The downside here is that these events tend to simply be opportunities for people to vent and are geographically confined to the region in which they are held. One way around these drawbacks is to hold public forums that have been carefully organized and that are held in different parts of the country.

Macro Level

The macro level typically looks at a problem from a societal level. This takes into consideration political and economic factors. Like micro level approaches, numerous methods may be used to determine specific problems for police, their administrators, and the public at large.

1. Gather the information from crime victims, either through the National Crime Victimization Study (NCVS) or some similar kind of study that includes complaints against police (e.g., Beral and Sisk, 1963; Regan, 1971; Box and Russell, 1975; Russell, 1976), administered by units like a citizens review bureau or board. Undoubtedly, this data would be a biased sample and would open only a small window into the world of policing.

2. Perform a content analysis of the mass or news media, such as television and/or radio news broadcasts as well as newspaper and magazine reporting, to see which policing-related issues are cited most frequently (e.g., Krippendorf, 1981). One could look at all stories on the police during a specific period. Although this will provide some insight with respect to the important issues, this approach will be biased. The drawback here is that these reports may simply be snapshots in time and could suffer from the same constraints as do scholarly journals.

3. Collect and analyze so-called social indicators (i.e., data on factors such as crime rates, victimization patterns, and incarceration rates) located in a variety of governmental sources such as the Uniform Crime Reports (UCR).

Finally, a number of research methods could be used, including quantitative methods, qualitative methods, and/or case studies. Ideally, one would employ an integrated methodological approach, thus increasing the number of sources and methodologies, which should lead us to a more accurate understanding of any problem.

A Satisficing Strategy

In the end, although each method and form of data has its advantages, almost all have disadvantages as well. Instead, combining all these methods and data sources may be the most useful and would come closest to achieving a balanced approach. To do this properly, however, researchers need adequate resources.

That being said, my original attempts to identify the "special" problems facing municipal policing were quite rudimentary. I began with a sample of convenience: students enrolled in my criminology/criminal justice classes. I asked them to list and rank in order the problems they believed were the most important facing municipal police in the United States.

As expected, the problems varied according to the identifying constituency: the police themselves, their administrators, government officials, or the public. Also, just because we have a list that ranks the order of the problems does not mean that we can simply take those topics and develop a logically coherent course or a text around them. Nevertheless, I used this information as a heuristic device to organize the subject matter of my undergraduate course and this text.

Thus, this effort deviates from a typical introduction to policing text because of its arrangement of topics and the focus it provides to students. This text, like the majority of research in this field, typically focuses on municipal policing.

One must take into consideration the unique circumstance of each city and its police department. Every police department cannot be reformed, improved, or changed in the same way. Just because a similar police agency changed in a positive way does not mean that all others can do so. Therefore, there must be a greater appreciation of context.

In addition to providing a traditional literature review, I observed, corresponded with, and/or interviewed numerous policing practitioners, experts, and scholars; visited several police departments; and went on those all-too-familiar voyeuristic ride-alongs, not only in the United States but elsewhere as well. I also contextualized the numerous problems (citing statistics where appropriate), and proposed what I believe are realistic solutions. Some of the problems—like too much red tape, a common complaint of all bureaucracies—were too ambiguous and not given much attention.

Solutions to Problems

Few of the proposed solutions are easy to implement, and all may lead to unintended consequences (e.g., Merton, 1936; Preston and Roots, 2004). In general, it might be easiest to achieve success at the institutional level (i.e., individual police department) rather than at the state or federal level of policing. There is also a realization that many problems seem to simply snowball; problems can be linked together and affect each other, and the population interviewed or surveyed may not be able to disentangle them.

It is also clear that the history of police reform is fraught with problems (Walker, 1977). Moreover, solutions to policing issues may be initiated by or may originate from several sources, including politicians, the state (especially policymakers), the private sector, religious bodies, police associations, and communities/citizens. Some of the solutions that specifically address problems regarding police officers and departments are intended to solve numerous types of issues. Finally, some of the more extreme suggestions—like the abolition of police—are not widely held and are perhaps impractical now.

Unintended Consequences. It must be understood that policing is ultimately a system in which each component has a part or role to play. As systems theory suggests, if you tinker with one aspect of the organization, it will have an effect somewhere else. It is like a domino effect, and the ripples are felt in many places that are often not immediately apparent or easy to distinguish. What do I mean by this statement? In simple terms, some of the solutions implemented by practitioners can and do have negative and unintended consequences that police planners failed to account for, no matter how sophisticated their original predictions were or how much they minimized the negative impact they might have. Granted, nothing in life is perfect. But some of the negative effects might be controlled. The challenge in proper criminal justice planning is to adequately predict and prepare for this possibility with contingency plans (Welsh and Harris, 2004).

Survey of End Users. Given that I do not have the kind of resources to conduct the more comprehensive kinds of studies, as previously mentioned, I survey my students nearly every semester and ask them to rank in order what they think are the most important problems facing the field. Not all the responses fit into distinct categories, but over the years, I have discovered a number of consistent themes. Indeed, the problems will not strike the reader as anything new, but the organization and rendering in this book should. Additionally, to the extent possible, the problems identified in each chapter are presented from least to most important in terms of how they affect policing. Certainly, there will be disagreements among police officers, administrators, policing experts, and citizens with respect to what they think are most important.

I believe that a textbook author's most important job is to contextualize things. Some may also question the utility of students' perceptions as an organizational tool, as many students have not yet been exposed to the realities of the criminal justice system. However, the reader should understand that my approach is meant to serve as a benchmark and a pedagogical starting point for discussing policing problems with students and not as an end in itself.

Problems for Police Officers, Citizens, and Criminals. One set of difficulties I've identified focuses on the problems for citizens and the other challenges encountered by police officers and administrators. It is with this knowledge that I organize my courses, lectures, and this book. As I have argued in my other books (Ross, 1995/2000, 2000c), although it is important to discuss problems (and, in general, most people are reasonably good at doing so), it is more important to propose and implement realistic solutions that address or solve these difficulties. The reader should also realize that some of the solutions proposed in one part of the book reappear frequently because they are capable of solving more than one difficulty.

Other Issues That Are Important to Readers of This Book

There are a handful of other issues that readers of this book should keep in mind. These matters include the importance of a social-justice approach to crime, criminals, victims, and criminal justice; the acknowledgement of the best-practices approach to organizational behavior; neglected subject matter; terminology; and the realization that policing is a global phenomenon.

The Relevance of Social Justice. Mention should be made of the social-justice (e.g., Arrigo, 1999) and restorative-justice approach (e.g., Braithwaite, 1989). Many observers of policing recognize the limitations with the current criminal justice system, particularly its emphasis on retributive justice and its inability to address the higher-order societal goals of human respect and dignity. That is why the criminal justice system and policing in particular should be working in this direction. To the extent possible, this book emphasizes these themes.

Best Practices. Another issue that should be addressed is the best practices approach. Over the past two decades, there has been a tendency in many policy circles to admire "what works" in institutional settings and quickly apply this from one agency to another and from one industry to another (e.g., private sector to nonprofit). Supporters of this strategy often fail to recognize that, given the diversity of agencies, it is not as simple as it might appear to transfer methods from one setting to another, without much consideration of context. It is short-sighted to assume that all one needs to do is some simple tinkering before the best practices approach will work in the new institutional setting.

Missing Subject Matter. The reader will notice that some problems were not included (or at least not in any detail). These include police handling of certain populations (e.g., juveniles, the mentally ill), racism, and terrorism. This is not to suggest that these issues are not important or problematic; their omission or minimization of coverage reflects the consensus of those to whom I administered my survey. Also, despite their importance, both state and federal law enforcement agencies were neglected as subjects of this book.

Terminology. A note on terminology is in order. Some of the terms the public uses to label police officers are unnecessarily derogatory, pejorative, or colloquial, as they disregard the professional nature of this occupation. Thus, to the extent possible, the labels "cop" or "pig" are avoided as synonyms. True, some police officers act in a deviant manner, but in a scholarly text such as this, nuance should be observed.

Also, as I will reiterate later, although all police officers are law enforcement agents, not all law enforcement officers are police officers. Regardless, I will occasionally use the term *law enforcement* to reduce redundancy, but it should be understood that I am referring to police officers. Likewise, throughout the text when referring to police departments, I will interchangeably use the expression *police agency* as a synonym.

Exhibit Boxes. In order for students to better appreciate the subject matter of each chapter and to break up the flow of the text, I have included exhibit boxes that provide overviews of a well-known piece of relevant research, historical event, and/or a movie that they or their instructors might find helpful.

Policing as a Global Experience. Finally, policing is not only an American phenomenon, but also a global one (Bayley, 1971, 1979, 1990). However, for the sake of focus, the majority of examples marshaled within this book are rooted in the United States. In sum, this book reviews and examines the critical, longstanding, and emerging issues that affect how police organizations operate and how citizens, criminals, police officers, and administrators experience this unique setting. Yet it does not stop there. It reviews solutions that have been advanced and critically analyzes them.

Acknowledgments

The process of developing, researching, and writing this book has been a journey of sorts. Maintaining my focus has been a constant challenge, given the competing pressures on my time.

In any given project, however, there are many people to thank, and this one is no different. I would like to extend my appreciation initially to the folks at Jones & Bartlett Learning, including Jeremy Spiegel, former acquisitions editor, for signing this book, and then to Sean Connelly, acquisitions editor, for stepping in as cheerleader and coach and for providing the necessary carrot and stick to help me make good on my promises. He demonstrated impeccable patience and maintained confidence that this manuscript would eventually make its way into print.

As always, I would like to thank Catherine Leidemer and Rachel Hildebrandt, who tidied up my prose when it was clear that my thoughts were a bit scattered, and to Chris Hart, who helped me seed some of this material as op-eds in various publications. I also extend my gratitude to my students—many of whom are former or current convicts, police officers and administrators, or other criminal justice practitioners—for enduring portions of this work through lectures and/or required readings.

Thanks to the many invaluable sources who gave freely of their time to respond to my numerous questions and to help me contextualize this material.

I'm also indebted to Marvin Ross and Dawn L. Rothe, who volunteered (or, more appropriately, were pressed into service) to look at selected chapters. Thanks to Christine Bevans, research assistant extraordinaire, who also provided input on chapters. I also extend my gratitude to several anonymous reviewers for their helpful comments; these individuals encouraged me to rethink many of the ideas I initially presented at both the proposal and manuscript review stages.

Thanks to Vic Kappeler for writing the foreword. Finally, I would like to extend my appreciation to my numerous policing colleagues, such as Ben Bowling, Dorothy Bracey, Gary Cordner, Mengyan Dai, James Frank, Don Gerkin, Larry Gould, Donna Hale, Stephen Holmes, Robert Kaminski, Dennis J. Kenney, Peter Manning, Gary Marx, Phyllis Parshall McDonald, Phil Stinson, Lawrence Travis, Ron Weitzer, and Benjamin S. Wright, and to my departmental colleagues, who provided a supportive community of sorts.

Thanks to the production people at Jones & Bartlett Learning, especially Jenny Corriveau, and the people at Shepherd Incorporated, especially Mary Grivetti and Karen Bankston.

Last, but certainly not least, I extend my never-ending gratitude to my wonderful family. I thank Natasha J. Cabrera, my wife and fellow scholar, for providing encouragement and feedback at several critical times, for serving as a sounding board for my ideas, and for trying her best to keep me focused. I also recognize Keanu and Dakota Ross-Cabrera, our children, who are a constant source of inspiration and joy and who reluctantly tolerate their father's divided attention more times than necessary.

About the Author

Jeffrey Ian Ross, PhD, is an Associate Professor in the School of Criminal Justice, College of Public Affairs, and a Research Fellow of the Center for Comparative and International Law at the University of Baltimore.

He has researched, written, and lectured on national security, political violence, political crime, violent crime, corrections, policing, cybercrime, and crime and justice in Indian Country for over two decades. Ross's work has appeared in many academic journals and books, as well as popular media. He is the author or editor of fifteen books, including *Making News of Police Violence: A Comparative Study of Toronto and New York City* (Praeger, 2000) and the forthcoming *Political Terrorism: An Interdisciplinary Approach*, Second Edition (Jones & Bartlett Learning, 2013).

Ross is a frequent and respected subject matter expert for local, regional, national, and international news media. He has made live appearances on CNN, including Jack Cafferty's *In the Money* and *Larry King Live*; CNBC, including *Geraldo Live*; and Fox National News, including *Hannity and Colmes* and *The O'Reilly Factor*. Additionally Ross has written op-eds for *The* (Baltimore) *Sun, The* (Maryland) *Daily Record, The Gazette* (weekly community newspaper serving Maryland's Montgomery, Frederick, Prince Georges, and Carroll counties), the *Baltimore Examiner*, and the *Tampa Tribune*.

From 1995 to 1998, Ross was a social science analyst with the National Institute of Justice, a Division of the U.S. Department of Justice. In 2003, he was awarded the University of Baltimore's Distinguished Chair in Research Award. His website is www.jeffreyianross.com.

Foreword

Jeffrey Ian Ross brings an exceptional amount of experience and motivation to the subject matter of policing in America. From a childhood interest in policing, to a position at the research arm of the National Institute of Justice, and teaching policing classes at university for more than a decade, it is clear that Ross' scholarly biography crafts the pages of *Policing Issues: Challenges and Controversies*. Motivated by the desire to contribute to our understanding of the issues surrounding policing as well as a dearth of critical scholarship designed specifically for classroom use, this book brings to the forefront of academic consideration not only "police problems," but problems and issues confronting the institution of policing. Far too often authors take for granted that "police problems," the challenges those in policing are willing to see and address, are "the" problems of policing. Ross does not fall into this conceptual trap. As one might expect from an author with such a diverse motivational biography, his approach to police problems is not merely the run of the mill "problem-solving" method that plagues traditional policing literature and thought. Ross' approach to the formulation of problems is derived from the assorted positional gazes of diffuse audiences and stakeholders who view the police—the police officers, community members, subordinate workers, victims of crime, criminal offenders, and political leaders.

With a clear and eyes-wide-open understanding that solutions to problems are not detached from the very formulation of problems themselves, Ross' mission is to identify the most important social problems and solutions in policing by bringing "sound empirical research" to bear on the issues he methodically confronts. As one might expect from someone with Ross' background, "sound empirical research" is given the same careful complexity of treatment afforded the notion of police problems. Highly quantitative and deeply qualitative studies crafted in the academy, as well as their less rigorous "best practices" counterparts, conjured by functionaries deep in the heart of the justice system apparatus are all given a weighted and measured level of consideration and presentation. The practitioner/academic divide often found in policing literature is bridged by Ross' thoughtful treatment of the research in policing. Not only is the research brought to bear on Ross' treatment of policing inspected for its scientific rigor, but this work also evidences conscious concern with the political construction of the knowledge that becomes policing research and how that information becomes a political interdiction into the institution of policing itself. In essence, Ross subjects the research in policing not only to an inspection of the adequacy of its execution, but also a critique of how it is used to forge the way we understand both the police and the perception of issues and problems. Unlike many academics who venture into this problem-filled world of policing, Ross offers us solutions by bringing a wealth of information to bear on the topic; information constructed, collected and proffered by those most capable of giving us an insight into policing. In doing so, he brings a balance to the often-unnoticed influences on viewers, writers and researchers of the police bringing a whole-sightedness to the topic that often eludes other authors.

This way of understanding the motivated author and this gaze on the world of policing brings to light the importance of the understated meaning of the title, *Policing Issues: Challenges and Controversies*. The work is a uniquely structured and well-considered array of issues both confronting and confronted by the police institution, not merely from a problem-solving perspective, but from an academic gaze that recognizes the political realities that give rise to "controversies" that "challenge" the police as a viable democratic institution—in all a very bold and tall order.

Policing Issues: Challenges and Controversies not only confronts the police, but it confronts its readers. If one is looking for a traditional read of the police, one that presents little challenge to the reader's expectations about structure, the required formulation and rote ordering of issues, and a voice free of purpose or political tone, this may not be the book to spend your time with. If on the other hand, one really wants to examine policing with an unexpected diverse political pose, a juxtaposition of voices that are confronting and confronting, a complex presentation crafted with an ease of understanding and classroom utility in mind; this is a book that can be enjoyed for its thoughtful difference.

Victor E. Kappeler, PhD
Foundation Professor and Chair
College of Justice and Safety
Eastern Kentucky University

PART

1

Introduction to Policing

Introduction to Policing

Introduction

The police perform numerous functions including investigating crime, responding to emergency calls, stopping, questioning, searching (e.g., frisking) and arresting suspects. The courts criminally charge and try these individuals. Once convicted, the corrections industry punishes, protects society from, and sometimes rehabilitates criminals. If we are lucky, this entire process sometimes deters criminals and/or the wider society from committing future crimes.

The police are important for a variety of reasons, but for the criminal justice system, they are the gatekeepers of individuals who enter the process. "The police begin the initial processing of individuals who violate the law" (Roberg and Kuykendall, 1993, p. 16). In addition to providing law enforcement, the police "maintain order (keeping the peace) and provide needed government and social services" (Roberg and Kuykendall, 1993, p. 14). This is why they are often referred to as a social service and/or as social workers with badges and guns.

Defining the Police

Although each state and municipality in its legal documents defines police officers slightly differently, in general, police can be described as paramilitary government workers and organizations "who are given the general right by government to use coercive force to enforce the law . . . [and whose] primary purpose is to respond to . . . conflict that involve[s] illegal behavior. Although the military can be given police powers, this is not the . . . [collectivity] with which we are concerned" (Roberg and Kuykendall, 1993, p. 13).

Though, by definition, police are authorized to use coercive force, most officers "rarely" threaten or use violence (Roberg and Kuykendall, 1993, p. 13). The majority of the time they maintain order and keep the peace, ensuring that society runs with a minimum of hassles. In the case of policing, this means directing traffic, assisting the fire department, providing crowd control, responding to noise complaints, and dealing with quality-of-living problems.

The Study of Policing

Throughout this book, I will use the terms *police, law enforcement officers,* and *cops* interchangeably. The term *cop* is not derogatory. It is simply an acronym that stands for "constable on patrol" and refers to the copper badge historically used by those working in this profession. (Modern badges are now made of brass.) Today, this acronym is most often understood to stand for "community-oriented policing."

Also, we should distinguish between police and law enforcement. The term *police* refers to a narrow occupational category within the field of criminal justice, whereas *law enforcement* includes not only the police, but also correctional, probation, and parole officers. Although all police officers are law enforcement officers, not all law enforcement officers are police.

How We Learn About Policing

Most people learn about policing through personal experience or through the mass media. For the average citizen, this means receiving a parking ticket or moving violation, being involved in a traffic accident, making a noise complaint, or reporting some sort of victimization, like a theft or assault. In terms of the news media, we can usually learn about the police through the 6 or 11 p.m. news broadcasts and on news magazine shows like *Dateline, Investigative Reports, 20/20, 60 Minutes,* and *Cops.* Or we might learn about the police through the variety of fictional shows on television such as *Law and Order, CSI,* or *Criminal Minds.*

However, if you want more rigorous information on policing, you could turn to the written media. Here I'm not referring to the *National Enquirer,* but instead to a number of magazines, such as *Newsweek, U.S. News & World Report,* or *Time,* which are geared to the average citizen. Unfortunately, the information gathered, analyzed, and presented in these publications is generally not particularly comprehensive.

Alternatively, one might turn to the publications produced by professional organizations that represent police officers. Here, one could consult issues of *Police Chief* or *American Police Beat Magazine* or Web sites like www.officer.com. Undoubtedly, the articles published in these venues are helpful, but they are not written and presented in accordance with the high standards of peer-review research (see Exhibit 1.1).

Scholarly articles on policing can be found in journals such as *American Sociological Review* or *American Journal of Sociology* or in criminology or criminal justice journals such as *Criminology* or *Justice Quarterly.* More specifically, a handful of academic journals now specialize in policing, including *Police & Society, Police Quarterly, Journal of Police Strategies and Management,* and *Police Practice and Research.*

Why does the distinction between mass media and scholarly journals matter? In the mass media, editors and producers select stories that they believe the public is most interested in. The veracity of the story varies based on the type of media outlet. In peer-reviewed journals, however, the editor

Exhibit 1.1   **Getting a Paper Published in a Peer-Reviewed Journal**

After academic investigators have conducted research, they typically compile their findings in a paper and may present their results at a public forum like a conference and/or submit it to a respectable and/or recognized peer-reviewed scholarly journal. The journal editor (or board) makes an initial determination about the suitability of the paper (if he or she thinks that the subject matter and approach of the paper will be of interest to the journal's readership and if it is of appropriate sophistication).

If the paper holds merit, the editor then sends it out to three or more subject matter expert reviewers. The writer's identity is concealed, as is the identity of the reviewers (also known as referees). This process of quality control, called "blind review," is meant to guard against bias. Reviewers try to determine whether the paper is thorough, if it offers an empirical analysis, and if the methods, data tested, and results seem appropriate. Referees generally make one of three recommendations: accept, reject, or revise and resubmit. Authors may resubmit, but if their work does not show improvement, the editor may refuse them the opportunity to submit again.

There is a hope that the findings from the research process will have an impact on policy and practice, but unfortunately, due to a multitude of factors, this is rarely the case. Peer-reviewed research is more credible than non-peer-reviewed research. Peer review strengthens the validity and reliability of the paper. It is the highest standard of research in academia. It is important for the career of a scholar to be published in a peer-reviewed journal. Not all academic or scholarly journals are peer reviewed. In order to determine whether a journal is peer reviewed, you have to check the submission criteria, typically listed at the back of the journal or on the journal's Web site. Also, a paper is not an article until it has been published.

examines the paper and, if he or she feels the manuscript is appropriate, sends it on to experts for blind review. This means that neither the paper's author(s) nor its reviewer(s) know the others' identities. The reviewers, who are not paid for their services, ultimately offer one of three responses: accept, reject, or revise and resubmit.

Where to Learn About Policing

In English-speaking countries, the academic study of policing is typically conducted by scholars who work for universities. Although it varies from state to state, many community colleges offer programs of study for those interested in becoming law enforcement officers. Also, those individuals who are already police officers can seek more advanced education at the Federal Bureau of Investigation Police Academy in Quantico, Va., or at the Federal Law Enforcement Training Center in Glynco, Ga.

You can study policing at many universities in the United States. Most academic study of policing goes on in sociology, political science, or criminal justice/criminology departments; there are very few departments of law enforcement. Exceptions include the John Jay School of Criminal Justice, Western Illinois University, and Eastern Kentucky University, all of which offer a disproportionate number of classes in policing.

One of the first academic courses in policing was offered in the 1920s at Wichita State University in Kansas by then-police chief Orlando W. Wilson. Later, he moved to the University of California-Berkeley, where he established the well-respected, but now defunct School of Criminology. Wilson also wrote a classic book on police administration, first published in 1943.

During the 1960s, there was an increase in the number of criminal justice and criminology programs in the United States after President Lyndon Johnson signed into law the creation of a separate branch of the Department of Justice called the Law Enforcement Assistance Administration (LEAA) to deal with the recommendations of a series of commissions that investigated racial riots and increasing crime across the nation (President's Commission on Law Enforcement and Administration of Justice, 1967; U.S. Crime Commission, 1967; National Advisory Commission on Civil Disorders, 1968).

The LEAA attempted to increase general knowledge about police and to improve education for the field of law enforcement. During this time, many law enforcement officers earned bachelor's degrees thanks to this government financial assistance. Others completed graduate and doctoral degrees. In fact, a handful of former police chiefs and commissioners—such as Willy Williams, former chief of the Philadelphia and Los Angeles police departments, and Lee Brown, former commissioner of the New York Police Department, former chief of the Houston police department, and former Houston mayor (1998–2004)—hold PhDs. Although the LEAA no longer exists on its own, it has since transformed into the National Institute of Justice. In sum, this infusion of money led to the increased academic respectability of the study of policing.

Academic Organizations Specializing in Research on Policing

There are no autonomous organizations that specialize in the scholarly study of policing; however, the Academy of Criminal Justice Sciences (one of the most well-respected academic associations for criminal justice) has a section that specializes in policing.

The policing section meets each year when the Academy of Criminal Justice Sciences holds its annual conference. At these meetings, selected academics, practitioners, and professionals who both study and practice law enforcement generally present papers and comment on them. The policing section hopes that authors will then submit the manuscripts to an academic journal that will review and publish these papers, a process that could ultimately advance our knowledge and understanding of policing.

Professional Organizations That Focus on the Police

Currently, several professional organizations are responsible for monitoring policing, including the Fraternal Order of Police (FOP), International Union of Police Associations (IUPA), the International Association of Chiefs of Police (IACP), the National Sheriff's Association (NSA), the Police Foundation, the Police Executive Research Forum (PERF), and the National Organization of Black Law Enforcement Executives (NOBLE). Almost all of these organizations have headquarters located in or around Washington, D.C. The Patrolmen's Benevolent Association represents the interests of line police officers. There are also organizations that represent the interests of female, Hispanic, Asian-American, Native-American, and gay and lesbian police officers.

Police and Democracy

Although police are found in all types of political systems, police and their organizations have an intimate connection to democracy. In fact, "[T]he word police derives from the Greek word politeuin, which means 'to be a citizen or engage in political activity,' and polis, which means 'city' or 'state.' . . . All governments are [given] police power to regulate matters of health, welfare, safety, and morality" (Roberg and Kuykendall, 1993, p. 4). Governments typically achieve this regulation through their law enforcement agencies and the people who work for them.

Consequently, "Police form an important link between citizens and government. Police, in carrying out the police power of government, as it relates to crime and order-maintenance problems, are not only enforcing the laws but the individual officer also represents a direct connection between the citizen and appointed officials and political leaders" (Roberg and Kuykendall, 1993, p. 6). In many cases, with the exception of public school teachers, the only face-to-face contact a person may have in his or her lifetime with a government representative is through a police officer.

In most cities, police agencies seem to be a magnet for controversy (Roberg and Kuykendall, 1993), which can create what is known as the democracy-police conflict. Herman Goldstein—a well-respected authority on policing, a former law professor at the University of Wisconsin, and a keen observer of the police—restates Rousseau's social contract to frame the democracy-police conflict as follows: "The police, by the very nature of their function are an anomaly in a free society. They are [given] a great deal of authority under a system of government in which authority is reluctantly granted and, when granted, sharply curtailed" (1977, p. 1).

In fact, it is more appropriate to describe police as having relative autonomy (Marenin, 1990), which means that they have a great deal of freedom to set their own priorities. How does this apply to the police? Most police officers work on their own and are at liberty to do their job the way they know best or seem fit to do.

Police and Rule of Law

In order to direct and regulate the activities of police officers, societies rely on a number of controls. One of the most important is the law.

We can divide the subject of law many different ways. One of the most crucial distinctions for those studying criminology and criminal justice, especially practitioners, is that laws are either civil or criminal and either substantive or procedural. The following section reviews the distinctions between these categories to better understand this fundamental concept as they apply to policing.

Criminal Versus Civil Law

Criminal justice personnel need to know the difference between criminal and civil types of law. For instance, when observing a dispute or asked to mediate it, practitioners should determine quickly if it can be solved through the application of civil or criminal law. Criminal justice practitioners do not want to give the wrong information to citizens, nor can they afford to waste valuable resources (e.g., their time) in matters unrelated to their basic job functions.

Civil law relates to a person's property interests and to relationships between or among private parties; it includes such mechanisms as contracts (verbal and written), business transactions, and family relations (marriages, divorces, child custody). Typical disputes in this realm are between or among businesses, consumers, or family members over the custody of a child or the division of property in a divorce or inheritance. Criminal law deals with behaviors that are perceived to be harmful to society as a whole, such as homicide, robbery, or sexual assault (Roberg and Kuykendall, 1993).

Crimes are considered to be actions that disturb the good order and safety of society as they affect both the victim's and the accused's liberty interest. For example, if someone is stealing Joe's car, unless Joe is a friend or relative, why should I care? The simple answer is because the thief might feel bold enough to steal my car later on.

The state has a responsibility here. Some may question why the government has to be involved at all. Why don't we simply get a crowbar or a shotgun and settle this matter ourselves? In democracies, citizens have accorded the government (either implicitly or explicitly) certain powers, and we supposedly benefit from these actions, which include enforcing the law. The state is supposed to help in all matters that deal with public order. Through selected agencies (e.g., the Department of Homeland Security), the state protects us from internal threats and from foreign enemies. This is called the *Social Contract* (Rousseau, 1763/1983). In return, the government provides certain benefits, including reducing anarchy that we may see in some states in which society is very loose or disorganized.

Both civil and criminal law have different burdens of proof and procedures that must be followed if the criminal justice system process is perceived to be fair. With matters that fall under criminal law, the case is brought forward in a court by prosecutors in the name of the state. In a criminal trial, for example, the judge and/or jury must decide if the accused is guilty "beyond a reasonable doubt." With matters that fall under civil law, typically the aggrieved individual or organization sues the "offending person" or entity. In a civil proceeding, the judge and/or jury only has to decide the case for the plaintiff or defendant based on "a preponderance of evidence" standard. In other words, the plaintiff has, more likely than not, showed the allegations or causes of action to be true and is entitled to relief (i.e., usually a monetary award or transferring of property). This latter threshold is a lower standard to achieve than in criminal cases.

Indeed, there are connections between criminal and civil law. We see these most dramatically in famous criminal cases, particularly those that have garnered considerable media attention. Famous defendants frequently have more assets than the average person, and after being charged with a criminal offense, celebrities may try to hide or protect their property by, for example, transferring assets to their relatives or closest friends. Naturally, the civil law is complicated in this area, but it does allow some transference of assets.

For instance, in June 1994, former Buffalo Bills running back, ABC sports commentator, and B-level movie star O. J. Simpson was accused of murdering his wife, Nicole Brown Simpson, and her friend, Ron Goldman.

Simpson had a series of run-ins with the law in connection with alleged and verified domestic abuse against his wife. The criminal trial, which was lengthy, widely publicized, and televised, depicted a crafty legal team (led by attorneys Robert Shapiro and the now-deceased Johnny Cochran) that knew how to work the jury and the media and that was able to suppress some evidence and to convince the jury to acquit Simpson of all charges. The state was unwilling to retry Simpson, who paid quite handsomely for his legal defense. However, in 1996, the subsequent civil trial against Simpson was decided in favor of one of the plaintiffs (i.e., the Goldman family). The plaintiff won a financial judgment because of the lower burden of proof and was able to garner assets from Simpson and exact a measure of justice, reminding him that he is not above the law.

Although this was not the case in Simpson's criminal trial, a prior criminal conviction against the defendant sometimes benefits the plaintiff in a civil trial. It is one more piece of evidence that a plaintiff's lawyer can use against the accused or the defendant to demonstrate liability or bad character.

Substantive Versus Procedural Law

A subtle difference exists between substantive and procedural law. The former specifies the kind of behavior that must be present if a person violates a particular law (i.e., who, what, when, where, how, and why?). Substantive law may also include a sanction (e.g., a fine or period of incarceration) for engaging in that kind of action. Although the name of the offense can vary from state to state, a good example is "driving under the influence" or "driving while impaired." To sustain this charge, a person must have a certain "percentage of alcohol in the bloodstream and actually [be] driving the car on a public road" (Roberg and Kuykendal, 1993, p. 9). A person found guilty of this charge may be punished by a fine, imprisonment, and/or license suspension. In Maryland, for example, a driver only has to be in control of the vehicle, which means that the key is in the ignition and the engine is running.

Procedural law outlines how criminal justice personnel "go about enforcing the substantive laws. For instance, police must have probable cause to believe a person has committed a crime. If that individual is arrested, he or she must be advised of the right to remain silent and to have an attorney" (Roberg and Kuykendall, 1993, p. 9). The basic framework of procedural criminal laws hinges upon the existing criminal codes of each state.

A typical example of procedural law in action is an officer pulling a driver over, searching the car, and finding illegal drugs, leading to the driver being arrested for drug possession. In order for the officer to legally search the vehicle, s/he must have probable cause (e.g., a suspicion that the vehicle operator has illegal drugs). In general, an officer cannot stop someone at random and search that person's car. To appropriately justify the stop during any subsequent court proceedings, the officer will likely say to the judge that he was conducting a routine patrol, noticed the car driving erratically, and either smelled or saw marijuana or other drug paraphernalia upon pulling the vehicle (also known as "in plain sight") over. This ritual, repeated every day in courtrooms all over America, means that the officer is essentially covering the procedural legal bases. If the police officer does not follow these steps, s/he is guilty of violating the accused's right to privacy and, unless the accused has a poor lawyer, the case will likely be dismissed.

When criminal justice personnel enforce substantive laws, they must take specific steps and adhere to particular criteria. For example, law enforcement personnel must have probable cause to stop, question, and/or arrest an individual. Or, to enter a private dwelling, police must have a warrant or sufficient evidence that a crime is occurring or has occurred on the premises. In general, it is recognized that law enforcement decision making is subordinate to the fundamental rights of citizens.

Not surprisingly, the police and other criminal justice personnel do not always follow the procedural law. In general, they are given a disproportionate amount of discretion—a decision made by criminal justice personnel to invoke a legal sanction. This process differs from decision making, which is simply making a choice among alternatives (Davis, 1969, 1971, 1975; Rosett, 1972; Goldstein, 1998). Many of us have met police officers who, because of personal experiences (often involving a family member or a friend) appear as though they are on a mission to stop particular types of crime (e.g., drunk driving).

Law enforcement organizations also have limited resources, so they must make decisions with respect to which laws they will enforce and under what circumstances they will do so. This can be done in consultation with the public, through internal discussions, or based on experience and/or empirical research. Complete enforcement of the law, also known as "zero-tolerance policing" (e.g., Dennis, 1997), on the other hand, can lead to some disastrous effects, including clogging the court system with less important cases and causing a situation in which the jails and prisons would be more crowded/overcrowded than they currently are. In these scenarios, officers may feel that they are simply treated like robots without the ability to make decisions.

In some communities, in which minor or victimless crimes are rampant, the police may ignore these violations. In other areas that have significant community outcry, law enforcement officers may vigorously enforce the law.

The police are not only influenced by the law, but also affected by personal values, citizens' expectations, and the nature of the interaction. In some departments (or in parts of a city), police officers must enforce every law; this is typically called zero-tolerance policing. In general, though, police agencies do not have the resources to enforce all the laws all the time. They make decisions about which laws to enforce based on a number of factors, including political input, citizen complaints, and their own perceptions of what is important. For further discussion about this process, see chapter 6 on police discretion.

Many police ignore both procedural and substantive laws. "Some police officers even come to believe such violations are unavoidable if they are to obtain results they considerable[y] desire. For some police officers, the ends of enforcement of substantive law (i.e., catching a criminal) become so important they neglect to observe the means, represented by procedural laws and organizational guidelines, required in that enforcement. This ends-means dilemma is an important part of police discretion" (Roberg and Kuykendall, 1993, p. 12).

In short, police have relative autonomy. This term was refined by political sociologist Nicos Poulantzas (1973), who argued that many government organizations have considerable latitude to make their own decisions about what is important in order to achieve their mission, depending upon various conditions. Police, in general, are no different.

Types of Policing

Up until now, the discussion has focused on municipal policing. Yet there are different kinds of policing (Roberg and Kuykendall, 1993), and knowing this now will help the reader better contextualize the subject matter of this course.

The Citizen Police Officer

Dating back to British magistrate Sir Robert Peel, who said, "The police are the public and the public are the police," there has been an understanding that citizens are allowed some of the functions of police. In democracies, citizens are permitted, if not encouraged, to participate in the legal process. They have limited powers of arrest, they are encouraged to report crimes, and they serve as witnesses for the prosecution (Roberg and Kuykendall, 1993, p. 14). Two terms are important here:

Posse Comitatus. Historically, citizens were more involved in law enforcement duties within their communities. In the United States, a historical precedent for involvement was the *Posse Comitatus Act* (1878), which allowed sheriffs to temporarily deputize citizens so they would have police powers. Over time this phenomenon has changed.

Vigilantes. Some citizens have been known to "take the law into their own hands," either because they perceived or because of an actual lack of law enforcement presence or because of the belief that law enforcement officers are not doing their job properly. These citizens then become judge, jury, and executioner, thereby subverting the principle of fairness in criminal proceedings. "Such groups were commonplace in the nineteenth century, and such groups usually developed as the result of a public perception that the existing law enforcement system was inadequate and corrupt. . . . Although this type of citizen involvement in law enforcement has been less pronounced in the twentieth century, it still occurs" (Roberg and Kuykendall, 1993, p. 15). The western states of Montana, Idaho, and Colorado have some of the richest histories of the vigilante tradition.

Citizen participation in the legal process also varies based on the degree to which people feel a civic obligation and the extent to which such actions are encouraged by the police (Roberg and Kuykendall, 1993).

Private and Public Organized Police

In the United States and elsewhere, there are two basic types of police: those paid by tax dollars and those funded by private entities. According to Roberg and Kuykendall (1993):

> Public police refer to those police employed, trained, and paid by a government agency, whose purpose is to serve the general interest of all citizens through enforcement of democratically developed laws. Private police refer to those police employed and paid to serve the specific purposes, within the law, of an individual or organization. A municipal police officer is a public police officer, whereas a guard at a bank or department store is a private police officer, usually referred to as a security officer.
>
> However, there is also a combination of public-private policing in the United States. An example of this combination is off-duty police officers working as private security guards at a Baltimore Orioles (baseball) game. (p. 15)

Although it might be helpful to understand policing in all contexts, since the majority of research on policing focuses on public and municipal policing, and most undergraduates looking for a career in law enforcement want to work for a police department, this book focuses on this narrow but important subject.

This book "further emphasizes local police, more than state and federal law enforcement because local, or community, police organizations employ most personnel. . . [are the most expensive], and have more of an impact on citizens' lives than do state and federal agencies. In addition, municipal police agencies, particularly large ones, have been studied far more extensively than have other types of law enforcement organizations" (Roberg and Kuykendall, 1993, p. 15).

Organizational Structure of Law Enforcement

To best understand policing, one must become familiar with a number of well-used terms which, on first usage, may seem simple enough to understand but actually refer to specific kinds of arrangements. One of the most important is *jurisdiction* or *venue*. This refers to the geographic area or to the type of law for which an officer has authority. Thus, for example, if a Baltimore City police officer vacations in Miami and sees a crime in progress, s/he cannot arrest an individual with full police powers. On the other hand, if a person committed a crime in Baltimore County and then drives through the city of Baltimore, the Baltimore County police officer can pursue the individual—known as fresh or hot pursuit—if the officer keeps his/her eyes on the suspect at all times during the chase. Alternatively, if a Baltimore County officer had an arrest warrant for a suspect in the city of Baltimore, a Baltimore city officer must accompany the county officer in order to make the arrest. In these cases, a longstanding arrangement has been worked out between the two police agencies to share the responsibilities.

Other Organizational Forms of Law Enforcement

In addition to the basic structure of police work, there are a number of different organizational forms of law enforcement with which students should be familiar.

Public Safety Model/Concept. Under this arrangement, a city or region's police, fire, and emergency medical services squad are integrated under one municipal department. The leader of this organization is usually called the director of public safety. This kind of design can lead to cost savings in terms of communications, training, purchases, cost of vehicle repair, and payroll and human resources (Roberg and Kuykendall, 1993). The public safety model allows municipalities to leverage their resources.

Consolidation/Amalgamation. Two or more police agencies may be combined. "This integration can be either by function or by combining organizations. Functional, or partial, integration involves the combining of the same organizational function, perhaps communication or training" (Roberg and Kuykendall, 1993, p. 18).

Mutual Aid. The temporary sharing of police resources (e.g., personnel) may occur when one law enforcement agency is incapable of handling the situation alone (e.g., crisis, riot, inauguration) or could benefit from additional help. This can occasionally include "other public resources such as fire-fighting and medical personnel, among two or more jurisdictions during emergencies" (Roberg and Kuykendall, 1993, p. 18). This structure accommodates for a lack of resources within some jurisdictions.

Special Jurisdiction Police. These police are primarily used to monitor a special jurisdiction and have limited police powers (e.g., your university's police department). In other words, these police operate in special areas of a jurisdiction and/or have a special kind of crime they are responsible for enforcing (e.g., FBI, Secret Service Police, University of Baltimore police).

Task Force Approach. A police unit may be composed of selected officers from different law enforcement agencies (e.g., local, state, and federal) with particular areas of expertise to investigate specific crime-related problems, such as terrorism or organized crime. A task force may be multijurisdictional.

Contract Law Enforcement or Policing. In this arrangement between two or more units of government, one agrees to provide law enforcement services for the other. This typically happens in smaller jurisdictions. In the United States, rural policing is generally performed by highway patrol or by the state police.

Police Employment and Expenditures

Every four years, the Bureau of Justice Statistics, a division of the US Department of Justice, sends a survey to and compiles basic statistical information on and from almost all individual state and local agencies with 100 or more officers in the United States. The latest version (2004) includes data on expenditures, the number of employees at different ranks, and the racial and ethnic composition of the police department, operations, community policing, policies and programs, equipment, and computers and information systems. Originally called the Law Enforcement Management and Administrative Statistics, in 2008 it was renamed the Census of State and Local Law Enforcement Agencies.

In 2003, there were 452,000 full-time, sworn police officers (those with arrest powers) operating at the local level. During that year, 67% of all police agencies operated at the local level, and the balance operated at the county, state, or federal level (Hickman and Reaves, 2004). Keep in mind that police departments do not simply consist of sworn officers. Many positions are staffed by civilians; they often perform functions in human resources, accounting, and dispatch. Employment and expenditure patterns of police departments vary based on numerous factors, including population dynamics and crime rates.

Conclusion

This chapter introduced the reader to the definition of policing and explained where policing is taught, why it is a respectable academic offering at universities throughout the United States, which constituencies have an interest in policing, and what the different types of police officers are. Policing is complex but understandable. Despite variations in the early years, big-city police departments have increasingly come to resemble each other. Police departments and policing have become more professional, recognizing a body of knowledge and skills that are highly specialized. Meanwhile, police agencies and the profession itself over time have expressed a general willingness to experiment and to learn from their mistakes. These are the basics. It is important to know this information because it serves as the foundation for the information that follows.

Glossary

Consolidation: Integration/combination of two or more police agencies.

Contract law enforcement: Arrangement between two or more units of government in which one agrees to provide law enforcement services for the other.

Cop (colloquial): Historical term, slang for police officer, that originated from the term "constable on patrol." Term also said to originate from the copper badge that the police historically wore.

COP: Acronym for "community-oriented policing," also known as community policing.

Discretion: A decision made by criminal justice practitioners to invoke the law/criminal sanction. In the case of police, it includes the decision to stop, question, search, arrest, and use force against a suspect.

Jurisdiction/venue: Geographic area or type of law for which the officer has authority.

Law enforcement: Professional individuals who ensure that criminal laws are upheld/not broken. Term encompasses police, sheriffs, and corrections, probation, and parole officers.

LEMAS: Acronym for Law Enforcement Management and Administrative Statistics. Biannual survey conducted by the Bureau of Justice Statistics to determine basic features of law enforcement agencies (primarily those related to police, sheriffs, and federal police) in the United States.

Multijurisdictional policing: A temporary unit composed of selected police officers from different law enforcement agencies (e.g., local, state, and federal) with particular expertise to investigate specific crime-related problems (e.g., terrorism, organized crime).

Mutual aid: Temporary sharing of police resources (e.g., personnel) when one agency is incapable of handling the situation alone (e.g., crisis, riot, inauguration).

Order maintenance: Making sure that society runs with a minimum of hassles. In the case of policing, this includes directing traffic, assisting the fire department and emergency medical services, crowd control, responding to public disturbances/noise complaints, giving information, helping the public with lost items, etc.

Peer review: Processes used in scholarly research where the editor of a scholarly journal examines the unpublished manuscript and then, if he or she feels it is appropriate, sends it to experts for blind review. This means that neither the author/s of the paper nor the reviewer/s know the others' identities. The reviewers, who are not paid for their services, offer one of three responses: accept, reject, or revise and resubmit.

Police: Nonmilitary government workers and organizations "who are given the general right by government to use coercive force to enforce the law . . . [and whose] primary purpose is to respond to . . . conflict that involves illegal behavior. Although [the] military can be given police powers, this is not the . . . [collectivity] with which we are concerned" (Roberg and Kuykendall, 1993, p. 13).

Police-democracy conflict idea: "The police, by the very nature of their function are an anomaly in a free society. They are given a great deal of authority under a system of government in which authority is reluctantly granted, and when granted is sharply curtailed" (Goldstein, 1977).

Posse Commitatus Act: Federal law that permitted local residents to assume temporary police powers and come to the assistance of a sheriff or marshal.

Procedural law: The proper steps that criminal justice personnel must follow to enforce substantive laws.

Private police: Police paid by private dollars (e.g., security officers).

Public police: Police paid by tax dollars (e.g., local, state, and federal officers).

Public safety model/concept: An arrangement whereby a city's or region's police, fire, and emergency medical services are integrated under one municipal department.

Special jurisdiction police: Individuals who have normal police powers but are typically responsible for law enforcement in a limited area.

Substantive law: Behavior that must be present if a person violates a particular law.

Victimless crime: Crimes that are less severe or that may involve the active participation of the so-called victim, including prostitution, gambling, and illegal drug possession.

Vigilantes: Citizens who "take the law into their own hands" because of a perceived or actual lack of law enforcement presence or a belief that law enforcement officers are not doing their job properly. These individuals become judge, jury, and executioner, thereby subverting the principle of fairness in criminal proceeding.

Chapter Questions

Part One: Multiple Choice Questions

Choose the most appropriate answer.

1. The focus of this book is on which type of law enforcement?
   a. federal
   b. national
   c. municipal
   d. regional
   e. state

2. Among the following choices, which is the most common way the majority of people learn about policing?
   a. academic journals
   b. police academies
   c. newspapers
   d. joining the police
   e. Uniform Crime Reports

3. At which U.S. university was the first college class in policing taught?
   a. Harvard
   b. New York University
   c. University of California-Berkeley
   d. Wichita State University
   e. Yale

4. Which academic organization specializes in the scholarly study of the police?
   a. American Society of Criminology
   b. the policing section of the Academy of Criminal Justice Sciences
   c. Police Educators Society of America
   d. Federal Law Enforcement Training Center
   e. none of the above

5. Who is responsible for putting forward the "police-democracy conflict" idea?
   a. Dunham and Alpert
   b. Vold
   c. Goldstein
   d. Reiss
   e. None of the above

6. Which option identifies behavior that must be present if a person violates a particular law?
   a. criminal law
   b. civil law
   c. substantive law
   d. procedural law
   e. none of the above

7. What is the acronym for the organization that promotes the interests of chiefs of police?
   a. COPS
   b. IACP
   c. NOBLE
   d. PBA
   e. PERF

8. Which of the following organizations represents the interests of line police officers?
   a. Police Executive Research Forum
   b. International Association of Chiefs of Police
   c. National Sheriffs Association
   d. Patrolmen's Benevolent Association
   e. National Institute of Justice

9. What is the acronym for the national database that assembles information concerning personnel issues in police departments?
   a. NDBPD
   b. LEAA
   c. LEMAS
   d. PERF
   e. none of the above

10. Which of the following statements is true?
    a. There are more public police than private police.
    b. There are less public police than private police.
    c. There is relatively the same number of public police as there are private police.
    d. There is no relatively reliable method to count the number of private and public police.
    e. none of the above

11. What is the term used to describe a situation in which police officers enforce all criminal laws all the time?
    a. political enforcement
    b. absolutist policy
    c. discretion
    d. good police work
    e. zero-tolerance policing

12. What is the name of the organizational structure characterized by selected police officers from federal, state, and local governments combining forces to combat a crime-related problem for a limited period?
    a. consolidation
    b. contract law enforcement
    c. mutual aid
    d. multijurisdictional task force approach
    e. special jurisdiction police

13. In the context of municipal policing, what is mutual aid?
    a. an insurance policy in which many police officers enroll
    b. when police from federal, state, and local governments combine forces to combat a crime-related problem for a limited period
    c. when smaller departments depend on larger departments to train their people
    d. when law enforcement officers temporarily assist a neighboring or nearby law enforcement agency due to understaffing
    e. all of the above

14. In the United States, rural policing is generally performed by which type of police force?
    a. highway patrol or state police
    b. marshal service
    c. municipal police
    d. FBI
    e. ATF

15. Which option is NOT an organizational form of law enforcement?
    a. consolidation
    b. mutual aid
    c. public safety
    d. special jurisdiction police
    e. none of the above

16. What is the public safety model?
    a. when police primarily patrol and portray the image that they are keeping the public safe
    b. when the police strategize on how to be more effective on how to protect the public
    c. a model that involves keeping citizens safe and the streets clean
    d. the amalgamation of policing, fire, and emergency medical services squads in a jurisdiction
    e. none of the above

17. What is the term used to describe when police direct traffic, assist the fire department, engage in crowd control, and respond to noise complaints?
    a. community policing
    b. law enforcement
    c. order maintenance
    d. police sting
    e. problem-oriented policing

18. Which of the following best describes a cooperative effort between police and the communities they serve to solve crime and crime-related problems?
    a. community policing
    b. door-to-door canvassing
    c. propaganda
    d. public relations
    e. none of the above

Part Two: Short-Answer Questions

Answer each question. Be as detailed and specific as possible.

1. Define the police.

2. What is the difference between discretion and decision making?

3. For what type of police department do the majority of law enforcement officers in the United States work?

4. Who is O.W. Wilson, and for what was he responsible?

5. List three common ways most people learn about policing.

6. What does the historical origin of the acronym COP?

7. What is jurisdiction?

8. What is the difference between order maintenance and law enforcement?

9. What are four organizational forms of the police?

10. What is the public safety model?

Part Three: Essay Questions

Present a logical argument with supporting facts that takes into consideration multiple interpretations. Answer in paragraph form. Be as specific and detailed as possible; avoid generalizations.

1. Is there and/or should there be a relationship among the organizations and institutions in which policing is taught, academic organizations specializing in conducting and promoting research on policing, and professional organizations that advocate on behalf of the police?

2. How would you systematically identify the problems with municipal policing in the United States? Is one way better than another?

3. What do you believe is the most important aspect of policing and why?

The History of Municipal Policing in the United States

Introduction

It is difficult to present a comprehensive overview of the history of municipal policing in the United States.[1] Why? Because its development was uneven and urban police agencies varied from one jurisdiction to another. To be sure, unique practices were implemented in different cities; some persisted while others were abandoned. As a result of advances in communications, training, and education, growth in one place eventually resembled what was occurring in another (Kelling and Moore, 1988). This chapter reviews the early history of policing in the United States from the 17th century until the present.

Early History of Policing

All groups have norms and mechanisms to sanction those who deviate from the rules, policies, or laws. They also choose individuals to enforce the rules and to punish any rule breakers.

Shortly after the colonists and settlers arrived in the United States (1648–1850s), they established unique forms of law enforcement and policing. These approaches were based on geographical location, resources at their disposal, and the cultures and ethnicities of the different people who settled throughout the developing nation. In general, the immigrants established mechanisms of law enforcement with which they were the most familiar (Johnson, 1981; Richardson, 1974).

When the early English and Dutch colonists first settled in the northeast in the 1600s and 1700s, they established a night-watch system and then, somewhat later, a day-watch system—both of which were prevalent in Western Europe during that time. Similar to what occurred in England, the voluntary watch was not liked; those on rotation were typically inadequate for the job, and citizens soon switched over to a paid watch and then to a paid police force.

In the southern part of the United States (e.g., Georgia, Alabama, the Carolinas) in the mid 1700s, patrols were established to watch over slaves, capture them if they escaped, and to put down their revolts. Like the watch, slave patrol duty was an obligatory responsibility of males in the community.

In the Southwest, which was originally a Spanish possession and later part of Mexico, the alcade— a "combination of sheriff and justice of the peace" (Roberg and Kuykendall, 1993, p. 57)—was established. This was tied into the municipal style of governance that was established before the Southwest became part of United States. Over time, these systems of law enforcement were modified in favor of the full-time constable, who was paid for providing both day and night watch duties.

The Beginning of Modern Policing in the United States

Modern-style policing refers to the period beginning with the establishment of the first police department in London, England, in 1829 to present day. The city of London was plagued with crime in the early 1800s, and members of Parliament struggled with an appropriate mechanism to keep this under control. One of the controversial suggestions that made its way into legislation (i.e., the *London Metropolitan Police Act*) involved the creation of a full-time, uniformed police force responsible for patrolling the city and arresting suspected offenders. The unit, later called the "Bobbies," was suggested by then-Home Secretary Sir Robert Peel.

Regional Diversity

Uchida (2010) shares this history of policing in the northeast part of the United States, where newly arrived immigrants originally settled:

> The county sheriff, appointed by the government, became the most important law enforcement agent particularly when the colonies remained small and primarily rural. The sheriff's duties included apprehending criminals, serving subpoenae, appearing in court, and collecting taxes. The sheriff was paid a fixed amount for each task he performed. Since sheriffs received higher fees based on the taxes they collected, apprehending criminals was not a primary concern. (p. 19–20)

In its earliest incarnation, the sheriff was appointed by the governor, whereas today's sheriffs are typically elected. Their duties vary from one jurisdiction to another, but sheriffs typically have greater responsibilities than do municipal police departments. In years past, sheriffs also had the power to invoke the *Posse Comitatus Act*, which allowed them to deputize citizens to come to their aid.

In the first half of the 1800s, cities became increasingly aware that the constable night-watch system was inadequate, so they shifted over to "paid daytime police forces. . . . Eventually, the daytime force joined the night watch to create integrated day-night, or modern, police departments" (Roberg and Kuykendall, 1993, p. 57).

During this time, Uchida (1997) notes,

> American cities and towns encountered problems similar to those in England. Cities grew at phenomenal rates; civil disorders swept the nation, and crime was perceived to be increasing. . . . Foreign immigrants, particularly Irish and Germans, accounted for a large portion of the increase. Traveling to America in search of employment and better life-styles, the immigrants competed with native-born Americans for skilled and unskilled positions. As a result, the American worker saw Irishman and German as social and economic threats. (p. 22)

Theories of Police Development

By the mid- to late 1800s, most cities, towns, or villages with expanding populations had police departments (Fogelson, 1977; Monkkonen, 1981). Four theories, explanations, or models have been advanced to describe why these jurisdictions decided to create such departments: disorder–control, crime control, class control, and urban dispersion theories.

The *disorder–control theory* argues that police forces were created because of the need felt by cities to control actual or potential mob violence.

The *crime control theory* "suggests that increases in criminal activity resulted in a perceived need for a new type of police. Threats to social order, such as highway robbers and violent pickpockets, created a climate of fear" (Roberg and Kuykendall, 1993, p. 57). With this explanation, the overwhelming reason for the creation of a police department was because of fear of or an actual increase in crime.

The *class control theory* argues that police departments were created because of fears of lower- and working-class-based revolution. Urban and industrial growth coincided with the development of a new labor force that increasingly demanded rights. During this period, many people of different social and ethnic backgrounds competed for opportunities that would enhance their economic status. The resulting disruption prompted the middle and upper classes — usually white Anglo-Saxon Protestants — to develop a means to control the people involved, usually poor immigrants who were not always Anglo and often not Protestant.

Finally, the *urban dispersion theory* suggests that police departments were established because mayors and other members of the city administration learned about the existence of police departments in other jurisdictions and thought they might be useful in their own city. Here, the simple fact that other jurisdictions had police departments was reason enough to justify the creation of a new police department. It was also something that a local politician could sell to his constituency; no jurisdiction wanted to be left behind, and thus having a police department could be seen as being current and keeping up with the times.

Which is the correct explanation? According to Roberg and Kuykendall (1993, p. 58), "There is some evidence to support all four theories; however, no single theory provides an adequate explanation. While some cities had major urban disturbances before they established new police departments,

| Exhibit 2.1 | Book/Movie: *Gangs of New York* |

Written in 1927, this book by journalist Herbert Asbury details the underbelly of New York City during the mid-1800s and documents the various gangs of the day—including the Dead Rabbits and Bowery Boys—corrupt politicians, and police officers. In 2002, director Martin Scorsese borrowed the name of the book and converted the story to a movie. The film begins during the 1840s during massive Irish immigration to New York City, and moves through the 1860s, around the time of the Draft Riots (July 13–16, 1863). The movie stars actors Leonardo DiCaprio, Daniel Day Lewis, and Cameron Diaz. Lewis plays Bill "the Butcher" Cutting, the head of an immigrant gang, and DiCaprio portrays Amsterdam, who is connected to the Dead Rabbits, an Irish immigrant gang. Meanwhile, Lewis is beholden to William "Boss" Tweed, the infamous (and corrupt) Tammany Hall politician. Numerous battles and vendettas are carried out by the rival gangs while the police support Cutting's group.

others did not." Nevertheless, the authors note, "By the 1870s, most cities had a police department even if it consisted of only one person. In more rural areas, the county sheriff was the dominant law enforcement officer. In the territories of the western United States, federal marshals were primarily responsible for law enforcement activities" (p. 59).

Eras/Periods/Stages of Modern Policing in the United States

Different theorists and commentators divide the history of modern policing in various ways. During each era, period, or stage, certain approaches to crime control were emphasized. For example, Kelling and Moore (1988) break the history of municipal policing in the United States into the political, reform, and community problem-solving eras. Roberg and Kuykendall (1993) divide the history of policing in the United States into the political model, the bureaucratic/legalistic model, and the service and contingency model. Stevens (2009) organizes the history into eras: political, reform, community, and quality of life.[2] In short, there is no real hard-and-fast rule as to when these eras begin and end. For ease of presentation, however, I break up the periods or stages of modern policing in the United States into the Political Era, the Bureaucratic/Legalistic Model/Scientific and Reform Era, and the Community Service Era.

The Political Era

The first stage started during the mid-1840s and lasted until the 1920s. During this time frame, the long arm of politics reached into police departments and affected who was employed, which positions they held, and ultimately who became the chief of police. In short, getting a job with the police department depended on political connections. Selection criteria for recruitment were minimal, and background checks were absent. In terms of the job, since policing was disproportionately a decentralized profession, supervision was minimal during this era, and so police officers had considerable freedom to apply the law in the manner they felt necessary. Thus, both political and economic corruption was prevalent, if not rampant. Most importantly, political machines (i.e., political parties that had almost exclusive control on the reins of municipal power) dominated many city services.

During this time, there was a chicken-and-egg scenario happening. Roberg and Kuykendall (1993) suggest:

> To be elected to public office, politicians had to make promises to citizens. One of the most important promises was related to employment. Public jobs became a reward for some individuals who supported the political party in power. Police jobs became an important part of a political patronage system. These types of jobs were popular because they required little or no skill and paid well when compared with other jobs that also required minimal ability. (p. 63)

This era reflects political involvement in law enforcement. Police officers were very important to political machine bosses. There was a sort of mutual dependence. During election time, police would help "get the vote out" by transporting individuals who would vote for the machine bosses and their team, therefore frustrating efforts by citizens who would vote for the opposition. The white middle and upper class supported legislation that controlled and wanted the police to enforce "morality" laws (i.e., to control gambling, drinking, and prostitution) which was primarily perpetrated—or so they believed—by the poor and by certain ethnic groups.

By the end of the 19th century, many police were Irish immigrants who did not always enforce these morality laws. Not only were they quite tolerant of gambling, public intoxication, and prostitution, but it is possible they even participated in these activities. As cities physically expanded, it became more difficult for local government to manage them. There was an increase in crime and population, traffic congestion, health problems, and inadequate housing. Understandably, criticisms against the police increased.

Nevertheless, one of the changes involved the way in which police officers and chiefs were recruited onto the forces. The *Pendleton Act* was passed in 1983 in an effort to stamp out corruption at the federal level. The legislation made it illegal to terminate employees because of their political affiliations. Shortly after its passage, the states and municipalities instituted similar laws.

From 1890 to 1920—generally identified as the Progressive Era—many social problems (e.g., child labor, poor work conditions) were addressed by the government and by elites. The progressives (i.e., middle- and upper-class educated Protestants who were influential during the turn of the century) encouraged honesty and efficiency among government workers, more authority for public officials, and the use of experts for specific problems. They also wanted to reform government services based on principles of industrial management (i.e., efficiency; increased quality of service at a low cost; centralized control; good leadership; and rational set of rules, regulations, and specialization). These changes also applied to police agencies. This leads us toward a new model and/or era with a different approach to law enforcement.

Bureaucratic/Legalistic/Scientific and Reform Era

This period, which took place approximately between 1920 and 1960, established the foundations for the professionalization of law enforcement. Policing became recognized as having a distinct body of knowledge and skills that needed to be taught to recruits. During this time, police departments adopted elements of the bureaucratic process, a focus on the law, and the use of the scientific model. The police used their mission to fight crime to improve their public image, and to mobilize support for their reforms. They also began to emphasize the dramatic aspect of their work. Some of the other changes that took place during this era included less political meddling, increased efficiency and centralized management, and a commitment to professionalism. These changes were due to the introduction of science into police work, changes in American society and politics, and the growth of the police reform movement (Roberg and Kuykendall, 1993).

Application of the Scientific Method. Efforts were made to apply the scientific method to European police work. Scientific developments—such as the Bertillon system for identifying suspects—were introduced into law enforcement. The Bertillon system was based on precise physical measurements, detailed descriptions of criminal and suspects (e.g., scars), crime scenes, photographs of criminals, and use of fingerprints. This approach was rational and detached, and it provided part of the body of knowledge for training. This was also the beginning of the introduction of the Uniform Crime Reports started by the Federal Bureau of Investigation.

American Society Changed. Shortly after the mass production (and consumption) of the automobile and the construction of highways, middle-class whites started leaving the big cities and moving to the suburbs. The inner cities were disproportionately left with the poor, unskilled, and powerless—typically meaning minorities (e.g., primarily African Americans, Hispanics and newly arrived immigrants) who were in great need of city services. The inner cities became increasingly dangerous. Police were frequently accused of mistreating immigrants and minorities. The racist actions led to increased tension between minorities and the police. This conflict was an important factor in numerous urban riots of the 20th century. Meanwhile, suburbanites expected efficient and quality-driven government services. Police were expected to be well trained and courteous, to have the best equipment, and to operate in accordance with the latest management techniques. Many of the progressive-era and legalistic-model qualities had the most positive impact in the suburbs.

Reform. Reform was often instituted as a reaction to numerous crime commissions. Prominent citizens and experts were appointed to these bodies (e.g., the Chicago Crime Commission) to investigate and make recommendations for change in police departments. Over time, many of these commissions became permanent fixtures in the urban locales in which they were started.

Why was this necessary? "By 1931, there were seven local, sixteen state, and two national crime commissions established to investigate the police. . . . The most well-known of these was the National Commission on Law Observance and Enforcement, established by Herbert Hoover in 1929" (Roberg and Kuykendall, 1993 p. 68). It was also known as the Wickersham Commission (1929–1931), so named for the prominent judge who headed the group. It produced 12 reports, including recommendations for minimizing police brutality and for improving officers' education and training.

August Vollmer (1876–1955), the chief of police in Berkeley, Calif., from 1905 to 1932 who also helped establish the criminology program at the University of California-Berkeley, was the main consultant to the Wickersham Commission (Carte and Carte, 1975). The report identified the most problematic issues in American policing, which were, at the time, excessive political influence, inadequate leadership and management, ineffective recruitment and training, and insufficient technological services.

After the Wickersham Commission, individuals like Vollmer and O.W. Wilson, the superintendent of the Chicago Police Department, championed the professionalization of the police, including the introduction of the legalistic approach to police work (i.e., criminal laws are enforced without concern for politics by well-trained, scientifically proficient professionals in centralized organizations). The police function mainly focused on fighting crime. Nevertheless, many police agencies remained dominated by politics well into the 1960s.

The Great Depression, which began in 1929, made police reform easier because there was less money available for the duplication of effort. This translated into decreased opposition to centralizing the police. As a result, many precincts were closed, officers in the field were better controlled, there was a decrease in meddling by politicians, and educated people became interested in police work as careers because they believed that it offered job security. Also, this period was marked by the beginning of collective bargaining between organized labor and management.

By the 1930s, the reform of police agencies was well established. Centralization had been accomplished. Standardization of behavior through professionalization was occurring, and new policies and procedures were being introduced. There was also increased education and training available to police officers. Selection and promotion was now primarily based on merit. Police departments became committed to crime fighting and to doing so using the latest science and technology. As Swanson, Territo, and Taylor (2008) note:

> Stimulated by high-profile cases, such as the kidnapping of Charles Lindbergh's baby in 1932, the Federal Bureau of Investigation (FBI), under the direction of J. Edgar Hoover, began to emerge as a dominant entity in American policing. In 1935, the FBI created the National Police Academy, where local police leaders and officials were educated in the 'professional' and 'scientific' aspects of law enforcement. (p. 14)

During World War II (1941–1945), police departments lost many of their most able officers to the military. Starting in the late 1950s and well into the 1960s, police behavior was significantly affected by the *due process revolution*, a period of American legal history during which important Supreme Court cases [e.g., *Mapp v. Ohio* (1961), *Gideon v. Wainwright* (1963), *Escobedo v. Illinois* (1964), *Miranda v. Arizona* (1966), *Terry v. Ohio* (1968)] reinforced the constitutional rights of suspects in cases of arrest, search, self-incrimination, freedom of speech, due process, and right to counsel.

Community Service Era

The 1960s

During the 1960s, large-scale protests and riots over demands of increased civil rights, racial inequality, and America's military participation in Indochina (Vietnam, in particular) kept municipal police busy. A number of questionable police-citizen encounters and shootings of unarmed African Americans resulted in widespread rioting and looting in many large urban centers.

These events prompted the federal government to initiate two federal criminal justice commissions. The first, the Commission on Law Enforcement and Criminal Justice, released its well-cited report *The Challenge of Crime in a Free Society* in 1967. The second, the National Advisory Commission on Civil Disorders (often referred to as the Kerner Commission) published its findings in 1968.

In the 1960s, a series of federally funded commissions, including the United States National Commission on the Causes of Crime and Disorder (1968), investigated race riots and increasing crime in the country. The reports made several recommendations, one of which was the passage of the Omnibus Crime Control and Safe Streets Act, which established a separate branch of the Department of Justice called the Law Enforcement Assistance Administration (Conley, 1994).

Its mission was to provide funds for postsecondary institutions of higher education to train criminal justice personnel; give out grants and low-cost loans to practitioners pursuing higher education; give money to universities to develop programs in criminology and criminal justice; increase specialized knowledge about criminology/criminal justice; and improve education for practitioners.

During this time, many criminal justice professionals earned bachelor's degrees through government financial assistance. Others completed master's or doctoral degrees. In fact, a handful of well-known and respected contemporary police chiefs, many of whom are now retiring, such as Willy Williams (former chief of the Philadelphia and Los Angeles police departments) and Lee Brown (former chief of the Houston and New York City police departments), hold PhDs that they earned with the assistance of LEAA funds. In 1982, the LEAA closed and then reconstituted as the National Institute of Justice. In sum, federal funding led to a general increase in the academic respectability of the criminology/criminal justice field.

Largely because of the advent of motorized patrol and partially because police departments wanted to isolate themselves from politics, police officers and their departments were now being interpreted as being too distant from the people they policed. From the 1920s on, selection standards increased and professionalization became not only a buzzword but also a practicality for most big-city police departments.

The 1970s

During the 1970s, there was an increase in the amount of long-term social scientific research on policing that made use of observational methods. This included groundbreaking research on police patrol (e.g., Kelling et al., 1974) and on criminal investigation (e.g., Greenwood, Chaiken, and Petersilia, 1977). This body of research called into question assumptions previously held by police professionals about police practices in these two areas. There was also an increase in municipal police efforts to reach out to the communities where they worked, which laid the foundation for later efforts in community policing and problem-oriented policing in particular. In the late 1970s, many police departments struggled to achieve accreditation, a method by which an agency's performance would be subject to national standards developed by experts in the field rather than simply the whims of local politicians and state boards of inspection. For additional information on the challenge of accreditation, see chapter 16.

The 1980s

During and since the 1980s, a handful of notable incidents, trends, and seminal pieces of research have affected policing. These include the introduction of community policing, the introduction of zero-tolerance policing and CompStat, the fear and reality of terrorism, and the preoccupation with undocumented immigrants. Since the 1960s, politicians, police administrators, and community leaders realized that old policing strategies such as motorized patrol as well as the racial and ethnic composition of police forces were not effective. As a result, selected police scholars, practitioners and police departments developed two complementary approaches: community policing and problem-oriented policing.

In 1979, University of Wisconsin–Madison law professor Herman Goldstein published his quintessential article on problem-oriented policing. He suggested that since the development of motorized patrol, police had become increasingly out of touch with the communities they served. This resulted in an increase in both crime and citizens' disrespect for the police. To change this state of affairs, police needed to shift their focus ever so slightly from crimes that have already occurred to the problems that lead to crime. Goldstein advocated that police departments form true partnerships with the communities in which they work to solve mutually identified problems. Problem-oriented policing became one of several strategies embedded in community policing. These concepts included bike patrols, mini-police stations, and problem-oriented policing. Shortly after the publication of Goldstein's ideas, a handful of police departments experimented with community policing. It took another 15 years for his ideas to result in the formation and passage of the 1994 Violent Crime Control and Law Enforcement Act (also known as the Crime Act), which, among its major components, led to the creation of the Office of Community-Oriented Policing in the Department of Justice. (For a more detailed discussion of this challenge, see chapter 8.)

In 1982, James Q. Wilson and George Kelling wrote a seminal article called "Broken Windows," which argued that small-scale deviance and neighborhood disorder (e.g., houses boarded up, in disrepair, lawns not cut, graffiti) can have a big effect on neighborhood deterioration and thus crime. This led to the slow and selected introduction of zero-tolerance policing— that is, the aggressive enforcement of one or more criminal laws in a particular jurisdiction and/or during a specific period; no discretion is allowed on the part of officers. It was also seminal for the introduction of CompStat (short form for Computer Analysis of Crime Statistics, or Comprehensive Computer Statistics) in the New York City Police Department. In essence, through the CompStat program, on a regular basis, the police department converts crime statistics into maps of criminal events. This information is then used by senior management to regularly monitor the performance of precinct level staff in crime reduction efforts. For more information on CompStat, see chapter 15.

The 1990s

In 1991, African-American motorist Rodney King was beaten by Los Angeles Police Department officers during a routine traffic stop. (For a more detailed discussion of this challenge, see chapter 10 on police violence/excessive force.) This was a turning point in American policing; it forced the federal government to take a renewed interest in this social problem. Initially, the government dispatched Warren Christopher, who later became Secretary of State in the Clinton Administration, to investigate the problem. The beating also stimulated the 1994 passage of the *Violent Crime Control and Law Enforcement Act* (also known as the Crime Act). Among its many provisions, it called for 10,000 police officers to be on the streets engaging in community policing. To receive the funds for this purpose, jurisdictions needed to apply through the newly created Office of Community-Oriented Policing, a division of the Department of Justice. The Crime Act also set aside money that allowed the National Institute of Justice to conduct research.

Toward the latter part of the 20th century, U.S. municipal police departments encountered numerous unforeseeable problems, including both domestic and international terrorism (Ross, 2006a). More of a problem for big-city police departments than smaller jurisdictions, it was clear that law enforcement agencies had a difficult time understanding and properly responding to this relatively new threat to public safety. New York City, because of previous terrorist incidents such as the World Trade Center bombing in 1986 and the 9/11 attacks, were a visible reminder that foreign terrorist organizations could attack large-scale symbols of American economic power and injure and kill numerous innocent civilians. For a more detailed description of this challenge, see chapter 17.

Changes were implemented in the way "police officers exercised their discretion, particularly when it came to the use of force. Gradually, many departments began to develop guidelines for officers in this area and to provide training in the use of appropriate methods" (Roberg and Kuykendall, 1993, p. 70). Other changes involved the hiring of more women and visible minorities, additional training for police officers in human relations, and a greater emphasis on crime prevention, training for officers, and management and administration for senior officers.

Finally, the perception that illegal immigration is out of control, primarily caused by problems of enforcement around the U.S.–Mexican border, has led to increased demands for municipal police throughout the country to help monitor and respond to this sector of the population. Some citizen complaints have their origins in public uneasiness surrounding the numerous day-labor centers/locations in the United States, where young Central American males wait for short-term employment; the intervention of police in robberies of Central Americans, who are typically paid in cash; and the periodic involvement of police in crime-related matters.

Conclusion

In sum, there have been three stages in the history of modern policing in the United States: the political, the bureaucratic/legalistic/scientific and reform, and the community service. At each stage, a series of challenges were addressed; while solutions were proposed and some were implemented, not all were successful. Policing is an evolving field, and police need to respond to these challenges. Living in a democratic society, police must be constantly aware of their mission and operate within the bounds of the law and the professionalism which they've fought so hard to achieve.

Notes

1. Clearly, the history of policing predates the existence of the United States, but for purposes of this book, a discussion of this period is not included.
2. The reader should also take into consideration that there is disagreement among experts on the history of municipal policing in the United States (e.g., Hartmann, 1988).

Glossary

Accreditation: A method to determine if a criminal justice agency meets standards established by a respected accrediting body (e.g., American Correctional Association, Commission on Accreditation for Law Enforcement Agencies).

Broken windows theory: Developed by George Kelling and James Q. Wilson, who argued that small-scale deviance and neighborhood disorder (e.g., houses boarded up and in disrepair, lawns not cut, graffiti) can have a big effect on neighborhood deterioration and thus crime.

Community (oriented) policing: A cooperative effort between police and the communities they serve where both work together to solve crime and crime-related problems. Also a series of strategies that bring the police closer to the community to reduce and solve crime and crime-related problems. It is often defined by the programs it subsumes, including bike patrol, storefront policing, and problem-oriented policing.

CompStat: A relatively new management technique that includes weekly meetings of senior police personnel (especially the chief/commissioner and district commanders) to review crime that has occurred in their sector/district/borough to monitor responses to reduce crime in those areas. This concept usually involves crime mapping and was pioneered in New York City during the early 1990s.

Day watch system: System of policing that predated modern policing whereby citizens were obligated to take turns patrolling the community during the day.

Due process revolution: A period of American legal history during which important supreme court cases [e.g., *Mapp v. Ohio* (1961), *Gideon v. Wainwright* (1963), *Escobedo v. Illinois* (1964), *Miranda v. Arizona* (1966), *Terry v. Ohio* (1968)] reinforced the constitutional rights of suspects in cases of arrest, search, self-incrimination, freedom of speech, due process, and right to counsel.

Law Enforcement Assistance Administration (LEAA): Formed during the late 1960s as one of the major recommendations that came out of the national riot commission. Established in the Department of Justice to provide grants and loans for police officers to improve their post-secondary education, extend research grants to criminologists, and offer funds to colleges and universities for the creation or enhancement of programs in criminology and criminal justice.

Modern policing: Period beginning with the establishment of the first police department in London (1812) to present day.

Night watch system: System of policing that predated modern policing whereby citizens were obligated to take turns patrolling the community during the night.

Problem-oriented policing: Getting police officers and departments to think creatively, recognizing connections across similar incidents that they may not have been able to see when they otherwise are responding to random incidents or reactively responding to calls for service.

Progressives: Middle- and upper-class educated Protestants in the United States who were influential during the late 19th and early 20th centuries.

Quality of life issues/indicators: Building upon Kelling and Wilson's broken window identifying a number of visible cues in a neighborhood that would indicate the neighborhood was declining, including the number of abandoned homes, presence of homeless people, and vagrancy.

Theories on the development of police agencies: Competing explanations underlying the reasons for the formation of municipal police agencies in the United States.

Zero-tolerance policing: The aggressive enforcement of one or more criminal laws in a particular jurisdiction and/or during a specific period; no discretion is allowed on the part of officer.

Chapter Questions

Part One: Multiple Choice Questions

1. The *London Metropolitan Police Act* established a full-time uniformed police force with the primary purpose of:
   a. arresting suspected offenders
   b. supervising public programs
   c. patrolling the city
   d. all of the above
   e. some of the above

2. Who proposed the first modern police department?
   a. Anderson
   b. Belnap
   c. Wilson
   d. Peel
   e. none; it evolved on its own

3. In what part of the United States were slave patrols originally formed?
   a. northeast
   b. southwest
   c. northwest
   d. deep south
   e. none of the above

4. Urban dispersion theory is concerned with which of the following?
   a. controlling the unruly masses
   b. increases in crime and the need for an organization to monitor and control crime
   c. cities wanting police departments because other similar cities had them
   d. all of the above
   e. none of the above

5. By about what time did most cities in the United States have police departments?
   a. 1860s
   b. 1870s
   c. 1880s
   d. 1890s
   e. 1900s

6. Around the dawn of the 21st century, what was the most important development in police practice?
   a. beat patrol
   b. finger printing
   c. community policing
   d. CompStat/crime mapping
   e. motorized patrol

7. Between the mid-1800s and the 1920s, police departments were known for:
   a. establishing policies and procedures
   b. political corruption
   c. establishing professionalism
   d. improved training, selection, organization, and management
   e. a and c

8. The Law Enforcement Assistance Administration was created:
   a. to improve the educational level of police
   b. to conduct research on causes of crime and the effectiveness of the criminal justice system
   c. as part of the National Institute of Justice
   d. a and b
   e. all of the above

9. What is the name of the law that states that citizens must come to the aid of a police officer when needed or if called?
   a. vigilantes
   b. Posse Comitatus
   c. substantive law
   d. procedural law
   e. none of the above

10. Why was the constable night-watch system abandoned?
    a. The work was voluntary.
    b. Substitutes were inadequately paid.
    c. Replacements were inefficient.
    d. Substitutes were poorly educated.
    e. all of the above

11. Modern policing consists of which stages?
    a. political
    b. legalistic
    c. community service
    d. some of the above
    e. all of the above

12. On which country's system of policing was the American system of policing modeled?
    a. England
    b. France
    c. Greece
    d. Spain
    e. none of the above

13. Which of the following Presidential Administrations created the LEAA?
    a. Bush (George W.)
    b. Clinton
    c. Kennedy
    d. Johnson
    e. Reagan

14. In recent times, who was one of the earliest theorists of community policing?
    a. Bayley
    b. Goldstein
    c. Marx
    d. Moore
    e. Ross

15. What are the four theories that have been identified to explain the development of police departments in the United States?
    a. causal, effects, pure, and applied
    b. classical, behavioral, legalistic, and paramilitary
    c. problem orientation, education, community needs, and political influence
    d. crime control, class control, urban dispersion, and disorder–control
    e. critical, interpretive, ontological, and formal

Part Two: Short-Answer Questions

1. List three scientific achievements introduced into policing between 1921 and 1960.

2. What is the difference between substantive and procedural law?

3. What was the night-watch system?

4. What is Posse Comitatus?

5. What are three stages in history of modern policing in America?

6. What is the service and contingency stage?

7. What are four explanations marshaled to explain the development of municipal police departments in the United States?

8. List three changes that occurred in police departments during the service and contingency era.

9. What is community policing?

10. What sorts of advances in investigative technology have been developed over the past few decades?

Part Three: Essay Questions

1. Why is it important to study the history of policing?

2. How important are politics for police departments of today?

3. How useful would it be for major police departments to hire professional historians?

The Mythology of Municipal Policing

Introduction

The majority of the public and some law enforcement officers see police work as "exciting," "dangerous," and "stressful." Combined, these attributes create "many negative side effects" for police officers, police organizations, and the communities they serve (Kappeler, Sluder, and Alpert, 1994, p. 209). The reader should keep in mind that no two police officers—or departments—function or react in the same manner. What does this mean? Creating a realistic picture of the "true" nature of policing is often difficult. Policing is indeed a demanding and dangerous job, a fact that should not be minimized by what follows. However, this chapter is meant to introduce the exaggerations, mythology, misrepresentations, and stereotypes of policing. These perceptions can have negative side effects in terms of recruitment of appropriate police candidates and unrealistic expectations about police capabilities among members of the public.

Included in this discussion is a brief review of the power of various political actors to create, bolster, and engage in mythmaking. First, some caveats are in order. Some individuals may know police officers who experience exciting work details or suffer from particular problems (e.g., stress), but these stories are only anecdotal evidence. And although good policy and practice considers this type of information, informed police managers and administrators are best advised to base their decisions on evidence gathered in a scientific (empirical) fashion; otherwise, they will end up drawing broad generalizations from the isolated incidents. Because of this, empirical research should play a critical role in departmental planning processes (e.g., Manheim and Rich, 1986). Exhibit 3.1 provides one example of mythmaking on the big screen.

Exhibit 3.1   *Cop Land*

Written and directed by James Mangold, this 1997 film examines how Freddy Heflin (played by Sylvester Stallone), a small town New Jersey sheriff, almost single-handedly confronts the corruption engaged in by a group of rogue NYPD officers led by Ray Donlan, a corrupt senior-ranking NYPD police officer, (played by Harvey Keitel). As time has passed, Freddy has become a drunk, and he is shown hanging out at the local bar, where the NYPD cops also drink. Some years earlier, Freddy saved the wife of a NYPD officer, Joey Randone, from drowning when her car careened off a bridge and into the water. Freddy originally wanted to become an NYPD officer, but was not hired because he had sustained a bad ear injury from the rescue.

The film begins with NYPD officers attending a party for a fellow officer, nicknamed Superboy. Superboy, slightly intoxicated, returns home, but his car is sideswiped en route. He pursues the car, and the passenger of the car pulls out what Superboy thinks is a machine gun. Superboy panics and shoots the car several times, killing the driver and the passenger. When the other officers show up, they determine that the gun was actually a club (a steering wheel locking mechanism). One of the officers places a plant-down gun at the scene of the crime and challenges the ambulance driver who disputes the officers' explanation of events. Superboy feigns his own suicide by jumping off a bridge into the Hudson River.

Ray has enormous power. He arrives at a NYPD police funeral attended by Freddy and the police commissioner. After that, Freddy approaches Figgs, another NYPD officer (played by Ray Liotta), at the cop bar and asks him to help bring the officer corruption to the attention of the police administration. Freddy approaches the Internal Affairs (IA) office, which is run by Moe Tilden, an officer portrayed by Robert DeNiro, and is not taken seriously. Freddy sees sensitive files that are lying around the office and takes them back to his office to try to learn more about what is going on in the NYPD. Freddy figures out that a high-level conspiracy is active in the NYPD, knowledge that causes him to be threatened by the NYPD officers living in his town. Superboy, who has been hiding at Ray's, is threatened by Ray and his group of officers. At the very end of the movie, Freddy, with the assistance of Figgs, manages to take Superboy to the IA office to get some closure on this case. The ending is the most dramatic of the movie.

All in all, there are several realistic and unrealistic aspects to this film, which are worthy of classroom discussion.

Sources of Myths About Police Work

As mentioned in the previous chapter, in addition to personal experience, details about policing can be learned from a variety of sources, including contacts with police officers and administrators, researchers or consultants, victims, and criminals. However, most impressions about police officers are developed through mass media exposure. The mass media consists of a number of cultural institutions and entertainment vehicles, including Hollywood films, fictional books, newspapers and magazines, television, music, and the Internet (Inciardi and Dee, 1987; Kaskinsky, 1994; Leishman and Mason, 2003; Perlmutter, 2000).

One of the most important media forms is television. The majority of Americans watch television. This is their primary source of entertainment and often their main venue of information about current affairs. Television programs not only educate the public, but also provide entertainment. In many cases, it is through this medium that viewers form and create many of their impressions about individuals, society, and cultural institutions.

A serious crime is a newsworthy event. Media coverage of such an event typically involves a sympathetic victim, an interview with a police officer or spokesperson, some dramatic footage, video recordings of a car chase or a robbery in progress, and occasionally the arrest of an individual. Indeed, the depiction of police officers as working in an exciting profession is not a new aspect to media coverage. In the late 1800s, newspapers like the *Times* (London), for example, featured stories about courageous police officers chasing criminals and solving crimes.

One of the most dominant messages that television series and Hollywood movies produce is the notion that policing is exciting, dangerous and stressful (Crew, 1990; Crawford, 1999).

The Crime Fighter Image

The epitome of police-related thematic character types emphasized by the mass media, especially television and Hollywood movies, is the crime fighter image. At its basic level, this projection involves the well-used icon of police officers as solitary and misunderstood individuals, combating criminals while being forced to work within the confines of an indifferent and overly bureaucratic police department. Other important iterations of this motif can include "high-speed pursuits of wanted felons, questioning persons suspected of having committed serious crimes, shooting it out with dangerous criminals, and in other law enforcement tasks requiring precision skills and often under threatening conditions" (Kappeler et al., 1994, p. 211). Occasionally this crime fighter type includes the "police officer single-handedly or sometimes with a minor partner, fighting diabolical, sophisticated and well-armed criminals. These are not run-of-the mill criminals like the drunk driver, the thief or the check forger. [In the movies] police officers are pitted against . . . serial murderers and international terrorists" (Kappeler et al., 1994, p. 210). The sad reality is that policing is rarely as exciting, dangerous and stressful as the mass media make it out to be.

Police officers and police departments are largely responsible for creating and maintaining many of the myths of policing and the crime fighter image. This is mainly done through their capable public relations units. The myths and the image have a number of benefits, and can potentially intimidate and deter criminals and create or maintain the power, prestige, and respect of the police. Some officers believe that these effects make police work easier. This is perhaps why police departments have willingly allowed camera crews to accompany them on all sorts of dangerous operations, including drug raids (Kappeler et al., 1994). Moreover, if members of the public wanted information that is contrary to that which is portrayed in the media, they would need to actively search through scholarly research and/or interview experts in the field. Unfortunately, the public does not have the resources (i.e., time, money, access) or necessarily the desire to do this.

It must be understood that not everyone who is exposed to the myths believes them. In all likelihood, those who are young and who are less educated are most susceptible to the stereotypes and misinterpretation. As people mature, enter the workforce, and have more experiences with law enforcement professionals, they start to question the claims of so-called authorities such as the media (Exhibit 3.2).

The media image contrasts sharply with reality. "Police officers do considerably less 'crime fighting' than one might imagine" (Kappeler et al., 1994, p. 211). The majority of a police officer's job is dedicated to peace keeping, order maintenance (e.g., giving directions to people), or problem solving, and considerably less to law enforcement (Walker and Katz, 2004).

Naturally, police professionals do not readily try to debunk this perception. Why? Because the stereotype can help them achieve their goals. In general, one of the most important objectives of a police department is the

Exhibit 3.2 **Popular Hollywood Movies on Policing**	
Naked City (1948)	*A Man in a Uniform* (1993)
French Connection (1971)	*L.A. Confidential* (1997)
Serpico (1973)	*Cop Land* (1997)
Prince of the City (1981)	*Training Day* (2001)
Die Hard (1988)	*Pride and Glory* (2008)
Q and A (1990)	*Righteous Kill* (2008)
Internal Affairs (1990)	

ability to maintain or increase its resources. If the public thought that the police profession was an easy one, then less government spending would be devoted to public safety.

The Myths of Policing Examined in Detail

Several myths about police officers exist. Some of the most important ones relate to deaths caused by officers, dangers of police work, calls for domestic violence, stress, suicide, drug and alcohol abuse, police mortality, and divorce rates (Kappeler et al., 1994).

Deaths by Police Officers

Although there are no national statistics on the number of individuals who are killed each year by police officers, one can establish an approximate number of police shootings by examining the separate list of Deaths by Legal Intervention contained in the Vital Statistics, which are essentially "the birth and death records that are collected and published by the federal government's United States Public Health Service" (Kappeler et al., 1994, p. 213) and the Supplementary Homicide Report (SHR), which is part of the Uniform Crime Report (UCR). In a comparative analysis between the two data sources looking at the years 1976-1998, Loftin and colleagues (2003) reported 8,658 (SHR) and 6,686 (NCSS) deaths by police officers. Over the 22 years of the data collection, there was an average of 309 (SHR) and 239 (NCSS) justifiable homicides each year.

According to Kappeler and colleagues (1994), "not only are killings caused by police rare events, but the[y] are becoming even more infrequent. . . . In effect, law enforcement personnel were killing about half as many people in 1984 as they were in 1971" (p. 214). What has caused this development? Police departments have developed tighter policies and practices around the use of lethal force, including better training of police officers. This improvement is the direct result of the famous Supreme Court case, *Garner v. Tennessee* (1985), which allows plaintiffs (typically the deceased victims' loved ones) to sue police departments and their related cities for amounts in excess of 1 million dollars. In reality, "the majority of police officers will go their entire career and never shoot anybody" (Kappeler et al., 1994, p. 215). In short, the number of people killed by police officers has declined significantly.

The Dangers of Police Work

The media continuously portrays policing as a dangerous occupation. For example, when a police officer dies in the line of duty, there is typically copious local news coverage of the sad event, accompanied by emotion-laden images of the widow, the children, the murder scene, and the funeral (Kappeler et al., 1994). But what is the reality of the prevalence of police deaths? Since 1996, the FBI has collected data and published an annual report, *Law Enforcement Officers Killed and Assaulted* (http://www.fbi.gov/ucr/killed/2008). Over the past eight cycles of data collection, a high point of 105 deaths was reached in 2001, which is largely attributable to the officers who died in the World Trade Center, and a low statistic of 22 municipal officers killed in the line of duty was recorded in 2008. These numbers clearly indicate that the killing of police officers is exceptionally rare.

To help gauge the level of danger inherent to the policing profession, it is helpful to compare policing to other types of jobs. As it turns out, according to data collected by the Bureau of Labor Statistics, policing is not even included in the top 10 list of dangerous occupations. This information can be found in the Bureau of Labor Statistics' semi-annual report "National Census of Fatal Occupational Injuries 2008" (http://www.bls.gov/news.release/pdf/cfoi.pdf).

The introduction of bulletproof vests to the police field has lessened the likelihood that officers will die of gunshot wounds while on duty. Not all officers, however, wear bulletproof vests; some find them very uncomfortable because they do not fit well. Some departments require officers to have their vests near them at all times, and many keep their vests in the trunks of their cars. Various officers may not wear the vests because they have heard about officers who are shot in the head, a part of the body the vest cannot protect. The perception of the vest's weakness may cause some officers to choose not to wear the vests. With this in mind, how are most officers killed in the line of duty? Traffic accidents, usually involving high-speed chases, is the most prevalent cause of police officer injury and death. "Research shows that officers who are engaged in pursuit of criminals on highways experience a collision of some type in 32 percent of those pursuits; in 13 percent of those cases, officers are injured" (Stevens, 2009, p. 303). (See Exhibit 3.3.)

Dangerousness of Calls Involving Domestic Violence

During the 1980s, numerous stories circulated about officers responding to domestic calls/domestic disturbances and, through the course of the interaction, being seriously injured and sometimes killed. The violence sometimes occurred at the hands of one or both of the parties involved. While they could understand why a man who abused his wife or girlfriend might lash out at a police officer, many observers were surprised when the woman who was allegedly abused struck out against the officer. Due to the unpredictable nature of domestic violence events, many people believe that the domestic call is the most dangerous one to which an officer can respond (Kappeler et al., 1994, p. 217).

The empirical evidence, however, contradicts this perception. Kappeler and colleagues (1994) cite an analysis of the situational characteristics of on-the-job police killings that occurred in the United States between 1978 and 1980; only 5.2% of deaths occurred in situations in which officers had responded to domestic disturbances. Other investigators, such as Garner

| Exhibit 3.3   The Ten Most Dangerous Jobs in the United States |

Occupation Fatalities per 100,000 workers	
Fishers and related fishing workers	128.9
Logging workers	115.7
Aircraft pilots and flight engineers	72.4
Structural iron and steel workers	46.4
Farmers and ranchers	39.5
Refuse and recyclable material collectors	36.8
Roofers	34.4
Electrical power-line installers and repairers	29.8
Driver/sales workers and truck drivers	22.8
Taxi drivers and chauffeurs	19.3

Source: Bureau of Labor Statistics; Selected occupations with high fatality rates, 2008 (http://www.bls.gov/news.release/pdf/cfoi.pdf).

and Clemmer (1986), examined existing statistics and determined that deaths to officers responding to domestic disturbances were overstated and that other kinds of calls for service (i.e., robbery and burglary) were far more risky to patrol officers.

Police Stress

Police officers experience numerous sources of stress. It has been argued by some that the stress among officers leads to higher rates of suicide, alcohol and drug use and abuse, and death than among workers in other occupations (Kappeler et al., 1994). The following discussion will critically look at this assumption.

Police Suicide

Many people seem to believe that high suicide rates are both a cause and an effect of the excessive amount of stress in the policing field. The evidence, however, appears to be contradictory. Indeed one early study of 36 occupations discovered that police officers had the second highest frequency of suicide (Labovitz and Hagedorn, 1971). A follow up study by Lester (1983) indicated that police officer's suicide rates were comparable to individuals who were self-employed and those working on an assembly line. In short, "Uncritical readings of these findings are often offered as direct evidence of the stress inherent in police work" (Kappeler et al., 1994, p. 221).

The literature and statistics related to suicide rates are contradictory in their findings. One should not assume that stress causes police officers to kill themselves, anymore than those who join the army actively wish to die. Despite the lack of a concrete link between policing and suicide, the following issue should be kept in mind: "It is difficult to obtain accurate statistics about police suicide because officer deaths are often not reported as suicides, largely because officer death benefits would not be available to the individual's survivors and because officer suicide is seen as a weakness of a 'fallen brother'" (Stevens, 2009, p. 361).

Drug and Alcohol Abuse

Many people think that police officers suffer from a higher rate of alcoholism and drug abuse than those in other professions. Indeed, several studies on this problem have been conducted (Reiss, 1971; Barker, 1983; Kraska and Kappeler, 1988). With respect to alcohol abuse, the figures tend to be relatively high, but the validity of the statistics is compromised by a number of agency problems. Police departments typically do not want to tell researchers about the alcoholics in their midst, which leads to a skewing of the statistical pool. One of the more recent studies (Lindsay, Taylor and Shelly, 2008) of 1328 Mississippi municipal, sheriff, and state law enforcement officers indicated that their alcohol consumption was consistent with levels found in the general population and that approximately 70 percent of them either did not drink at all or only drank once a month. Meanwhile, the empirical research indicates that very few police officers use illegal drugs. When drugs are used, it is typically for recreational purposes and is not the result of stress (Kappeler et al., 1994).

Police Mortality

According to one popular belief, the high levels of stress that police are under result in shorter life spans when compared to other occupations. "When one links the dangers, the suicide rate, and the stress myths, it is a natural inference that police officers must experience a greater rate of work-related mortality" (Kappeler et al., 1994, p. 224). According to empirical research, compared to the rest of the population, police officers do not lead shorter-than-average lives (Raub, 1988).

Police Divorces

Many people believe that police officers have higher divorce rates then other kinds of professions. Some of the causes for marital failures are as follows: shift work; the stress created by the need to work nights, weekends, overtime, and holidays; frequent interactions with members of the public, which could lead to greater opportunities for officers to cheat on their spouses; and exposure to the worst aspects of humanity, which could lead to emotional distance. Despite these plausible reasons for increased divorce rates, "the findings from various studies are contradictory" (Kappeler et al., 1994, p. 226).

Conclusion: Solving the Problem

The aim of this chapter is to sensitize students to the myths about police by focusing on seven issues and seeking to explain the reality of each.

Undoubtedly, Hollywood movies and prime-time television cop shows are dramatized for effect. In reality, police officers spend a considerable amount of time doing boring activities, such as driving around in their cars, responding to often repetitious and irrelevant questions, and filling out numerous pages of paperwork. In order to counter the myths of policing, more efforts should focus on educating the public. Police officers and their organizations need to be more accessible to the public through police citizens' academies (i.e., short-term classroom/instructional programs administered by police departments to educate the public about police practices), seminars, public forums, and presentations at public schools and institutions of higher learning.

Police departments could also increase the frequency with which they offer ride-alongs to interested members of the public (e.g., students and prospective police officers). Over the past three decades, one of the best ways that the reality of policing has been conveyed to local residents has been through community policing programs. Under the community policing model, increased contact between police officers and citizens is a major goal. In the post 9/11 era, because of budget cutbacks, the growth of Comp-Stat, and the fear of terrorism, it appears that community policing, however, is now a thing of the past.

Law enforcement agencies, policy makers, and the public seem to have a difficult time agreeing on the best way in which the reality of policing should be understood and disseminated. This uncertainty is not only grounded in the technical aspects of policing, but police officers are typically distrustful of outsiders and are reluctant to speak openly to citizens, something that has been referred to as the "blue wall" of silence (Becker, 1963).

Criminologists and other interested social scientists might be encouraged to conduct, use and disseminate more scholarly research on police practices. This could be expanded to offering and teaching more courses that critically analyze these myths. Researchers need to make the data they gather about policing more available to the public. Their work should make its way beyond the scholarly journals and into the popular press. Investigators could also focus on determining why people have so many misconceptions about the police field and make suggestions on how the stereotypes can be lessened. This begs several subsidiary issues including: 1. How frequent should scholarly research or courses that demystify police be done/offered? and 2. Who should pay for it? Unfortunately, the reward structure in academia does not encourage this.

Although it could be helpful and honest to debunk the myths, changing the view of policing could be detrimental to police agencies' funding sources. Police departments depend on the public believing that their main purpose is to be out in communities fighting crime and those officers are the essential "thin blue line" between good and evil. Presenting the reality of policing, particularly the monotonous, less glamorous aspects of the profession, might make the public think that police departments are not as essential as we think they are.

One should keep in mind, however, that a movie or television series that is extremely precise and realistic might not be ideal, since criminals could learn from it how to better exploit the weaknesses of police procedures. If this were the case, the safety of police officers and the public could be jeopardized. And even if one were to wish otherwise, the media, because it is so prominent, will long have a disproportionate influence on people in comparison to the impact of researchers, policy makers, and the police themselves. Despite this reality, it may be difficult, but not impossible, to challenge long and deeply held personal beliefs.

Glossary

Citizen police academies: Short-term classroom/instructional programs administered by police departments to educate the public about police practices.

Corruption: Acts involving the misuse of authority by police officers. These lead to personal gain for the officers in question or others.

Crime fighter image: A characterization developed by the mass media (especially television and Hollywood films) of police officers who are portrayed as solitary and misunderstood individuals combating criminals while also working within the confines of an indifferent and overly bureaucratic police department.

Death by legal intervention: When a person dies at the hands of a criminal justice practitioner (i.e., police officer or other law enforcement officer including corrections, probation, and parole) in the course of doing their job.

Ride-along: An arrangement for a civilian to spend a shift (or part thereof) in the passenger or back seat of a police car. This allows civilians to observe the work day of a police officer.

Thin Blue Line: The perception that if it was not for the police, society would devolve into anarchy.

Uniform Crime Reports: These reports contain official data on the crimes that are reported to law enforcement agencies in the United States.

Vital Statistics: Statistical data collected and maintained by the federal government on the births and deaths of individuals in the United States.

Chapter Questions

Part One: Multiple Choice Questions

1. What is the most prominent source of myths related to policing?
   a. Personal experience
   b. Mass media
   c. Scholarly research
   d. Victims
   e. All the above

2. Which of the following is a myth of policing?
   a. Policing is one of the most dangerous professions.
   b. Officers' lives are full of stress.
   c. Shoot-outs occur on a regular basis.
   d. Compared to other professions, police officers have a higher number of suicides.
   e. All of the above

3. What are the drawbacks of the myths about policing?
   a. Inability to recruit the right kinds of people to the job
   b. Unrealistic public expectations of the role of police officers
   c. Excessive taxpayer resources are given to the police department
   d. All of the above
   e. None of the above

4. What kind of data is included in Vital Statistics?
   a. The grade point averages of students at a particular university
   b. Blood pressure and breathing rates
   c. Profit and loss statements
   d. Birth and death records
   e. All of the above

5. What is the name of the best data source for statistics on the number of people killed by law enforcement professionals each year?
   a. NCVS
   b. UCR
   c. Vital Statistics
   d. Some of the above
   e. None of the above

6. What is the name of the police officer image developed by the mass media (especially television and Hollywood films)? This character is a solitary and misunderstood individual who combats criminals while working within the confines of an indifferent police department?
   a. Community-oriented policing image
   b. Crime fighter image
   c. Dirty Harry image
   d. Vic Mackey image
   e. None of the above

7. What is the title of the federal statistical publication that records the births and deaths of individuals in the United States?
   a. B and D report
   b. Uniform Crime Reports
   c. Victimization reports
   d. Vital Statistics
   e. None of the above

8. For which of the following myths of policing is the empirical evidence poor?
   a. Police have a higher rate of suicide than other professions.
   b. Police have a higher rate of divorce than other professions.
   c. Police have a higher mortality rate than other professions.
   d. Police are more susceptible to alcohol and drug abuse than other professions.
   e. None of the above.

9. Based on this chapter which of the following has the highest risk of committing suicide?
   a. An EMT
   b. A police officer
   c. A firefighter
   d. A professor
   e. They all have an equal chance of committing suicide.

10. Among the following professions, which one is the most dangerous?
    a. Drivers/sales workers
    b. Timber cutters
    c. Police officers
    d. Fishermen
    e. Ice cream vendors

11. Why are deaths by police officers decreasing?
    a. Better-trained police officers
    b. Better information provided to police officers responding to calls
    c. Stricter protocols for the use of force
    d. Better response times by EMTs
    e. All of the above

12. According to this chapter, what is the most dangerous call to which police officers can respond?
    a. Robbery
    b. Traffic disputes
    c. Domestic disputes
    d. All of the above
    e. None of the above

13. Which of the following methods may NOT help the public debunk the myths of policing?
    a. Read scholarly research on policing
    b. Watch *Lethal Weapon* and *Die Hard* movies
    c. Take relevant classes at reputable institutions of higher learning
    d. Attend a citizen police academy
    e. Go on a ride-along

Part Two: Short Answer Questions

1. What is the crime fighter image?

2. List three of the most important reasons why the number of police officers killed in the line of duty has been decreasing in recent years.

3. List two reasons why police officers typically do not dissuade the public from thinking that their jobs are dangerous, exciting, or stressful.

4. What are the three most dominant myths of policing?

5. What are three sources of policing myths?

6. How do most police die in the line of service?

Part Three: Essay Questions

1. What methods would you use to debunk the myths of policing?

2. What would you recommend police officers, policy makers, and researchers do to present a more realistic picture of policing? Will the public be well served by this?

3. If policing is NOT as dangerous as the media portray it to be, then why does the public continue to believe this?

PART

Problems for Citizens
and the Community

Emphasizing Public Relations over Crime Reduction

Introduction

Several persistent questions about police behavior exist: "Why do police behave as they do? How can differences in police behavior be characterized? What are the most important factors in the decisions that police officers make? What is good and bad police work, or what is deviant police behavior?" (Roberg and Kuykendall, 1993, p. 161). This chapter develops and outlines a typology of police behavior, reviews factors that influence police behavior, focuses on the challenges of public relations efforts of police departments, and then provides a brief conclusion.

Typologies of Police Behavior

Police behavior can be divided generally into two categories: appropriate and inappropriate (Roberg and Kuykendall, 1993). What counts as acceptable police behavior versus unacceptable police behavior? Police actions can be considered appropriate when they conform to the rules and regulations of a police force and obey the confines of the law. In this context, three types of appropriate behavior have been identified and studied. From the least to most frequently researched issues, they include public relations, discretion, detective work, and patrol (the subject matter of this chapter and the following two ones). On the other hand, when police behavior that violates the rules and regulations of a police department and the law is considered unacceptable behavior, sometimes called "deviant behavior," and includes the following: acceptance or solicitation of gratuities, corruption, illegal surveillance, and excessive force.

Factors That Influence Police Behavior

Two major theories are used to explain police behavior: predispositional and socialization. In order to better understand these typologies, the following discussion briefly outlines these perspectives, followed by an alternative, and in some ways more reasonable, explanation of why police officers do what they do.

Predispositional Theory

This theoretical framework incorporates and analyzes the values, habits, and work styles (i.e., attitudes and behavior) of a police officer. This approach focuses primarily on the characteristics, values, and attitudes that an individual exhibits before he or she is employed as an officer. For example, "if an officer is dishonest or honest, brutal or temperate in the use of force, he or she probably had those positive or negative traits before being hired as a police officer" (Roberg and Kuykendall, 1993, pp. 161–162). Although holding some merit, this explanation is too simplistic on its own.

Socialization Theory

In this perspective, the behavior of a police officer is determined mainly through work experiences, especially interactions with coworkers, supervisors, and individuals who are met on the job. The complex process of socialization results in the police subculture, which is the "learned objectives, shared job activities, similar use of nonmaterial and material items, and veteran officers who act as gatekeepers (as opposed to supervisors) and who transmit job obligations, responsibilities, and expectations of the job" (Stevens, 2009, p. 11). Work-related socialization also helps to create what has often been identified as a police personality.

For example, "if a police officer becomes corrupt, it is because the police organization fosters the development of corrupting values; in other words, corruption is learned within the organization" (Roberg and Kuykendall, 1993, p. 162). Nevertheless, socialization is more complex than meets the eyes. There are primarily three types of socialization that police officers may experience: anticipatory, formal, and informal.

> [The *anticipatory*] socialization of some police officers begins before they are employed in law enforcement. Individuals interested in law enforcement as a career often are acquainted with or may be related to a police officer. Those individuals interested in a career may actually begin to acquire the values of those friends or relatives prior to being employed in law enforcement. (Roberg and Kuykendall, 1993, p. 162)

Formal socialization is "the result of what transpires in the selection process and the training program, what is learned about policies and procedures, and what officers are told by supervisors and managers" (Roberg and Kuykendall, 1993, p. 162).

Lastly, *informal socialization* occurs when "recruits interact with older, more experienced officers. One's peers play an important role in determining behavior, not only in the police occupation, but also in other jobs. . . .

What one learns on the job and from one's peers may contradict what is learned during the formal socialization process" (Roberg and Kuykendall, 1993, p. 162). A good example of informal socialization is the classic situation when a seasoned veteran tells a rookie police officer, on the first day of the job, to forget what was learned in the police academy and to just do what the senior officer does.

An applicant's character, as formed before joining the force, has an effect on his or her behavior after becoming a sworn police officer. This is why most police departments invest considerable resources trying to weed out inappropriate candidates. On the other hand, it is often argued that the screening process is only of limited usefulness in preventing poor behavior. Most bad work-related behavior is learned on the job (Roberg and Kuykendall, 1993, p. 162). Unfortunately, predispositional and socialization theories are, in the end, too simplistic to provide satisfactory explanations of police behavior.

An Alternate Explanation

Factors that influence police behavior can be divided into a number of categories. Some of the better-known explanations fall under the rubrics of psychological perspectives, situational/role expectations, and departmental characteristics. These variables intersect with each other and are connected to discretionary decisions. This present review, however, will be confined to the more general factors that impact police behavior, the police personality, police role considerations, and departmental characteristics.

Police Psychology

Most of the early research into police behavior focused on trying to understand if any generalizations could be made about an overarching police personality (Hanewicz, 1978; Adlam, 1982). Investigators singled out authoritarianism and cynicism as common traits among officers.

Authoritarianism includes, but is not limited to, a propensity for conventional thinking, aggressiveness, concern for exerting power, and a cynical disposition. Research on authoritarianism has focused on the role and demands of police work (e.g., Balch, 1972), the selection procedures of police departments (e.g., Tifft, 1974), and the attraction of police work for various people (Hanewicz, 1978).

Police cynicism, on the other hand, refers to a sense of frustration that officers may develop after working some time in a police department. Although their motivations for becoming and joining a law enforcement agency may have had been noble when they joined, over time when faced with the daily reality of police work their attitudes towards the public, criminals, co-workers and supervisors may become jaded (Niederhoffer, 1969). In order to survive in their job Neiderhoffer argued that officers make one of three adaptations: participation in a deviant activities, alienation, and/or the development of a more mature professional attitude towards ones job. Future empirical research on police cynicism (e.g., Regoli, 1976) further specified the relative contribution of different factors on an officer's proclivity to be cynical. None of this research, however, suggested that cynicism was central to a police officers' personality.

The conclusions of these studies were quite mixed and did not offer a homogenous image of a police personality. In the end, there is no certainty about whether or not a collective "cop personality" exists or if authoritarian and cynical tendencies are defining elements among most police officers.

Some of these research studies incorporated data obtained from psychological tests administered to screen prospective police officers. The most popular tests are the standard written tests, such as the Minnesota Multiphasic Personality Inventory (MMPI) and the California Personality Inventory (CPI). Tests designed to more specifically determine the prospective performance of law enforcement applicants, as based on a number of traits, include the Inwald Personality Inventory and the Law Enforcement Personal History Questionnaire. Unfortunately, these tests yield mixed results in terms of their predictive reliability.

Recent efforts to set up elaborate psychiatric screenings of recruits have been based on the assumption that the major problem with policing is the inclusion of defective and unsuitable candidates in the hiring process. Other observers suggest that the question of what an individual is like before joining the force is not as critical as the impact of the situations that are encountered after someone becomes a police officer. Although the police profession may attract some people with psychological problems, the screening process attempts to weed out inappropriate recruits.

The contradictions inherent in the two previously mentioned theories are related to the issue of proportion. Although it is reasonable to suppose that police departments will unknowingly employ, on occasion, officers who engage in inappropriate behavior, this should be viewed as the exception and not the rule. All of the available evidence indicates that police recruits are not, on average, more sadistic, cynical, or authoritarian than the average citizen.

Role of Police Officer

A police officer's behavior varies based on a number of factors. One of the most important causal factors is the type of beat to which officers have been assigned (Roberg and Kuykendall, 1993). Banton, in his book *The Policeman in the Community* (1964), discovered that the type of beat that an officer was assigned to and their specialization in the police force had an effect on their behavior. "Uniformed patrol officers were essentially peacekeepers because they interacted with a wide range of people who were not suspects and tended to do many things other than enforce the law" (Roberg and Kuykendall, 1993, p. 165).

Departmental Characteristics

Departmental size, command structure, officer-citizen ratio, and other departmental factors can have an effect on police behavior. Perhaps the most classic study examining the type of police department as an independent variable is Wilson's (1968) *Varieties of Police Behavior*. He identified three types/styles of law enforcement that at the time were commonly displayed by various departments: the watchman, the service, and the legalistic. The first style is mainly oriented to the maintenance of order, the second emphasizes service to the community, and the third involves the strict enforcement of all laws. Since the publication of Wilson's book, other researchers (e.g., Gardiner, 1969) have sought to explain the differing approaches to traffic law enforcement by distinguishing and exploring the distinct leadership styles of the chiefs of different communities. Moreover, over the past half-century, since the publication of Wilson's book, there has been a tendency toward increasing homogenization among police departments. A number of reasons explain this trend: amalgamation of police agencies, dissemination of information through conferences, and the growth of information availability through the World Wide Web. In other words, the relative contribution of departmental characteristics to differences in police behavior may have lessened over time.

Summary

Frequent access to police organizations present an important stumbling block in the pursuit of studies related to police work and behavior. Sensationalized acts involving police officers, however, are given copious media coverage, further hindering a clear understanding of one of the most complex jobs in urban America. This lack of balance naturally leads to one of the least understood aspects of police behavior: public relations.

Public Relations

Leaders, politicians, and organizations actively seek to create positive impressions of themselves to maintain or create support among the public. They do this through a variety of techniques, including public relations.

The reader may wonder: What is the difference among public relations, propaganda, and publicity? *Public relations* is an umbrella term that covers a collection of communication techniques used by individuals or organizations to convince an audience about the merits of an organization, program, or policy. Public relations methods primarily make appeals based on reason. *Propaganda* is a variety of communication techniques used by individuals or organizations to convince the public and/or news media about the merits of an organization, program, or policy. Propaganda mainly relies on appealing to its audience's emotions and does not normally emphasize facts or logic. *Publicity*, on the other hand, "seeks to gain maximum and rapid exposure for a client and his program by this exposure per se, as an end in itself. Public relations may also seek wide exposure for a client and his program, but behind this desire for exposure is a detailed program designed to capitalize on the attention won from the public" (Carlson, 1968, p. 211). Public relations actions employ symbols, myths, and "activities directed at creating and maintaining favorable impressions of a product, a firm or an institution—in Madison Avenue terms, building an image. The emphasis is on looking good, not necessarily on being good" (Radelet and Carter, 1994, p. 31).

The publicity profession is not a recent development. This work has its roots in the efforts of publicists "who made their appearance during the 18th century. These writers turned out pamphlets and tracts in support of social, political, and religious causes" (Carlson, 1968, p. 209). However, as a profession, public relations first came to prominence in the 20th century with the advent of large organizations such as corporations and governmental entities. Public relations techniques are used to overcome negative perceptions that the public may have of organizations. These negative assumptions may be motivated by the actions that an organization has taken or is expected to take in the future. These views are exacerbated if an organization is seen as remote-geographically or metaphorically (Carlson, 1968). Both for-profit and nonprofit entities (e.g., political parties, labor unions) use public relations efforts to further their agendas.

The Necessity of Public Relations Efforts

There are several reasons why public relations activities are needed. The public often wants to know the reasons why organizations take a particular course of action or how they will respond to changes in their environment. The organization aims to present itself in a positive light. In some cases, there may be so many contradictory communications circulating amongst the public that it is in the organization's best interest to present its side of the story in a favorable light (Carlson, 1968). In many cases, the leaders of an organization no longer have the time or the expertise to project a positive image of their organization. Finally, a need to prevent miscommunication and a desire to overcome the lack of public trust are issues that many organizations seek to ameliorate via public relations efforts.

Functions of Public Relations Personnel

Public relations professionals and departments are inextricably linked to almost all forms of external corporate communication. These communications can include the writing of speeches, press releases, and letters on behalf of senior personnel. Public relations employees may also coordinate with the news media; write, edit, and/or supervise their organization's newsletter; respond to requests from the media; conduct tours of the organization; supervise the museum or archives; and maintain the Web site (Carlson, 1968).

Police Public Relations

During the 1960s, public attitudes toward police were at an all-time low. Riots against controversial police actions were taking place almost on a regular basis. Much of the civil unrest was in response to police brutality directed toward African Americans. This perceived selective, racial targeting was the source of many problems faced by police departments during this period. Since that decade, through a series of calculated reforms, including federally mandated affirmative action guidelines, new legislation affecting police policies and practices, better training in police use of deadly force, and the institutionalization of public relations divisions in most municipal police departments, municipal police have attempted to sell themselves to different audiences. As Manning (1971) notes:

> The audience for the police is diverse; it should be considered many audiences. For the police must convince the politicians that they have used their allocated resources efficiently; they must persuade the criminals that they are effective crime-fighters; they must assure the broader public that they are controlling crime. (p.153)

Understanding Police Public Relations

In the context of police organizations, public relations actions are used to manipulate public and governmental reactions and external control initiatives (Ross, 1995b; Souryal, 1995). The process of public relations has a series of causes and effects that can be detrimental to both the police and the constituencies they serve and protect. If a police department disproportionately focuses on public relations, it risks the proliferation of the following perceptions:

1. More energy is being expended on public relations efforts promoting policing than in the implementation of actual policing programs that might solve community problems.
2. Public relations methods that promote policing receive more resources than the implementation of new policing initiatives.
3. Policing may come to be seen as simply a public relations exercise.

In general, there are at least seven interrelated reasons that police departments engage in public relations efforts. Ranked from least to most important, these factors include:

1. a highly partisan context
2. crises of legitimacy
3. cost effectiveness
4. the need for alternative or additional public relations tools
5. the availability of police resources

6. media propagation and/or cooperation

7. an apathetic, alienated, deferent, or uneducated public.

Regardless of the causes for these related issues, the public, at least in most advanced industrialized countries, is relatively content to allow the police to take responsibility for formal social control within their nation's borders. Nonetheless, public relations efforts are so crucial to police departments that they have given rise to numerous books and guides (e.g. Garner, 1982, 1984, 1987), and workshops are regularly offered to assist senior command officers with this important duty.

Effects of Police Public Relations

Building on the previous discussion, there are a variety of interrelated problems with police public relations. These effects, from least to most important, are ranked in accord with the severity of disturbance:

1. utilizing scarce resources
2. implementing a defensive strategy
3. fostering an unrealistic expectation of police capabilities
4. legitimatizing state rather than community forms of social control
5. temporarily diverting attention from civilian processes that could reduce crime and fear of crime
6. increasing public disaffection
7. increasing public complacency
8. temporarily satisfying the public
9. increasing officer dissatisfaction

What are the ramifications each of these effects?

First, public relations efforts undoubtedly consume valuable resources that could be invested in more profitable or concrete policy initiatives and programs inside the police department or other related agencies (Turque et al., 1990). According to Leighton (1991):

> During the 1960s and 1970s, when crime rates were increasing rapidly, police chiefs could argue for more officers and resources on the grounds of a crime wave. With overall crime rates settling down, chiefs have had to shift their argument from "quantity policing" to "quality policing." . . . That is, in order to deliver high quality policing services, as represented by community policing, then they require additional officers and resources. (p. 508)

Second, public relations is often a defensive strategy used by law enforcement agencies to deal with actual or potential media coverage. Some scholars have detected a similarity behind the goals of public relations efforts and other police programs. In turn, public relations helps the police maintain their monopoly on their official right to implement social control measures.

If public relations efforts to appease citizen dissatisfaction and unrest were minimized, there would be a subsequent reduction of police ability (i.e., power) to exercise independent control over their organizations (both legally and symbolically). Thus, public relations efforts, particularly the promotion of community policing programs, constitute attempts by police to minimize community and governmental criticism and to maximize interdepartmental control over policing operations. This then helps the police maintain their position as the primary mediators of community conflict.

Third, in promising that police strategies will cure most societal ills, the police can be accused of fostering unrealistic expectations in their communities. Klockars (1988) argues that this is major problem in modern policing efforts:

> Police can no more create communities or solve the problems of urban anomie than they can be legalized into agents of the courts or depoliticized into pure professionals. There is no more reason to expect that they can prevent crime than to expect that they can fight or win a war against it. (p. 257)

Fourth, police public relations help to legitimize state forms of social control. Police public relations efforts continue to place the onus of social control on mechanisms beyond the family, peers, schools, and other social institutions.

Fifth, public relations tactics temporarily divert attention from concrete strategies that could conceivably achieve the goals of policing. Informal social controls (e.g., the family, Big Brothers/Big Sisters) that can be less coercive than police intervention and might provide the same results as policing programs. As it is, alternative techniques that might solve community problems are usually not introduced. And it may be that some community problems are in fact irresolvable.

Sixth, when police fail to achieve their stated and perceived objectives, this can increase citizen disaffection and cynicism in connection with the police and those agencies responsible for monitoring them. This situation diminishes police officers' legitimacy as keepers of public order. Citizens may continue or begin to withdraw support from the police in a variety of ways. For example, they may fail to report crimes or come to the assistance of a police officer in need.

Seventh, public relations may lead to external complacency about crime, police, and community values, because the non-police community may perceive that the police's idea of community has only minimal effect on the level and type of problems that community policing was supposed to solve. This external apathy, accompanied by feelings of alienation, helps maintain and advance the power of the police organization. By the same token, it might lead to diminished respect in the community. Citizens and politicians may want to reduce funding to police agencies because they believe that they are not effectively addressing their needs.

Eighth, police public relations may satisfy the public only temporarily. When programs are primarily reactive and are implemented quickly with minimal or no evaluations, the public gets the impression that the police are actively and quickly engaging in their communities. However, when a program is evaluated by critical observers and is found to fall short of its stated or inferred objectives, community dissatisfaction is the typical reaction.

Ninth and finally, many police officers resist changes in departmental policies and practices unless they perceive that they will be beneficial to their profession, the organization, or the community in which they police. Forced to comply, officers may become cynical, thus minimizing the proper implementation of community policing (e.g., Turque et. al., 1990). This cynicism may lead to an increased number of job actions and deviance, such as the "blue flu" or "cooping."

Police officers, their agencies, and other local government offices and agencies are now using such popular catchwords and labels such as "community ownership," "stakeholder participation," and "partnerships" to sell their communities on new programs, but unfortunately widespread cynicism in many communities prevents the police efforts from being taken seriously.

Defining Police Public Relations

The public is generally ignorant about how a police department operates. Thus, police public relations can create or develop a positive image for the department. Good public relations programs inform the public and "instill pride and confidence in the police force, its competence, and its sense of professionalism" (Radelet and Carter, 1994, p. 202). Public relations methods can also maintain perceptions of integrity, trust, and security and can minimize the possibility of hostility and litigation against police departments.

Initially, police departments, like most governmental agencies, actively campaign to promote favorable images of their agency and to minimize negative characterizations. Public relations efforts may entail convincing the community and politicians that social control could be maintained better if the police are supplied with better cars, better crime laboratories, better equipment, better trained police officers, and more enabling laws, for example.

The effort to expand departmental resources is reflected in extensive public relations efforts, including follow-up interviews with victims of crime to provide updates on the progress in the investigation (Greenwood et al., 1975; Sanders, 1977; Ericson, 1981), displays at shopping plazas, lectures and talks to selected groups in the community, employment of public relations officers who generate contacts with the media and supply them with information (Fishman, 1978, 1980), and a variety of other methods of police rhetoric (Beare, 1987).

In order to properly structure its projected message, the police department needs to understand the recipients of its communications. This can include youth, senior citizens, minority groups, and other selected groups. A good relationship with the public promotes confidence between citizens and the police. If citizens have confidence in the police, then they will be more likely to report crimes to the police and support the police force's objectives, especially increased salaries and benefits and improved equipment to help them do their jobs.

The Police Public Information Officer

Police public relations personnel are responsible for responding to inquiries by the public and the news media about activities of the police, including details about crimes and ongoing investigations into crimes and scandals. These responsibilities include holding press conferences, maintaining the department's Web site, and releasing statistics on crime.

Over the past half-century, large urban police departments have typically employed Public Information Officers (PIOs). The PIO tries to stay well informed of the situations that occur on a daily basis. When a potentially controversial incident occurs (such as a police-involved shooting), the PIO often responds to the scene to gather relevant facts. After the PIO has figured out what has transpired, he or she usually gives a statement to the press. If the story is withheld for any length of time, the press will try to get the story through other sources or channels, and the information might not always be accurate. The PIO is responsible for coordinating tasks related to most internal and external communications: editing departmental documents, advertising/commercials, open houses, citizen police academies, and Web pages.

Policing Programs That Function Primarily as Public Relations Efforts

Over the past 90 years, police departments in the United States have created and implemented a host of programs that have been very popular and were designed to help members of the community in a way that would have a positive public relations impact. These include the Police Athletic League, gun buy-back programs, ride-alongs, citizen police academies, Drug Awareness and Resistance Education (DARE), and Officer Friendly. Some, but not all, have been subject to process and impact professionally conducted evaluations.

Police Athletic League

Starting in the 1920s, many police departments in the United States created Police Athletic Leagues (PALs). Typically, police officers and occasionally volunteers (e.g., from the federally sponsored AmeriCorps program) devote their time to teaching, helping with homework, mentoring, and coaching "at-risk" children in different sports. Occasionally the organized teams play others from different parts of the city or other cities. The implementation of these programs has varied over time and from one jurisdiction to another. PALs may operate once or twice a week at a drop-in center or in a separate building named for the Police Athletic League. Some PAL programs (e.g., Baltimore) run after-school programs for disadvantaged children. This program ostensibly brings children off the streets and teaches them teamwork, morals, and responsibility. The children spend their time engaged in activities designed to further their education and physical well-being. Otherwise, they might be getting into trouble by committing crime or engaging in drug use or risky sexual encounters.

PAL provides an opportunity for the public to see the police doing something visible besides patrol, and the facility serves as a surrogate child care center. Parents know that their children are involved in prosocial activities while ensuring that their education is a priority. Children interact with someone who seems to care (i.e., the police officer or AmeriCorps volunteer), which allows them the opportunity to connect with a positive role model. The program organizers hope that the children involved with PAL will be less inclined to be involved in crime than they otherwise might have been. In 2004, the Baltimore PAL program was evaluated by Child Trends, a Washington, DC based consulting firm and it was found to have numerous valuable impacts including raising the academic ability of its clients/participants. Unfortunately, in 2009, due to budgetary constraints, the Baltimore Police Department relinquished control of the PAL system to the Department of Parks and Recreation, and thus the public relations benefits to the BPD are unknown at this time.

Gun Buy-Back Programs

Each year many police departments hold gun buy-back events in which citizens are encouraged to turn in any firearm for money or other items of value, like toys or gift certificates. In most jurisdictions, the police organization does not ask questions with respect to where the gun was purchased or how it was acquired. This activity demonstrates to the public that the police are keeping guns off the streets and ostensibly out of criminal hands. It also indicates that the police are more interested in public safety than prosecutions. The trouble with this approach is that most of the guns that are returned are nonfunctioning, and this program has not led to a discernible reduction in crime. In 2004, a National Academy of Sciences report (Welford, Pepper, Petrie, and the Committee to Improve Research on Firearms, 2004) concluded that gun buy-back programs are ineffective.

Ride-Alongs

This program typically involves a uniformed patrol officer escorting a member of the media, a politician, a visiting dignitary, a scholar, or a student for a police shift or a portion thereof in a marked patrol car. This activity helps citizens to see firsthand how boring and routine much police work is and how much paperwork is required of each officer (Exhibit 4.1).

Exhibit 4.1   **Conducting a Meaningful Ride-Along**

Many students—as part of a class on criminal justice or policing/law enforcement or because they are interested in entering the police/law enforcement profession—will be required or may want to do a police ride-along. In general, students contact a local police, sheriff's, or law enforcement agency that conducts patrols. They will get some sort of official clearance. Students should obtain and provide their instructors with accurate documentation of their ride-along from a person in authority at the criminal justice agency they observed. In the case of a law enforcement agency (i.e., municipal, county, or state police), it is often easier to do the ride-along during daylight hours and spend a minimum of two hours in this context. Students should document what they observed, what they overheard, and with whom they talked.

Students should also try to interpret (at a bare minimum):

- How does this agency work in terms of the relationships, both formal and informal, among workers, administrators, and the clients they serve?
- What type of people work in these agencies (e.g., age, training)?
- Where are these agencies located and why?
- Why do you suppose they are located here?
- Who do these agencies serve (i.e., their clientele)?

Documentation of the ride-along should also cover any other factors they believe are important, in order to develop as comprehensive a portrait as possible of this agency. Students are encouraged to talk about themselves, including their reaction to the setting.

Citizen Police Academies

Over the past two decades, many police departments in the United States have offered citizen police academies. These classes meet once a week over a number of weeks and provide a forum for citizens to learn about the police department. At the end of the course, students are given a certificate, and there is a quasi-graduation ceremony. A national Citizen Police Academy Association helps to promote these programs around the country (Ellis, 1997; Weinblatt, 1997; Maffe and Burke, 1999; Kanable, 1999).

Drug Awareness and Resistance Education (DARE)

Started in 1983 by the Los Angeles Police Department, under the direction of Chief Darryl Gates, the DARE program involves uniformed police officers who enter fifth and sixth grade classrooms to talk about the dangers of drugs. The officers present a negative image of drugs, discuss the hazards of drug use, and offer positive role models and ways students can use interpersonal skills to avoid using drugs. The program lasts approximately 17 hours and extends through the middle school grades. In general, teachers, school administrators, and parents like this program. This resource is now provided by different police departments around the United States. In many respects, DARE is an example of proactive policing that attempts to convince children that police officers are intelligent, personable, and not out to harass them.

During the early 1990s, several well-respected researchers evaluated DARE to determine its utility (e.g., Clayton et al., 1991; Lynam et al., 1999; Dukes, Ullman, and Stein, 1996; Dukes, Stein, and Ullman, 1997; Rosenbaum, 1997). Unfortunately, they discovered that DARE had only a minimal impact on a child's likelihood to take drugs.

Officer Friendly

During the 1970s, the Sears-Roebuck Foundation sponsored a program called the Officer Friendly program. It was designed to "humanize children's perceptions of police officers and their work, improve rapport between children and police, increase awareness of safety and civic responsibility, and reduce crime involving children" ("The Officer Friendly Program," 1979). In order to accomplish this task, police officers made regular visits to public schools, and teachers conducted exercises connected to the visit.

Summary

There are a multitude of public relations programs that police departments participate in and believe will pay dividends in public trust and confidence. These activities often have an army of willing supporters in the wider community who, based on personal or anecdotal evidence, and the absence of empirical support are their biggest champions too. Indeed public relations programs may break down some of the myths of policing. Too often, however, these activities have little actual influence on crime rates or proclivity to commit crime in later years. Community policing, for example, has devolved into a public relations program (Ross, 1995b).

Conclusion

Police public relations programs are typically perceived to be low-cost, high-impact options for police departments. They are approved and implemented because they make sense intuitively but rarely are they are scientifically evaluated. Police public relations efforts may help the police organization increase pride in its work and cultivate confidence and legitimacy among its workers and some local politicians and members of the public. On the other hand, if law enforcement agencies are doing this in order to cover up corruption or types of abuses, the public relations efforts function only as a thinly veiled propaganda campaign and can lead to cynicism toward the police organization.

Glossary

Authoritarianism: A personality characteristic sometimes ascribed to the police. This includes, but is not limited to, conventional thinking, aggressiveness, concern for exerting power, and cynical dispositions.

California Personality Inventory (CPI): A written psychological test used to determine the attitudes, mental processes, and behaviors of test subjects to screen them for the presence of mental disorders.

Drug Awareness Resistance Education (DARE): An educational program implemented by selected police departments in the public schools. It is designed to warn children of the dangers of drug use.

Gun buy-back program: A periodic program administered by police departments or local governments to purchase guns, regardless of their condition, from community members with no questions asked.

Minnesota Multiphasic Personality Inventory (MMPI): A written psychological test used to determine the attitudes, mental processes, and behaviors of test subjects to screen them for the presence of mental disorders.

Police citizen academies: Classroom programs created and administered by police departments to educate the public about police practices.

Police subculture: The "learned objectives, shared job activities, similar use of nonmaterial and material items, and veteran officers who act as gatekeepers (as opposed to supervisors) and who transmit job obligations, responsibilities, and expectations of the job" (Stevens, 2009, p. 11). This subculture has supposedly helped to create what has often been identified as a police personality.

Predispositional theory: Theory that the values, attitudes, habits, and work styles of a police officer is primarily explained by the characteristics, values, and attitudes that the individual had before he or she was employed as an officer.

Propaganda: A collection of communication techniques used by individuals and/or organizations to convince the public and news media about the merits of an organization, program, or policy. It primarily makes appeals based on emotions.

Publicity: An action that results in drawing attention to a particular individual, program, or project.

Public Information Officer (PIO): An individual employed on behalf of an organization whose responsibility is to communicate with the news media by responding to inquiries and writing and disseminating press releases. This officer aims to portray the organization in a positive light.

Public relations: A collection of communication techniques used by individuals or organizations to convince an audience about the merits of an organization, program, or policy. It primarily makes appeals to its audience based on reason.

Ride-along: An arrangement for a civilian to spend a shift or portion thereof in the passenger or back seat of a police car to observe the work day of a police officer.

Socialization theory: Theory that the behavior of a police officer is mainly determined through work experiences, especially interactions with coworkers and individuals with whom the officer comes into contact while on the job.

Chapter Questions

Part One: Multiple Choice Questions

1. What are three basic types of appropriate police behavior?
   a. public relations, detective work, and patrol work
   b. corruption, excessive violence, and deviance
   c. grass eating, meat eating, and accepting gratuities
   d. All of the above
   e. None of the above

2. Which of the following are personality tests that may be required of potential police recruits?
   a. California Personality Inventory
   b. Ends-Means test
   c. Minnesota Multiphasic Personality Inventory
   d. Some of the above
   e. None of the above

3. What is socialization theory?
   a. When the police socialize with the community to do their job
   b. A theory based on the premise that polices officer need to socialize with the public to gain their trust and confidence
   c. A theoretical framework based on the social habits of a person within a community
   d. An understanding that through interaction with others, individuals come to adopt certain values, habits, and work styles
   e. None of the above

4. Which of the following can be used for police public relations efforts?
   a. gun buy-back programs
   b. ride-alongs
   c. community policing
   d. DARE
   e. All of the above

5. What is the difference between public relations and propaganda?
    a. There is no difference.
    b. Public relations involves the management of the flow of information between an organization and its audiences. It encourages a rationale response by its audience.
    c. Propaganda involves the crafting of messages aimed at changing the orientations or actions of its audience and encourages an emotional response from its audience.
    d. None of the above
    e. Both b and c.

6. Which of the following is not a style of policing identified by James Q. Wilson in his classic study *Varieties of Police Behavior*?
    a. Community
    b. Watchman
    c. Legalistic
    d. Service
    e. None of the above are styles listed by Wilson.

7. What important police-related center started at Michigan State University?
    a. National Institute of Police & Community Relations
    b. Police Athletic League
    c. Technical Assistance, Technology and Training Center
    d. Crime Mapping Research Center
    e. Community Safety Information System

Part Two: Short Answer Questions

1. What is predispositional theory?

2. In a typical big-city police department, where is the public relations function located?

3. List two explanations advanced to explain police psychology.

4. List three types of socialization police may experience.

5. According to Manning, what are three ways that the police try to influence the public's perception of them?

6. What is the difference between proactive and reactive policing?

Part Three: Essay Questions

1. Some have argued that public relations efforts by police departments can be detrimental to their organizations. Do you agree or disagree with this statement and why?

2. How can police departments improve their public relations? How should the organizations test to gauge the effectiveness of their strategies?

3. Should police public relations efforts be administered by police officers who are trained in public relations, or be run by outsider professionals on contract? Justify your answer.

Failure to Properly Investigate Crime: Problems with the Detective Function

Introduction

In most police departments, after being dispatched to a call location or after noticing something unusual, patrol officers complete an initial (also called preliminary) investigation. Done properly, this action helps the police department determine if a possible crime has been committed. If the officers believe a crime has occurred, they will usually gather readily available evidence, such as witness statements or physical evidence (e.g., weapons). In addition, they typically secure the crime scene for the detectives (also known as investigators) and the crime lab, if the situation so merits, who will arrive shortly thereafter.

Detectives are the officers who try to solve crimes by determining who the perpetrator and victim are, ascertaining the involvement of accomplices, locating stolen property, and tracking down suspects. The ultimate aims of investigators' efforts are the arrest and conviction of the perpetrator(s) (the so-called disposing or closing of a case). Detectives accomplish this task by using their experience, the information uncovered by a crime lab, and their contacts within the community in which they work. This process may also include the cultivation of informants and cooperative citizens. Wrobleski and Hess (2006) outline critical steps in this process: protecting the crime scene, recording the pertinent facts surrounding the case/incident, recording the incident through photographs, measuring and perhaps drawing a diagram of what happened, locating relevant evidence, securing this information, and interviewing witnesses and potential suspects.

By gathering suspect and witness statements, physical evidence, and records, detectives strive to determine if they are pursuing a viable case that could lead not only to a criminal charge but also to a conviction in court. Depending on the importance of the crime, detectives may search for additional evidence or may drop a case entirely. In some jurisdictions, the development of a case is pursued in tandem with the local prosecutor, while in others it is solely the job of the detective (Roberg, Kuykendall, and Crank, 2000).

History of the Detective Profession

Early History

During the 1800s, private detectives were hired by those who could afford them to locate stolen property. During the late 19th century, "thieftakers" played a prominent role in the professionalization of the police field. These individuals would work with their contacts in the criminal underworld to locate stolen merchandise, and for a small fee, they would arrange the return of items to their rightful owners. Sometimes this activity bordered on the unscrupulous, since the thieftakers would periodically carry out criminal activities simply to receive the finders' fee. In the United States, private detective agencies, such as the Pinkerton National Detective Agency (or Pinkertons for short), were employed by corporations (especially banks) to recover stolen property and to manage less savoury activities such as strike breaking.

At the turn of the 20th century, criminal investigation increasingly became the responsibility of the police "because of a desire to prosecute suspected criminals and a general disproval of the methods employed by private detectives. In addition, the emergence of insurance companies tended gradually to lessen the victim's concern about the return of stolen property" (Roberg, Kuykendall, and Crank, 2000, p. 246). In the early part of the 1900s, police detectives were similarly secretive in their work. Their methods were mostly clandestine in nature. In some police departments, detectives hid their identity by wearing disguises and altering their appearance in different ways. This practice was the precursor to police undercover work. Although periodically romanticized by literary characters such as Sherlock Holmes, detectives of this era were often criticized for either perceived or actual corruption, and they did not do their assigned job particularly well, as reflected in the percentage of closed cases (Roberg, Kuykendall, and Crank, 2000).

The Introduction of Forensic Evidence into Detective Work

At the turn of the 20th century, public dislike for police informants (also colloquially called "snitches" and "stool pigeons") and the potential corruption of the legal system fueled the need to collect evidence using scientifically derived methods. Eventually the detective's role was affected by the integration of scientific methods into policing. This included developments such as:

- blood typing
- fingerprint evidence
- mug shots
- ballistics
- lie detector tests

During the early part of the 20th century, police detectives were primarily solving cases after the crime was committed. Due to the nature of police work at this time, the newly introduced scientific methods were not viewed as essential since most cases did not require this kind of expertise to be closed. As Roberg, Kuykendall, and Crank (2000) note, "the information that became most important in making arrests and ensuring successful prosecutions was derived from witnesses, informers, and suspects. As detectives stopped being secretive rogues . . . [they] often coerced information from suspects to make cases" (p. 248). Although not all of the new techniques held up over time (e.g., the lie detector test), most became an asset to police detective work.

Due Process Revolution

Another development in the detective's role was the effect of the Due Process Revolution that took place during the 1960s. At this time, a number of criminal procedural laws concerning search and seizure, advising suspects about their constitutional rights, and the admissibility of evidence were clarified through the passage of pivotal Supreme Court decisions. The standardization of due process procedures shifted detectives from being super sleuths to functioning as bureaucrats, resulting in a shift from a proactive to a reactive mode (Roberg, Kuykendall, and Crank, 2000). This also meant that detectives needed to be creative in order to simultaneously achieve their objectives and not violate an individuals constitutional rights.

The Rank of Detective

Approximately 7% of all sworn police officers are detectives (Meesig, Lee, and Horvath, 2002). The rank of detective is typically above that of patrol officers, and among the detectives as a group, individuals are categorized by the usual police ranks, such as Sergeant, Lieutenant, and Commander.

There are a number of advantages to being a detective as opposed to a patrol officer:

First, the assignment may involve a promotion and pay raise. Second, detectives have much more control over their work and are more independent. Patrol officers frequently race from call to call, while detectives are assigned to specific cases and are given substantial latitude in investigating those cases. . . . Detectives also have more normal work hours and are able to work in civilian clothes as opposed to uniforms. Perhaps most importantly, detectives have a very clear measure of success: the arrest of a suspect. (White, 2007, pp. 142–144)

Most police officers must serve a total of one to five years before becoming a detective.

Exhibit 5.1	Subdivisions of Detective Squads
Homicide	Criminal Intelligence
Robbery	Sex Crimes
Stolen Vehicles	Street Crime (mugging)
Organized Crime	Computer Crime
Fraud	Crimes Against Children
Burglary	Surveillance
Narcotics	Arson
Forgery	

Organization of Detectives and the Collection of Forensic Evidence

In bigger police departments, detectives are often divided into numerous squads based on a particular type of crime or criminal. Usually the subdivided units are arranged according to the categories of various major crimes. Smaller police departments often do not possess the resources to have specialized detective units. In departments that have 10 or fewer officers, only one detective may be employed, and he or she is solely responsible for investigating all crimes. Alternatively, the patrol officers may be given some of the responsibilities of the detective (White, 2007). (See Exhibit 5.1.)

Throughout history, police departments, particularly the detective branch, have benefited from the introduction of scientific methods of criminal investigation. Numerous kinds of evidence can be collected by detectives, all of which may help them identify a victim and/or criminal. These techniques have been brought into policing through the hard sciences of biology, medicine, physical anthropology, and physics. Evidence collected by investigators is usually broken down into two types: physical evidence, and paper/electronic evidence that provides background information on the suspect(s) (see Exhibit 5.2). In addition to accumulating and analyzing information, detectives may be required to appear in court to provide testimony on the specific cases they have worked.

Scholarly Research on the Detective Function

Although numerous studies on the patrol functions of police officers have been conducted, there are relatively few specific analyses of detective work (Skolnick, 1966; Greenwood, Chaiken, and Petersilia, 1977; Sanders, 1977; Wilson, 1978; Manning, 1980; Ericson, 1981). One reason for this paucity of research may be that general investigation detectives represent only a small fraction of police force membership.

Exhibit 5.2	**Types of Evidence Collected**

A. Physical evidence
  Ballistics/shell casings
  Blood type and splatter
  Chemical traces
  Computer hard drives
  Crime scene reconstruction
  DNA analysis
  Fingerprints
  Footprints or tire tracks
  Position of objects
  Tool marks
  Trace fibers
B. Public and private records that provide background information on the suspect
  Answering machine messages
  Cell phone activity
  Credit card receipts/activity
  Credit reports
  Criminal history of suspect (i.e., arrests and convictions)
  Electronic mail
  GPS logs
  Hotel, airline, train, bus reservations
  Mug shot(s) and/or photo ID
  Motor vehicle records
  Online purchases
  Text messages, Internet usage, Web sites visited

Results from Observational Studies

An important part of detective work involves "cooling out" citizens (also known as "cooling out a mark"), which refers to reassuring crime victims that they are doing everything in their power to take their case seriously) and pursuing cases in such a manner that the threat of legal or administrative problems is minimized. Detective activity is primarily geared toward the disposition of cases.

In the most comprehensive study to date, detectives were observed directly while on the job. After analyzing 193 shifts of a specific detective unit of a major metropolitan police force, the researchers made a number of conclusions about detective work in large urban North American cities (Ericson, 1981). According to this study, the primary investigative activity entails interviewing victims, complainants, witnesses, and informants in the hope of obtaining information relevant to an investigation. Another major form of detective activity involves contacting suspects. Arrests are not a dominant shift activity, nor is patrol activity or spending time in court. Almost half of the detective work time in this study was spent in the office. On average, detectives spend most of their time sitting at their desks, typing reports, reviewing files, calling citizens connected with case investigations, and holding both formal and informal meetings about a variety of matters relating to investigation priorities and procedures with their coworkers and superiors. In other words, most investigations are mundane and routine.

Another issue that has been examined by researchers is the percentage of police personnel assigned to the detective function and the related work teams. Some researchers have tried to determine the ideal number of investigators that should be assigned to detective work. Some have used a ten percent rule, however, this number needs to take into consideration the amount and type of crime a jurisdiction experiences, existing departmental policies, the level of training, and experience of the current pool of officers working this detail (Roberg, Kuykendall, and Crank, 2000, p. 248).

Bigger police departments tend to have specialists organized into investigation units. These detectives focus on specific types of crime (e.g., homicide, fraud, robbery, sex crimes, drugs, arson, auto theft), or they may monitor particular types of criminals (e.g., gangs, organized crime) (Roberg, Kuykendall, and Crank, 2000).

Results from Investigative Effectiveness Studies

One of the most important studies of detectives was conducted during the mid-1970s by Greenwood, Chaiken, and Petersilia (1977).

> [They] observed operations in 25 detective units and administered surveys in 156 units. The major findings of this study indicated that (1) most serious crimes are solved through information obtained from victims rather than through leads developed by detectives; (2) in 75 percent of the cases, the suspect's identity is known or easily determined at the time the crime is reported to the police; and (3) the major block of detective time is devoted to reviewing reports, documenting files, and attempting to locate and interview victims on cases that experience has shown are unlikely to be solved but are carried out to satisfy the victims' expectations. (Roberg, Kuykendall, and Crank, 2000, p. 249)

The 1977 study concluded that most detective units operated ineffectively and inefficiently.

Several years later, Willman and Snortum (1984) replicated the study with a medium-sized police department, and unlike the earlier research, they examined the handling of all crimes regardless of whether or not the cases were ultimately solved. Willman and Snortum observed similar patterns to those described in the Greenwood et al. (1977) study. However, they concluded that detectives play a valuable role particularly because of their ability to properly interrogate witnesses and suspects and their expertise in monitoring the cases they were given. Echoing the conclusions from the Willman and Snortum study, Eck (1984) concluded that in criminal incidents where the officers did not find a lead, the follow-up investigations by detectives provided suitable lead 14 percent of the time, and an arrest 8 percent of the time.

To help understand more fully the role and status of detectives, Farmer (1984) advocated a more comprehensive framework for evaluating the role played by police detectives: "the notion of case clearance as the sole objective of detective work is as inadequate as is the idea that the principal function of a detective is to solve crime" (p. 49). Farmer pointed out that detectives' proactive work included interaction with their communities: "investigators may pursue other equally important goals to aid citizens—including increasing citizen satisfaction, reducing fear, counselling victims, and deterring further crime" (p. 50).

Since the 1980s, very few empirical studies of detective work in the United States have been conducted.

Clearance Rates

All sorts of crimes come to the attention of police departments. Once reported, a succession of prescribed steps occurs. One of the most important issues to address is whether the crime warrants some sort of arrest. Once arrested, the suspect is fingerprinted. Fingerprint information is submitted to the FBI and is used to tabulate the crime clearance. This information is typically tabulated by the police and is then sent to a state Statistical Analysis Center (SAC) department or to the FBI, which then produces the Uniform Crime Report (UCR). In order for a crime to be considered cleared, an individual must be arrested and charged with the commission of the crime, and the case must then be sent to a court for processing. Even if a case is sent to court, the individual(s) will not necessarily be convicted of the crime.

> In 2006, 44.3 percent of all violent crimes and 15.8 percent of all property crimes in the United States were cleared by arrest or exceptional means. Of the violent crimes of murder and non-negligent manslaughter, forcible rape, robbery, and aggravated assault, murder had the highest clearance rate. . . . Most of these crimes had been investigated by an investigative unit. (Stevens, 2009, p.13)

In light of these statistics, it is obvious that the detective function appears to have a minimal impact on actual clearance rates. Most of the public think that clearance is the same as a case being solved. Nothing can be further from the truth.

Why Do Some Cases Get More Attention than Others?

Not all cases requiring criminal investigations receive equal attention from police detectives. Members of the public often complain that police detectives, and by extension their agencies, ignore or focus their energies on particular types of crimes. In general, there are four basic reasons that motivate the police to take a case seriously:

1. dollar value of stolen or damaged property or illegal goods exchanged
2. degree/type of violence/brutality that was committed
3. profile of victim
4. media attention

The Chandra Levy case is a good example of how some of these factors may have influenced the police investigation. In May 2001, Levy, who was working as an intern with the Federal Bureau of Prisons in Washington, D.C., went missing. As information about the case was revealed in the news, the public learned that Levy was having an affair with then Congressman Gary Condit (Democrat, California). Levy was last seen jogging in Rock Creek Park (a national park located in Washington, D.C.). Despite the sensationalism of the case, when few leads and little evidence were found that incontrovertibly linked Condit or anyone else to Levy, the Washington, D.C., police effectively sent it into a "cold case" or "backburner" status. Had it not been for the dogged determination of Levy's parents (who hired William "Billy" Martin, a well-known Washington, D.C., lawyer), two former District of Columbia Police detectives, and Condit's initial denial of the affair, the Washington, D.C., police would have probably dropped the case earlier. Nevertheless, it was not until 2002 that Levy's remains were found in Rock Creek Park and 2009 that an arrest was made in connection with her death.

Another criminal case that received a considerable amount of attention was the 2002 disappearance of a Modesto, California, woman, Laci Peterson, and the eventual arrest of her husband, Scott Peterson. In the United States, men kill their spouses (or significant others) every day. Why did this case receive a disproportionate amount of attention? Two particular factors motivated the Modesto Police Department to take the case seriously: first, the media frenzy over the story of a seemingly all-American couple with a storybook marriage and, second, Scott Peterson's denials of committing the murder.

Undercover and Sting Operations

Police officers frequently engage in undercover (i.e., plain clothes) operations. This involves officers pretending to be accomplices or willing victims of crimes. Undercover officers typically alter their appearances by wearing appropriate civilian clothing and may also take on the mannerisms and speech of the relevant criminal element in order to gain the confidence of real or alleged criminals and/or to infiltrate a criminal organization. Agent provocateurs also engage in covert activities. These undercover police or law enforcement officers who provoke individuals and/or groups to engage in illegal behaviour (e.g., building bombs, participating in violent protests, taking up arms). During the 1960s and 1970s, law enforcement agencies often infiltrated progressive (i.e., left of center) organizations and acted not only as "spies" but as agents provocateurs (Marx, 1981, 1988).

Sting Operation

A sting is a longstanding police practice that involves undercover police officers and/or detectives who, posing as either criminals or victims of a crime, set up situations to specifically arrest criminals. Stings are planned and executed to capture individuals engaging in drug sales and purchases, illegal alcohol and/or cigarette sales and consumption, solicitation of prostitution, hate crime, computer crimes, or gambling activities. Some undercover operations involve the creation of fencing operations.

A fencing operation appears to be a real criminal enterprise or business, but in actuality, it is established by the police in order to purchase or sell stolen goods. The operation is designed to arrest criminals who make use of this enterprise.

Examples of stings include:

- purchasing illegal drugs or guns to catch a supplier
- posing as a client to catch a prostitute, pimp, or escort agency
- pretending to be a prostitute to catch a client
- posing as someone who likes child pornography to catch a supplier
- pretending to be a supplier of child pornography to lure a pedophile
- posing as a child in a chat room to lure a pedophile
- arranging for someone under the legal drinking age to ask an adult to buy an alcoholic beverage on his or her behalf
- posing as a hit man to catch gang members or wanted murderers

A similar situation results when police officers park an expensive car in a specific location in the hopes that car thieves will try to either steal it or steal items from it (e.g., radio, tires, GPS system). In police circles, this is called a honey trap. In the context of computing crimes, a honey trap can be used to gain information about an individual who is a potential hacker (i.e., someone who wants to gain illegal access into a computer system). Law enforcement officers must be careful not to provoke the commission of a crime by someone who would not normally be inclined to do so. If this occurs in a common law jurisdiction, the defendant is within his or her right to invoke the defense of entrapment.

Sting operations can be executed in cooperation with other law enforcement agencies and with officers at different ranks of the police profession. They also frequently involve the use of informants to help with the operation.

One of the biggest problems connected to stings is entrapment. "Police are allowed to engage in deceit, pretense, and trickery to determine whether an individual has a predisposition to commit a crime, and they can provide an opportunity for an individual to commit that crime, all without being guilty of entrapment" (Stevens, 2009, p. 431). A rich legislative history exists around the legal defense against entrapment and is embedded in the following Supreme Court cases: *Sorrells v. United States* (1932), *Jackobson v. United States* (1992), and *United States v. Jimenez Recio* (2003).

There are both advantages and disadvantages to sting operations. On the plus side, these kinds of police operations can potentially ensnare criminals who are often too difficult for the police to otherwise catch. Stings can also serve as deterrents to individuals who violate the law. In terms of disadvantages, if they are not careful, police officers can be charged with entrapment. In other cases, police officers may be forced to befriend criminals to keep up their ruse and may purposefully or inadvertently adopt some criminal values in the process.

> [A sting] puts officers at the greatest risk of corrupting their own integrity. Uncommitted undercover officers can easily lose perspective. Some officers may become emotionally attached to their job and sometimes to the suspects, such that they compromise their own values and try drugs. Danger and temptation can play a role in the late stages of the operation. . . . They may feel insecure and anxious about regular work and continued employment with the department once the mission is closing down. Some become paranoid about danger and arm themselves with secret weapons. Sometimes other forms of self-survival may emerge, such as surveillance of their police supervisors or handlers. Undercover officers who have 'gone too native' can become dependent on drugs, alcohol, and sex. (Stevens, 2007, pp. 423–424).

Another problem with sting operations is that they have been frequently criticized for generating an increased number of crime victims. For example, if criminals can easily sell stolen property for a comparatively higher price to police undercover operators, they will end up stealing more and thus victimizing more citizens (Langworthy, 1989).

In order to protect officers involved in high-risk sting operations, a number of safeguards must be instituted. First, hiring the right kind of people to be undercover police officers is important. It is also critical to recruit the "right" kind of officers. One option is to hire officers who have finished their training requirements: "They may have been interviewed and identified for such duty while attending the training academy or while waiting on some civil service eligibility list" (Stevens, 2009, p, 424).

Physical attributes matter greatly in the context of sting operations. Undercover officers must be able to pass scrutiny (i.e., look the part). Attention to detail is important in terms of their age, demeanor, body language, dress, vehicles, and mannerisms. It is essential that the officers handle themselves appropriately in situations that could build trust among the people to which they are trying to get close (i.e., the criminals). On average, undercover recruits have recently completed their first year as a rookie police officer or they are officers from other jurisdictions who are unknown in the one where they will be working.

> The Commission on Accreditation for Law Enforcement Agencies requires "written procedures for conducting vice, drug, and organized crime surveillance, undercover, decoy and rapid operations." These procedures cover the processing of officers supplied with false identification, disguises, and other necessary credentials as needed on the job, and require that the department follow specific supervisor guidelines. (Stevens, 2009, p. 425)

How Interrogations Are Conducted

The subject and process of police interrogations is often highly contentious (Leo, 2008). Needless to say, there are numerous books filled with helpful advice on how to conduct investigations and interrogate suspects. One of the most popular methods is the Reid technique (Inbau, Reid, Buckley, and Jane, 2005), which advocates that police detectives quickly establish a baseline of each suspect's normal behavior and responses. This information will help the detectives to read the subject more thoroughly and to better understand when he or she is lying. The Reid method involves nine basic steps, including: confronting the suspect, developing a plausible story why the individual committed the crime, preventing the suspect from denying his or her actions, overcoming objections, maintaining the subject's focus, watching for the suspect to lose resolve, giving the suspect a couple of alternative explanations for the crime, forcing the suspect into one of the alternatives, and then securing the confession.

However popular it may be, this method has been criticized because of the assumption "that every criminal is motivated by guilt and that he or she lives in constant fear of discovery" (Stevens, 2009, p. 397). The Reid technique assumes that a suspect, once relieved of the so-called psychological and emotional burden of providing a confession, "will let them over past the act and get on with their lives" (Stevens, 2009, p. 397). This may be true with unsophisticated first-timers, those who may feel guilty about the crime they have committed, but it may not be as effective when dealing with experienced convicts. Furthermore, full-fledged and articulate confessions by suspects are rare.

Many strategies have been developed to help minimize error in police interrogation work. The array of options includes using Rossmo's approach, such as improving a suspect's self-respect, changing the mind-set of the investigator, and improving the training of the detective. Rossmo (2006) outlines a number of strategies for investigators: having a team member serve as a devil's advocate, being careful to systematically question how certain conclusions have been drawn, obtaining the opinions and advice of experts at critical moments in time, debriefing members of the team after major investigations, and reviewing the merits and drawbacks of the investigation to proactively prevent intelligence failures.

Another technique involves creating a situation that encourages the suspect to tell the truth during the early part of the investigation. Investigators must be careful not to automatically assume that a suspect is guilty, and they should try to minimize any premature or unsubstantiated expectations about the crime and the criminal. Admittedly, it is very difficult to remain totally unbiased during the course of a criminal investigation, particularly if the crime is particularly hideous.

As one final precaution, detectives must receive appropriate training for their tasks. This is usually carried out at a state training academy or through the Federal Bureau of Investigation (FBI) in Quantico, VA, or the Federal Law Enforcement Training Centers (FLETC) in Georgia. Currently there are seven FLETC locations providing advanced course to over 80 federal agencies.

Intelligence-Driven Policing

Over the past decade the U.S Department of Justice, along with a number of policing practitioners have advocated intelligence-driven policing. This practice involves "the collection and analysis of information to produce an intelligence end product designed to inform police decision making at both the tactical and strategic levels" (Schmalleger and Worrall, 2010, p. 203). Policing experts suggest that this goes beyond the normal activities of CIB or CIDs. They add that "Not every agency has the staff or resources needed to create a dedicated intelligence unit. Even without an intelligence unit, however, a law enforcement organization should have the ability to effectively utilize the information and intelligence products that are developed and disseminated by organizations at all levels of government" (p. 203). Just as there are several types of police patrol, there are numerous kinds of intelligence collection types. One is tactical intelligence (i.e., primarily concerned with criminal and terror threats and the best way to arrest offender or frustrate their ability to engage in crime), and the other is strategic intelligence (i.e., providing information to criminal justice administrators to enable them to make appropriate decisions concerning the appropriate course of action).

The CSI Effect

One of the side effects of living in a society where there is phenomenal mass media (particularly, television) saturation is the proliferation of popular television shows such *CSI*, *CSI Miami*, and *Criminal Minds* that emphasize the role of forensic analysis techniques in the solving of complicated crimes. "Television and movies depict detective work as exciting and dangerous, with detectives possessing extraordinary skill and courage, capable of solving any crime if given enough time and resources" (White, 2007, p. 143). This phenomenon has led some analysts to propose the *CSI effect*, in which the message underlying fictional portrayals of forensic investigation "offers glamour, certainty, self-discipline, objectivity, truth, and justice all rolled into one, and in doing so effortlessly accommodates much-heralded successes" (Stevens 2007, p. 405). As White (2007) notes, "The popularity of crime scene investigation on television has fostered the impression that all crimes can be solved within an hour through sophisticated scientific techniques, DNA, and fingerprints" (p. 143). Although forensic science has helped the detective function immensely, the television shows have heightened (unfortunately) the expectations of both victims and the public in regard to the investigative process and its success rate.

Conclusion

A number of factors can influence the outcome of any investigation, including the amount of resources the police department has. Typically resources are gauged by the number of police officers or detectives who are assigned to a specific case: "too few, too many, or from too many jurisdictions, of which some do not communicate with other agencies . . . the detectives' caseloads, and budgetary and financial concerns can all influence the outcome of the investigation" (Stevens, 2009, p. 386). Not only are staff shortages a too-common reality, but a police department might also face problems related to lack of adequate "equipment, staff and forensic analysis," Stevens continues. "Another reason a case may go unsolved is because of poor interview and interrogation strategies provided by detectives."

Many recruits dream of the day that they will receive their gold detective shields. There is good reason for this. In comparison to patrol officers, detectives enjoy higher prestige and visibility among the public. In terms of the actual job, the hours worked by detectives are more regular. But like patrol officers, the daily work of a detective can end up being mundane. This is especially true when the detective functions primarily as a bureaucrat whose time is filled with filling out forms and making sure that the police department is protected from legal liability.

Glossary

Agent Provocateur: An individual, working undercover (e.g., an undercover police officer, a company spy, a member of the political opposition, or a subcontractor), who encourages others, particularly in a group setting, to engage in more extreme actions, including violence and illegal activities. When conducted by the police this practice is often labeled as entrapment.

Asset forfeiture: This occurs when police and law enforcement agencies specifically target convicted and suspected criminals for investigation and arrest because of the assets they have. Once seized, these assets can then be used by the police agency, rather than further harming the community at large.

CSI effect: The perception that forensic science as portrayed in popular television shows can solve crimes, identify criminals, and ensure that justice will be done quickly, exactly, and in a glamorous fashion.

Due process revolution: The result of several key rulings by the U.S. Supreme Court in the 1960s protecting the rights of the accused and placing additional pressures on police officers to alter their field practices related to the securing of convictions. The main goal now is to avoid instances in which a case can be thrown out of court because an officer has violated the defendant's constitutional rights.

Entrapment: This happens when a police officer coerces or tricks an individual into committing a crime that he or she would not have committed under normal circumstances.

Fencing operation: An alleged criminal enterprise or business, established by the police, through which stolen goods are purchased and sold. This operation is designed to result in the arrest of criminals tempted to use this enterprise/business.

Forensic evidence: The information collected by scientific and technical techniques that aid in crime-related investigations (e.g., fingerprints, blood splatter, DNA, ballistics).

Reid technique: An interrogation methodology by which police detectives quickly establish a baseline of a suspect's normal behavior and responses, which will help them to read the subject more thoroughly and to better understand when he or she is lying.

Sting operation: In this situation, undercover police officers set up a fencing operation in order to capture criminals engaged in illegal activity (especially thieves and purchasers of stolen goods).

Thieftaker: A private individual hired to capture thieves or recover stolen property. This profession predates the creation of the detective function in public police forces.

Undercover policing: This occurs when police officers pretend to be accomplices or willing victims of crimes. They do this by not only wearing civilian cloths and altering their appearance, but also by taking on the mannerisms of the criminal element in question. The primary goal of an undercover investigation is to gain the confidence of real or alleged criminals or to infiltrate a criminal organization.

Chapter Questions

Part One: Multiple Choice Questions

1. What is the name of an experienced individual familiar with the criminal underworld who would attempt, for a fee, to secure stolen property?
    a. magistrate
    b. constable
    c. thieftaker
    d. police officer
    e. frankpledge

2. In the history of policing, when were private detectives used instead of police detectives?
    a. early 1800s
    b. late 1800s
    c. early 1900s
    d. 1960s, during the police strikes
    e. 1980s, when some police departments were privatized

3. What kinds of forensic evidence are useful to law enforcement professionals in the solving of a crime?
    a. ballistics
    b. blood spatter
    c. blood type
    d. all of the above
    e. depends on the type of crime committed

4. What is a police sting?
    a. when police sit, wait, and watch to catch a person doing something wrong
    b. when police surround a suspected building or house and eventually break in unannounced
    c. the effect of police use of excessive force
    d. a police operation designed to catch a person committing a crime by means of deception
    e. when a police officer is physically assaulted

5. What does "cooling out a mark" mean?
    a. properly storing service revolvers
    b. when a police officer does not wear his or her hat while on duty
    c. reassuring crime victims
    d. going to a 7-11 for coffee and donuts
    e. refrigerating evidence

6. What is entrapment?
   a. a secret door in a police station that leads to the holding cells
   b. a term for entering the police academy
   c. performing a stakeout
   d. a practice used by fish and wildlife law enforcement officers
   e. forcing an individual to commit a crime in which they otherwise would not engage
7. What is the main problem connected with the practice of asset forfeiture by police departments?
   a. no place to store the items
   b. the need to hire a Certified Public Accountant
   c. a greater likelihood that police officers will be hurt or killed in the raid
   d. potential or actual criminals are targeted based on the amount of their assets rather than on the gravity of their crime
   e. the criminal justice system has difficulty disposing of the assets

Part Two: Short Answer Questions

1. What is the due process revolution?

2. What is a police sting?

3. List three kinds of forensic evidence that is useful to law enforcement officers in the solving of a crime?

4. What is order maintenance?

5. List three reasons why some cases receive a disproportionate amount of attention by police detectives.

Part Three: Essay Questions

1. Contrast the forensic techniques depicted in a television series, like CSI, with the actual empirical research methods used in detective work.

2. If most crimes are solved with little to no detective work, then why do we still have criminal investigation bureaus in police departments?

3. Many police officers aspire to be detectives. Why do you think this takes place? What are the advantages and disadvantages of this job category?

6
CHAPTER

Improper Discretion

Introduction

Police officers make decisions all the time. Police officers who have been sent out to a call by their dispatcher are legally and professionally obligated to respond. Officers who receive a call for service or who see something questionable while on patrol must answer two basic questions: Should they intervene; if so, how should they do so? More important, however, is why and how police officers become involved in a particular situation.

When no legal obligation exists, officers must rely on their personal discretion. In the framework of law enforcement, discretion involves a conscious decision made by criminal justice personnel to invoke a legal sanction. This process differs from decision making, which simply entails making a choice among various alternatives (Davis, 1969, 1971, 1975; Rosett, 1972; Goldstein, 1998). According to Davis (1969), among all of the professionals in the criminal justice system, the police make "far more discretionary determinations in individual cases than do any other class of administrators" (p. 222). As one may expect, police discretion is not value-free. To the contrary, it is quite subjective and controversial (McCabe and Sutcliffe, 1978; Williams, 1984).

Why Is Discretion Important?

Discretion is one of the most important tools that society has granted police officers. Moreover, it is a pervasive element in each officer's work, surrounding the typical decisions officers are empowered to make, such as stopping, questioning, searching, and arresting individuals (Brooks, 1997). Nonetheless, discretion is not monolithic. Discretion is influenced by a number of factors including decision-making, pervasiveness, and variability.

The Difference Between Discretion and Decision Making

The need to make discretionary judgments consumes a large part of a police officer's time, and it must be distinguished from simple decision making, which usually refers to when and how to intervene in situations. Discretion is more narrowly defined. The most commonly used definition is the decision not to invoke legal sanctions when circumstances are favorable for them. . . . In encounters with suspects, for example, police may be presented with a situation in which they have the legal basis for an arrest. They do not, however, always make an arrest. The decision not to make an arrest when it is legally justifiable is sometimes called non-enforcement discretion. (Roberg, Kuykendall, and Crank, 2000, p. 276)

In sum, "discretion involves both action and inaction" (Brooks, 1997, p. 151).

Another point worth mentioning is the distinction between delegated and unauthorized discretion. The phrase "delegated discretion" refers to the power that officers are typically given by virtue of their position, whereas officers who operate under "unauthorized discretion" are doing so without actual legal authority (Skolnick, 1966, pp. 71–90).

Pervasiveness

Who should be stopped, questioned, searched, or arrested? The answer to this ongoing question varies greatly. And what about the paperwork? When should it be completed, and how should it be filed? Some police actions require the extensive application of discretion, while others do not (Brooks, 1997). Minor crimes—that is, misdemeanors—that occur without bystanders and observers may require considerable discretion, whereas serious crimes, or felonies, that are committed while the police and/or bystanders are present require less discretion.

Variability of Discretion Among Police Officers

Every officer repeatedly makes decisions regarding who they should stop, question, search, or arrest. There are several reasons why an officer may decide not to intervene in a specific situation, including their perception that the criminal offence is not that important and being dispatched to another, more pressing criminal matter or emergency. Although all police officers use discretion, they do not apply it uniformly in all situations. Furthermore, the amount of discretion they exercise varies over the course of the number of days police officers have been on shift and where they are in their careers (Brooks, 1997; Linn, 2009).

Contextual Factors

Numerous contextual variables can influence police discretion. Research on police discretionary behavior has examined the effect of personality, situations, police organizations, and neighborhood factors on the discretionary behavior of police officers on the job (Brooks, 1997). A considerable amount of research on police discretion was motivated by police–community interactions during the 1950s and a report published by the American Bar Foundation, both of which inspired the due process revolution in the 1960s.

Personal Disposition Styles

In terms of personal disposition, researchers have studied the "response styles" exemplified by experienced officers while on the job and when placed in particular situations. For example, a police officer occasionally might feel sympathy for a suspect. An officer might also wait to see how a suspect reacts to police presence, all the while being prepared to make an arrest if a suspect resists or gets "smart-mouthed." In short, not all situations and individuals must be arrested (Brooks, 1997).

Situations

There are many reasons why a police officer may decide to ignore criminal infractions. The officer might be about to go off duty and want simply to wrap up his or her paperwork at the end of the shift. Perhaps the officer has a family obligation (e.g., pick up a child from day care) or a leisure activity (e.g., tickets to a sports event) lined up right after work. Alternatively, budgetary constraints may influence the officer. The police department may discourage end-of-shift arrests due to lack of funding for overtime. Or an arrest might be inconsistent with a specific officer's ethical and moral standards; for example, he or she may not be particularly motivated to arrest beer drinkers in public parks. Each police department may allow its officers a considerable amount of flexibility in certain situations (Brooks, 1997).

Departmental Rules

Police departments have numerous written and unwritten rules on police practices and behaviors. "The fewer the rules about handling incidents and situations, the more discretion officers have. Discretion involves both action and inaction" (Brooks, 1997, p. 151). Organizational rules greatly influence the degree of discretion that is accorded each police officer:

> Levels of discretion are contingent on the flexibility that police departments allow their officers in handling day-to-day calls for service. When organizational rules are strict, less discretion is afforded to police. Conversely, when rules are vague or lax, officers are allowed, or perhaps forced, to make their own decisions on how to conduct themselves. (Brooks, 1997, p. 149)

Rationale

There are numerous good reasons why police should be given the power of discretion:

1. vague laws that require officers to use their judgment
2. limited resources of the police department
3. the possibility of community alienation if officers fully enforce all of the laws all of the time
4. more time for officers to devote to more important activities
5. encouragement of cooperation from local residents

In the final analysis, if the police stopped and arrested people at every opportunity (i.e., zero-tolerance policing), the citizenry would become alienated, perhaps even hostile, against the police. In other words, discretion helps officers and the organization they represent maintain good relations with the public.

Styles of Policing

A considerable amount of scholarship has been devoted to understanding police discretion. One of the elements commonly studied is personal policing style. According to Brooks (1997), "officers may develop response styles and these styles may not only affect police perceptions, but they may also predispose them to act in certain ways" (p. 149).

In his pivotal study, *Police: Street Corner Politicians*, Muir (1977) identified four kinds of police officers: the professional, the reciprocator, the enforcer, and the avoider. Professional officers are both compassionate and comfortable with their authority. When necessary, these individuals do not hesitate to use coercion to accomplish a worthwhile purpose. Reciprocators are compassionate but are not comfortable with exercising their authority. These officers try to persuade individuals to cooperate without relying on coercion. Enforcers are comfortable in exercising authority, but they are not compassionate. These officers use coercion too often, primarily because they derive satisfaction from their ability to exercise power over others. Avoiders "are neither compassionate nor comfortable with their authority . . . they try to avoid as many difficult situations and problems as possible" (Roberg, Crank, and Kuykendall, 2000, p. 174).

Brown's 1981 study, *Working the Street: Police Discretion*, examined policing styles in three southern California cities. Brown pursued his study within the framework of two major issues: officer aggressiveness and crime selectivity. "Aggressiveness was the degree to which they actively seek out problems. Selectivity was the extent to which they were concerned only about serious crime problems" (Roberg, Crank, and Kuykendall, 2000, p. 273). Using these two variables, Brown identified four styles of police behavior/crime fighters: old style, clean-beat, service style, and professional style.

Old style officers are very aggressive and tend to be selective, concentrating primarily on felonies. These officers develop an extensive knowledge of the area in which they work, use informants, and tend to be coercive. They are sometimes willing to act illegally to get "results." Fictional examples include the title character in the 1971 movie *Dirty Harry*, starring Clint Eastwood, or the TV character Vic Mackey, portrayed by Michael Chiklis in the FX series *The Shield*.

Clean-beat officers believe in the importance of legal procedures. These officers are proactive and legalistic, but do not tend to be selective. Almost all violations of the law are considered significant.

Service-style officers do the minimum amount of work necessary to get by; that is, they are not aggressive but are selective. Only the most serious problems will result in their enforcing the law. Such officers tend to rely on informal solutions to problems rather than legalistic ones. Fictional examples typically come from 1960s television police shows such as *Andy of Mayberry* and *Barney Miller.*

Professional-style officers engage in limited proactivity and are not selective. They are situationally oriented, though "tough" when necessary, and at other times they may be service minded (Roberg, Crank, and Kuykendall, 2000, p. 274).

Though somewhat debatable by today's standards of social science research, Muir's and Brown's studies contributed significantly to the theories linked to the role of discretion in policing practices and to the impact of police personalities on the profession at large. These researchers also helped to further sensitize police departments to the importance of officer selection, training, and performance evaluations.

Mandatory Arrest Policies and Laws

In an attempt to limit the discretionary authority of police, some jurisdictions require police officers to arrest citizens they suspect or know to have committed particular kinds of crimes. Mandatory and/or presumptive arrest policy and practice compels officers to take into custody individuals especially when there is a legal requirement to intervene in domestic violence call or observation of same.

Given that police have considerable discretion to stop, question, and arrest individuals, one controversial area where police intervene is when they are dispatched to domestic violence calls. In some states, police officers are required by law to arrest the individual who appears to be the aggressor. Officers who fail to arrest in these situations are subject to disciplinary actions.

There are several reasons why some police officers are reluctant to make an arrest in a domestic violence incident. They may argue that it is a "private matter" between a man and a woman or that the courts will just end up releasing the individual who is arrested. They may contend that the definition of the situation changes when the police arrive or that an arrest will just increase their paperwork workload. Some officers interpret departmental philosophy to imply that some types of crime are more deserving of officers' time and effort than others. In some cases, the person who is the aggressor may be known to the officer; the aggressor may even be another law enforcement professional.

A mandatory arrest "policy eliminates police discretion and requires an arrest in all cases where officers have probable cause to believe that an act of domestic violence has occurred" (Stevens, 2009, p. 12). "During the late 1970s and early 1980s, a number of forces emerged that led to a shift toward mandatory arrest for domestic violence offenders" (White, 2007, p. 183). The Supreme Court case *Monell v. Department of Social Services of the City of New York* (436 U.S. 658) gave legal support to mandatory arrest practices. This decision upheld the notion that government employees and their agencies are liable for individual actions, even if these are considered normal practices. The main issue is whether an action or non-action violates the constitutional rights of an American citizen. In other words, an argument that an action is a normal and accepted practice is not a sufficient defense against an actual violation of constitutional protections. "The ruling in Monell put local governments at risk of being forced to pay large civil judgments as a result of the behavior of individual officials" (White, 2007, p. 183). This decision was "buttressed in 1984 by *Thurman v. Torrington, 595 F. Supp. 521* . . . [which] extended police liability to acts of omission, indicating that failure to protect victims of domestic violence . . . could result in civil litigation and large civil verdicts against the departments and city" (White, 2007, p. 184).

After these rulings were made, a major research study was conducted. In 1984, Sherman and Berk published the results of their Minneapolis Domestic Violence study, which indicated that when an abusive domestic partner was immediately arrested, the incidence of repeat offending dropped considerably in comparison to other kinds of police responses (e.g., warning). Shortly after the publication of this research, police departments across the country started to implement mandatory or presumptive arrest policies in cases of domestic assault (Gelles, 1996). Subsequently, the National Institute of Justice funded replications (a study using the same methods but in a different location to see if the results are similar to or different from the original study). The results, however, "clearly challenged the Minneapolis findings; specifically, results in three studies indicated that arrest led to increased frequency of subsequent domestic violence offenses" (White, 2007, p. 185). White goes on to note that a deeper examination of this issue reveals a multitude of problems related to mandatory arrest and the research it has generated:

> Inconsistent responses by prosecutors and courts is problematic for measuring the impact of arrest. . . . The shift to mandatory arrest has in some cases led to police reliance on dual arrest, where both participants in the incident are arrested. . . . Some jurisdictions have responded to this issue by adopting 'primary aggressor' laws (where police must identify and arrest only the initiator or aggressor) and by modifying police training and policy. (p. 184)

To try to cover as many issues as possible, a number of jurisdictions have adopted comprehensive policies on domestic abuse:

> [These] blend elements of each of these perspectives, employing mandatory arrest policies but also making an effort to establish a relationship with the victim and to connect her with a range of services that can help address her current situation. This approach often involves placing police officers with social workers as a crisis intervention team, with police focusing on arrest and building a case for a prosecutor while the social workers provide services to the victim including counseling, advocacy, shelter, support, and legal aid. (White, 2007, p. 185)

Zero Tolerance and Full Enforcement

Over the past two decades, considerable discussion has been devoted to zero-tolerance policing. This practice usually involves an aggressive enforcement of criminal laws in a particular jurisdiction or specific parts of a city (i.e., sectors, street corners or intersections, districts, zip codes) or with respect to some types of crime. It is also practiced in areas where particular kinds of crimes are known to occur. Often these areas are called "hot spots," "weed and seed areas," or High Intensity Drug Trafficking Areas (HIDTA). Under zero-tolerance policies, police officers are granted the right to stop, question, frisk, issue a citation or a summons, or arrest an individual if they believe the individual has committed a crime.

One of the most well-known adopters of zero-tolerance policing has been the New York Police Department in connection with the CompStat model. The impact of the CompStat model is difficult to measure, but many tourists and native New Yorkers remark that around major public places, like Times Square, the Port Authority, and the subways, they see less panhandling, graffiti, and homeless people (i.e., conventionally accepted typical indicators of disorder).

Why was zero-tolerance policing so widely adopted? One reason was the development and "uncritical" acceptance of the "broken windows theory" (Kelling and Wilson, 1982). This approach argues that when small-scale nuisances and deviance (e.g., panhandling, vagrancy) exist, especially in locations that are characterized by abandoned or poorly maintained houses and properties, the situation is ripe for the development of large-scale criminality. In such situations, police officers do not use discretion. Instead, officers focus on minor violations, such as disorderly conduct and traffic violations, by increased stopping, questioning, searching, and arrest of suspects and by stepping up the issuance of parking and moving violations/motor vehicle tickets.

Advantages

What are the advantages of this kind of policing? First among the commonly acknowledged benefits of zero tolerance is that many police officers and citizens believe that this approach is a strong deterrent to crime. On occasion, this practice can help police catch criminals more quickly than may be possible under other standards. Furthermore, there is a hope that this strategy will lead to the arrest of more important criminals. Finally, zero-tolerance minimizes criticisms of racial profiling (Brooks, 1997). One should keep in mind, though, that many of these advantages are built upon anecdotal and not empirical research.

Disadvantages

On the other hand, there are also many drawbacks to zero-tolerance practices. Zero tolerance can supplant the patrol officer's ability to use discretion.

This policy implies that an officer is incapable of adequately applying his or her discretionary ability to a particular situation. Zero tolerance can also lead to unintended side effects. For example, relatively law-abiding members of the public may dislike being stopped on a frequent basis, which may lead to citizen alienation and loss of support. Other side effects are crime displacement and an increasing clogging of judicial courts and correctional facilities. Finally, zero tolerance minimizes community participation and problem-solving techniques and emphasizes traditional law enforcement practices in the resolution of community problems.

Racial Profiling

The phrases "racial stereotyping" or the more pejorative "Driving While Black" (DWB) refer to the controversial practice in which important decisions (e.g., stopping, questioning, searching, arresting, charging, convicting, and sentencing) are made based on an individual's race, ethnicity, or religion. In the context of policing, the most common activities linked to racial stereotyping are stopping, questioning, searching, and arresting individuals. Although racial profiling has existed since the creation of the first modern police force, it was not until the 1980s that this practice was brought to the American public's attention (Engel, Calnon, and Bernard, 2002). As White (2007) notes:

> It is very difficult to determine the true extent of racial profiling, our ability to collect appropriate data is limited and it is hard to eliminate competing explanations. Nevertheless, an increasing number of police agencies are collecting racial information during traffic stops. By 2001, more than a dozen states required law enforcement agencies to record data on traffic stops; many other departments do so voluntarily. (p. 258)

During the mid 1990s, African-American drivers on the New Jersey Turnpike, one of the most important interstate highways in that state, complained that they were stopped and searched by the New Jersey State Patrol (NJSP) primarily because of their race. Through the efforts of the American Civil Liberties Union (ACLU), a legal case was brought to the New Jersey Attorney General, and in 1996, the State of New Jersey courts ruled that "state troopers were engaged in a state-condoned policy of racial profiling and that the NJSP had failed to monitor, control, or investigate claims of discrimination" (White, 2007, p. 260). In 2002 and 2003, legal claims were settled by the state. Because of these events, the NJSP was placed under a consent decree by the U.S. Department of Justice. The consent decree effectively placed the day-to-day management of the police force under federal government control until it was determined that appropriate changes had been made by the NJSP.

Advantages

Advocates argue that racial profiling is a time-tested, effective, and universal practice in law enforcement. The practice of stereotyping can make the job of policing much simpler. Police officers only need to use a handful of simple visual cues to make decisions to stop, question, search, and arrest suspected individuals. Also, racial profiling periodically leads to the arrest of an individual who has committed a crime.

Disadvantages

Simply being a member of a particular race that the police believe commits crime more than others is not an appropriate criterion for the decision to act on an individual basis. Critics of this practice, especially the National Association for the Advancement of Colored People (NAACP) and the ACLU, maintain that race should only be used when one subject needs to be distinguished from others; it should not be applied to help determine police practice of any kind. Some opponents to racial profiling claim that when a particular race is targeted by the criminal justice system, this is tantamount to discrimination or racial prejudice. Others argue that racial profiling is a violation of the U.S. Constitution's Fourth Amendment, which protects persons from unreasonable search and seizure.

Another difficulty is that when law enforcement officers disproportionately focus on people of a particular race, they risk ignoring potential suspects who belong to other races. In other words, police officers could miss considering other possible suspects and perpetrators of crimes. Finally, racial profiling casts the net too wide, which means that too many people are taken into police custody. This happens because the police officers stop, question, and arrest the wrong persons. This practice wastes valuable and limited police and criminal justice resources.

Policing in this manner can potentially open a police department up to a civil suit. Moreover, racial profiling typically creates hostility and decreases trust toward the police. In terms of the police officers as individuals, profiling perpetrates and reinforces negative stereotypes (http://www.aclu.org/racialjustice/racialprofiling/index.html).

Occasionally, community activists and those prone to believe conspiracy theories argue that because police departments target or concentrate their resources in particular areas (e.g., ghettos, barrios), the police are actually engaging in racial profiling. Although there may be some merit in this argument, this claim is rarely substantiated (see Exhibit 6.1).

Exhibit 6.1   **The Expansion of Racial Profiling**

Racial profiling is not only limited to street criminals, and traffic stops. Since September 11, 2001, American law enforcement officers from the municipal to the federal level have been accused of racially profiling individuals of Middle Eastern and Muslim descent, and assuming that Sikhs were Islamic Fundamentalists. Almost every day, we hear reports in the news media about the improper detention of individuals—both American citizens and foreigners—with Middle Eastern physical characteristics. These incidents are stressful and hurtful to the victims of racial profiling and make them distrust the criminal justice system in general and law enforcement in particular. If we think that terrorists live in only one geographic region of the world, or belong to one nationality, we forget that in reality many terrorist groups, particularly large ones, are all around the world. Focusing on one group may lead law enforcement to ignore other terrorist groups, thus helping them to grow stronger and to fine-tune the tactics they may use against American citizens and our allies. Many Muslims and those who can trace their origins to the Middle East were either born in the United States or have lived here for years and do not or no longer have any connections to Iraq, Afghanistan, or other Middle Eastern countries.

It is often difficult to differentiate between racial and behavioral profiling, and terrorism awareness requires a degree of knowledge and sensitivity that some law enforcement officers and their agencies lack. There are good and bad people in every race, ethnicity, and nationality, and law enforcement officers and agencies may need to be better educated regarding the diversity of people.

Conclusion

Discretion is an important aspect of municipal policing. Without it, our criminal justice system would be clogged with numerous noncritical, extraneous cases. Capable citizens would be discouraged from working as police officers since their ability to use their own judgment using an important legal sanction would be compromised. Nonetheless, since no one is infallible, controls on police discretion must be in place. The academic community has responded to this need by instituting studies and research, much of which has resulted in contradictory conclusions. Nevertheless, the consensus is that the behavior of the police organizations should be shaped in a way that will not unnecessarily hamper their valuable societal job or frustrate their employees. Since 9/11, the challenge of racial profiling is no longer restricted to African-Americans. Muslims and other individuals of Middle Eastern descent are routinely stopped, questioned, searched and arrested by municipal police, based not simply on the suspicion of having committed a crime, but on their physical characteristics. Finding appropriate solutions to this violation of procedural law is not easy given the heightened fear in America over the possibility of another catastrophic terrorist attack.

Glossary

Brown's four styles of police behavior: Typology based on aggressiveness versus selectivity of crime problems: (1) old style, (2) clean beat style, (3) service style, and (4) professional style.

Decision making: A choice among two or more alternatives.

Discretion: A decision made by criminal justice practitioners to invoke a legal or criminal sanction. In the case of police officers, acts of discretion include stopping, questioning, searching, and arresting suspects.

Full enforcement: Synonym for zero-tolerance policing.

High Intensity Drug Trafficking Area (HIDTA): Area identified by law enforcement and criminal justice planners in which a disproportionate amount of illegal drug dealing or other type of crime takes place.

Muir's four styles of police officers: Typology based on an officer's compassion and comfort levels as related to his or her authority: (1) professionals, (2) reciprocators, (3) enforcers, and (4) avoiders.

Racial profiling: This occurs when criminal justice system practitioners make important decisions primarily based on the race or ethnicity of the suspect/accused.

Zero-tolerance policing: The aggressive enforcement of one or more criminal laws in a particular jurisdiction or during a specific time frame. In this policy framework, no discretion is allowed on the part of officers. Typically, this type of policing relates to low level kinds of crime, like seat belt laws and open container laws.

Chapter Questions

Part One: Multiple Choice Questions

1. What are the four typical criteria that police officers depend on when exercising their discretionary authority?
   a. initiation, reaction, reduction, and causation
   b. norms, policies, practices, and rules of the police department
   c. counseling, deterrence, education, and visibility
   d. age, appearance, demeanor, and gender of suspects
   e. some of the above

2. How does discretion differ from decision making?
   a. Discretion involves action and inaction.
   b. Discretion requires a choice to be made between two competing alternatives.
   c. Police officers have the ability to invoke a criminal sanction.
   d. both a and c
   e. none of the above

3. It is Christmas Eve. A police officer clocks a rather jolly old man wearing a red suit and driving a herd of reindeer at 25 miles over the speed limit. Upon closer examination, he decides not to give the man a ticket. This is an example of what?
   a. accepting a gratuity
   b. corruption
   c. decision
   d. discretion
   e. all of the above

4. The scholarly research and public concern over police discretionary authority are usually attributed to what impetus?
   a. survey research conducted by the American Bar Association in the 1950s
   b. the Watts Riots
   c. the riots connected with the demonstrations during the Democratic Party convention in 1968
   d. the identification of racial profiling
   e. problems with the PATRIOT ACT

5. Who conducted one of the first studies of police discretion?
   a. Brooks
   b. Brown
   c. Fogelson
   d. Goldstein
   e. Ross

6. Which of the following is NOT one of the four styles of policing identified by Muir?
   a. Avoider
   b. Enforcer
   c. Old style
   d. Professional
   e. Reciprocator

7. What can police departments do to minimize bad decisions by police officers?
   a. more careful selection of recruits
   b. proper training
   c. the development and use of clear and understandable administrative guidelines
   d. accountability for police officers who break the rules
   e. all of the above

8. Racial profiling is
   a. the same as psychological profiling
   b. a highly controversial police practice
   c. rarely used
   d. all the above
   e. none of the above

Part Two: Short Answer Questions

1. What is the difference between discretion and decision making in the context of police officers and police departments?

2. Is police deviance a criminal action?

3. What is zero-tolerance policing?

4. How important is discretion as one of the tools available to police officers?

5. Is there a difference between racial profiling and racial prejudice? If so, what distinguishes them?

6. What are four disadvantages of racial profiling?

7. In which situations will police departments use a mandatory arrest policy?

Part Three: Essay Questions

1. Does Muir or Brown provide a better explanation of police discretionary behavior? Your answer should briefly describe both authors' studies, including their relevance for policing practices and theories. Present clear arguments about why you favor one author over the other.

2. Is racial profiling by police officers a good practice or a bad practice? What are the arguments for and against its use?

3. Which strategy is better: zero-tolerance policing or police discretion? Why?

4. Is mandatory arrest a useful police policy and practice?

Inability to Significantly Reduce Crime: Problems with Patrol and Domestic Violence Arrests

Introduction

Most police professionals engage in patrol activities (e.g., foot, bicycle, segway, horse, motorized, air, water) at various points in their careers. This function has been described as the "backbone of policing."

Over the history of modern policing, departments have expended considerable resources on making patrol activities more efficient through the adoption of new transportation technologies as they have become available. For example, foot patrol was aided by the introduction of bike and mounted (horse) patrols. These methods were eventually dwarfed by the introduction of motorized patrol (i.e., car and motorcycle). Moreover, as new and more portable communication technologies were invented, such as two-way radios, computers, and computer-aided dispatches, these were quickly placed at police officers' disposal in their patrol vehicles. All of these developments were supported because the police force management believed they would increase the effectiveness of police officers.

Patrol typically involves routine street stops, which, seasoned law enforcement practitioners have argued, help police officers to gather information on individuals committing crimes and sometimes lead to arrests. Street stops, it is argued, also serve as a deterrent to those thinking about committing a crime. During a typical police stop, the officer reviews the individual's identification, asks them to explain their presence in the area, and may even check their name in the National Crime Information Center (NCIC) criminal database. When officers stop an individual in a vehicle, they will also ask for the person's license, ownership, and insurance documents. This can provide information about outstanding warrants and criminal histories. In addition, through questioning, observation, and, when warranted, conducting appropriate searches, officers may find weapons, drugs, or other contraband, which may then lead to an arrest (Exhibit 7.1).

Exhibit 7.1   **Television Series Featuring Police Patrol**

Since the creation of the television, American programs have featured police officers, primarily depicting them on patrol. These programs have spanned different genres from comedy (e.g., *Car 54, Where Are You?, Reno 911, Hills Street Blues*) to drama (e.g., *Southland*) and typically echo the headlines and issues of their day, including race relations, terrorism, and gangs. These types of programs are a subset of police procedural shows that focus on a series of crimes being investigated rather than one crime. One of the very first television shows featuring police patrol was *Car 54, Where Are You?*, which ran seven seasons and focused on the antics of two New York City police officers as they went about their daily patrol. *Adam 12*, which ran from 1968 through 1975, featured the activities of two police officers, a seasoned Los Angeles police officer and his rookie partner, as they responded to different calls during the day. Finally, *Southland*, a relatively serious television drama which debuted in 2009, focused on the trials and tribulations of officers who worked the south Los Angeles beat. It involved issues of death, police deviance and camaraderie, and job discrimination. Over time, many of the same themes are repeated from series to series.

Importance of Patrol

In any given police department, patrol officers account for a minimum of 50% of all uniformed police officers. In some agencies, this allocation can be as high as 70%. The patrol function is the most visible aspect of any officer's work. Because of the enormous attention spent on patrol, it is often dubbed the backbone of policing. In addition to the belief that patrol aids in the reduction of crime, it has been noted that this police function is used for "(1) crime prevention and deterrence, (2) apprehension of offenders, (3) creation of a sense of community security and satisfaction, (4) provision of noncrime-related services, and (5) traffic control" (Roberg and Kuykendall, 1993, p. 308).

Different Types of Patrol

Patrol varies based on the available transportation means (e.g., foot, motorized, horse) and the manner in which it is pursued (e.g., proactive versus reactive). Although there are numerous ways police patrol, two basic methods are used: traditional/random, and directed/targeted. In the first instance "[o]fficers are assigned to a specific geographic area and move around that area in an unsystematic manner" (White, 2007, p. 140). Police departments assume that this practice will make officers seemingly omnipresent; on their random rounds, they may even be able to detect crimes in progress. In the second method, patrol, "officers focus on a particular area, such as a hot spot where crime and offenders are prevalent." This method is decidedly proactive in nature: "[It] often occurs at the same degree of crime analysis that detects the problem, but it can also be more informal. . . . Directed patrol may involve saturating a particular area with police for a specified period of time, with police aggressively enforcing laws, conducting random stops and frequent traffic stops" (p. 140). This kind of patrol falls under the umbrella of zero-tolerance policing and CompStat techniques.

Despite these objectives, most patrols are conducted by officers in their vehicles and these officers spend only a small fraction of their time dealing with situations that could potentially be construed as crimes. In actuality, officers have few contacts with citizens while on motorized patrols. Reiss (1971) was one of the first scholars to empirically document the low number of criminal arrests by officers on preventive patrol. In fact, less than 1% of the time spent on preventive patrol is occupied in handling criminal matters (Cumming, Cumming, and Edell, 1970; Cain, 1973; Punch and Naylor, 1973; Payne, 1973; Punch, 1979).

Despite the impressions promoted by the media, the solitary nature of patrol work has been well documented (Bittner 1967a, 1967b; Black, 1970; Black and Reiss, 1970; Reiss, 1971; Lundman, 1974a, 1974b, 1979; Pepinsky, 1975; Friedrich, 1980; Sykes and Brent, 1983). Although the majority of this research has focused on American police departments, the findings are generally similar in other Anglo-American democracies, such as England (Ekblom and Heal, 1982) and Canada (Ericson, 1982). As this depiction clearly demonstrates, contrary to popular culture, police work is far from glamorous.

Police officers on patrol engage in three basic functions: law enforcement, order maintenance, and service. "Law enforcement activities involve problems in which police make arrests, issue citations, or conduct investigations" (Roberg and Kuykendall, 1993, p. 308). Order-maintenance activities may or may not involve a violation of the law (usually minor). In dealing with them, many officers tend to use alternatives other than arrest. Examples of order-maintenance actions include responding to loud parties, teenagers consuming alcohol, or minor neighbor disputes. "Service activities involve taking reports and providing information and assistance to the public" (Roberg and Kuykendall, 1993, p. 308).

Police Patrol Issues

Numerous aspects of patrol are important and have been subject to scholarly research. Two of the most important are resource determination and resource allocation.

Resource Determination

Resource determination seeks to ascertain the appropriate numbers of full-time police that need to be hired in a particular police department, the number of employees who should be allocated to the patrol function, and the manner in which their services should be distributed throughout the day. There are essentially three ways to establish the "right" number of police personnel for a city: by intuition, comparison, and workload (Roberg and Kuykendall, 1993, pp. 313–315). The first approach typically depends on an educated guess by an experienced person who has a position of seniority in the department. This estimation is often calculated based on past trends. The second approach involves comparing a specific police department with another similar law enforcement agency and trying to match the number of resources. (This method resembles the efforts of real estate evaluators in determining the market price of a property.) The final technique, when done properly, involves gaining an understanding of the complex activities that fall to each sector in the police department, including the prioritization of tasks.

Resource Allocation

Most urban police departments operate 24 hours a day, 7 days a week. Thus, departments must staff their agencies in a manner that helps them deal with the numerous demands on their time over this continuous period. This aids them in establishing a good sense of the kind of workloads that may be encountered. As Roberg and Kuykendall (1993) note,

> Because the workload distribution is not equal across time periods, days, or patrol areas, it is apparent that the equal allocation of police resources would mean that some officers are being overused while others are being underused. Such an arrangement presents operational problems not only in attempting to respond to calls for service but also in not being able to perform directed or preventive patrol duties. (p. 315)

Allocation is dependent on the location and timing of problems. Developing a comprehensive understanding of these factors is difficult but not impossible. The growth of computer-aided dispatch (CAD) has helped many departments to better allocate their scarce resources.

> As a general rule, the greater the number of problems, the smaller the size of the beat, and thus the more concentrated the resources. The time it takes to respond to a problem is also important because the resource being allocated is a skilled officer's time, which needs to be managed in the most effective manner possible. Once data have been collected and analyzed with respect to these variables, beat boundaries, number of officers, and shift times are determined. Because of population-shift and demand-for-service changes, it is important that departments continually re-evaluate patrol beat boundaries and assignment of personnel. (Roberg and Kuykendall, 1993, p. 316)

Selected Research on Patrol

Since the 1960s, a vast number of scientific research studies have been conducted on the patrol function. Because they are resource intense, most of them have been funded by the National Institute of Justice, a division of the

U.S. Department of Justice. Many of the studies contradict previously held assumptions about what officers do on patrol and how successful they are in achieving the police agencies' and criminal justice planners' original goals.

To date, approximately eight basic types of patrol studies have been examined:

- preventive
- response time
- management of demand
- directed patrol
- police crackdowns
- covert patrol
- foot patrol
- one- versus two-person patrol models

The following section reviews the most important patrol studies conducted in the United States.

Kansas City (Missouri) Preventive Patrol Experiment (1974)

One of the earliest, most well-known, and oft-cited patrol experiments in the United States occurred in Kansas City and was led by George Kelling and a research team at the Police Foundation (Kelling, Pate, Dieckman, and Brown, 1974). The investigators wanted to determine the effect of random patrol on the rates of reported crimes, actual crime rates, citizens' perceptions of the police, response times of police, and citizens' feelings of security. For the purpose of their study, the researchers divided a section of the city into 15 beats. They identified five similar groups and further subdivided these into three subgroups. Each of the subgroups received a different kind of patrol: proactive (i.e., police performed two to three times the average level of patrol), reactive (i.e., police only responded if there was a call for service), and control (i.e., police did not change the way they normally conducted patrol). After allowing the study to run for several months, the results indicated that there was no difference in the identified measures based on the kind of patrol the officers used.

This study called into question the time-honored assumption about the impact of patrols. Contrary to common belief, preventative patrol, which occupied a disproportionate amount of officers' work days, actually had little effect on crime rates.

New Haven (Connecticut) Directed Patrol (1975)

In 1975, patrol officers in New Haven were instructed to arrive at certain times of day at specific locations that were known to experience higher-than-normal serious crime rates. At these particular locations, each officer was given a further set of instructions. For example, he or she might be told to patrol around a certain block slowly, park, walk around, get back in the car, and cruise down another street. These "D-runs" took up to one hour, and each officer completed two or three of these per shift. Favorable public attitudes for the patrol officers in the study were generally low, and the program did not reduce crime but rather displaced it. After a year's duration, the experiment quietly ended. This experiment was later replicated with the Minneapolis Hot Spot Patrol Experiment (Sherman and Weisburd, 1995).

Wilmington (Delaware) Split-Force Experiment (1976)

In 1976, researchers (Tien et al., 1977) tried to determine if, by splitting the approximately 250 uniformed patrol officers of the Wilmington Police Department into two different groups with different patrol styles, a discernible effect on crime rates, response times, and other relevant factors could be detected. Three-fourths of the officers were restricted to responding to calls for service, and the others were given "structured-saturation patrol" duties. The structured patrols were allocated to high-crime areas, were typically pursued as undercover operations, and allowed for engagement in surveillance and stakeouts. The evaluation of the experiment determined that the new patrol model reduced crime rates by approximately 20% and increased community satisfaction and accountability.

Kansas City Response Time Analysis (1977)

In 1977, the Kansas City Police Department attempted to determine if response time by patrol officers had any effect on an officer's ability to apprehend a suspected perpetrator (Pate, Bowers, Ferrara and Lorence, 1976). This study also looked at the impact of police vehicles driven by one officer versus two officers. The study reported that police response time had little or no effect on apprehension percentages. What was most effective in securing an arrest was the time it took citizens to report the incident and whether there were adequate and credible witnesses present when the police arrived. Additionally two person police cars do not have any advantage in crime reduction or apprehending criminals, nor are officers more likely to sustain injuries in one person cars.

Newark (New Jersey) (1978–1979) and Flint (Michigan) (1985) Foot Patrol Experiments

Between 1978 and 1979, the Police Foundation conducted a study in Newark, New Jersey to determine the effectiveness of taking officers out of their patrol cars and assigning them to walk their beats (Wilson and Kelling, 1982). The researchers concluded that the foot patrols had not reduced crime rates but that residents seemed to feel more secure because of them. A replication in Flint, Michigan, in 1985 found that officers on foot patrol were more satisfied with their jobs and felt safer than those in motorized patrol.

Project on Policing Neighborhoods (Indianapolis and St. Petersburg) (1995)

In 1995, Stephen Mastrofski, Roger Parks, Robert Worden, and Al Reiss began an observational study of the Indianapolis, Indiana, and St. Petersburg, Florida, police departments (Parks et al., 1999). Not only did the researchers (and their assistants) observe patrol officers, but they also examined police administrators and the effectiveness of community policing meetings. In addition, the study involved conducting interviews with the individuals who were being observed. The researchers hoped to determine if policing methods differed substantially between the two communities: St. Petersburg had an established program in community policing, and Indianapolis was in the early stages of implementing a similar program. The study, which cost $2.2 million, concluded that police officers engaged in community policing programs found their work and tasks to be satisfying and that residents of the cities in question were, in general, happy with the level of police services they were receiving.

Summary

The patrol experiments have not escaped criticism: "given their narrow focus, some argue, the studies relate to only a small segment of actual police experiences and are not reliable. In practice, it was recognized that specific initiatives were not as efficient as expected. Nevertheless, the results of these studies, through trial and error, can aid police performance" (Stevens, 2009, p. 312). Another issue, which is often ignored, is the possibility of the displacement of crime, which can occur when criminals seeing or hearing about a heightened police presence temporarily stopping crime in a neighborhood and start victimizing people and businesses in another jurisdiction (typically very close to the area in which they had previously engaged in illegal activities). Moreover, patrols typically affect street crimes (e.g., muggings, vandalism, drug sales) and do not influence those activities that take place beyond the police officer's immediate view (e.g., domestic violence, white collar crime, corporate crime).

Conclusion

After reading this chapter, one may be left wondering about the utility of police patrol. If patrol is only minimally effective as a method to reduce crime, then why do police forces still invest incredible resources in this practice? Although no concrete information exists to answer this question, one reason may be linked to public relations efforts. Regardless of their reasons, police departments are constantly experimenting with new ways to reduce crime. In the 1990s, law enforcement agencies started experimenting with community policing, problem-oriented policing, CompStat, and zero tolerance methods of policing. However, research into the effectiveness of these strategies has produced mixed findings. For example, "There is some empirical support for problem-oriented and community policing, but contradictory findings have also emerged to prevent definitive conclusions from being drawn" (White, 2007, p.121).

Glossary

Crime displacement: Migration of crime from an area with a heightened police presence as criminals shift to another, typically nearby, jurisdiction.

Kansas City Preventive Patrol Study: Earliest, most well-known police patrol experiments in the United States. It concluded that preventive patrol had little effect on crime rates.

National Institute of Justice: Research wing of the U.S. Department of Justice that funds criminal justice studies designed to be helpful to state and local criminal justice agencies.

Patrol: The process whereby officers walk or drive through an area to observe and respond to crimes in progress or that have occurred.

Patrol experiments: A series of experiments conducted in selected jurisdictions to determine if the way police conduct patrols has an effect on crime rates, citizens' sense of security, and/or citizens' opinions of the police.

Street stops: These are believed to help police officers gather information on individuals committing crimes, resulting in arrests as needed. A typical stop involves a review of the individual's identification and running his or her name through the National Crime Information Center (NCIC).

Chapter Questions

Part One: Multiple Choice Questions

1. A typical stop by a police officer involves
   a. an arrest
   b. questioning the individual
   c. a search
   d. checking the individuals' information against the National Crime Information Center
   e. none of the above

2. In the typical police department, what percentage of officers are assigned to patrol?
   a. 10–25%
   b. 25–50%
   c. 50–75%
   d. 76–90%
   e. 90%

3. Typically the largest operations area in mid- to large-sized police departments is
   a. patrol
   b. criminal investigations
   c. special operations
   d. vice and narcotics
   e. public relations

4. What is the type of police patrol where officers patrol in dissimilar patterns and not always taking the same streets?
   a. Traditional/Random Patrol
   b. Directed/Targeted Patrol
   c. Same District Patrol
   d. Saturation Patrol
   e. none of the above

5. What were the findings of the Kansas City Patrol Experiment?
   a. Police officers, when unsupervised, tended to be more corrupt than others who had to report to their lieutenants on an hourly basis.
   b. Police officers were told to enforce every law or issue citations for every law violation witnessed.
   c. Empty patrol cars were parked on the roadsides to gauge the public's reaction.
   d. The greater the number of patrol units, the fewer the number of crimes.
   e. The type of patrol had no effect on the level of crime.

6. What was the name of the patrol study, conducted in the 1990s, that examined the police departments in St. Petersburg and Indianapolis?
   a. Kansas City Patrol Experiment
   b. Delaware Foot Patrol Experiment
   c. Newark Foot Patrol Experiment
   d. Project on Policing Neighborhoods
   e. none of the above

7. What do many criminals do after learning the patterns of police patrol?
   a. commit crimes in a neighboring jurisdiction
   b. temporarily cease or desist from committing crime
   c. take more care with respect to where and when they commit crime
   d. none of the above
   e. all the above

8. What is one of the most important findings of police patrol studies?
   a. The type of patrol had an effect on the ability to catch a criminal.
   b. The type of patrol had an effect on officer morale.
   c. The type of patrol varies over time.
   d. The type of patrol affects administrator job satisfaction.
   e. The type of patrol had a minimal effect on the crime rate.

Part Two: Short-Answer Questions

1. List four major patrol studies.

2. What are three types of police patrol?

3. Why do experts say that police patrol is the backbone of policing?

4. Why do police patrol? (Give two reasons)

5. What kind of information do police officers gather during a street stop?

6. What were the two different groups in the Delaware split force experiment divided into?

Part Three: Essay Questions

1. If patrol has a minimal effect on reducing crime, why do police departments continue to expend a disproportionate amount of their resources on this function?

2. What areas of police patrol need additional research and why?

3. Under what conditions are police officers reluctant to arrest a husband for domestic violence? What moral and ethical reasons do you think enter into a police officer's decision to arrest in this situation?

8
CHAPTER

Poor Police–Community Relations

Introduction

There are many reasons why the police have difficult interactions with the communities they are supposed to "serve and protect." Many of these stem from the fact that overall, police departments have contrasting "perspectives, poor communications, and concerns about the nature of social control in a free society" (Radalet and Carter, 1994, p. 7).

The police deal with the community on several levels: individually, as a group/organization, and as political actors. When it appears that law enforcement represents the interests of the communities in which they police, there is general harmony. When police are out of sync with these sentiments, there is discontent and dissension. Also, keep in mind that "Different community groups view the police differently and have varying notions of the priorities and objectives of law enforcement and criminal justice" (Cordner and Scarborough, 2007: 10). Also, difficulty at one level of the interaction can have repercussions at another.

This chapter defines police–community relations; distinguishes it from public relations, community service, and community participation; reviews the history of improving police–community relations; and then analyzes the strategies of community policing and problem-solving policing. The remaining portion examines how community policing can be easily misused and what to do to put it back on course.

Definitional Issues

There are a considerable number of definitions for police–community relations. Nevertheless, this term generally refers to the sum total of attitudes and behaviors between police and the communities they serve. They can range from positive to negative in general or with respect to particular things police do. One of the ways that police–community relations has been understood (and defined) is by seeing it as part of a tripod, including public relations, community service, and community participation (Radalet and Carter, 1994). Taken as a whole this conceptualization makes sense.

However, if one of these component parts is all there is, police–community relations can be quite problematic.

Public Relations

Many times police–community relations is primarily the practice of public relations, which is a collection of communication techniques used by individuals or organizations to convince an audience about the merits of an idea, organization, program, practice, or policy. Public relations tries to convince an audience based on appeals to reason. Despite what might appear to be an innocuous kind of communication, the public relations process tends to be one way—from the police department to citizens. And if the community is consulted, sometimes only selected constituencies' ideas or preferences are taken into account (i.e., addressed), thus upsetting those who were ignored and/or left out.

The problem here is that "what a police department views as good for the department may not necessarily be good for the community; or it may be good only for that part of the community to whom the police are particularly responsive and not for other parts" (Radalet and Carter, 1994, p. 31).

Community Service

Alternatively, community service refers to the activities whereby police engage in prosocial activities to enhance the well-being of the community beyond law enforcement and order maintenance. Examples include running a Police Athletic League or night basketball league. Community service can provide a public relations benefit. Frequently the words and expressions *public relations* and *community relations* are used interchangeably. But in reality, there is a difference between the two. Although public relations was defined earlier in this book, a community relations program is best seen as "a long-range, full scale effort to acquaint the police and the community with each other's problems and to stimulate action aimed at solving those problems" (Radalet and Carter, 1994, p. 31).

Community Participation

Finally, community participation involves members of the community taking an active role in trying to genuinely help the police. "It is the widely used social work concept of community organization, with particular attention to the pivotal responsibility of the police and other criminal justice agencies" (Radalet and Carter, 1994, p. 34).

In the end police–community relations is a process where the entire police department (not a specialized unit) is engaged with the communities they serve in order to make it a safe and better place to live (Radalet and Carter, 1994, p. 32).

Importance of Police–Community Relations

When there is good police–community relations, police have a better understanding of the public's concerns (especially those that are crime related), and citizens are more inclined to report crimes that occur to the police, provide tips/intelligence to law enforcement, willingly serve as witnesses, and are happy to participate in jury trials. By extension, police also become more proactive, thereby preventing crimes before they occur or minimizing their impact, instead of simply reacting to calls for service. Good police–community relations prevent the possibility that the public thinks that police are simply a mechanism for intelligence collection.

When there are poor police–community relations, the police typically lack a basic understanding of community problems, goals, and desires, and the community, particularly those citizens who are experiencing high rates of crime, poverty, and homelessness, perceive police as an occupying and out-of-touch force that does more harm than good. In these situations, police departments primarily assume a reactive mode of response to community problems.

In sum, police–community relations refers to the ongoing and changing relationship between the police and the communities they serve. This includes issues of cooperation, race relations, fear of police, violence, and corruption.

Emergence of the Problem of Poor Police–Community Relations

The notion of police–community relations derives from Sir Robert Peel's principles of law enforcement. As you may recall, before the creation of the first modern police department, it was the duty of every able-bodied person to take their turn at the watch, thereby contribute to the policing of their community. If there was a threat to the community, the night watch would raise a hue and cry. This would wake up the community, and its citizens would collectively repel an attack from wild animals or intruders, help put out a fire, and so on. Why did this break down?

Early History of Police–Community Relations

Developments during the early part of the 20th century (e.g., the advent of motorized vehicles, the development of more efficient mass transportation systems, police officers not living in the same jurisdiction in which they patrolled) led to a breakdown in police–community relations. In short, there are numerous reasons for poor police community relations. These can include:

- Socialization of children by parents to fear/distrust the police
- Hostility toward the police

- Confidence in police ability has decreased
- Less contact by police with citizens
- Bad cops (rude, corrupt, violent)
- Some veteran officers would rather not deal with the community
- Police are not the best communicators
- Police and citizens have different perspectives on how crime is caused and how to respond to it.

These factors in whole or in part prompted police reformers to search for appropriate solutions. One of the more notable was the integration of the human relations movement into law enforcement The human relations movement and some astute police executives believed that police had to move beyond simply being responsible for enforcing the law and actually connect with the communities they policed (Radalet and Carter, 1994, p. 23). Some of the initial attempts to increase awareness and techniques of police–community relations were started with the introduction of human relations training into police training academies (Radalet and Carter, 1994; Bayley and Mendelsohn, 1969). Human relations consisted of a series of techniques to both better understand how individuals behaved in groups and to improve their productivity and cooperation in organizational contexts.

After World War II, there was a fledgling interest in human relations training for police officers and the communities they policed (Radalet and Carter, 1994, p. 23). Police administrators interested in having their departments improve interactions with the communities they police occasionally sent officers to summer workshops that were led by organizations such as the National Conference of Christians and Jews (NCCJ). "A few police officers enrolled in these workshops as early as 1947, seeking help in understanding human relations or in setting up departmental training programs on the subject" (Radalet and Carter, 1994, p. 23). In 1954, in Philadelphia, the International Association of Chiefs of Police and the National Association of Intergroup Relations Officials sponsored a two-day conference for police executives and other professionals involved in human relations.

The National Institute on Police and Community Relations

In 1955, based on the relative success of these initiatives, through the combined efforts of the NCCJ and the Michigan State University (MSU) School of Police Administration and Public Safety, the National Institute on Police and Community Relations (NIPCR) was formed. The NIPCR's training involved workshops and/or institutes. "The institute, a five-day conference, proved to be so popular that it was repeated each May until 1970. It brought together teams of police officers and other community leaders to discuss common problems and to develop leadership for similar programs at the local or state levels" (Radalet and Carter, 1994, p. 24).

The police–community relations programs during the 1950s and 1960s were useful in articulating the contours of the field. They also "encouraged a teamwork or interprofessional approach to problems of police–community relations, by using a kind of laboratory method that brought together citizens of widely diversified community interests and the police and other criminal justice people to discuss problems of common interest [and] promoted the idea of police–community relations program development on a national scale" (Radalet and Carter, 1994, pp. 25–26).

In 1961, through financial support from the Field Foundation, the School of Police Administration and Public Safety at MSU conducted a national survey of 168 law enforcement agencies that supported establishment of a National Center on Police and Community Relations. The center opened on the Michigan State campus in August 1965 with further financial assistance from the Field Foundation, the United States Commission on Civil Rights, and the Law Enforcement Assistance Administration. Moreover, a handful of Jewish organizations (e.g., Anti-Defamation League of the B'nai Brith) and prominent African-American organizations (e.g., National Association for the Advancement of Colored People) also encouraged this kind of program (Radalet and Carter, p. 27).

Post-Riot Phase: 1969–1994

During the 1960s race riots and student demonstrations in the United States called into question the efforts that were initiated in the field of police–community relations during the previous decade (Radalet and Carter, 1994, p. 27; Bayley and Mendelsohn, 1969). "Traditional patterns of community organization (block committees, precinct councils, and so on) were evidently not doing the job; many police officers and others began to express skepticism about whether it was 'worth the effort' and to ask 'What have we done wrong?'" (Radalet and Carter, 1994, pp. 27–28).

Why had many of the police–community relations programs not done the job? One of the reasons why is because proper (i.e., rigorous and scientific) evaluations had not been conducted. "In fact, there was even some resistance to such research by eager program developers who preferred not to be reminded that the attitudes of many people were not being changed and that many people were not being reached . . . [and there was] little or no progress in solving basic societal problems that vitally affect police–community relations" (Radalet and Carter, 1994, p. 28). This, however, did not stop the creation of new police–community relations programs in selected jurisdictions between the years 1967 and 1973. Although many of these programs focused mainly on public relations, a few government-funded programs did offer innovative features.

For reasons that are not completely known, in 1969 the National Institute on Police and Community Relations was closed. Since then most of the police–community relations programs changed to "community-based crime prevention efforts" (Radalet and Carter, 1994, p. 30). This was largely stimulated by the public concern over "predatory crime, with acknowledgement of the necessity for police–community cooperation to achieve anything significant in preventing crime" (p. 30).

Problem-Oriented Policing (POP)

In 1979, law professor Herman Goldstein published a seminal article on problem-oriented policing. Goldstein argued that police need to look at crime more proactively and try to find solutions that address the underlying causes of crime.

How does one go about doing problem-oriented policing? In short, the community, in cooperation with the police department, identifies issues that need to be fixed that are within the realm of the law enforcement agency's mandate. In an effort to improve this process, Piquero and Piquero (2001) developed a schema to identify and solve problems encountered by police departments. Much like all new kinds of policies, there are problems with obtaining appropriate resources and resistance to change in most departments. Overall, although crime rates do not appear to have changed much, police officers reported more job satisfaction with problem-oriented policing.

One of the most important techniques used in POP is SARA, an acronym for scanning, analysis, response, and assessment. Swanson, Territo, and Taylor (2008) define those four elements as follows:

- *Scanning*—"officers are encouraged to group individual related incidents that come to their attention as 'problems' and define these problems in more precise and useful terms."

- *Analysis*—"officers working on a well-defined problem then collect information from a variety of public and private sources, not just traditional police data, such as criminal records and past offense reports."

- *Response*—"the knowledge gained in the analysis stage is then used to develop and implement solutions. Officers seek the assistance of [a broad array of constituencies] who can help develop a program of action. Solutions may go well beyond traditional police responses to include other community agencies and/or municipal organizations."

- *Assessment*—"officers evaluate the impact and the effectiveness of their responses. Were the original problems actually solved or alleviated? They may use the results to revise a response, to collect more data, or even to redefine the problem." (pp. 40–41)

Problem-oriented policing has been implemented in numerous jurisdictions, and empirical research indicates that it has been relatively successful (e.g., Eck and Spellman, 1987; Green-Mazerolle and Terrill, 1997; Kennedy, 1997; White, Fyfe, Campbell, and Goldkamp, 2003). Nevertheless, there are significant shortcomings with this technique.

Because police departments may interpret problem-oriented policing as a passing fad, they may not embrace the philosophy and the practices and thus do not significantly invest organizational resources in properly implementing it. Moreover, "The police culture is notoriously resistant to change, and problem-oriented policing represents a significant and fundamental shift in the police paradigm. Others have argued that the typical rank and file officer does not have the necessary skill-set to engage in the problem solving process" (White, 2007, pp. 101–102). White continues:

> Experts recognize that the problem-solving process may produce solutions that are not necessarily transferable to other problems and other jurisdictions (Reitzel et al., 2005). In fact, a central element of problem-oriented policing is that the problem-solving process should produce a solution that is specifically tailored to the identified problem and underlying condition. (pp. 97–98)

In addition, relatively recent research on the San Diego Police Department (Cordner and Biebel, 2005) suggests that even in law enforcement agencies that have gained a considerable amount of exposure to the POP model, it may not be implemented entirely and in the same way throughout the entire rank and file, and officers may be experiencing fatigue over its use.

Problem-oriented policing experts suggest that law enforcement agencies keep good records on the situations in which they intervene and the strategies that worked and ones that failed. This will become an important part of institutional knowledge that other officers and police management can draw on in the future.

Solutions: Community Policing and Problem-Oriented Policing[1]

An outgrowth of problem-oriented policing was community-oriented policing, or community policing for short. This practice involves a cooperative effort between police and the communities they serve where both work together to solve crime and crime-related problems. It also includes a series of strategies that bring the police closer to the community to reduce and solve crime and crime-related problems. Community policing is often defined by the programs it subsumes, including bike patrol; kobans; storefront or mini police stations; problem-oriented policing, "Policing by Objectives"; neighborhood meetings with the police; crime prevention programs; foot patrol by beat cops; and police getting more involved in community activities. In 1994 Congress passed the Crime Bill. Not only did it establish the Office of Community Policing as a part of the Department of Justice, but it provided funds to eligible law enforcement agencies to hire 10,000 new police officers who would be doing community policing. It also provided funding for research on community policing.

Over the past two decades, no self-respecting chief or commissioner of police will admit to not having community policing. There are many reasons for this. Community policing is good public relations. It could reduce the number and kind of stereotypes both the public and the police have of each other. And it could open up more channels of communication.

Nevertheless, two important evaluations of community policing have occurred. First, Skogan and Harnett (1997) evaluated the Chicago Alternative Policing Strategy (CAPS). This program, initiated by the Chicago Police Department, was implemented over a five year period. The evaluation was done on five districts. The program had a number of objectives. "Through regular meetings between police and citizens, a wide range of problems were identified. Drug dealing was the most commonly cited problem, but many of the other most prominent issues involved disorder-type problems . . . Based on the issues that arose in specific neighborhoods, police and residents engaged in a multitude of approaches to alleviate the problems" (White, 2007, pp. 109–110).

Predictably, the measures were mixed. "Some goals were achieved while others were not. Importantly, in the evaluated districts there was less crime, less fear of crime, less gang activity, and more positive attitudes toward the police" (White, 2007, p. 110). There were some drawbacks, however, particularly that there was "the lack of citizen involvement in certain poor, high-crime areas. In particular, Latinos, low-income households, and those without high school diplomas were not engaged by the CAPS program" (p. 110).

Second, Cordner (2005) examined the practice in 60 police departments. He looked at seven basic elements. There appeared to be some decreases in crime, fear of crime, disorder, and calls for service, but these improvements were either mixed or not across the board. Similarly, there were some moderate improvements in community relations, police officer attitudes, and police officer behavior.

Adoption of community policing can backfire (Oliver and Meier, 2001) or be seen as increased surveillance of the poor by the police (Websdale, 2001). Even though community policing has a series of laudable goals, and in some contexts has solved a number of community problems, many police, academics, politicians, and community organizations have overstated the success of this approach. Moreover, there has been a disproportionate emphasis on public relations programs in support of community policing initiatives in lieu of implementing community policing as its originators (e.g., Goldstein, 1979) intended it to be (Manning, 1988; Klockars, 1988).

The remainder of this chapter reviews how community policing is too often implemented as a public relations tactic; outlines some of the effects of community policing as public relations; and suggests a number of strategies to minimize community policing as public relations in order to maximize what the framers of community policing conceived it to achieve.

Literature Review[2]

Without question, several academics (e.g., Alderson, 1979; Goldstein, 1987; Skolnick and Bayley, 1986, 1988), police professionals (e.g., Darryl

Stephens), and the federal government through the establishment of the Office of Community Oriented Policing Services (COPS) (as a consequence of the 1994 Crime Bill) have advocated and facilitated community policing. Most of these political actors stress the prosocial goals and achievements of community policing.

At the same time, some individuals and organizations have difficulties with community policing as it currently exists and question both the assumptions for its implementation and the evidence marshaled to demonstrate the success of these types of initiatives. There are several general critiques (e.g., Manning, 1984, 1988; Smith, 1987; Weatheritt, 1988) and analyses of obstacles (Skolnick and Bayley, 1988) to community policing. More common are specific difficulties with respect to particular assumptions underlying the concept of community policing.

Conceptually, community policing has been criticized for being built upon fallacious assumptions about crime, criminals, and communities; definitional problems (Manning, 1984); and the variety of methods it entails (Ekblom and Heal, 1982).

Other problems with community policing include its inability to reduce crime and fear; poorly conceptualized evaluation studies; lack of transferability of community policing models from one setting to another; insensitivity to cultural differences among and inside advanced industrialized states; failure to build the partnership between the police and the community; poor response time to citizens and crime; police officers' negative view of community policing; emphasis on intelligence gathering rather than attempts to reach out to the community; increased politicization of the police; greater potential for police corruption; and the use of community policing as public relations (Weatheritt, 1983, 1988; Trojanowicz, Steele, and Trojanowicz, 1986; Morgan, 1987; Bayley, 1988; Klockars, 1988; Manning, 1988).

Although the literature makes a good case that community policing is a public relations technique, it does not outline strategies that academics, community activists, or well-informed and well-intentioned police officers and administrators can use to either stop or minimize the public relations aspect of community policing and redirect it into what it is supposed to accomplish.

The notion of community policing as public relations can be interpreted in three ways: the characterization of community policing as public relations, its causes, and effects. This section of the chapter is structured around these three processes and concludes with a series of recommendations for change (Ross, 1995b). The following are recommendations to control and change how community policing is implemented.

Overcoming Community Policing as Public Relations

A number of experts have offered suggestions on how to improve the implementation of community policing programs. Bayley (1988), for example, outlines four improvements, including systematically monitoring the effectiveness "of community policing as a crime-control strategy" (p. 236); giving "an institution outside the police . . . the authority and capacity to determine whether community police operations conform to the rule of law" (pp. 236–237); improving the selection and training of police officers who will engage in community policing; and "develop[ing] the capacity to formulate and implement general policies of policing, calling on all resources both public and private so as to provide effective and equal protection to all segments of the population" (p. 237).

According to Manning (1984), "If a community police scheme is to be successful it will require: structural and legal change, changes in habits of dispute settlement and definition, in organizational structure, performance evaluation and in reward structures within the police" (p. 224). These suggestions are necessary to help community policing become a concrete reality, but are not in and of themselves sufficient. As formulated, these proposed changes do not minimize the problems and their unflattering effects on community policing.

Methods to Implement Change

Opinion leaders, academics, observers of the police, the media, community activists, and well-informed police officers and administrators should oppose the use of community policing for public relations purposes. This constituency can accomplish this task by persistently explaining the causes for and negative effects of using public relations techniques in lieu of implementing community policing and by suggesting alternative methods for improving implementation of this latest development in modern policing. Six basic interrelated strategies should be employed by those who may be called "devil's advocates" of community policing to minimize its unnecessary public relations component. These interrelated methods are, from least to most important:

1. Refuse to be co-opted into public relations legitimating exercises.
2. Educate others.
3. Organize concerned community actors to influence the process of community policing.
4. Become knowledgeable on the subject.
5. Conduct research on community policing programs.
6. Assist the police in the implementation and evaluation of community policing.

These techniques are a handful of many possibilities that are limited only by our creativity and imagination. By becoming involved in community policing, its true advocates will develop a repertoire of experience from which to draw the best way to approach the police, government officials, media, and public in order to prevent uncritical acceptance of actual or postured community policing initiatives (see Exhibit 8.1).

Exhibit 8.1 "Stop Snitchin" and the Baltimore Police Department Response

In 2000, a controversial video entitled "Stop Snitchin," which included shots of the back streets of Baltimore set to a hip-hop soundtrack, was surreptitiously shot and released. Eventually posted on the popular Web site www.youtube.com, it suggested that anyone who cooperates with local law enforcement in the prosecution of someone who has been charged criminally would be subjected to violence or even killed. It also mentioned that local police officers were corrupt. The DVD gained national attention because it featured Carmelo Anthony, a former Baltimore resident and well-known National Basketball Association player in one of the scenes.

This led to a considerable amount of media attention through cable television news personalities such as Fox National News' Bill O'Reilly, who claimed the video was evidence of how morally decadent professional basketball, Baltimore, and, by extension, society was becoming. As a way to address the negative public relations storm, selected members of the Baltimore Police Department decided to create a counter-video entitled "Keep Talking," along with a t-shirt bearing a specially designed logo. This was not the first time that police departments (or other state-run agencies, such as the military) have used the Internet and popular music to get their message out and create the impression that they are hip and in touch with the community. Having a band composed of police officers playing contemporary music to reach out to the community is perceived by many police departments to be good public relations.

Conclusion

Community policing, like majority rule or equal rights, is perceived by many to be a widely accepted and/or sacred institution. Challenging community policing is not welcomed by most police administrators, politicians, or citizens who have championed its implementation. The actions of advocates for true and effective community policing may well be interpreted as counterproductive. Criticisms against the implementation, methods, and effectiveness of community policing as it is commonly perceived will be interpreted as an attack against its goals and the core values and assumptions of the processes (e.g., Klockars, 1988). However, the drawbacks of using community policing as public relations is far more damaging to a city and its police force than being branded as unsympathetic to this change in policing. In sum, it is preferable to be an informed realist rather than a naive idealist.

In many respects community policing is a thing of the past. It has been replaced by CompStat (a relatively new management technique that includes weekly meetings of senior police personnel, especially the chief/commissioner and district commanders, to review crime that has occurred in their sector/district/borough in order to monitor their responses and to reduce crime in those areas) and by the pressing concerns of the possibility of terrorism in the wake of 9/11. More will be said about CompStat in chapter 12 and terrorism in chapter 18.

As we move into the post-9/11 era and with the current economic insecurity, almost all criminal justice budgets have been slashed and all "nonessential activities" are being cut. This includes community policing, which is mostly perceived as soft policing.

Notes

1. An earlier version of this section appeared as Ross (1995b).
2. This section builds on Ross (1995b).

Glossary

Chicago Alternative Police Strategy (CAPS): A well-funded and highly publicized and evaluated community policing initiative in Chicago that started in 1992.

Community-oriented policing: A cooperative effort between police and the communities they serve where both work together to solve crime and crime-related problems. Also, a series of strategies that bring the police closer to the community to reduce and solve crime and crime-related problems. It is often defined by the programs it subsumes, including bike patrol, kobans, storefront policing, and problem-oriented policing.

Community participation: When members of the community participate/help police in achieving their mission. Typically this goes beyond simply reporting crimes and serving as witnesses to crimes.

Co-optation: When an individual or group is forced to join the mission/support the mission of an individual or organization.

Crisis of legitimacy: When an individual or organization faces a situation in which its legitimacy is called into question.

Devil's advocate: A person or group who calls into question the assumptions and evidence that organizations and individuals proffer as common or accepted knowledge.

Koban: A stand-alone, often portable, hut strategically placed in a jurisdiction where police officers can work. Typically, no more than two officers can comfortably work in this location. This concept originated in Japan and has had experimental use in selected jurisdictions in the United States.

National Institute on Police and Community Relations: Founded in 1955 at Michigan State University, this organization pioneered programs and research to improve relations between communities and police on a national basis.

Police–community relations: The ongoing and changing relationship between the police and the communities they serve. This includes issues of race relations, fear of police, violence, and corruption.

Proactive policing: When police act to prevent crime and other police-related concerns before they occur.

Problem-oriented policing: A process in which police and the community work together to understand the sources of crime or crime-related problems in their communities and come up with a plan they believe will systematically minimize or eliminate the causes.

Public Relations: Collection of communication techniques used by individuals or organizations to convince the public/news media about the merits of an organization, program, or policy. Primarily makes appeals based on reason.

Reactive policing: When police respond to crime (or calls for service) after it occurs.

SARA: an acronym for scanning, analysis, response, and assessment. Steps used in problem-oriented policing.

Chapter Questions

Part One: Multiple Choice Questions

1. In which way has police–community relations benefited the most through active problem-solving strategies?
   a. public relations
   b. neighborhood watch
   c. community participation
   d. community service
   e. all of the above

2. Where was the National Institute on Police and Community Relations established?
   a. John Jay College of Criminal Justice
   b. Western Illinois University
   c. Eastern Kentucky University
   d. Michigan State University
   e. Penn State University

3. Starting after WWII, which organization started offering classes in reducing tensions between elements of the African-American community and the police?
   a. National Institute of Justice
   b. National Conference on Christians and Jews
   c. Law Enforcement Assistance Administration
   d. President's Commission on Law Enforcement
   e. International Association of Chiefs of Police

4. Community policing and problem-oriented policing are:
   a. the same thing
   b. unrelated to each other
   c. related techniques
   d. both in danger of being simply public relations
   e. none of the above

5. What is one of the biggest problems with community policing?
   a. Too often it is simply public relations.
   b. Rural police already do it.
   c. There is no commonly accepted definition.
   d. We do not know why police departments implement it.
   e. It is too frequently confused with problem-oriented policing.

6. The history of community policing can be traced back to the principles written by
   a. Chambliss
   b. Manning
   c. Peel
   d. Sherman
   e. Vold

7. Who is regarded as one of the most important theorists of community policing?
   a. Brownstein
   b. Goldstein
   c. Reiss
   d. Ross
   e. Williams

8. Which organization did the 1994 crime bill establish?
   a. OST
   b. NIJ
   c. COPS
   d. Knapp Commission
   e. National Institute on Police and Community

9. In advanced industrialized democracies, if the police ignored the public, the public would
   a. report more crimes
   b. not report crimes
   c. not testify in court
   d. both b and c
   e. none of the above

Part Two: Short Answer Questions

1. What is the National Institute on Police and Community Relations?

2. What is a koban?

3. What are three reasons why good police–community relations are important?

4. What is meant by the expression "community policing is public relations"?

5. What is the difference between public relations and community relations in the context of police–community relations?

6. What is the difference between proactive and reactive policing?

7. What does the acronym SARA stand for?

Part Three: Essay Questions

1. What are three problems with community policing? How can we address these challenges?

2. What are the implications of community policing used disproportionately as public relations?

3. What are three realistic ways you could better interact with police in your neighbourhood that would have a positive effect on police–community relations?

4. Why is it difficult to improve police–community relations?

9 CHAPTER

Deviance and Corruption

Introduction

Deviance is an action or behavior that violates the generally accepted norms of a group, organization, or society (Adler, 2005). Many societies' and organizations' policies, practices, and laws are developed from this normative foundation. Policies (and sometimes laws) are written because entities, ranging in size from organizations to countries, codify acts of deviance. Deviance can and does occur in all workplaces and throughout all professions. When public officials violate organizational rules and/or break the law these acts are also called malfeasance, misfeasance, and nonfeasance. Yet the scholarly literature typically prefers to use the term deviance.

Many criminal justice agencies have codes of ethics or standards of conduct that are taught to recruits and reinforced by veterans of the organization. One term closely related to deviance is corruption, also known as graft. According to McCarthy (1996), this practice includes "the intentional violation of organizational norms (i.e., rules and regulations) by public employees for personal material gain" (p. 231). This behavioral category subsumes theft, smuggling contraband, embezzlement, and misuse of authority (p. 232). Corruption, however, is not a synonym for deviance, although it is a subset of this practice.

Police deviance occurs when law enforcement officers behave in a manner that is "inconsistent with the officer's legal authority, organizational authority, and standards of ethical conduct" (Barker and Carter, 1986, pp. 2–3).

Police deviance includes but is not limited to:

- discrimination
- misconduct
- intimidation
- sexual harassment
- corruption
- excessive force
- use of restricted weapons
- illegal surveillance

This chapter reviews how widespread deviance is in police departments in the United States. It will also present a typology of police deviance, introduce the research methods that scholars use to conduct studies on police corruption, and examine the causes and effects of deviance (particularly the controls on corruption).[1]

How Widespread Is the Problem?

It is hard to determine how much deviance exists in specific police departments, which makes it almost impossible to gauge the pervasiveness of deviance across the country. One thing keen observers can be sure of is that because of the numerous policies, procedures, and rules that exist in police agencies, most officers have at one point or another in their career violated at least one regulation.

> Many of the violations are minor in nature—for example, officers not wearing their hats when required to do so. . . . [E]ven the more serious deviations are widespread and frequent occurrences. Examples would be some form of unnecessary verbal or physical abuse, misrepresenting or leaving out facts in police reports, committing perjury when testifying in court, or violating important organizational policies, such as those governing high-speed pursuits. . . . In fact, such behavior is so common in many agencies that it has become the 'way of doing business' and is no longer considered serious enough to warrant a formal organizational response. (Roberg and Kuykendall, 1993, p. 186)

Typology of Police Deviance

In general, police deviance can be divided into two types: occupational deviance, which involves "criminal and noncriminal [behavior] committed during the course of normal work activities or committed under the guise of the police officer's authority" (Barker and Carter, 1986, pp. 4–7), and abuse of authority, which involves the violation of the trust placed in police officers.

Occupational deviance usually falls under the categories of corruption and misconduct. The abuse of authority includes "any action by a police officer without regard to motive, intent, or malice that tends to injure, insult, trespass upon human dignity, manifest feelings of inferiority, and/or violate an inherent legal right of a member of the police constituency in the course of performing 'police work' (e.g., physical, psychological and legal abuse)" (Roberg and Kuykendall, 1993, p. 186). There are two subcategories of occupational deviance: police misconduct and police corruption. Police misconduct involves violations of organizational policies, procedures, rules, and other standards, whereas police corruption covers any criminal act in the commission of one's job, which benefits either the officer in question or someone else.

Police Gratuities

One of the most frequent problems commonly confused with corruption is the solicitation or acceptance of gratuities by police officers. A gratuity is something of minor value—a cup of coffee, for example, or other gift or small reward—offered as a "token of appreciation" in return for non-enforcement of a criminal law. Accepting gratuities "is a common practice in many police departments, but this practice is considered to be unethical by" influential police organizations, such as the International Association of Chiefs of Police (Roberg and Kuykendall, 1993, p. 187). Even though a police agency may have a written policy against the acceptance of gratuities, a disproportionate number of its rank and file ignore this rule.

There are both positive and negative issues involved in accepting gratuities. On the positive side, for example, business owners may believe that a police presence minimizes the possibility of victimization by shoplifters or juveniles. The gratuities also may reflect business owners' and managers' appreciation for police officers. The general public also may not be aware of the problematic nature of giving police gratuities. Refusal of an offer may sometimes be interpreted as an insult.

On the negative side, gratuities may compromise a police officer's ability to "operate in a democracy in a balanced and fair fashion" (Roberg and Kuykendall, 1993, p. 188). In other words, police officers may be in danger of granting preferential treatment to those who give gratuities and thus apply the law unequally. Acceptance of gratuities may even result in "police officers thinking of themselves as 'special' in the sense that they deserve benefits that others do not" (p. 188). Critics of the acceptance of gratuities also think that this "may lead to more serious forms of corruption" (p. 188).

Regardless of one's personal opinion, one must take into consideration that deviance is situational, meaning that in one police department, a behavior can be interpreted as normative, while in another it is perceived as deviant. This relativity is especially pronounced in the use of profanity, sleeping (i.e., "cooping") on the job, and engaging in personal business (i.e., going to the bank) while on duty.

Corruption

As stated earlier, "police corruption, the second subcategory of occupational deviancy, involves overt criminal activity by police officers. This includes committing crimes like theft or robbery, selling drugs, or taking money or something of value to not enforce the law" (Roberg and Kuykendall, 1993, p. 190). These types of actions are known among police officers as "going on the pad, collecting a steady note, or collecting the rent" (Barker, 1977). Police officers may receive money or other items of value, both legal and illegal, in exchange for not citing or arresting an individual for prostitution, illegal gambling, or drug possession or dealing.

Situations for corruption have existed for a long time. As Fogelson (1977) commented, during the political era, "the police did not suppress vice; they licensed it" (p. 32). Throughout the country, "they permitted gamblers, prostitutes, and saloon keepers to do business under certain well understood conditions. These entrepreneurs were required to make regular payoffs to the police" (Roberg and Kuykendall, 1993, p. 192). Some jurisdictions, like New York City, have a long history of police corruption. Over the history of the NYPD, at least nine major corruption investigations have been exposed and investigated.[2]

What is the difference between corruption and bribery? In short, bribery involves the acceptance or solicitation of bribes and gratuities (which usually involve money or some sort of economic benefit, gift, or favor) in exchange for past, current, or future actions that will benefit the individual or organization that gives the bribe.

Types of Police Corruption

Corruption is a broad and varied issue. Examples include: corruption of authority (e.g., through the offering of free meals and drinks—especially alcohol—services, or discounts); kickbacks (money, goods, and services); opportunistic threats (victims, burglary, or unlocked buildings); shakedowns of criminals; protection of illegal activities (vice operators, business people); traffic citation fixes; misdemeanor or felony charge fixes; direct criminal activities (burglary, robbery); and internal payoffs (off-days, work assignments). Some experts have rank-ordered the seriousness of different kinds of corruption (Caplan and Murphy, 1991).

In general, corrupt officers can be divided into two types. On the one hand, so-called "grass eaters" are officers who engage in minor (i.e., low-level) corruption. These kinds of actions are usually reactive and are generally not frowned upon by other officers. On the other hand, "meat eaters" are police officers who actively engage in crimes, including burglary and drug dealing, on a regular basis. These officers are proactive in their endeavors. Police departments commonly protect reactive grafters but not proactive grafters. Meat eaters are usually ostracized by other officers.

Many police officers may accept low-level bribes, which they call "clean graft," but they usually refuse to take drugs or money from drug dealers, which they consider "dirty graft." Clean graft includes taking money found on the street or valuables left behind in public places by drunken, distracted, or belligerent middle- or high-class individuals. For example, an honest citizen who has found a wallet, flags down a police officer, reports the discovery, and turns over the wallet to the police officer. The police officer looks through the wallet, finds $100, and decides to pocket a $20 bill before logging the property in with the department. Dirty graft involves actively taking items of value from drug dealers, cop killers, and other serious criminals.

Causes

The problem of deviance and corruption is plagued with numerous misperceptions. Nevertheless, two basic perspectives exist to explain the causes of corruption: popular and scholarly.

Popular Conceptions

Police chiefs and their directors of public information traditionally suggest that deviance and corruption are the result of the "bad or rotten apples" in their ranks. "The 'rotten or bad apples' are either weak individuals who have slipped through the elaborate screening process of most police departments and succumbed to the temptations inherent in police work, or deviant individuals who continue their deviant practices in an environment which provides them ample opportunity" (Barker, 1977, p. 354). Despite the logic that seems to support this conclusion, this explanation can be easily discounted.

The bad or rotten apple explanation suggests that despite the elaborate screening mechanisms that police departments use, one or more corrupt police officers may, nonetheless, be hired. On the other hand, political and community activists and some pundits offer a "bad barrel" explanation. This is the claim that the entire police department is deviant or corrupt. In most cases, this perspective is a vast overgeneralization.

Scholarly/Expert Conceptions

Over the past five decades, numerous dominant causal explanations for police corruption have been offered: irresistible opportunities for corruption presented to police officers; low pay rates; cynicism surrounding the pay and promotion mechanism; socialization and reinforcement; extent of corruption in the community and broader society; tolerance among citizens and the police; and inadequate leadership (Barker, 1977; Roberg and Kuykendall, 1993; White, 2007).

Opportunity

First, police officers "are constantly exposed to situations in which the decisions they make can have a positive or negative impact on an individual's freedom and well-being. Citizens may try to influence this discretion by offering ... any item of value that will result in a favorable decision" (Roberg and Kuykendall, 1993, p. 192). Because of the way that policing is designed, including a lack of direct supervision and the clientele police must deal with on a daily basis, multiple opportunities for corruption may present themselves during any given week (Barker, 1977).

In the area of so called "victimless crimes" (e.g., gambling, prostitution, drug use and dealing), police officers are placed in an untenable position. They have a great deal of discretionary power to invoke a criminal sanction

(Barker, 1977). Because the police regulate vice activities, they face numerous opportunities to collect graft on a regular basis.

If, for example, officers respond to a burglary at a store or a residence, they might take items of value that do not belong to them. They may rationalize that the goods are insured, and the rightful owner will be reimbursed for the loss (Barker, 1977). Occasionally, officers will lie on the stand (i.e., commit perjury while testifying in court) during a criminal trial in exchange for some sort of benefit. Some police officers believe in a sense of entitlement. They argue that because they work hard or because they put their lives on the line, they should receive extra perks from their job situations.

Pay Rates and Cynicism Surrounding Remuneration and Upward Career Mobility

Another cause for corruption may be the belief of some police officers that they are not paid enough (Barker, 1977). They may believe that the risks they take deserve more compensation than what they are paid, and thus, they may feel entitled to more money than their standard pay and benefits. Additionally, the career advancement model in most police departments may serve as a cause for corruption, White (2007) suggests:

> Opportunities for advancement in police department . . . is limited, yet the only way to get a significant pay increase is through promotion. . . . Structural elements of the promotion process can also frustrate officers. . . . The lack of opportunity for promotion clearly limits officers . . . who are unhappy with their pay may be tempted to seek illegitimate means to add to their salary, particularly if they believe that their performance has not been evaluated fairly. (p. 245)

Socialization and Reinforcement

Police officers share both their history and their identity. By interacting with other officers and being exposed to similar situations (e.g., boredom, fear, excitement), officers can form deep and often hidden emotional bonds. Through this process, similar norms and values are transmitted and shared (Barker, 1977).

Many officers may view the world as a "we versus they" environment (Becker, 1963). "Police tend to see the world as being composed of insiders and outsiders—police and persons who are not police officers are considered outsiders and are viewed with suspicion" (Kappeler, Sluder, and Alpert, 1994, p. 60).

Despite individual convictions, the work group of police officers remains a powerful influence on each officer (Barker, 1977). In the police academy context, the building of communal officer identity begins, an identity that is further developed once work on the force starts. Shortly after graduating from the academy, through a combined process of working on the streets plus interactions with senior police personnel, officers soon become cynical and a have a higher proclivity to engage in deviance. Specifically, this cynicism may pave the way to corruption.

Extent of Corruption in Society

The community and political environment are influential in establishing attitudes toward corrupt activities. When corruption is found in other government agencies, among judges, prosecutors, and politicians, and in the business world, it contributes to the ability of the police officer to rationalize his or her own behavior (Newfield and Barret, 1988; Roberg and Kuykendall, 1993).

Tolerance by Citizens and the Police Department

This rationalization can lead to tolerance of abuses, as Roberg and Kuykendall (1993) write:

> In police departments, there are often many standards of behavior for officers to follow. In fact, there are so many standards that it is difficult to adhere to all of them. . . . Many officers even come to believe that if they are to be good police officers, they have to violate some of the standards they are supposed to follow. (p. 194)

Inadequate Leadership

An environment in which many officers either accept the existence of corruption or participate in corrupt activities calls into question the quality of leadership. Roberg and Kuykendall (1993) note that:

> Even nondeviant officers are both tolerant and tolerated because few will break the code of silence among officers. This belief can even carry over to the chief executive and managers in the organization, particularly if they have, or are, participating in the deviant behavior themselves. In addition, executives and managers may be 'blamed' and lose their jobs if the deviancy is exposed, even if they are not involved. (p. 194)

In the aftermath of the 1972 Commission to Investigate Alleged Police Corruption (also known as the Knapp Commission), the frequency and pervasiveness of corruption in our nations' police departments have decreased.

In the end, a variety of reasons may motivate police officers to engage in corrupt acts. Officers may lose respect for their superior officers, and they may see corruption in other parts of the criminal justice system (including among judges and prosecutors). They may abuse drugs and alcohol, which can impair their judgment. Meanwhile, the pressures to perform well in their duties are high. All too frequently, their contributions to the mission of the police department are not appreciated. Thus, officers may end up believing that engaging in corruption is an acceptable decision.

Solution: Controlling Police Corruption[3]

Police corruption has numerous effects, including an attrition of public trust, the possibility that corruption will seep into other government organizations, the lessening of police moral, and the loosening of controls. Most of the arguments about controlling police deviance, including corruption, have their origins in the study of large bureaucratic organizations. Additionally, those mechanisms established to control various police practices, such as illegal surveillance and police violence, are broadly applicable to the bigger problem of police corruption. Nevertheless, formidable obstacles mitigate the implementation of the control mechanisms, most significantly the lack of sufficient resources, information, discretion, and sanctions (Sherman, 1978). In addition, in many police departments, officers' behaviors/actions concerning what is considered corrupt changes over time. Furthermore, the networks that engage in corruption continuously shift their activities, whenever they sense they are under the watchful eye of Internal Affairs officers or the news media.

Admittedly, allegations of corruption have existed since the establishment of the first police department. Some of these episodes have led to high-profile corruption scandals. Better controls on police officers and their departments have been advocated by members of the public, government officials, and honest police officers and administrators. Prominent anti-corruption policies and practices have been implemented in most big city police departments. Some of these recommendations are proactive, while others are reactive.

One should not forget that police officers are under constant scrutiny. This new level of supervision has been fueled by the introduction of police vehicles with dashboard video capability, cell phones, and Internet-based technology. Most cell phones now come equipped with photographic and video capabilities. It is now much easier for citizens to record conversations between themselves and police officers, which can be used as evidence in departmental or legal proceedings. A combination of internal and external controls can be effective in the control of police deviance and corruption.

Improved Pay Scales for Officers

Of primary importance, paying police officers a respectable and living wage is an important step in minimizing corruption. As previously mentioned, during the early history of policing, police departments did not pay officers well, but income was not the reason why individuals chose that occupation. The appeal of policing lay in the opportunity to benefit from the gratuities and corruption that were presented to officers. During the "professional era" (1920–1960), this practice changed. Through the creation of police unions and the introduction of other civil service reforms, police officers were given better pay and benefits. Still, some law enforcement officers, regardless of the level of their incomes, will always want more or think they deserve more than they are earning.

Teaching Ethics to Police Officers

Teaching ethics to police officers, either as part of the training academy or as in-service workshops, has been advocated by many police professionals and scholars. Courses on ethics are frequently taught in police training academies. Police commissioners boast about the number of hours or the complexity of the assignments tied to these courses. The scholarly journal *Criminal Justice Ethics* helps to further develop the field of police ethics by publishing articles on the subject. The downside to this approach is that ethics education too often just helps police officers to better rationalize their deviance or corrupt actions.

Routine Transfers of Police Officers

Routinely transferring police officers who are likely to fall into the temptation of corruption (particularly those on vice and drug details) to different assignments or beats is a method used by some law enforcement organizations to decrease corruption. The downside to this practice is that it may destroy the human capital expertise that has been accumulated by specific officers. In order to decrease this loss, police departments only change a handful of police officers in specialized details each rotation. Nevertheless, on many occasions, corrupt networks persist even though individual officers are transferred. Even after rotations, some officers may seek out new means to extract an illegal benefit from their new assignments.

Internal Affairs Bureaus/Departments

Sometimes also called the Office of Professional Standards or Responsibility, Internal Affairs departments or bureaus (IAD/IAB) exist to enact a measure of accountability and quality control over police officers and their actions. Information comes to the departments through civilian review boards, public complaints, and the criminal investigations of officers. Violations pertain to written policies, procedures, and criminal laws. Most Internal Affairs efforts have been reactive, but in recent years, larger police departments have tried to make these offices more proactive using early warning systems and integrity tests. Internal Affairs officers are often distrusted by outsiders and police officers alike. In various communities, citizens have come to believe that Internal Affairs was simply hiding or excusing the misconduct of the police officers. On the other hand, some officers have also felt that Internal Affairs is composed of officers who are seeking a degree of revenge for past grievances (White, 2007). (See Exhibit 9.1.)

The existence of IAB units is important, but this presupposes that they can fulfill their mandate. The creation of properly functioning Internal Affairs departments has lessened the frequency of hiring and continuing the employment of corrupt police officers. These units are limited only by the resources they have at their disposal and by the relationship the administrators have with the chief or commissioner of police.

| Exhibit 9.1 | *Prince of the City* |

This movie, based on the Richard Daley book with the same title (1978), chronicles the activities of Robert (Bob) Leuci, who during the 1970s was part of the Special Investigations Unit of the NYPD. Leuci's unit had a stellar track record of arrests and convictions of drug users and dealers. During the process, however, Leuci was known to take both drugs and money for personal use and to give drugs as incentives to his informants. In order to accomplish his unit's goals, Leuci established an elaborate web of informers. He rationalized his actions as the cost of doing business. As a police officer, he argued that many people treat police officers as the lowest rung on the socioeconomic ladder, and moving up the police ladder commanded a certain amount of respect. Under scrutiny, Leuci agreed to participate in a federal investigation and wore a wire on his former associates. This led to additional convictions. The subject of Bob Leuci's rise and fall was made into a movie directed by Sidney Lumet.

Accreditation

Accreditation is another solution that can help alleviate deviance and corruption, as well as with other officer transgressions (Mastrofski, 1986). In 1979, the Commission on Accreditation for Law Enforcement Agencies (CALEA) was formed. Over the years, CALEA has developed a system of standards that police and other law enforcement agencies are expected to adopt in order to meet the requirements of this organization. CALEA membership is voluntary, and the approval process can require a considerable amount of agency resources to complete. The accreditation process takes place over three stages. An agency applies to be certified and then fills out a self-questionnaire. Upon completion, a CALEA team comes to the department to assess compliance issues and the accuracy of the information provided on the application form. Then the assessment team writes a report. If departmental deficiencies are found, the police department must make the appropriate changes. Accreditation lasts for five years, after which time the agency must apply for reaccreditation. There are distinctive advantages to accreditation. According to McCabe and Fajardo (2001), accredited agencies were more likely to require regular drug tests of their officers, place higher educational requirements on recruits, and provide more training to recruits.

Integrity Officers

Integrity officers are frequently used by large police organizations. In New York City, in the wake of the Knapp Commission recommendations, each

---

Exhibit 9.2   **Frank Serpico**

Frank Serpico is a retired NYPD detective who was instrumental in providing information about incidents of police corruption to the Knapp Commission. Serpico revealed information about the corruption to the *New York Times*. His story was the focus of a bestselling book written by Peter Maas (1973), a Hollywood movie starring Al Pacino (1973), and an A&E-televised *Biography* episode (2000). Serpico grew up in a working-class Italian family in which police officers were respected. During the 1960s, corruption was rampant at all ranks throughout the NYPD. In his testimony, Serpico suggested that police corruption is part of the police socialization process. Rookie police officers learn early on how to break the rules and cut corners in order to survive in the police organization. Because Serpico did not accept graft, he was ostracized by his fellow officers. As a result of officer appre-hension, Serpico was shot while on a drug bust. He survived and shortly after testifying in front of the Knapp Commission, he moved to Switzerland out of fear of police-related retaliation. He has since returned to the United States.

---

precinct is required to employ an Integrity Officer (IO) who is accountable to the Internal Affairs Division in headquarters. The IOs, who are placed strategically in the district houses rather than headquarters, serve as the eyes and ears of Internal Affairs units and are responsible for investigating allega-tions of possible corruption and police deviance. These officers, often ostra-cized by their colleagues, pass on valuable information to their superiors. Attempts have recently been made to shift the role and work of IA from being mostly reactive to being proactive. (See Exhibit 9.2.)

Corruption Investigations/Commissions

Widespread and "gut-wrenching" corruption investigations are often initi-ated in the wake of the disclosure of severe police wrongdoing. This reaction is usually the work of an outside body or Internal Affairs. In order to properly conduct an investigation, sufficient resources need to be allocated to it. If these resources are not available in police or municipal budgets, then the state or even the federal government should step in to provide sufficient per-sonnel to complete the investigation. Unfortunately, with each new investi-gation, typically only a handful of officers are identified and sanctioned.

Hiring Police Administrators from Outside of Departments

Finally, hiring police administrators, particularly police chiefs and commis-sioners, from outside of a specific department has become a routine practice. Since the Knapp Commission, many mayors, city managers, and police boards seek to hire new chiefs from other police departments. This practice typically lacks approval from the rank and file and those higher up in the chain of command who hoped they would one day be promoted to this position. The new head of the organization, however, has few loyalties in the department and can be in the best position to make drastic departmental changes, including the dismissal of corrupt administrators.

Obviously, stemming the tide of any unpleasant practice requires a multipronged effort. The use of the previously reviewed practices should go a long way to minimize the occurrence of police corruption. It is to be hoped that these approaches may also have ripple effects on other forms of police deviance and crime.

Conclusion

Police deviancy and corruption is an everyday problem for most police departments. Law Enforcement officers have an extremely important duty to serve and protect society. They hold the public's trust, but the legitimacy of that trust can erode quickly if an officer or group engages in corruption. When evidence of corruption emerges, police departments must make bold steps to fairly investigate and eradicate it as soon as possible. Anything short of this will perpetuate fear and distrust among the public.

Notes

1. Some authors (e.g., Stevens, 2009) suggest that police deviance and corruption (along with police misconduct) is best seen as part of the wrongful acts perpetrated by police officers.

2. In 1895 (by the Lexow Committee); in 1900 (by the Mazet Committee); in 1913 (as a result of the Curran investigations); in 1932 (by the Seabury Committee); in 1942 (as a result of the Amen investigation); in 1952 (by the Brooklyn Grand Jury); in the 1970s by the Knapp Commission (as a result of the Serpico revelations); in the late 1970s (by the "Prince of the City" investigations); in 1986 (in the Buddy Boys investigation); and in 1993 (by the Mollen Commission) (McAlary, 1987).

3. This section builds on Ross (2004). Other authors (e.g., Stevens, 2009) have created similar lists. Stevens, for example, under internal monitoring, singles out supervision, close supervision, performance evaluations, early warning/intervention systems, internal affairs and professional standards. Under external monitoring, he includes: monitoring committees, the courts (especially through Supreme Court cases), and civil liability.

Glossary

Bad barrel explanation: The claim that an entire police department is deviant or corrupt.

Bad or rotten apple explanation: A situation in which only one or a small number of police officers in a police department are deviant or corrupt.

Bribe: Money, items, or services given to a public official with the explicit understanding that the public official will assist the individual in receiving favorable treatment by the government. Favorable treatment can also include failing to enforce the law.

Clean graft: Bribes, gratuities, and corruption that are not frowned upon by fellow police officers and by the administration.

Corruption: Any criminal act engaged in by a police officer in the commission of his or her job as a police officer that results in some sort of gain.

Deviance: An action or behavior that violates generally accepted norms in a group, organization, or society.

Dirty graft: Bribes, gratuities, and corruption that is frowned upon by fellow police officers and by the administration.

Frank Serpico: NYPD officer who during the 1960s and early 1970s attempted to stop corruption. His complaints were largely ignored by his superiors.

Graft: Illegally obtained money or benefits a police officer receives through corrupt practices.

Grass eater: A police officer who engages in minor, unplanned corruption.

Gratuity: In law enforcement circles, this involves receiving something of minor value (often referred to as a token of appreciation) for non-enforcement of a criminal law.

Illegal surveillance: This involves eavesdropping without out a warrant or collecting information in violation of an individual's right to privacy.

Integrity Officer (IO): An officer who works for the Internal Affairs Bureau/Division (IAB/IAD). He or she is strategically placed in the district houses rather than at headquarters in order to serve as the eyes and ears of IAB / IAD. This officer detects and reports on instances of police corruption or other breaches of ethical conduct. This position was first introduced in the NYPD after the revelations of Frank Serpico to the Knapp Commission. Recently, there have been attempts to shift the role and work of IA from being mostly reactive to being proactive.

Knapp Commission: The federal commission established to investigate the allegations of Officer Frank Serpico of corruption in the NYPD.

Meat eater: A police officer who engages in serious corruption (e.g., protecting drug dealers or smugglers, armed robbery) that is planned or proactive.

On the take: A colloquial expression indicating that an officer is corrupt and receives regular payments from illegal sources.

Police deviance: Activities that are inconsistent with an officer's legal authority, organizational authority, and standards of ethical conduct.

Chapter Questions

Part One: Multiple Choice Questions

1. The acceptance of gratuities by police officers involves/is
   a. receiving something of value
   b. a common practice
   c. considered by respected policing organizations to be unethical
   d. some of the above
   e. all of the above

2. Why is there disapproval of gratuities given to police officers?
   a. It causes unnecessary competition among police officers.
   b. It forces police to be super-cops instead of being a police unit.
   c. It could lead to corruption.
   d. There is not enough to go around.
   e. none of the above

3. An officer who is considered a "grass eater"
   a. engages in minor corruption
   b. is respected by others officers
   c. is frowned upon by other officers
   d. some of the above
   e. all of the above

4. What is a meat eater?
   a. a police officer who engages in illegal behavior to cover up evidence
   b. a police officer who engages in major police corruption
   c. a police officer who solicits money or services
   d. a proactive crime fighter
   e. a police officer who consistently uses aggressive violence in effecting an arrest

5. The owner of a local Dunkin Donuts store offers a police officer two donuts and a large coffee. The officer accepts. This occurs despite a police department policy that under no circumstances shall officers take gratuities. How would a police expert interpret this action?
   a. The officer is exercising his constitutional rights.
   b. This action would be considered police misconduct.
   c. There is no wrongdoing.
   d. This would be considered police corruption.
   e. It creates an obligation.

6. Which commission investigated the alleged corruption in the NYPD that was brought to public attention by Frank Serpico?
   a. Garrison
   b. Knapp
   c. Mollen
   d. Pretty Boy
   e. Warren

7. Who was Knapp?
   a. one of Serpico's partners
   b. former Commissioner of the NYPD
   c. police chief
   d. former mayor of New York City
   e. leader of famous corruption investigation

8. In which city did the Knapp Commission take place?
   a. New York
   b. Austin, Texas
   c. Albany, New York
   d. Sacramento, California
   e. Washington, D.C.

9. What is one type of police corruption?
   a. coming into work late
   b. being a grass eater
   c. being a meat eater
   d. both b and c
   e. none of the above

10. Police officers who investigate police officer misconduct in an organized unit represent what kind of control?
    a. external
    b. formal
    c. informal
    d. internal
    e. none of the above

11. The NYPD was "relatively successful" in stemming corruption through what practice?
    a. utilization of the citizen's complaint bureau
    b. recruiting police chiefs from outside the force
    c. the revelations of Frank Serpico
    d. reports of investigative journalists
    e. none of the above

12. Which of the following is NOT a drawback to gratuities?
    a. They compromise officers' ability to operate fairly.
    b. Officers think they are special and deserve special favors.
    c. Giving gratuities is costly to shop owners.
    d. Acceptance of gratuities may lead to corruption.
    e. none of the above

13. Which of the following is an action or behavior that violates generally accepted norms?
    a. misconduct
    b. rotten apple
    c. deviance
    d. corruption
    e. none of the above

14. Which of the following is NOT police jargon for participating in corruption?
    a. going on the pad
    b. collecting the rent
    c. on the down low
    d. collecting a steady note
    e. none of the above

15. Which of the following is a cause of corruption?
    a. poor pay rates
    b. inadequate leadership
    c. the opportunity structure
    d. socialization and reinforcement
    e. all of the above

16. Why might it be difficult to determine how widespread police corruption is?
    a. The corruption might be considered normative behavior.
    b. Most of it is hidden.
    c. Empirical research is not comprehensive.
    d. Police departments are not reliable sources for this kind of information.
    e. all of the above

17. What is a minor temporary gift given to and accepted by an officer that is not in itself illegal but is seen as inappropriate?
    a. bribe
    b. graft
    c. gratuity
    d. corruption
    e. misdemeanor

18. Which of the following is the term used for a situation when an entire police department is seen as corrupt?
    a. bad apple
    b. grass eater
    c. bad barrel
    d. meat eater
    e. none of the above

Part Two: Short Answer Questions

1. What is the difference between police deviance and corruption?

2. What is the difference between the bad apple and bad barrel explanations?

3. What is an Integrity Officer?

4. What is the difference between a gratuity given to a waitress and a gratuity given to a police officer?

5. How did Frank Serpico deal with the knowledge that corruption took place in the NYPD?

6. What are four causes of police corruption?

7. What are four effects of police corruption?

8. What are two types of corrupt police officers?

9. What is the difference between clean and dirty graft?

Part Three: Essay Questions

1. Discuss the following statement: The corruption of police officers would cease to exist if police departments would only properly screen candidates before offering them spots in the police training academy.

2. How would you effectively educate the public about the problems of police corruption?

3. What is the best way to reduce the amount of corruption in police departments in the United States?

4. Some commentators have argued that as long as police officers occupy positions of power, we will never be able to eliminate police corruption. Do you agree with this statement? If so, why? If not, why?

Police Violence/Excessive Force

Introduction

On March 3, 1991, African-American motorist Rodney King and two passengers were pulled over by Los Angeles Police Department (LAPD) officers. King was slow in heeding the officers' commands and during the subsequent interaction was beaten. The entire event was videotaped, a select portion of which quickly aired on local and national television stations. The episode created considerable public outrage and led to a criminal trial against the officers. In May 1992, officers Stacey Koons and Laurence Powell were acquitted of the charges. The verdict prompted devastating riots in Los Angeles and in a handful of other cities across the country. The federal government, through the U.S. Department of Justice, quickly filed charges against the officers alleging that they had violated King's civil rights. Later that year, a conviction was achieved, and Koons and Powell went to federal prison (Ross, 2000a).

Over the past two decades, the problem of police violence and excessive force (terms that are used interchangeably in this chapter) has become a prominent issue of public, police, governmental, and media concern. To better understand this challenge, this chapter reviews the definitional issues, the types of police violence, and the amount of excessive force that exists. It also provides a review of the scholarly literature on police violence, the research on its causes, and the problems of controlling this form of state violence. The chapter ends with a discussion of some of the more prominent solutions to the problem of police violence.

Definitional Issues[1]

Not all police violence/excessive force is the same. This kind of police behavior is defined as a type of misconduct, deviance, or police abuse and is used as an all-encompassing term for brutality, extra-legal force, riots, torture, shootings, killings, and deadly force.[2] Police violence/excessive force usually refers to violence in excess of what is typically permitted according to training protocols and the law. It is important to understand that police violence occurs in contexts that usually affect the way it is perceived. Indeed, one of the most important perceptually constructed dimensions of police violence is that it falls within both the public and the private domain (Ross, 1992, 1998).

The public/private context is rooted in what Torrance (1986) calls *public violence*. After distinguishing among several types of violence, she focuses on the subcategories of public and private. According to Torrance, public violence "comprises those incidents that are widely regarded as having a significant impact on society or are an important part of it" (pp. 14–15). While admitting that "there is no hard and fast line dividing public from private violence," she suggests that these two types of violence differ on several more or less arbitrary dimensions.

When applying Torrance's distinction to police violence, instances of officers using excessive force that are detected by the police hierarchy or civilians can be considered public, while those that are not detected are private. Detection—in the form of officers' notes, citizen or witness complaints, or media reports—has the potential to create public reactions, therefore making the event public. Unless violent events create negative public reactions, the police have little motivation to change their policies and practices in regard to this type of behavior. In fact, sufficient and sustained civilian acknowledgment of police violence presumably plays an important role in law enforcement reform (Ross, 2000a).

Few acts of police violence, however, receive public attention. Among the possible factors that may explain the lack of publicity are the following: the officers' ability to conceal their activities; the victims' decision and/or ability to complain; journalistic/editorial constraints; or dissemination through other formal or informal mediums of communication. In sum, the public/private distinction is important because, to respond to an issue, the community of concern must first be aware that police violence exists.[3]

Types of Police Violence

Numerous types of police violence occur. However, seven distinct types are discussed most frequently in scholarly literature: torture, deaths in custody, police riots, police use of deadly force, SWAT teams, police vehicle chases, and dog bites. Following are a series of definitions of these police behaviors.

Torture

Over the past decade, particularly because of the U.S. detention of terrorist suspects in Guantanamo Bay, Cuba, what counts as torture has been heavily discussed and debated. Nevertheless, for purposes of simplicity, torture can be defined as any act by which severe pain or suffering, whether physical or mental, is intentionally inflicted by or at the instigation of a public official on a person to obtain information or a confession, inflict punishment for an act or a suspected act, or to create intimidation.

Death in Custody

Death in custody involves a person who has been detained by the criminal justice system or the military and who subsequently dies because of excessive force or lack of action (e.g., positional asphyxiation) on the part of a police/military/correctional officer or by inmates. This kind of death may also involve a failure to provide adequate or proper medical care. This is especially true if the detained individual experiences a medical problem (e.g., a heart attack or an epileptic seizure), and the criminal justice agency neglects to transport the individual to the appropriate hospital or to allow medical personnel to provide treatment.

Police Riots

Police riots involve the use of excessive violence, primarily by riot squads, in response to events such as public demonstrations, protests, and labor strikes.

Police Use of Deadly Force

This concept refers to a situation in which a law enforcement officer kills an individual using a weapon or technique that is designed to result in death. Typically, this is done by gun but can involve a baton or another blunt force instrument, choke holds, or other stronghold methods.

The Special Case of SWAT Teams

Over the past three decades, police departments throughout the country have developed specialized teams of police officers who respond to crisis events. Known as Special Weapons and Tactical (SWAT) teams or units, they have helped in complex negotiations with kidnappers and hostage takers (particularly in the context of bank robberies). In recent times, they have come under intense scrutiny after a series of incidents during which innocent people were injured or killed.

Police Vehicle Chases/Pursuits

For better or for worse, police are inextricably linked to chasing motorists suspected of moving violations, individuals who fail to yield to commands to pull over while driving, and persons who the police believe to have recently committed a crime. In many instances, the suspects, innocent civilians (i.e., bystanders), and sometimes the officers are injured or killed, and the extent of the property damage can be high (Alpert and Fridell, 1992; Alpert, Kenney, Dunham, and Smith, 2000). According to the National Law Enforcement and Corrections Technology Center, more than 70 percent of pursuits end with the successful apprehension of suspects, yet collisions occur in 32 percent of pursuits, property damage occurs in 20 percent, personal injury in 13 percent, and fatalities in 1.2 percent. . . . Police departments have been under increasing pressure to control officers' discretion in hot pursuits. . . . PERF [Police Executive Research Foundation] found that 91 percent of departments have a written policy governing pursuits, and nearly half have modified their policy within the last two years. (White, 2007, p. 251)

Dog Bites

A number of police departments have integrated dogs into their departments, not simply for search and rescue, but also to chase and intimidate suspects. Not only have suspects been bitten by dogs, but so have officers. "During a foot chase, it is not uncommon for . . . officers to be bitten if they do not heed the handler's instructions to stay behind him or her" (White, 2007, p. 250). In some jurisdictions (e.g., Prince George's County, Maryland, during the 1990s), the police came under intense scrutiny and a handful of civil suits resulted from their use of dogs during chase and arrest situations involving African-American males.

How Much Police Violence Is There?

Evidence concerning the incidence of police violence is mixed. Because of its controversial and hidden nature, it is impossible to determine with any degree of reliability the amount, types, and frequency of police violence in any jurisdiction.

One of the most recent attempts to address this shortcoming is Section 210402 of the 1994 Violent Crime Control and Law Enforcement Act which states, "The Attorney General shall, through appropriate means, acquire data about the use of excessive force by law enforcement officers." This initiated a data collection program managed by the United States Department of Justice.

Thus, in general, events that come to public attention are available for intense scrutiny. However, some recent data bears on this subject. According to the relatively recent "Contacts between Police and the Public, 2005" report, produced and published by the Bureau of Justice Statistics of the U.S. Department of Justice,

> an estimated 707,520 persons age 16 or older had force used against them during their most recent contact with the police in 2005. . . . This estimate is about 1.6 % of the 43.5 million people reporting face-to-face police contact during 2005. The percentage of contacts involving police use of force was relatively unchanged from 2002 to 2005. (Durose, Smith, and Langan, 2007)

If we are to believe this self-reported statistic, at least in recent history, very few people in the United States are victims of police violence. This is not to say that there have not been periods of considerable police violence in the United States. Moreover, when we deconstruct what police violence really signifies, the comparison between actual and perceived levels of police violence becomes extremely important.

Literature Review of Police Violence

Attitudinal Research

When considering the scope of published research, few studies have analyzed the public's perceptions of police use of excessive force (e.g., Westley, 1970; Gamson and McEvoy, 1970; Williams, Thomas, and Singh, 1983; Tuch and Weitzer, 1997). Since 1973, the General Social Survey has been used to collect citizens' perceptions of police use of excessive force.

These data indicate that educated, white males with incomes greater than $15,000 support police use or limited use of excessive force. In a review of the literature, Flanagan and Vaughn (1995) suggest that "public opinion may act as a method of social control" (126). Furthermore, "different segments of society and incongruous community groups want different kinds of police practices. Individuals who have never had an unsatisfactory encounter with the police are generally supportive of the police or at least ambivalent" (Flanagan and Vaughn, p. 126). If one believes that the public incorrectly perceives the application of excessive force, then efforts are needed to educate the public about the realities of police work and the infrequency of the abuse of force. On the other hand, if we think that these public perceptions are accurate and that they reveal a serious trend of police brutality in the United States, then organizational and structural changes in the way police agencies conduct their operations may be needed. The most likely situation is that both conclusions are valid.

Interesting insights can be gained from a handful of studies that examine citizens' attitudes toward police after critical incidents that involve police use of force (e.g., Lasley, 1994; Jefferis, Kaminski, Holmes, and Hanley, 1997). Lasley (1994) analyzed citizens' attitudes related to the Rodney King beating; results from a time-series analysis revealed that the event adversely affected people's attitudes toward the police. When the data were analyzed by race, Lasley reported that the incident generated more disdain for the police among African Americans than among Hispanics.

Alternatively, Jefferis, Kaminski, Holmes, and Hanley (1997) studied citizens' attitudes after "critical incidents within local jurisdictions." They explained how a widely publicized incident of police violence that took place in Cincinnati in 1995 resulted in a "negative impact on citizens' perceptions of force used by police during arrest situations, but that the effect was substantially greater among non-Caucasians" (p. 381).

Even fewer studies have examined police perceptions of extra-legal force (e.g., Koenig, 1975). Lester (1995), after reviewing the literature on police attitudes toward the use of force, concluded that although "the study of attitudes in general and police officer attitudes in particular is important for advancing understanding of police behavior[,] [a]t present, the study of police attitudes toward the use of excessive force is in only an embryonic stage" (p. 185).

Regardless of the sample group questioned, perceptions are usually based on partial information. As many scholars have pointed out, attitudes sometimes—but not always—may predict behavior.

Government Reports

Often, after a well-publicized incident of police violence, a government inquiry by a commission takes place. Most of these investigations then produce a report. Although these documents record citizens' reactions, occasionally they make a series of recommendations aimed at minimizing the proclivity of police use of excessive force. Several examples of prominent American reports include those released by the Wickersham Commission (National Commission on Law Observance and Enforcement, 1931), the National Advisory Commission on Civil Disorders (also known as the Kerner Commission, 1968), the National Commission on the Causes and Prevention of Violence (headed by Milton Eisenhower, 1968), which released the "Rights in Conflict" report in the wake of the 1968 Chicago riots during the Democratic Convention (Walker, 1968).

Most of the reports' recommendations are relatively straightforward; however, they rarely prescribe guidelines for implementation/process or outcome evaluations after these changes have been introduced.

The Causes of Excessive Police Violence

In general, research on excessive police violence can be divided into two categories: analyses of causes and works examining effects. The majority of literature falls under the former category. These studies contain a wealth of knowledge but are flawed in several respects. To improve this state of affairs, this chapter will examine the subdivisions of the research and assess their individual contributions and problems. This section reviews the available literature and organizes the main ideas in a way that could potentially lead to a more systematic method of studying excessive police violence.

In short, police violence depends on many of the factors already included in more general studies of police behavior, misconduct, deviance, and complaints against the police. These variables can be classified into individual, situational, organizational, community, and legal attributes. Many of these factors interact with each other, in turn creating complex explanations for police violence.

General Studies

The majority of research on police violence deals with its causes (e.g., Reiss, 1968). This work can also be divided into two types: studies examining a broad range of police violence and works focusing on particular forms. Although some scholars (e.g., Feld, 1971; Westley, 1953; 1970; Manning, 1980a) have studied the causes of police use of excessive force in general, most researchers have focused on single factors integral to the commission of police violence. Concurrently, causes for police violence are often broken down into internal and external factors (e.g., Stark, 1972). The former entails influences such as a patrol officer's personality, attitudes and values, working environment, police culture, relationship to the courts, and professionalization (e.g., Kania and Mackay, 1977). The latter, on the other hand, usually includes community structure and social polarization (e.g., Feld, 1971). General studies have not demarcated the contribution of different influences important in the causation of police violence. Often ignored is the fact that police violence is indirectly connected to frequency of street stops, crime in a community, the number of police deployed in a particular area, and the number and type of arrests. In short, the greater the number of these factors, the more opportunities there are for police officers to engage in violence.

Numerous individual, situational, organizational, community, and legal attributes have been posited or tested as causes leading to police violence against citizens. All said, there are several problems with the general literature dealing with the causes of police violence. To begin with, most of the studies are atheoretical; no theories have been developed or analyzed. The data are limited in scope, usually collected in the context of observational studies that are often not comparable from one jurisdiction to another. The work is predominantly ahistorical, and none of the analyses examine attempts to remove the presumed causes of police violence. Finally, because the literature primarily focuses on the American context, the generalizability of these findings beyond the United States is unknown.

Research on the Causes of Specific Types of Police Violence[4]

Only five specific types of police violence have been investigated in any detail: police torture, police death-squad activity, deaths in police custody, police riots, and the use of deadly force. The last type of excessive force has produced the greatest volume of research on police violence to date. In general, literature on police violence focuses on 10 areas of explanation: the information sources on this activity; the actions it includes; the types of political systems in which it takes place; the geographical locations of the violence; the perpetrators; the causes of violence and its purpose, effects, and victims; and data quality.

Police Torture

Incidents of police torture have been chronicled in mainstream and alternative media outlets and have been investigated by both nongovernmental organizations (e.g., Amnesty International, Human Rights Watch) and academic contexts. Police torture techniques include dry submarining (also known as water boarding), electroshock, beatings, and burnings. These practices have occurred in all types of political systems, but are most prominent in lesser developed countries and happen both in rural and urban locales. The main purpose of torture is to extract information or confessions regarding crimes, although it can also be applied for other purposes: "[as] punishment for undetermined guilt," "[to] extract money from the victim or because somebody has given the police money to thrash him/her," "[as] animal brutality," and "[because of a] desire for revenge" (Balagopal, 1986, p. 2029). Victims include actual and suspected criminals, members of political opposition groups, activists, trade union leaders and members, and peasants. Balagopal (1986) emphasizes that torture "takes particularly vicious forms when the suspect has done injury to the police themselves" (p. 2029). The academic literature on torture by police has ascertained three dominant causes at the individual level: psychoanalytic processes (Daraki-Mallet, 1976), obedience to authority (Miligram, 1974, 1977), and obedience to the authority of violence (Haritos-Fatouros, 1988).

Death Squad Activity

The activities and methods of death squads (also known as hit squads), particularly assassinations, have been documented in popular and alternative media accounts, in the reports of international monitoring agencies, and in various academic publications. These types of incidents are forms of state violence and crime, and they fall within an array of other types of violence, such as kidnapping, rape, and torture, all of which might result in murder as a final act. These actions occur primarily in lesser developed countries, at various levels of the police hierarchy, and in both rural and urban locales. Victims are generally actual and suspected criminals and political opponents (including activists, trade union leaders and members, and peasants) to the regime in power.

In general, death squad activity consists of military, paramilitary, and irregular units engaging in violent acts against citizens to deter them from lending support to opposition groups. "Death Squad violence" exemplifies repressive violence intended to induce compliance through fear. It may be employed reactively or proactively. Its most critical distinguishing feature is that the violence is usually sanctioned by the governmental regime in power, either explicitly through policy pronouncements or implicitly through a lack of effort to curtail such acts (Mason and Krane, 1989).

Sometimes, the offenders are police officers; many times, they are vigilantes who are led, trained, or directed by the police. According to Mason and Krane (1989), "Death squads are most prevalent in societies where an authoritarian alliance between the military and powerful economic elite is faced with a serious challenge to its legitimacy and authority" (p. 178).

Jakubs (1977) suggests four reasons, albeit at the organizational level, to explain the causes of the death squads in Brazil as "a conscious resolution on the part of the police delegados to take justice into their own hands, to do away with as many common criminals as possible," (p. 100) "revenge," (p. 100) "attempts to hide the extent to which the Brazilian police are involved in illegal drug traffic," (p. 101) and "the expansion of the boundaries of public and official tolerance for police violence in times of acute political tension and social disruption" (p. 101). The extent to which these findings may be generalizable beyond the Brazilian context is uncertain (e.g., Argentina during the so-called Dirty War, Chile during the Pinochet regime).

Deaths in Police Custody

The death of citizens while in police custody have been exposed in popular and alternative media accounts, governmental commission reports, coroners' inquests, autopsy reports, nongovernmental reports, and academic research. Although deaths in police custody may be the result of suicide (e.g., hanging), they can also be caused by a violent struggle between a citizen and a police officer before arrest, during an arrest, and while in custody, a struggle with other prisoners, or torture by police officers. Death in police custody occurs in all types of political systems, at different jurisdictional levels of police forces, and in both large and small cities.

In lesser developed countries, there is often confusion over which deaths were caused by police, defense, or security forces, all of which may maintain ambiguous positions. Explanations for deaths in police custody are usually linked to the inadequate supervision of both prisoners and guards, which may be complicated by the state's questionable responses when a victim dies or commits suicide while in custody (e.g., Hazelhurst, 1991; Home Affairs Committee. 1980). Reports of deaths in custody are based on autopsy evidence and commissions of inquiry, the reliability of which is debatable. Moreover, explanations rely on many of the same factors as torture and do not explore a variety of other reasons.

Police Riots

Well-known police riots have primarily been chronicled in popular and alternative media accounts, governmental commission reports, and academic treatments. These incidents involve the rampaging of police during public strike and protest conditions and have occurred in all types of political systems. This violence is primarily perpetrated by riot squads active in both large and small cities (Marx, 1970a).

Police Use of Deadly Force

The bulk of research on police violence has focused on the use of deadly force. These incidents have been discussed in popular and alternative media accounts, reports of governmental inquiries, and academic research. This focus on deadly force is directly related to the relative ease of documenting these acts. Victims of police use of deadly force are typically minorities and males. A plethora of variables and levels of analysis have been examined as plausible causes of police use of deadly force. The major finding is that a particular police department's policy on the use of deadly force is the most important determinant of the number of citizens shot and killed by police (Fyfe, 1979, 1988; Sherman, 1980a).

Nevertheless, research on the causes of police use of deadly force has produced its share of criticisms. These studies commonly lack internal validity, and disagreements exist about the precise nature of the dependent variables used in the research process (i.e., justifiable homicides versus shots fired)

(Binder and Scharf, 1980; Fyfe, 1981, 1988; Geller, 1982; Scharf and Binder, 1983; Binder and Fridell, 1984; Fridell, 1985). Based on a review of 20 articles, Horvath (1987) concludes, "most research has been carried out only in large cities and large urban areas" and "has involved only incidents in which fatalities of citizens occurred" (p. 226). Horvath also points out that "there are substantial methodological differences between studies making it difficult to draw meaningful comparisons or to generalize from any one group of apparently similar findings" (p. 266). Moreover, some police techniques that can cause death are rarely included in deadly force statistics (e.g., choke holds, death by baton). Finally, most studies are confined to the U.S. context.

Summary

Although the literature on general and specific types of police violence has contributed a considerable amount to our understanding of this controversial type of police behavior, it has a series of drawbacks (Horvath, 1987), including:

- a paucity of valid and reliable data
- a difficulty in distinguishing the perpetrators (i.e., sometimes the military is involved, and at other times, the police are active; periodically, the government directs the activities, while at other times private citizens are hired by the government)
- a problem in generalizing one incident to another
- causal explanations that have focused on the individual
- only rare instances in which the focus extends beyond the situational or organizational context to include structural issues
- reports often based on victim accounts
- questionable reliability of reports
- difficulty in generalizing from one country to another
- mostly descriptive data
- disagreements over exactly what has been measured (i.e., justifiable homicide versus deadly force versus shots fired)
- a concentration of research from large cities and urban areas

Another weakness in the studies relates to the methods of collecting data, which vary among jurisdictions and studies. Finally, with the exception of the subtypes of police violence, no research exists that posits a comprehensive theory, develops a model, or tests the relative influence of possible causal factors.

Controlling Excessive Police Violence

In general, research on police violence can be divided into two categories: analyses of causes and examinations of effects. Of the two, less work has been conducted on the effects. When effects—also known as consequences, outcomes, reactions, and responses—are addressed, they are usually and narrowly framed in the context of "control mechanisms" instituted by the public, government, or the police to affect future acts of police violence.

Controlling police use of excessive force has been problematic since the first modern force was developed. In fact, some of the early debates over the creation of the London Metropolitan police, particularly the legislation enabling its creation, centered on the problem of control.

Controlling police violence is part of a larger debate about the autonomy and control of government organizations. Consequently, control usually is addressed in research studies on the larger issues of public administration and local bureaucracies (Lipsky, 1971, 1980). When control is discussed in the context of policing, scholars often look at the typologies of control in police settings, police reform and change, police discretion, and police deviance.

Although a considerable amount of work has been done in this area, the majority of research has focused on definitional and typological development, descriptions, and case study analysis. In most studies, primary emphasis has been placed on the police use of deadly force in the American setting. While definitions and typology development are necessary, this field is underdeveloped and disproportionately uses case study analysis, which mitigates the ability to draw broad conclusions. This narrow approach prevents the development of a comprehensive theoretical framework and minimizes the ability of researchers and policy makers to realistically, successfully, and efficaciously control police violence.

This section briefly reviews the definitional issues and research on controlling police use of excessive force in order to demonstrate the shortcomings of this literature. This section then concludes with a series of recommendations for improving the control of police violence.

Definitional Issues

Not all researchers define "control" in the same way. Nevertheless, the thread uniting these processes is the notion that organizations and their members should perform their duties according to a set of agreed-upon standards and that these guidelines should constrain, restrict, or restrain behavior within the organization. Moreover, the process of control should be both proactive and reactive and, thus, be ongoing in nature.

Literature Review

Scholars have identified a variety of factors that are believed to be important in controlling police in general (e.g., Ackroyd, 1975; Bayley, 1979, 1985) or, in particular, "deviant" actions such as undercover operations (e.g., Marx, 1988), corruption (e.g., Sherman, 1978), and the use of deadly force (e.g., Fyfe, 1980). The notion of controlling police officers is covered by several studies that focus on typologies, leading in some cases to intricate combinations. For example, Bayley (1985) categorized the mechanisms for promoting control into four types. He conceded, however, that in practice, police and their communities rely on several types of control at the same time. Although Bayley developed a typology and made a series of informal propositions, he did not construct a theory. He also neglected to discuss the effect of the proposed controls. As he rightly pointed out,

> formal description . . . is only the first step. It is necessary to go further and determine whether mechanisms in place are actually used. . . . Studies of police control must start, not stop, with descriptions of mechanisms. They must describe the actual operation. (pp. 171–172)

In sum, the relative influence of these controls varies among police departments, units in the police organization, individual police officers, and the actions in which they engage. Despite the energy devoted to developing typologies, these factors have not been assembled into a workable theory or model. The typologies, however, can be used to develop a series of hypotheses related to this topic.

Internal and External Control Initiatives

Essentially, there are two categories of methods that are used to control police violence/excessive force: internal and external (Hudson, 1972; Tifft, 1975).

The first involves the introduction, resurrection, or implementation of different *internal control initiatives*. The mechanisms are part the police's own methods to minimize future acts of police violence. In general, police officers are more amenable to the implementation of their own internal controls than they are to implementing—in whole or in part—external controls. Internal control mechanisms give a police department the power to interpret a problem and approve the changes that are required. Unfortunately, internal controls are difficult for outsiders to detect.

Examples of internal control initiatives against an *entire* police force include changes in supervision and reporting methods. First, new supervisory bodies and intra-force policies may be established, such as an internal affairs or public complaints department, automatic evaluations of police officers' actions by internal review committees, transfers, immediate suspensions or temporary leaves, automatic visits to the force's psychologist, and the revision of guidelines on the use of certain controversial practices (e.g., choke holds, stun guns). Secondly, changes may be made in reporting requirements (e.g., directly to the chief).

Internal control initiatives against the entire police department generally prompt officers to better conceal their deviant behavior or to set into motion the processes similar to those initiated when external controls are resisted. Furthermore, internal controls directed against the entire organization may stimulate a police union or association, which may protest on behalf of the rank and file of a police department.

Internal control initiatives against *individual* officers (i.e., administrative or disciplinary measures) may consist of reprimanding, retraining, demoting, transferring, reassigning, suspending, fining, firing, or criminally charging an officer.[5] Internal mechanisms against individual officers are normally better accepted than external measures placed on the entire organization. As is true for internal controls directed against the whole organization, actions against individual police officers may involve the input of a police association.

The second category of mechanisms, *external control initiatives*, requires, imposes, or legislates additional control in and of the police department. These kinds of controls are typically met with three possible responses by the police force: resistance, public relations, and internal controls. External controls are typically limited in scope and impact.

Caveats to Keep in Mind: Resistance and Public Relations Efforts

In addition to internal and external controls, two parallel processes may also be operating in a police department: resistance and public relations. *Resistance* consists of the conscious or unconscious blockage by police of demands by the public and the government regarding changes in departmental policies and practices. When facing a crisis, police departments, like most other organizations, may experience internal conflict over the appropriate course of action, and may respond defensively and rigidly (e.g., Niederhoffer, 1967; Watson, 1967; Fink, Beak, and Tadded, 1971). It is difficult for organizations to share or relinquish their power to other groups. Furthermore, changes in policies and practices may increase the financial burdens already placed on resource-strapped departments. A defensive reaction by a police department may involve the police chief writing a letter to other governmental agencies or to a newspaper explaining why certain mandates will be ignored, providing alternative recommendations, or justifying the organization's position. The stonewalling of the implementation of new regulations is a common practice.

Additionally, the police may engage in overt expressions of dissent, sometimes in a violent fashion (e.g., strikes or riots). Resistance may also be combined with public relations efforts. For example, a police department may try to use a police association to stir up public discontent with the external policy recommendation.

Public relations actions at this stage employ symbols and myths to counter external governmental control initiatives. These public relations practices may include continued posturing, such as introducing vague policies and practices, minimizing the severity of the events, blaming the victim, criminally charging the victim, suggesting a "bad-apple" explanation for the officer(s) in question, releasing dubious reports about the violent event(s), agreeing to reorganization, engaging in co-optation, or creating new rules and regulations (Murphy, 1977).

Other practices may involve

- having a department investigate similar problems
- drawing media attention to recent efforts to combat crime
- increasing the use of community policing and other community relations efforts to improve or restore favorable images of the police
- minimizing the perception of the officer's guilt and therefore preventing a criminal charge from being laid
- hampering the successful prosecution of a case (Ross, 1995a)

Specifically, police public relations efforts may consist of

- lifting the suspension on an officer
- terminating an investigation
- dismissing a departmental charge
- rejecting a complaint
- submitting letters to the editor of a newspaper or magazine
- publicizing the agency's ability to combat crime
- refusing to answer reporters' questions
- censoring reporters or holding a press conference to present the department's side of the story (Ross, 1995a)

Public relations is commonly carried out through the police chief's office, the public affairs office, police conduits such as the Police Athletic League, community crime prevention divisions, and favorable insider police reporters (Radelet, 1977; Beare, 1987; Garner, 1987). Rather than resolving the initial problem, public relations efforts temporarily divert attention from the specific incident(s) of police violence. Most of the programs, policies, and practices that will effect genuine change are not introduced at this time.

In short, the event that led to the crisis of legitimacy is ignored, forgotten, or inadequately addressed. If the problem of police violence was actually solved through external controls, it would lead to a reduction in the ability (i.e., power) of police to exercise independent control over their organizations. Consequently, public relations is a method that police use to maintain and advance their organizational interests (Reiner, 1983). Moreover, public relations efforts may generate external complacency or increased agitation, but they will not change police policies.

If officers are receptive to control initiatives that are both realistic and adequately implemented, there is a high probability that police violence will be reduced. If resistance is encountered, however, the problem will persist and may even worsen. Ironically, public relations may either calm the public and the government or increase the frustration of those involved.

Types of Controls on Police

In recent years, prominent control measures have been implemented to affect police violence (see Exhibit 10.1). With a certain amount of creativity, these mechanisms can be categorized into eight complementary typologies, which, in turn, can serve as the basis for hypotheses to be tested. In the context of the hypotheses, each will inspire a corollary and other implications.

Police officers and, by extension, their departments can be located at various positions along each of the continuums. In the context of the scholarly literature, the positions include the following categories (as ranked from least to most prominent): premonitory/investigative; high intensity/low intensity; conventional/unconventional; community, political-legal, and occupational culture; administrative/organizational versus political and legal constraints; inclusive/exclusive; formal/informal; and internal/external.

Exhibit 10.1 **Prominent Types of Controls on Police**	
• selection procedures	• police monitoring units
• training	• police commissions
• demotion/promotion	• citizen advisory boards
• transfer	• negative public opinion
• dismissal	• negative media attention
• peer review panels	• letters to elected or appointed officials
• retraining	
• policy manuals	• public protest
• guidelines	• education activities
• standing orders	• lobbying
• memos	• critical international attention
• shoot teams	
• Internal Affairs	• riots
• hierarchy	• armed attacks
• complaints bureaus	• revolutionary warfare
• civilian review boards	• laws
• community police boards	• supervisory accountability

Outlining the Controls

Some of these processes clearly refer to proactive actions, while others encompass reactive actions. Although before-the-fact mechanisms can act as deterrents to the commission of violence, after-the-fact ones can improve accountability. Obviously, a connection between the two mechanism types exists.

To begin, Sherman (1978), for instance, distinguishes between premonitory/administrative strategies, which limit the possibilities for misconduct, and proactive/investigative initiatives, which can help detect officers whose behavior is problematic. Since unorganized strategies are the least amenable to control by administrative policies, strategies, and tactics, an organization is always most vulnerable to the least-organized forms of misconduct (Reiss, preface in Sherman, 1978).

One should keep in mind, however, that Sherman was primarily referring to corruption rather than to any other form of police behavior. Excessive police violence, on the other hand, is usually unorganized or limited to a small number of officers in a department. Thus, Sherman's generalization may not be directly applicable to excessive force, and when police violence is sporadic, it is difficult to control it.

Second, controls can be rank ordered on a continuum from low to high intensity. Intensity, in this context, refers to the amount of effort that controllers require to implement these mechanisms. An example of a low-intensity control might be victims' communications with elected or appointed government officials. Examples of high-intensity actions include revenge killings, riots by the public, armed attacks, and all-out revolutionary warfare.

Third, controls can be divided into conventional and unconventional mechanisms. In this context, normative actions are the key element. If, for example, an officer has been repeatedly investigated by the complaints division, then his or her troublesome actions would be considered conventional. However, when a chief of police intervenes and fires an individual, then this decision would be considered atypical and thus unconventional. Moreover, controls are primarily conventional and legal, while informal controls are mostly unconventional and non-legislative. In most instances, conventional controls are more readily accepted by officers than are unconventional ones.

Fourth, there is a distinction among community, political-legal, and occupational culture types of controls (e.g., Manning, 1980a). These processes include: public standards constituted from public opinion, mass media attitudes, and politicians' statements and reactions to an incident of violence; the official departmental standard, sometimes a clear statement of conditions under which force will be employed; and finally, the response and reactions of the police occupational culture.

In general, Manning (1980a) contends that occupational controls are the most powerful ways to control the police. He points out at least three ways to improve control of police violence: increasingly moving the police into a regulatory mode, disarming the police, and "chang[ing] the reward structure that serves to define and reinforce role priorities" (p. 139).

Fifth, one can easily distinguish between administrative/organizational, political, and legal constraints (Roberg and Kuykendall, 1993). A number of legal controls affect police officers and are derived from either criminal or civil law.[6] One of the more important controls in the United States has been a series of civil rights decisions established under the 1978 Supreme Court case *Monell v. Department of Social Services*, whereby a municipality's liability can increase if a victim of police violence can prove a pattern of "persistent and widespread discriminatory practices of abuse."

Sixth, controls may also differ on an inclusivity/exclusivity dimension (Bayley, 1985). According to Bayley (1990), "civilian review boards in the United States, for example, deal single-mindedly with police; legislatures, on the other hand, regulate the police as part of a larger mandate to regulate governmental processes generally" (p. 161). Likewise, Bayley (1985) maintains that although some mechanisms in police departments are specifically designed to control officers others simply help in this process. In some ways, the controlling of police officers is similar to the adjusting of brakes on a car. Make them too loose, and you risk the chance of crashing your vehicle; adjust them too tightly, and you might not be able to use the vehicle for its intended purpose.

Seventh, controls may be divided into "formal" (also known as explicit) or "informal" (implicit) measures (Stark, 1972; Bayley, 1985). Formal controls include legislation, legislative oversight, congressional committees, courts, advisory boards, review boards, ombudsmen, ethics committees, commissions of inquiry, governmental regulation, monetary appropriations, prosecutors, and interagency competition.[7]

Informal controls may consist of negative public opinions, media attention, public protest, education activities, lobbying, and critical international attention. Formal methods entail bureaucratic solutions to department problems, while informal controls are more unstructured, fluid, and spontaneous. Informal controls are often the last resort for citizens, and they have the ability to influence both formal external measures as well as informal and formal internal controls.

Eighth, internal and external mechanisms (e.g., Watchorn, 1966; Hudson, 1972; Moodie, 1972; Stark, 1972; White, 1972; Cooper, 1975; Sherman, 1974b; Tifft, 1975) are important for police accountability. Nadel (1976) suggests that the problem of internal control concerns the question of who has the ultimate decision-making power inside particular organizations. The problem of external control focuses on who has that same authority outside the institution.

Some of the internal controls in organizations are related to hiring, training, supervision, hierarchy, disciplinary codes, policy manuals/guidelines, collective agreements, review boards, and intra-agency competition. Examples of external controls are review boards, legislation, and competition. In general, both internal and external controls result in either reviews or sanctions (e.g., suspension, dismissal of members/employees).

Moreover, it can be assumed that when internal controls break down or are circumvented or ineffective, external agencies and citizens must rely more on external controls. Four major internal entities exert control within police organizations. First, recruitment divisions screen applicants. Second, training personnel provide educational and socialization opportunities. Third, policy manuals and standing orders outline both guidelines and standard operating procedures. Fourth, supervisors and administrators engage in supervisory and inspection actions and exert authority through sub-bureaus and review boards designed to oversee police behavior (e.g., Internal Affairs and trials departments).

The prominent external mechanisms that exert control are the courts, prosecutors, legislatures, executive branches, auditors, and coordinating supervising agencies. They exert control through federal, state/provincial, and municipal constitutions, statutes, and laws that proscribe and outline the situations in which force (deadly or otherwise) can be used.

The courts may also impose special standards or initiate injunctions. Medical examiners or coroners may inspect victims of police use of deadly force. Legislative bodies (through the passage of statutes, oversight hearings, appropriations, and the ratification of appointments) also exercise some control. Executive branch authorities, such as governors, premiers, mayors, city managers, agency heads, and police commissions are also influential in the control of police departments via the mechanisms of appointments, resource allocation, persuasion, and policy directives. Finally, review boards (e.g., civilian, partially civilian, or partisan) can provide analyses of police violence and recommendations for improvement. Grand juries and district attorneys can also act as mechanisms of control.

Summary

Control has been the dominant focus of outcome-based research on the topic of police violence. However, research on controlling police use of excessive force has a number of shortcomings that must be overcome if solutions to this problem are to be improved. Citizens and police officers alike must examine this process in greater detail, encourage specialists in other areas to analyze control of police violence through their specific disciplinary lenses, move beyond the narrow context of police use of deadly force, engage in theory development and model building and testing, and study alternative methods to reduce violence.

To properly address some of the previously outlined problems, scholars and others should examine police forces in detail, develop a model of the typical process by which police violence comes to public attention, document the reaction of different members of the community, government, and police, and, finally, test the model or theory that has come out of the research process.

Although the studies included in this chapter only offer a tentative framework, common problems run through all of them. First, difficulties exist in distinguishing between violence committed by the police and that executed by other coercive agencies of the state. In other words, uncertainty exists about whether the same causal factors apply to all state agencies that use violence as a method of coercion. Second, police violence and its subtypes are mired in many definitional vagaries that make distinctions among them difficult. Third, few studies evaluate potential methods of violence reduction. Fourth, few researchers make recommendations for change. Fifth, many studies are ideologically biased; thus their objectivity is hampered. Sixth, questionable research methods are used (e.g., victims' personal reports). Seventh, many studies are ahistorical, outdated, or limited to one police organization or to a small number of police forces. Eighth, little theoretical or empirical analysis has been produced.

This means that hypotheses are rarely derived according to empirical methods and that the consequences of each event (e.g., from allegation to conviction or dismissal) are not traced. Finally, few researchers have looked at the effects of police violence. When outcomes are addressed, they are usually narrowly framed in the context of "control mechanisms" instituted by the public, government, or police departments to affect future acts of police violence. These shortcomings must be singularly and collectively addressed in order to better understand the causes of police violence and its outcomes and to ultimately attempt to reduce these issues.

Solutions

Although a police department may engage in one or more prescreening processes, approximately nine methods can be used to minimize future police violence and to control police officers: use and reliance on less-than-lethal weaponry; implementation of an early warning system; use of Internal Affairs divisions; instruction on the continuum of force process; teaching of ethics to police officers; employment of integrity officers; investigations by commissions; hiring of senior police personnel from outside the police department; and civil litigation.

Less-Than-Lethal (LTL) Weapons

Over the past two decades, many police departments have introduced the use of less-than-lethal weapons. During the early development of these weapons, it was determined that many (e.g., rubber bullets) were not appropriate for their intended use and often caused physical injury. Advancements since that time have included less potentially harmful weapons, such as pepper spray and tasers. These weapons, if properly integrated into a continuum of force training, are effective means of controlling unruly/uncooperative members of the public. At the same time, certain techniques, like choke holds, are not allowed by police officers because of the preponderance of evidence that they cause death. Tasers, despite their popularity, have also been called into question. A 2004 report by Amnesty International reported on 70 citizen deaths caused by police officer tasers. The report called for a moratorium on their use by law enforcement agencies. (See chapter 11, "Failure to Integrate New Technology" for a lengthy discussion of less-than-lethal weapons.)

Early Warning Systems

The phenomenon of the "problem officer" was first identified in the 1970s. At this time, Goldstein (1977) noted that problem officers "are well known to their supervisors, to the top administrators, to their peers, and to the residents of the areas in which they work" but that "little is done to alter their conduct" (p. 171). In 1981, the U.S. Commission on Civil Rights advocated the creation of "early warning systems to identify problem officers—those 'who are frequently the subject of complaints or who demonstrate identifiable patterns of inappropriate behavior'" (Swanson et al., 2008; p. 434).

> An early warning system is a data-based police management tool designed to identify officers whose behaviour is problematic and provide a form of intervention to correct that performance. As an early response, a department intervenes before such an officer is in a situation that warrants formal disciplinary action. The system alerts the department to these individuals and warns the officers while providing counseling or training to help them change their problematic behaviour. (Swanson et al., 2008, p. 434)

Use of Internal Affairs Divisions

Most big-city police departments have Internal Affairs offices that are answerable to the chief or to the commissioner of the police. The creation of properly functioning Internal Affairs departments has been credited with lessening the frequency of hiring and maintaining corrupt, violent, and crime-prone police officers. These units are limited only by the resources that they have at their disposal and by the relationship the administrators have with the police chief or with the police commissioner.

Continuum of Force

Over the past two decades, most police officers have been taught and trained in the "use of force continuum." This is a practice whereby officers use no more force than is necessary to control or apprehend a suspect. In other words, this policy and practice seeks to minimize the possibility that officers will use excessive force. The continuum of force idea had its origins in the *Tennessee v. Garner* Supreme Court case. In October 1974, two white Memphis (Tennessee) officers were dispatched to a reported robbery. When they arrived at the location, they discovered Garner, an unarmed African-American youth who fled the scene. Just as he was about to climb a chain-link fence, Garner was shot in the back of the head, and he died on the way to the hospital. The case was brought to the Supreme Court, and it was determined that the Memphis police officers had violated Garner's constitutional rights. As a result of this decision, police departments can now be sued for violations of suspects' civil rights in wrongful death events. This decision also brought about the creation of the fleeing felon rule and the continuum of force policy.

Teaching Ethics to Police Officers

Teaching ethics to police officers, either as part of the training academy or as in-service workshops, has been advocated by some experts. Courses on ethics are frequently taught in police training academies. Police commissioners often boast about the number of departmental hours and the complexity of the assignments tied to ethics courses. To help further the development of the field, a respected academic journal entitled *Criminal Justice Ethics* promotes scholarship on law enforcement-related ethics. The downside of this approach is that this course too often just helps police officers to better rationalize their corrupt actions.

Integrity Officers

The use of integrity officers is frequently promoted by large police organizations. For example, in the wake of several corruption scandals in the New York City Police Department, each precinct now employs an officer who is directly accountable to the Internal Affairs Division. This individual is responsible for investigating allegations of possible corruption and police deviance. These integrity officers, often ostracized by their colleagues, pass on valuable information to their superiors about deviant officers.

Investigations/Commissions

Investigations and commissions are often initiated in the wake of the disclosure of severe police wrongdoing. This reaction is usually initiated by an outside body or an Internal Affairs department. To conduct an internal investigation properly, a sufficient amount of resources must be available. If the police or municipal budget cannot support it, then the state or even the federal government should step in to provide adequate or sufficient personnel to complete the investigation. Unfortunately, each new investigation typically only identifies and sanctions a handful of officers.

External Hiring of Senior Police Personnel

Finally, hiring police administrators, particularly police chiefs and commissioners, from outside a specific department is now considered routine policy. Since the revelations of Frank Serpico, mayors and city managers make concerted efforts to hire new chiefs from other police departments. (See chapter 9 for an in-depth description of Serpico's importance.)

This practice is typically met with disapproval from the rank and file and from those higher up in the chain of command who thought that they would someday be promoted to this position. A new outside chief, however, has few loyalties built up in a department and can be in the best position to make drastic changes, such as the dismissal of corrupt administrators.

Increased Use of Civil Litigation

Police officers and the departments they work for are regularly sued by citizens and liberal organizations arguing that various civil rights have been violated in the arrest process. *Tennessee v. Garner* set the precedent that allows civilians to sue police departments over the alleged denial of their civil rights. In particular, this can occur when officers use deadly force against an unarmed real or suspected felon.

Conclusion

The use of force is integral to each police officer's duties. Through the threat of coercion, law enforcement officers seek to motivate individuals to comply with their demands. Over the history of policing, the situations under which officers are allowed to use force have been circumscribed through court actions and judicious training. Unfortunately, academic research on this subject is still in its infancy. Over time, through the collection of better statistics and more sophisticated research, we will be in a better position to understand the array of factors that contribute to this complex police behavior and minimize unnecessary force and deaths of civilians.

Notes

1. This section builds on Ross (2000b: chapter 1).
2. Thus, this field of study excludes police actions against violence and violence targeted against police. Instead, the studies included in this chapter focus on violent acts committed by police personnel. See Sherman (1980a) for a distinction among the three types of violence.
3. All future references to police violence and the use of excessive force, unless otherwise stated, generally refer to "public" police violence.
4. For a more in-depth treatment of this subject, see Ross (2001).
5. Many of these actions are coterminous.
6. For research on the legal controls on police violence, see Edwards (1966); Weiler (1968); Wilson and Alprin (1971); Davis (1974); Littlejohn (1981).

Glossary

Civilian review board: An internal or external body that reviews complaints of police misconduct. Depending on the laws governing its operations, the board may or may not have the power to institute sanctions against police officers, and may or may not be fully composed of civilians. In other words, the board may have a requisite number of officers from the police department as employees or investigators.

Control: Methods that either prevent or provide a suitable reaction to undesirable behavior in order to minimize its occurrence.

Conventional controls: Methods that are normally used by the police or by public or political actors.

Deadly force: The act of killing a person by a criminal justice system employee. This typically involves a gun, but it can include a baton, other blunt-force instruments, choke holds, or other similar weapons or tactics.

Death in police custody: This happens when a suspect dies while under the supervision of the police. This can include in a cruiser, in a holding cell, or in any other location related to the investigation or incarceration process. Deaths are most commonly the result of police violence/excessive force, substandard care, inadequate care, or improper security.

Death squad activity: An undercover police or militia activity that is intended to terrorize the local civilian population through violent acts, such as rapes, mutilations, and killings. After death has occurred, the responsible group typically wants the body to be found in order to strike terror into the hearts of the population.

External controls: Controls that exist outside the police department.

Fleeing felon rule: Derived from the *Tennessee v. Garner* [471 U.S. 1 (1985)] ruling. It states that officers cannot use deadly force "unless necessary to prevent the escape and the officer has probable cause to believe that the suspect poses a significant threat of death or serious physical injury to the officer or others."

Internal controls: Controls that originate inside a police department.

Police riot: The rampaging of police or use of excessive force against protesters during public demonstrations.

Police torture: Actions of police officers to inflict severe mental or physical pain in order to obtain confessions or as punishment for real or perceived transgressions.

Police violence/excessive force: The misconduct, deviance, or abuse perpetrated by police officers. This phrase encompasses all brutality, extra-legal force, riots, torture, shootings, killings, and deadly force caused by police officers. Police violence generally refers to violence in excess of what is typically permitted according to training protocols and the law.

Premonitory controls: Controls that are preventive in nature. These are also known as proactive controls.

Public police violence: Police violence that takes places in front of witnesses or is revealed in a public context (e.g., courtroom).

Reactive controls: These take place after the occurrence of an event that needs to be addressed.

Shoot team: A small group of police officers, typically from the Criminal Investigation Division, who respond after an officer-involved shooting occurs in order to determine if the shooting was "clean" (i.e., it conformed to departmental policies and practices and to the law).

Tennessee v. Garner: A landmark Supreme Court case from the 1980s that set the precedent that allows civilians to sue police departments for the alleged denial of their civil rights. In particular, this occurs when officers use deadly force against a fleeing, unarmed real or suspected felon.

Unconventional controls: Controls that are unusual, abnormal, and/or rarely used.

Use of force continuum: The policy and practice whereby officers shall not use more force than is necessary to control or apprehend a suspect.

Chapter Questions

Part One: Multiple Choice Questions

1. Scholarly research on police violence is limited because:
   a. It primarily focuses on security agencies.
   b. It is mainly limited to the United States.
   c. It focuses almost exclusively on causes and ignores the effects of police violence.
   d. none of the above
   e. both b and c

2. Research on police violence can be divided into which two categories?
   a. oppositional and state
   b. violent and nonviolent
   c. analyses of causes and works examining effects
   d. all of the above
   e. none of the above

3. Most studies on police violence focus on:
   a. isolated factors important to the commission of a crime
   b. longitudinal studies on criminogenic police agencies
   c. the aftermath of police violence within congressional sentencing
   d. racially motivated police brutality
   e. none of the above

4. In the aftermath of the Rodney King beating and as part of the 1994 Crime Bill, the federal government instructed the Department of Justice to conduct a study to determine the frequency of police violence. What were the results?
   a. There was considerable police violence.
   b. Police violence was an infrequent occurrence.
   c. Only those who disrespected the police were victims of police violence.
   d. The study was never done due to bureaucratic mismanagement.
   e. none of the above

5. Which kind of police violence has been studied the most by police scholars?
   a. deadly force
   b. deaths in custody
   c. death squad activity
   d. riots
   e. torture

6. Which statement does not apply to research on police torture? According to the literature, victims of police torture are usually:
   a. actual or suspected criminals
   b. activists or peasants
   c. members of political oppositions
   d. trade union leaders and members
   e. law-abiding citizens

7. Most research on police violence:
   a. offers recommendations for change
   b. evaluates methods of violence reduction
   c. focuses primarily on deaths in police custody
   d. focuses almost exclusively on its causes
   e. focuses disproportionately on its effects

8. What is the term best used to describe military, paramilitary, or police units that engage in violent acts against (or selectively kill members of) a population to deter them from lending support to opposition groups?
   a. police use of deadly force
   b. death squad activity
   c. police torture
   d. deaths in police custody
   e. both b and c

9. Research conducted during the early 1960s on police violence suggested that the major cause of this problem was:
   a. insufficient number of police officers
   b. police officers' racist attitudes
   c. officers' sense of being disrespected
   d. the increase in crime incidents
   e. all of the above

10. Which Supreme Court decision has had a lasting impact on the fleeing felon problem in American policing?
    a. *Coker v. Georgia*
    b. *Mapp v. Ohio*
    c. *Monell v. Department of Social Services*
    d. *Tennessee v. Garner*
    e. none of the above

11. Which of the following is the most important predictor of police use of deadly force?
    a. the amount of training a police officer receives
    b. the internal policy on situations under which deadly force can be used
    c. legislative policy
    d. all of the above
    e. none of the above

12. The majority of people who are killed in advanced industrialized countries by the police are killed:
    a. by torture
    b. by genocide
    c. by police riots
    d. by police use of deadly force
    e. in custody

13. Which of the following is NOT an example of control on police violence?
    a. training
    b. riots
    c. policy manuals
    d. patrols
    e. police commissions

14. Controls on police violence are most commonly broken down into:
    a. internal factors
    b. external factors
    c. psychological factors
    d. judicially legislated factors
    e. both a and b

15. Which of the following is NOT an internal control on police violence/excessive force?
    a. Internal Affairs
    b. mayor
    c. police commissioner
    d. human resources department
    e. policy manuals

16. Which of the following is an external control on police violence?
    a. shoot team
    b. hiring /firing practices
    c. policy manuals
    d. legislation
    e. power of chief

17. What is the name of the policy that states that a police officer should use only as much force as is necessary to effectively convince a citizen to comply with his or her orders?
    a. situational factor
    b. reaction rule
    c. clear and present danger
    d. continuum of force
    e. none of the above

18. Punishing police officers for physical abuse is very difficult because:
    a. there are usually few witnesses
    b. other officers follow a code of secrecy
    c. victims are usually powerless
    d. courts are reluctant to believe the complainants
    e. all of the above

19. What is the significance of having continuums of controls?
    a. to point out to officers the range of available possibilities when confronted with an uncooperative suspect
    b. to complicate matters for criminal justice students
    c. to once and for all control police
    d. to demonstrate how important internal and external controls are
    e. none of the above

20. What would be an example of an unconventional control?
    a. existing laws
    b. an armed attack of a police station
    c. an investigation by Internal Affairs
    d. writing a letter of complaint to the chief of police
    e. none of the above

21. What is a shoot team?
    a. a small group of police officers, typically from the Criminal Investigation Division, who respond after an officer-involved shooting to determine if the shot was clean (e.g., it conformed to departmental policies and practices)
    b. another term for a police sniper team
    c. another term for a SWAT team
    d. a group of police officers assigned to direct traffic at a basketball game
    e. none of the above

Part Two: Short-Answer Questions

1. Which effect of police violence is most studied by scholars?

2. What is a shoot team?

3. What is the continuum of force?

4. What is a civilian review board?

5. In the context of police violence, what role does a medical examiner play?

6. What are three possible explanations as to why someone might die in police custody?

7. What five different types of police violence are outlined in this chapter?

8. In what policing context are early warning indicators used?

Part Three: Essay Questions

1. Compared to all the problems that face the police, how important is excessive police violence?

2. What can senior management officers in police departments do to reduce the frequency of unnecessary police violence/excessive force?

3. What are the effects of police violence? Which ones are positive, and which ones are negative?

PART

Problems for Police Officers and Administrators

11

Failure to Adopt and/or Properly Use New Technology

Introduction

The history of municipal policing in the United States is inextricably linked with the development, implementation, and use of new technology. Some examples of technological advances that have been integrated into police work include motorized vehicles, call boxes, two-way radio communications, and in-vehicle computer systems. New technology, if implemented and used properly, has the ability to improve policing, solve crimes, and protect the property and lives of citizens (Foster, 2005; Downs, 2007). If used in an improper fashion, technology can result in purposeful or accidental harm to citizens and police officers. In the technology acquisitions process, large police departments are at an advantage, as they have greater financial resources with which to purchase new equipment and to properly train their officers in its use. Smaller police departments are at a disadvantage because they do not have sufficient resources to accomplish these goals. During the 1990s, in an effort to find civilian uses for defense technology and thereby recuperate some of the Department of Defense's original investment, private military contractors started testing the application of new technology in American police departments and other criminal justice agencies. As a result of this experimentation, private entities began to commercialize the technology process.

This chapter examines examples of new technology that have been implemented in five areas of policing: traffic enforcement, less-than-lethal weapons, officer safety technology, criminal investigations, and communications. This chapter will then explore the benefits and drawbacks of this technology and review the reasons why police departments might fail to adopt new technology and how this situation could be improved. In conclusion, this chapter will discuss the federal government's attempts to enable this process.

Technology Used In Traffic Enforcement

For many years, technology has routinely been used in traffic enforcement. Over the past decade, several new inventions have been integrated into the policing repertoire. For example, a wide variety of systems are used by police departments to detect individuals who are speeding or violating other kinds of traffic laws.

Red Light Running Devices and Speed Cameras

One method for recording red light running and speed violations involves capturing four types of photographic information: the face of the person driving a vehicle, the traffic light's color, the time when the front wheels of the vehicle hit the intersection, and the time when the vehicle exits the intersection. With red light running devices, a police department or a city department of public works typically selects the intersections and installs the cameras.

Undoubtedly, problems have occurred in determining accurately the timing of the amber/yellow warning lights. Sometimes this light phase can be too short, so there is practically no warning to the driver before a light changes to red. Also, if a camera only takes photos of license plates, sometimes photos of the drivers are not taken; thus, the owners of ticketed vehicles are required to either pay the citation or provide information on who was driving it at the time of the ticketing. Moreover, most speed camera units have no central calibration, so the courts must depend on the police officers' assurance that the unit in question was functioning properly.

These kinds of systems can be a temporary deterrent to speeders and red light runners. On the other hand, these devices will probably have no effect on drivers who frequent intersections and certain stretches of roads that have no cameras or who are tipped off by the local media reports on these devices. Over time, however, once media reports and stories from colleagues and friends about being caught by the photo radars subside, drivers often forget that the cameras are in place and periodically will be caught speeding.

Less-Than-Lethal/Non-Lethal Weapons[1]

Developing less-than-lethal (LTL) weapons and technologies represents a top priority for law enforcement professionals. The 1985 *Garner v. Tennessee* landmark Supreme Court decision ruled that the use of deadly force against an escaping, non-violent suspect is unjustified. The decision also called for the law enforcement community to develop appropriate equipment to apprehend suspects safely. Lawsuits and bad publicity have motivated the private sector to meet this new need and have motivated police departments to introduce a broad array of LTLs. These weapons include, but are not limited to, tear gas, rubber bullets, ballistic rounds, oleoresin capsicum (pepper) spray (or OC spray, for short), foams, tasers, phasers, bean bag projectiles, and nets. On the surface, this strategy makes sense; however, this kind of equipment is not without its disadvantages. Although LTLs lead to fewer deaths, some police officers use LTLs in an indiscriminate or improper manner. If used improperly, these weapons can cause harm and even death (Vilke and Chan, 2007).

Many of the LTL weapons have been introduced by recent military veterans who become law enforcement officers or by officers who are also in the military reserves and return to their police departments after their tours of duty. They bring new pieces of technology to the attention of their superiors and they are slowly integrated into the police arsenal. "Despite their popularity and nearly widespread adoption, most of these ... weapons have not been thoroughly examined in terms of their use, consequences, and effectiveness" (White, 2007, p. 249). Also although many departments have experimented with these LTLs, some have chosen not to continue with their use.

Pepper Spray/Oleoresin Capsicum

Over the past two decades, advances have been made in the kind and type of chemical irritants that police can use against noncompliant suspects. Although officers have long used tear gas to dispel riot situations, many police departments now use Oleoresin (pepper) Spray. Kaminski, Edwards, and Johnson (1998) reported that because of the widespread implementation of pepper spray, it can be considered successful as deterrent measure on suspects. According to Nowicki's 2001 study on OC spray, it is effective in gaining suspect compliance 80% to 90% of the time. Nowicki did note, however, that the level of success depends on the accuracy of the officer using the spray. Furthermore, there is a possibility that both officers and those standing nearby will experience the spray's effects.

Bean Bag Technology

Police officers in many jurisdictions commonly use bean bag projectiles that can be shot from a gun-like weapon. Upon impact the bean bag can simultaneously bruise, stun, and disorient the individual. Often this method is used with individuals who are threatening but who are not in a position to possibly kill an officer.

Taser[2]

The taser, which is a conducted-energy device, fires a cartridge with two wires and attached hooks and shoots an electric charge into the suspect. In order to use this weapon, an officer must be no more than 20 feet from the suspect. Safety issues have been raised about the use of tasers. White (2007) notes:

> Despite its adoption by more than 6,000 law enforcement agencies in the United States . . . , there appears to be serious questions regarding its effectiveness and potential to cause serious injury or death, particularly when used against mentally ill in crisis, those under the influence of drugs or alcohol, and those with heart and respiratory conditions. (p. 249)

Strobe-and-Goggle Technology

Due to the limitations of flashlight generators and flash bang devices (i.e., stun grenades), some police departments are now using strobe-and-goggle technology. This system, designed to temporarily blind and disorient subjects, uses a bright flashing light and is employed during raids or assaults on barricaded structures, allowing officers to enter the premises. The officers wear goggles that protect their eyes from the effects of the light. In this case, new technology did not need to be developed, since the kinds of goggles needed for this technique already existed. Both military pilots and commercial welders wear goggles designed to darken when exposed to bright light.

Remote-Control Barrier Strips

Although police departments have long employed spiked strips or stop sticks to blow out the tires of a pursued vehicle, the need for safer ways to stop fleeing suspects has led to the creation of technology that allows officers to remotely activate and control strips of needles that can pop out of a road and puncture a vehicle's tires. The police can then retract the needles so that their cars or others are not damaged. The ability to activate the system remotely prevents injury to law enforcement officers and innocent civilians (Stevens, 2009).

Fleeing Vehicle Tagging System

Because of the danger of high-speed chases to suspects, citizens, and police officers, some police departments are now using marking systems. Officers fire a "tagging" projectile, much like a GPS tracking device, at a fleeing vehicle. This projectile has a radio transmitter that then permits the police to follow the vehicle from a safe distance minimizing the possibility of endangering lives or allowing the suspect to escape.

Technology That Protects or Improves Officer Safety

Although weapons, both lethal and less-than-lethal, can protect officers, other advances in technology have made police officers even safer. These improvements include the inventions of smart guns, personal monitoring devices, and Kevlar vests.

Smart Gun

One-sixth of all law enforcement officers killed each year are shot with their own weapons, often in the course of a struggle with a suspect. Now, a national laboratory is testing a variety of sensors, which, when placed in the handgrip of a weapon, would "recognize" the authorized user and refuse to fire for anyone else. The resulting "smart gun" could never be used against its owner. In addition to saving the lives of law enforcement officers, smart guns might also save the lives of children who kill themselves, either accidentally or intentionally, with their parents' weapons. Another benefit is that criminals who obtain weapons illegally would be unable to fire them.

Personnel Monitoring System

Originally developed for Army medics, a personnel monitoring system can enable law enforcement and other public service personnel to remain in direct contact with their departments at all times. A miniature camera transmits full-color video of the scenes encountered during the course of a day, while wireless networks allow audio communication and data transmissions. A Global Positioning System (GPS) provides the officer's exact street location and a personal status monitor tracks the officer's vital signs. As a result, an agency could locate and monitor an officer in distress, quickly assess the situation, and respond accordingly.

Kevlar Vests/Bulletproof Vests

In 1975, because of technology used in the manufacture of heavy-duty, bulletproof military tires, scientists at the National Institute of Justice experimented with the development of bulletproof vests to be worn by officers. The protective material, perhaps best known by its trademark Kevlar, could be woven into the soft body armor worn by law enforcement personnel. Since the mid-1970s, bulletproof vests have saved the lives of thousands of police officers and are essential equipment for police departments to be accredited through the Commission for Law Enforcement Accreditation CELEA.

Technology That Improves Criminal Investigations

At the forefront of criminal investigations is a whole host of forensic tools and processes. During the 1960s, police departments started to videotape interactions with suspects (Grant, 1980; Baldwin, 1992; Chu, 2001). Over the past four decades, police departments have also integrated DNA analysis and gunshot detection systems into their investigations. Although police detectives and forensic technicians still collect and process fingerprints and bodily fluids found at crime scenes, police departments now utilize numerous kinds of technology that allow them to collect other evidence that can be helpful in the detection, arrest, and prosecution of criminals and criminal acts. One of the most important and controversial methods is Close Circuit Television (CCTV).

Gunshot Detection System

During the 1990s the Shotspotter Corporation (www.shotspotter.com) was formed. Although the technology developed by this corporation was first applied in the military context, a gunshot detection system can identify from afar the time, location, and possible weapon that fired a particular bullet. The very first test of this technology in a municipal policing environment took place in Redwood City, Calif., in 1995. Since then, the system has been installed in numerous cities: Los Angeles and Oakland, Calif.; Glendale, Ariz.; Rochester, N.Y.; Minneapolis, Minn.; Birmingham, Ala.; Gary, Ind.; and Washington, D.C. The system has also been evaluated by the National Institute of Justice (1998). This system can generate numerous calls for service each day when shot identifications are made. In almost all instances, by the time officers arrive at the scene, the shooter is not present nor can he or she be found.

On the positive side, this technology's greatest value may be that knowledge of the system appears to be a deterrent. The system can help locate victims of gunfire, especially if the person is close to where the shot was fired. There may also be some value in placing decoy recording devices to reduce additional crimes. Gunshot detection is a great example of the implementation of technology with minimal or no research findings or data. To date, no academic research has been published on this new technology (Waters, 2007).

On the downside, the system costs approximately $4,100 per sensor installed. In order to cover a respectable distance, the system requires a significant initial investment. What is almost as important as the technology is the response time of the officers. If they respond too quickly without backup, they put their lives and those of citizens in danger. Moreover, shortly after a shot, the police often respond with the sirens on. This reduces the element of surprise, which can be critical in apprehending the shooter. Finally, the sensors can be shot out, which require expensive repairs.

Closed Circuit Television (CCTV)

CCTV, a common technology that can be found in many cities such as London, England, provides traffic supervision as vehicles move both in and out of a city. For example, almost all vehicles entering London have their license plates photographed. The plate numbers are then run through central databases. Because of the years of violence and unrest caused by the Irish Republican Army, these protocols were developed to prevent or reduce terrorist attacks and to collect evidence to aid national security organizations in the capture of the individual/s who placed a bomb. Nonetheless, the attacks that continued to occur demonstrate that continuous, comprehensive security cannot be provided in open democratic societies. The *Baltimore Sun* (September 11, 2007) reported on the use of similar technology:

> In Baltimore, police began using surveillance cameras in 2005. There are now 300 throughout the city, and police say violent crime has dropped by 15 percent in the places where the cameras are installed. Prosecutors, though, aren't impressed. . . . In 2006, the cameras led to nearly 2,000 arrests in Baltimore, according to figures from the state's attorney's office. About a fourth of those arrests . . . led to guilty verdicts, [while another quarter led to] charges being dropped because of insufficient evidence—mostly surveillance camera tapes [which] was too poor to even file charges.

Closely related to CCTV, is vehicle license plate and facial recognition technology. This allows security personnel to take a digital picture of a license plate and/or individual and compare it with known license plate numbers and/or in the case of faces, criminals, terrorists, or individuals for whom there are outstanding warrants. The license plate technology has been used in England with moderate success. Evidence gathered through facial recognition software has been successfully used in a number of trails.

The Magic Wand

During the 1990s, the Alaska Crime Laboratory developed and distributed a Fingerprint Visualization System. Called the Magic Wand, it allows police officers to retrieve fingerprints from surfaces and quickly transmit this information electronically to a central database. This technology speeds up the identification of suspects to be questioned and/or arrested and minimizes the time that forensic examiners must spend at the scene of a crime.

Communications

From the introduction of the telephone in 1877 through the launch of iPhone in 2007, police departments have continuously improved their ability to remain in touch with their rank and file and to make it easier for the public to contact the police. Police officers doing patrol need information to be easily obtainable. One advancement in communication is the COPLINK network.

> [This is] a single easy-to-use interface that integrates different data sources such as incident record, mug shots, and gang information. It allows diverse police agencies to share data easily, on a 24/7 basis. COPLINK's cross-reference database enables information sharing, is the most efficient means of police communications available, and can expedite case investigations. An officer can provide little or partial information, such as an incomplete license plate number or an identifying tattoo, which the database cross-references and processes. The system's cross-referencing capabilities enable the officer to access information that other law enforcement agencies may have compiled about the suspect if the suspect had a previous run-in with the law in another county or jurisdiction. (Stevens, 2009, p. 364)

Although the inventor, Hsinchun Chen of the University of Arizona, claims that COPLINK is a huge success, officers must be trained in its use, and until they learn all of the necessary details, they may find the network quite frustrating to use.

Conclusion

Small police departments usually do not have the resources to implement new technologies. Even larger departments with the funds may not have access to the information needed to make the right or best purchase decisions. In fact, law enforcement agencies as a group may not possess the buying power to encourage manufacturers to research and develop the products their officers need at affordable prices.

Adapting technology to serve in a field other than the one for which it was originally intended frequently costs almost as much as developing it from scratch. Multiple-use technologies save money by targeting several related fields, such as the military, public service, and law enforcement realms. This process has been aided through the establishment of the Department of Justice's National Law Enforcement Technology Center, which is responsible for identifying, developing, and manufacturing new products and applications specifically designed with law enforcement in mind. (See Exhibit 11.1.)

When considering the purchase and implementation of new technology or a new system, a Chief of Technology or Acquisitions Officer for a police department faces a difficult task. It can be difficult for chiefs, commissioners, and those who are responsible for new technology acquisition to see past the often-slick sales presentations that are given to them. Unfortunately, few empirical studies have been published in peer-reviewed journals on the effectiveness of many contemporary technological advances. Thus, most evaluations are anecdotal or are produced or paid for by the companies that are trying to sell the systems.

Technology can provide the tools to make law enforcement more efficient and effective, limit the consequences of poor judgment, and improve the safety of the police and the public. It can also save lives. Technology, however, cannot fix every crime-related or order-maintenance problem. Technology cannot make up for poor judgment or compensate for inadequate or nonexistent training. It cannot fix the problems that result from poor officer screening or selection, nor can it replace incompetent leadership.

Nevertheless, chiefs, commissioners, and other senior officers should comprehensively examine all available published scientific research and not simply depend on corporate advertising and propaganda. Scholarly studies can provide valuable information about the manner in which jurisdictions have implemented and used various systems. Departments considering major purchases should also make contact with the appropriate administrators in other jurisdictions to ascertain their satisfaction or lack thereof with new technology.

Departments also need to consider the classic cost-benefit balance. Chiefs and commissioners should, as accurately as possible, predict what kind of benefits can be achieved (e.g., increased revenues, deterrence of speeders and red light runners, safer roads) versus the expenses of the purchase and the ongoing maintenance and replacement of a system. Unfortunately, once the first step of purchase has been made, it is harder to terminate a new system if a chief or commissioner comes to feel that the costs of maintenance are too exorbitant. Finally, police officers must be properly trained in the use of new technology. Failure to do so can open up a police department to numerous civil liability suits.

Exhibit 11.1   *RoboCop* Movies and Their Use of Technology

Since the 1960s, select Hollywood-created and -produced movies have featured police officers and departments deploying new technology. One of the most significant of these types of films is the *RoboCop* trilogy.

In *RoboCop 1*, (1987), directed by Paul Verhoeven, patrol officer Alex Murphy (played by actor Peter Weller) is almost killed when he and his partner enter a warehouse in pursuit of Clarence Boddicker's gang who are trying to takeover the deteriorating city of Detroit. In another part of town, Omni Consumer Products (OCP) is attempting to perfect a robotic police officer (ED 209) and create Delta City where old Detroit stands. ED 209 is an "urban pacification robot" that has undergone severe cost overruns and is the creation of corporate executive Dick Jones. It malfunctions when it kills an officer during a demonstration.

Bob Morton, a young and ambitious corporate member, suggests an alternative, called "RoboCop." Despite the hi-tech gadgetry, RoboCop cannot operate without a human brain. The brain of Murphy, who is on life support, is selected and the robot is transformed into a 21st-century advanced state-of-the-art, armor-resistant cyborg with four primary directives. Meanwhile, a workplace struggle between Jones and Morton ensues. Jones, the more devious of the two, hires Boddicker to kill Morton. "Robo" figures the plot out, arrests Boddicker then goes back to OCP to arrest Jones for aiding and abetting a known felon. Robo, however, cannot activate his last directive, arresting a senior officer of OCP, until Jones is officially fired by the president during a corporate board meeting.

In *RoboCop 2*, (1990), directed by Irvin Kershner, Murphy (aka RoboCop, also played by Weller), despite recurrent and debilitating flashbacks, continues to make Detroit safe from criminals. However, the police are on strike and mayhem is being wreaked by Cain, a drug cult leader responsible for introducing a new substance called Nuke to city residents. Robo locates Cain's operations, but is attacked by a mangy group of thugs using magnets, sledgehammers, electric shock devices, jackhammers, and machine guns.

He is reduced to a pile of twitching electrically disconnected body parts. OCP decides after consulting representatives from community organizations, to reprogram Robo to have less law-and-order functions and more community values. The result is a docile RoboCop. After a near suicide, Robo goes after Cain and his reconstituted gang. The police, in solidarity and acknowledging professional courtesy, take a break from their strike, join Robo and raid Cain's hideout.

Exhibit 11.1   Continued

They pulverize Cain's gang, leaving him hospitalized and hooked up to a life-support system. Worrying that Robo is becoming obsolete, OCP creates an improved RoboCop. Juliette Faxx, the corporation's project psychologist, and portrayed as someone trying to climb the corporate ladder, selects Cain's brain to complete RoboCop 2. In the meantime, the city is on the verge of bankruptcy, politicians are trying to raise money, and OCP is going to foreclose on the city. RoboCop 2, with Cain's brain, tears apart his reconstituted gang at their sludge plant hideout while they are trying to cut a deal with city politicians. RoboCop 1 finally confronts RoboCop 2 and a fight to the finish ensues, with predictable results.

While several themes are covered in these films, and they have led to a third sequel, video games, a television series, and comic books, three important conflicts relevant to students and practitioners of policing dominate the movies:

- the drawbacks of disproportionately relying on technological fixes to complex social problems;
- the efficiency but callousness of private enterprise versus the inefficiency but humaneness of public administration;
- the difference in the level and intensity in the amount of violence as a function of old versus new forms of technology.

Notes

1. This chapter does not include a discussion of conducted esoteric devices, such as high energy beams and sticky foam, because of their lack of widespread implementation.

2. The public frequently confuses the taser with the phaser, which is an LTL that emits an electric shock when placed on the exposed skin of an individual. An officer must be in close proximity to a suspect to properly use a phaser.

Glossary

Bean bag projectile: A less-than-lethal shotgun-like weapon that ejects a bean bag at an individual and can cause bruising.

Close Circuit Television (CCTV): This allows viewers (e.g., police/law enforcement personnel) to monitor the activities of individuals and groups in a circumscribed area where cameras have been installed.

Crime mapping: Visual display of criminal occurrences/incidents based on their reported location of occurrence.

Facial recognition software: Technology that allows security personnel to take a digital picture of an individual and compare it with known criminals, terrorists, or individuals for whom there are outstanding warrants.

Foam-type system: This foam can be sprayed on the ground or on a road in order to slow down an individual who is fleeing from the police.

Less-than-lethal (LTL) weapons: Weapons that do not seriously injure or kill the individuals to whom they are applied.

Net: This can be thrown on top of an individual and is intended for persons who are difficult to control, mentally impaired, or on drugs.

Office of Science and Technology: Office of the National Institute of Justice responsible for testing law enforcement-related technology brought to its attention by manufacturers and the U.S. Department of Defense.

Pepper spray: Also known as oleoresin capsicum spray, a less-than-lethal weapon that allows law enforcement officers to temporarily cause a burning sensation if the spray is applied to a suspect's skin or eyes.

Phaser: This less-than-lethal weapon emits an electric shock when placed on the exposed skin of an individual. Officer must be in close proximity to the suspect to properly use this device.

Red light running device: A technology and process that allows police/law enforcement agencies to record the license plate of a vehicle (and sometimes the image of the person) that fails to stop at a red light.

Shotspotter Gunshot Detection System: This system uses sensors installed in one or more parts of a city that help police officers to identify the location where a weapon was discharged, and thus sometimes, the location of a deceased person.

Taser: A less-than-lethal weapon that emits electroshock to the individuals to whom it is applied.

Chapter Questions

Part One: Multiple Choice Questions

1. The implementation of new technology into municipal police departments usually:
   a. is welcomed by all constituencies
   b. is always resisted
   c. is carefully monitored by all constituencies
   d. improves policing regardless of the department
   e. none of the above

2. Which of the following is NOT a less-than-lethal weapon?
   a. taser
   b. net
   c. pepper spray
   d. gun
   e. foam-type system

3. In which situation is a trained police officer most likely to use pepper spray?
   a. traffic enforcement
   b. investigation
   c. encounter with noncompliant citizen
   d. to season his or her food
   e. to mask bad odors in his or her patrol car

4. What is the name given to technology that allows a police or law enforcement agency to record the license plate of a vehicle that fails to stop at a red light?
   a. blue light
   b. CCTV
   c. red light running device
   d. spyware
   e. none of the above

5. Gunshot detection systems are probably most useful in helping police:
   a. locate a deceased victim of gunshot wounds
   b. detect the shooter
   c. locate the weapon discharged
   d. identify the make and model of a weapon
   e. none of the above

6. In police technology acquisitions, which type of department is at an advantage?
   a. large
   b. small
   c. those located in the south
   d. those located in the north
   e. those with lots of crime

Part Two: Short Answer Questions

1. What is a gunshot detection system?

2. What is the Office of Science and Technology?

3. What is CCTV?

4. What is facial recognition software?

5. What is Shotspotter Gunshot Detection System?

6. What is the source of most police less-than-lethal technology?

Part Three: Essay Questions

1. Can the adoption of new technologies lead to a situation in which the police are all-powerful?

2. As a police administrator, how would you best make decisions about which technology to purchase and how to implement it in a rational and safe manner?

3. How has the federal government tried to facilitate the dual-purpose use of new technology?

12

Inability to Properly Manage, Supervise, and Lead Police Organizations

Introduction

Municipal police departments, especially those that serve jurisdictions with large populations and those that employ a considerable number of officers, are unquestionably difficult to manage and lead. Moreover, police administrators need to take into consideration and balance three complex and often competing constituencies or pressure sources: "the community, the law, and the police organization" (Roberg and Kuykendall, 1993, p. 91).

Making matters more challenging, upper management is often far removed, both physically and psychologically, from the rank-and-file members from whom they seek cooperation (Reuss-Ianni, 1984). Police management typically want their decisions to be implemented immediately according to their instructions. Meanwhile, many officers and some members of the public believe that police departments are compromised by an array of problems: They are overly bureaucratic; too much red tape exists; superiors are insensitive to subordinates; rank-and-file officers are too often treated with disrespect; and promotions seem to be given unfairly (i.e., they are based on favoritism rather than skill or competitive exams). Further, officers who deserve to be disciplined are quietly asked to resign; new policies are inconsistent with existing ones; management does not take into consideration the viewpoints of its rank-and-file employees; and communication from one rank to another is poor (Stevens, 2009).

This chapter explores the most dominant problems—lack of or poor communication and the failure to manage and lead efficiently—and the solutions that have been advocated, and where appropriate implemented in police departments around the country. This section will conclude with a discussion of CompStat. Before proceeding, it is important to understand that not only are police agencies paramilitary organizations, but they are also bureaucracies. This means that as public organizations, they are typically conservative and are slow to change their policies and practices.

Problems in Communication

All organizations deal with a wide variety of communication methods, and police departments are no different. Although communications come into a police department through the mail or via the Internet, most "calls for service" (requiring the police to respond in an expeditious fashion) come in by phone call. They can range from the urgent (i.e., a 911 call) to the mundane (i.e., the score in last night's baseball game). Although good police officers are adept at listening, talking, and problem solving, managers and leaders (i.e., those above the rank of patrolmen) should possess full mastery of these skills. According to Bennett and Hess (1996), "more than 50 percent of a manager's time is spent communicating. First-line supervisors usually spend about 15 percent of their time with superiors, 50 percent of their time with subordinates, and 35 percent with other managers and duties. These estimates emphasize the importance of communications in everyday . . . operations" (p. 85).

Organizational Systems of Communication

There are three basic types of communication inside a police department: upward, downward, and horizontal. Upward messages go up the chain of command. Downward communiqués flow from the higher levels of the police organization down to the rank and file. Horizontal communication occurs among individuals in the same job or rank category (Allen, 1977). Horizontal communication often evolves when both upward and downward communication is either poor or nonexistent. Horizontal communication is also used when people want to spread information that they do not want to share with superiors or subordinates. This form of communication is proverbially known as "the grapevine." The grapevine allows the transmission of informal, unofficial information among employees or members in an organization. Often news that one would not receive through official channels of communication is conveyed via the grapevine.

Communication via these different types of channels is not always done well. At almost any given juncture, there are numerous opportunities for oral, verbal, or written miscommunication. Needless to say, police departments, like most criminal justice institutions, prefer written communication. Although there are advantages to oral communication, including the added nuances of tone, intonation, and expression, in organizations where communication is open to review at higher levels, written communication is extremely important. Thus, effective managers and leaders must also be good written communicators.

What Is Communicated?

All sorts of information are passed among coworkers and throughout the chain of command. These can include instructions about a job, why the task needs to be done, procedures and practices, feedback, and other subtle aspects of organizational culture. Although communication between and among officers and their immediate supervisors typically takes place through two-way radios, over radio bands specifically dedicated to the police and emergency services, or through written reports, face-to-face contact is often next to impossible. Headquarters is often geographically distant from the location where patrol officers perform their daily duties, therefore creating another barrier for direct communication.

Failure to Lead

Police departments need to have managers who are not only good communicators, but who also are able to command the respect of their subordinates and lead their organization to achieve its diverse goals. Part of this ability is innate and intuitive, while other aspects of this skill are developed through training and experience on the job.

Differentiating Between Leadership, Authority, and Power

It is quite easy to confuse the three interrelated terms that are frequently used in descriptions of police managers: leadership, authority, and power. There are numerous definitions of *leadership*. In general, a leader is an individual who occupies a senior management position in an organization and who demonstrates vision for his or her organization. *Authority* "is a grant made by the formal organization to a position, the incumbent of which wields it in fulfilling his or her responsibilities. The fact that a formal grant of authority has been made does not mean that the person receiving it also is automatically able to influence others to perform at all, let alone willingly" (Swanson et al., 2008, p. 271). The word *power* relates to "the ability to compel a performance or make people do a certain thing; there is some power inherent in the exercise of formal authority" (p. 295). Effective leaders need not only the authority to make decisions but also the power to implement or enforce them. For leaders, this authority is often actualized in their ability to distribute benefits (i.e., higher pay, bonuses, specialized training privileges) and to met out sanctions, both formal (e.g., reprimands, dismissals) and informal (e.g., less desirable work schedules).

Leadership and Performance

According to Swanson, Territo, and Taylor (2008), a police administrator is required to meet several department needs and issues:

The police leader is responsible for equally important but essentially different broad responsibilities:

1. Fulfilling the mission of the police department
2. Making work productive and helping subordinates to achieve
3. Producing impacts. (p. 269)

Exhibit 12.1   **Reaching for the Brass Ring: Memoirs of Chiefs/Commissioners of American Municipal Police Departments**

Little is known about the reasons why individuals become police chiefs or commissioners, their backgrounds before entering this position, and their unique behaviors while in office. In some communities, police chiefs and commissioners have the same status as rock stars, while in others they are ridiculed and vilified by the public, the news media, and the rank and file. On occasion, those who have managed to weather the political storms have released autobiographies or memoirs (Bratton, 1998; Stamper, 2006; Timoney, 2010). Others have written about a particular anti-crime strategy but have injected the narrative with considerable autobiographical material (Moose, 2003). Needless to say, the autobiographies and memoirs provide a rare glimpse into the lives of one of the most challenging jobs in America.

The level of success met by each administrator is affected by an intersecting array of influences, which these authors list as

> chief's leadership style, community preferences, available resources, and the selection process for a chief. Police leaders chosen by a competitive process or who are perceived by subordinates in the department as competent are viewed consistently as having greater expertise and, consequently, have more influence and power. (p. 269)

Theories of Leadership

Numerous theories of leadership have been advanced over the years. These theoretical tools "attempt to explain the factors associated with the emergence of leadership or the nature of leadership. Included are (1) 'great man' and genetic theories, (2) the traits approach, (3) behavioral explanations, and (4) situational theories" (Swanson et al., 2008, p. 277). Many studies and reports have been written on these perspectives. In discussions of police departments, there appears to be a certain preoccupation with describing, in considerable detail, each and every theory of leadership. Unfortunately, these are more diagnostic tools and are only minimally helpful in aiding a police leader and organization to become more efficient and effective. (See Exhibit 12.1.)

Solutions

Many solutions have been advanced to help deal with the problems related to ineffective management and supervision. Unfortunately, most of these management solutions have proven to be faddish in nature (Peters and

Waterman, 1982). Often, when solutions are applied to the policing context, they fail to meet the discrete set of needs that are unique to this profession. In other words, what works in the private sector does not always function well in law enforcement. Those managers who implement far-reaching changes in their departments must also be cognizant of the significant forces of resistance that reside at most levels of the police agency. Many officers predictably develop a sense of cynicism when their managers' attempt to fix problem areas (Niederhoffer, 1967). This sentiment is caused by a number of factors, including the fact that policing tends to attract faddish approaches to reducing crime and managing police activities that vanish after their funding is cut or a new chief of police is hired. Additionally, many of the new policies and practices are developed without officer input, or if input is solicited, it is rarely integrated or taken seriously.

Departments can improve the supervision of subordinates through a number of mechanisms. For example, the span of control should never be overwhelming for supervisors. According to Walker and Katz (2004), sergeants should only supervise between 8 and 12 officers. Those responsible for more officers

> will likely find it difficult to provide sufficient supervision. The Special Counsel to the Los Angeles Sheriff's Department (1988) concluded that the higher rate of police shootings among officers assigned to the Century Station was caused, in part, by inadequate supervision: Each sergeant at the station was responsible for 20 to 25 officers, two to three times the recommended span of control. (White, 2007, p. 274)

Second, supervisors need to be properly trained by their senior officers. They should not simply be asked to learn their jobs as they go along or through on the job training. Third, managers need the power to both punish subordinates who fail to adhere to organizational policies and to reward officers under their command for exemplary service. Fourth, managers, especially those who have been recently promoted, should not be responsible for supervising individuals who graduated with them from the police academy or who were in the same class. Working with peers can prove to be difficult in such a situation.

Management by Objectives

Popularized by management guru Peter Drucker (1954/1977), the Management by Objectives (MBO) approach is based on an awareness that each worker at every level of an organization should be involved in the management process and should clearly understand his or her unique contribution to the organization's achievement of its objectives. In a police context, this means "police and patrol officers agree on goals and objectives within the police organization" (Stevens, 2009, p. 224). MBO prescribes a series of steps, including the giving and processing of feedback. Employees at each level of the organization should participate in the procedure and should be actively involved in reaching consensus on appropriate tasks, objectives, and goals of an organization. Furthermore, they should help develop ideas for accomplishing organizational goals. The MBO approach is not without its detractors. Deming (1994), for example, states that frequently workers are unclear about the objectives of their organizations or subunits, but they strive, sometimes to the detriment of quality of the end product, to achieve their managers' goals. Deming prefers increasing the quality of the managers and leaders in an organization as a prime motivation for employees to improve the work environment and process.

Total Quality Management (TQM)

During the 1970s, police administrators both acknowledged that the old style of managing police departments was in need of a change and were exposed to new theories in the business world. As a result, some police departments started experimenting with, and in some cases implementing, both corporate and participatory methods for running their organizations. This was frequently achieved through the creation of so-called quality circles: "groups of personnel who routinely come together to discuss policy, share information with other groups, and report on their progress to management" (Stevens, 2009, p. 224). Although TQM has its advantages, it does not work well in the framework of police organizations, which are traditionally top-down bureaucratic organizations. Thus, both rank and file and middle management find this process to be a frustrating experience. In the end, "police organizations [should] adapt a managerial strategy that fosters perspectives that relate to working smarter rather than 'working harder'" (p. 224). In general, TQM is more suitable as a mechanism to improve staff–inmate communication in the jail or penitentiary context. This is often fostered by having the staff offices located directly on the tiers.

The Learning Organization

During the 1980s, one of the most popular fads in management was the notion that in order for organizations to improve, they needed to become learning organizations. As related to police departments, they "should develop the capacity to reflect on organizational needs, plan toward fulfilling those needs, and implement changes to meet their objectives" (Stevens, 2009, p. 233). One example of this process was called "Bridging the Gap":

> This initiative, which was originally developed by the Royal Canadian Mounted Police, . . . relies on human performance technology (HPT) to find, assess, and remove performance barriers for police personnel. [It] use[s] a systematic methodology to find the root obstacles to quality performance and to fix the problems related to a specific performance deficit. (Stevens, 2009, p. 233)

In this model, officers are periodically asked to identify particular problems they are experiencing, to prioritize them, and to explain what has thwarted their efforts to solve their problems. Once this step is finished, management tries to implement the appropriate solutions.

Other Suggestions

In an effort to fix administrative problems, especially the overly bureaucratic and paramilitary ones, all kinds of suggestions have been put forward. Several of them warrant mention at this point. One approach involves the creation of a flat organization, and another uses a hospital model for administration. In the first case, the number of ranks is reduced to one homogenous whole. This recommendation, made by Angel (1975), advocated the flattening of police organizations in terms of their ranks and encouraging decision making to be more democratic. Some departments followed this advice with mixed results. For example, during the 1990s the Baltimore Police Department eliminated the rank of Captain, so now only lieutenants and below had civil service protection. Officers who were at the rank below were unhappy because it led to confusion, which meant that a promotion above the rank of lieutenant would have an effect on job security. This ultimately lowered morale among the rank and file. Furthermore, the abolition of various ranks led to confusion and lowered morale among the rank and file. In short, there is consistently a considerable backlash among the rank and file whenever the flat-organization model is implemented.

Another suggestion was related to the adoption of the hospital model (Guyot, 1991). Guyot noted that many of the functions and roles that are present in hospitals have equivalents in the context of large urban police departments. In particular, employees at the higher echelons are responsible for different responsibilities than those who work under them.

> The typical hospital is run by two separate and distinct management systems: administrative and medical. The medical management system is comprised of doctors and other medical staff who make the day-to-day decisions regarding the treatment and handling of patients. Hospital administrators are responsible for [more management-related kinds of issues]. (White, 2007, p. 150)

While Guyot's proposal has some merit, White points out the weaknesses of this model in the policing framework:

> Training of police officers can be measured in terms of weeks, not years. Police officers have tremendous authority, including the capacity to use force. Police officers are generally dealing with unwilling and uncooperative clients. Police have a wide range of complex and sometimes conflicting responsibilities. The history of police misconduct suggests that supervision is critically important to controlling police behavior. (p. 151)

Many managerial suggestions and changes have been implemented and subsequently only rarely evaluated in the organizations that applied them. At other times, the changes are simply fads that are quickly abandoned when a new solution is proposed.

CompStat

In 1994, Bill Bratton became Police Commissioner of the New York City Police Department (NYPD). Under his direction, the former New York Transit Police Commissioner implemented a program called CompStat,[1] a shortened name for two alternate program titles, Computer Analysis of Crime Statistics and Comprehensive Computer Statistics. Bratton and others credited this program with reducing the crime rate, in particular for felonies, in New York City (Bratton, 1997, 1998; Maple, 2000; McDonald, 2001). In order to better understand this program, the following section provides a brief description of CompStat, lists the police forces that have implemented similar programs, and outlines the difficulties caused by this program, including unanswerable questions and concerns.

What Is CompStat?

Zero-tolerance policing and CompStat are frequently confused. CompStat is designed to affect the overall quality of life in a specific community, while a commander might explore zero-tolerance policing methods in certain select neighborhoods. CompStat and zero tolerance are not the same thing. In short, through the CompStat program, a police department converts crime statistics into updatable maps of criminal events. This information is then used by senior management to regularly monitor the performance of precinct-level staff employees and place more officers in higher crime areas in order to reduce crime (McDonald, 2001).

In the NYPD, the police department uses computer-retrievable statistics "to quickly identify and respond to emerging crime patterns in each of the city's 76 precincts" (Marzulli and Mustain, 1995). Regularly scheduled, often tense meetings are held, during which time the senior administrators are expected to "explain crime in their commands and what they plan to do about it" (Marzulli and Mustain, 1995).

> CompStat has evolved from casual meetings around a conference table with a few people to a formal meeting of 50, with charts, maps and high-tech displays in the NYPD's eighth-floor command and control center. Borough chiefs, precinct captains and squad commanders are called to the podium to make presentations and to answer questions designed to test their knowledge, skill, and creativity. (Marzulli and Mustain, 1995)

The meetings take place at various intervals, usually either once or twice a week. By 1996, many individuals and organizations believed that CompStat was one of the most effective programs available. In 1996, CompStat won the Innovations in American Government award from the Ford Foundation and from Harvard University (Goldschlag and Lombardi, 1996).

In general, CompStat helps deploy police efforts (and resources) more effectively and increase middle management accountability for the crime and responses to it.

Each command goes once every five weeks. Borough chiefs, precinct captains and now even squad commanders can be called upon to take the podium. Before an audience of 50 that often includes the police commissioner and sometimes the mayor, they make presentations and take questions based on a freshly drawn statistical portrait of what's happening in their commands. . . . The sessions have become so important that pre-CompStat planning meetings now occur in each command and so central to the department's crime-fighting philosophy that mini-CompStats are now held for beat cops at roll call in some precincts. (Marzulli and Mustain, 1995)

As a result of this process, several senior commanders have been demoted, allegedly because of their poor responses under questioning.

According to Jack Maple (2000), one of the pioneers of CompStat, the approach consists of several interlocking pieces: accurate and timely intelligence; rapid deployment that is concentrated, synchronized, and focused; effective tactics; and relentless follow-up and assessment. In sum, it forces accountability on the police administration.

Bratton (1997) claims that before he was Police Commissioner, the inexperience of young or new officers was a major problem in the NYPD:

The emphasis on community policing had resulted in police being assigned to beats in the neighborhood with the responsibility to solve all crime problems. New police officers, many no more than 20 or 21 years old were expected to use problem-solving methodologies associated with community policing to address any crime problem, from youths loitering on street corners to rampant drug dealing on their beats. This approach was not working. Some neighborhoods were so crime-ridden that these young officers could not cope with such complex problems and issues. (p. 37)

Which Police Forces Have Implemented CompStat?

The CompStat program has been implemented in several jurisdictions in the United States and elsewhere. Although the use of crime statistics and crime-/geo-mapping has been introduced in many large urban police departments, most chiefs of police recognize the advantage of this kind of analysis; nonetheless, not all departments have implemented a force-wide program, like the NYPD. In 1999, just five years after it had been proposed, Weisburd et al. (2003) reported "A survey of large police departments (with 100 or more sworn officers) [reported that thirty-three percent] had implemented CompStat or a similar data-driven strategy and that another one-quarter were in the planning stages to implement such a program" (White, 2007, p.117).

In the United States, CompStat or variations of this program have been implemented in: Baltimore (1995), New Orleans (1997), Milwaukee (1997), and Chicago (1999). Additionally, some state police departments have experimented with the program. In June 1998, the State of New York implemented a pilot program called "Crime Analysis Partnerships to Upgrade Regional Enforcement," or CAPTURE, which had a strong

CompStat component. It was the governor's hope that the program would be in force in 10 counties in one year's time (Tulley, 1998).

In sum, CompStat allows for real-time analysis of crime data. Officers are able to determine crime trends by linking similar crimes by method or victim type and by mapping hot spots to a particular area. This is important for visually assessing the short-term effects of arrest rates and crime rates and for evaluating new programs and policies. The program can increase officer morale by allowing officers to become actively involved in crime fighting by presenting collaborative ideas and giving feedback. By having regularly scheduled meetings, communication is increased by using CompStat to discuss similarities between crimes that occur during different shifts. Also, potential problems and problem-solving options can be discussed among officers.

Difficulties with CompStat

As White (2007) notes,

> Although the adoption of CompStat has coincided with crime decreases in several cities, the exact contribution of CompStat to the reduction remains unknown. (pp. 121–122)

Unfortunately, a number of questions surrounding CompStat's usage have not been answered or have been answered insufficiently. The issues include the danger of the public debate being hijacked, problems with the crime statistics, the aggressive nature of CompStat, the reduction of community partnerships, and the small number of independent scientific evaluations of the program.

The Public Debate

Some commentators have argued that the ramifications of CompStat extend beyond the walls of the police headquarters:

> The public debate on policing is in danger of being hi-jacked by the superficial, high profile promotion of 'Zero-Tolerance.' This is the term ascribed by politicians and the media to the policing of New York, without proper analysis of what it means and what it has—or has not—achieved. In many respects, the love affair of CompStat reminds me of the bandwagon posturing that was taking place with community policing or problem-oriented policing. (Pollard, 1997, p. 52)

Problems with the Crime Statistics

Many observers and analysts do not believe that the NYPD had a direct influence on the reduction of the crime rate; instead, critics claim that societal factors, especially demographic processes, including a maturing out of criminals, led to the sharp declines in crime rates (Pollard, 1997). Moreover, some detractors are quick to point out that crime rates have been falling nationwide. Additionally, "the accuracy of the crime figures can be called into question" (p. 52). Some law enforcement agencies have been accused of selectively recoding their statistics to make an area appear safer than it really is. The Baltimore Police Department, for example, has been under news media scrutiny for changing "attempted murder" incidents to "1st degree assaults," which have occurred in the Inner Harbor (where a series of tourist attractions exist), in order to minimize fear among visitors to this part of the city.

Aggressive Policing Methods Against Alleged Criminals

Many commentators have argued that CompStat has led to more aggressive policing practices, including such techniques as saturation policing, zero-tolerance policing, and vertical raids, which involves numerous police descending upon "an apartment block and arresting all those who cannot account for being there" (Pollard, 1997, p. 44). Furthermore, CompStat has contributed to the formation of "confrontational accountability systems within NYPD [right down to the name of the place where CompStat meetings are held], [which is] known as the 'war room'" (p. 44). Some critics have suggested that the changes in the organizational culture has led to more aggressive policing methods, as exemplified by the Louima and Diallo incidents.[2]

Diminished Community Involvement and Partnerships

CompStat arguably places a disproportionate emphasis on police-directed solutions to crime and community-related problems. Rarely are citizens of the impacted jurisdiction or other criminal justice agencies consulted in the problem-solving process (Pollard, 1997). Bratton (1998) adamantly contends that these developments are the result of the improved quality of policing he introduced to the NYPD and that this alone is the reason for the decline in the crime rate. Bratton argues that the crime rate

> did not drop due to changes in socio-demographic trends. Crime is not down because of changes in the economy. The declines may have been affected somewhat by higher prisoner incarceration rates, but the drop in crime in the City has been so precipitous over such a short period that the traditional causes of crime, or what we believed to have been the principle causes of crime increases or reductions, just don't apply. (p. 40)

Some critics argue that the same types of results could have been achieved through community policing methods (Pollard, 1997).

Dearth of Independent Scientific Evaluations

A considerable amount of unfounded hype is written and publicized about CompStat's utility whenever the program is being implemented. Despite the claims of Bratton and other CompStat supporters, the program has not been independently evaluated in such a manner that would conform to normal scientific standards.

Primarily, two types of evaluation are used to determine the effectiveness of policies and practices: process and impact/outcome reviews. The former involves "systematic observation of a program's implementation and activities. The focus is on internal dynamics and how actual operations are organized and carried out. In process evaluations, the aim is to discover what actually is happening and how that compares with what was planned or expected" (Przybylski, 1995, p. 4). During impact/outcome reviews, researchers "attempt to discover outcomes and to attribute them to the program, rather than outside influences. In other words, impact evaluations aim to provide stakeholders information that clearly confirms that the program (or specific activities) does or does not work" (pp. 4–5).

Limited in Effectiveness by Ineffective Leadership

In some circumstances, information generated by CompStat may be seen simply as a way to negatively "bash" supervisors, rather than support crime-fighting efforts. In order to improve the applicability of CompStat statistics, substantial investment is needed to fund the training of officers on the system and to acquire the equipment needed to implement the program. Information from CompStat must be manually compiled into a database that must then be interpreted accurately. The results and speed of this process may differ based on the size and competence of the department.

Inadequately Answered or Unanswered Questions

In every location where CompStat has been implemented, a number of questions about its usage have arisen and not been satisfactorily answered:

1. Does CompStat work better in some jurisdictions than others? If so, why?
2. Is CompStat simply the realization that police middle management has failed to properly do their jobs?
3. Will CompStat supplant community policing?
4. Can CompStat exist simultaneously with community policing programs?

The actual management model created by the CompStat phenomenon has not been accepted wholeheartedly by everyone. According to Bratton (1998), CompStat resulted in a streamlining of the police management hierarchy:

> In 1994, precinct commanders had very little authority to do anything unless headquarters demanded it. We cut through the 'wedding cake' of centralized hierarchical bureaucracy and put the focus on crime prevention and disorder reduction back on the police in the precincts. In other words, we decentralized policing in New York City. (p. 35)

Some people have suggested that this model of policing is "too assertive and that citizens are being abused in significantly greater numbers" (Bratton, p. 41). Bratton and other supporters have suggested that this is not true:

"Did complaints against the police increase? Yes, they did, but it should be noted that there are over 38,000 police officers making over 300,000 arrests and issuing millions of summonses each year. Compare that activity to the approximately 9,000 citizen complaints that were filed in 1996" (p. 41).

To date, only a handful of experts have called into question the causal link between CompStat and crime rates. Although crime decreased in New York City at the same time that CompStat was introduced, crime rates also decreased in other similar cities throughout the United States where the program was nonexistent. Additionally, many experts suggest that there are other reasons for the supposed success of this program: "the maturation of drug markets, the aging and demographics of the country (i.e., baby boomers), declining unemployment rates and a healthy economy and the mass incarceration of drug offenders" (White, 2007, p.118). In New York City, CompStat has continued under Mayor Michael Bloomberg and his Commissioner Raymond Kelly.

Conclusion

Numerous disconnects exist between the rank and file and the management/leadership of police departments. In light of this demanding environment, it is often surprising that a police department can function at all. The willingness to experiment with new models of management bodes well for police departments in the future, despite the fact that bureaucratic and paramilitary organizations tend to change slowly. Programs such as CompStat however must be treated cautiously until more scientifically conducted evaluations are conducted.

Notes

1. Supposedly, the CompStat program was conceived by Jack Maple, NYPD's deputy commissioner of crime strategies. Maple, now deceased, was a former New York Transit Cop.
2. In 1999, Amadou Diallo, a Guinean immigrant, was shot on his doorstep by four plainclothes NYPD officers of the street crime unit who mistakenly thought he was carrying a weapon. The officers fired 41 rounds of ammunition. Amadou was only carrying a soft drink can. In 1997, Abner Louima was arrested, and while in custody, beaten and then sodomized in a station house by an NYPD officer with a nightstick. Both incidents caused considerable negative publicity against the NYPD.

Glossary

William Bratton: Former Police Commissioner of New York City (1994–1996), who is credited with reducing crime in the city by using both CompStat and zero-tolerance policing methods.

CompStat: A relatively new management technique that includes weekly meetings of senior police personnel (especially chief/commissioner, district commanders, etc.) to review the crimes that have occurred in their sector/district/borough in order to monitor crime-reduction responses in those areas. Usually this model involves crime mapping. It was pioneered in New York City during the early 1990s.

Crime mapping: This method uses geo-coded crime statistics to evaluate crime patterns by mapping the locations in which specific crimes take place. The goal is to visualize the patterns of crime.

Leader: An individual who occupies a senior management position in an organization and who demonstrates vision for the organization.

Leadership: The ability to demonstrate and to inspire confidence in the direction that the leaders want to move their organization.

Manager: This individual ensures that the policies and practices of an organization or a subunit are adhered to by monitoring the work of employees or subordinates.

Zero-tolerance policing: The aggressive enforcement of one or more criminal laws in a particular jurisdiction and/or during a specific time period; no discretion is allowed on part of officer.

Chapter Questions

Part One: Multiple Choice Questions

1. Who identified the difference between managers and street cop cultures?
   a. Peel
   b. Reiss
   c. Reuss-Ianni
   d. Vollmer
   e. Wilson

2. Which of the following are management practices that have been implemented in municipal policing in the United States?
   a. CompStat
   b. The Learning Organization
   c. Managing By Objectives
   d. Total Quality Management
   e. All of the above

3. Which chief of police championed the use of CompStat?
   a. Lee Brown
   b. William Bratton
   c. Rudolph Giuliani
   d. Lawrence Sherman
   e. Patrick Murphy

4. Who originally developed the CompStat program?
    a. Jack Maple
    b. Phyllis McDonald
    c. Bill Bratton
    d. Tom Frazier
    e. Lee Brown

5. Which of the following is a difficulty associated with CompStat?
    a. It can lead to aggressive policing.
    b. It has decreased community participation.
    c. It causes problems in the production of crime statistics.
    d. all of the above
    e. none of the above

6. Which of the following is NOT a core component of CompStat?
    a. zero-tolerance policing
    b. accurate and timely reporting of crime statistics
    c. the use of crime mapping techniques
    d. weekly meeting of senior management to review crime in selected sectors, districts, or boroughs
    e. relentless follow-up and assessment

7. Which city was the first, after New York City, to implement a version of CompStat?
    a. Baltimore
    b. Chicago
    c. Los Angeles
    d. Milwaukee
    e. New Orleans

Part Two: Short Answer Questions

1. What is crime mapping?

2. What is the Management by Objectives method, as applied to the context of police departments?

3. What is Total Quality Management?

4. Name two cities other than New York that have implemented CompStat.

5. What are two basic types of evaluation done in social science research?

6. List two reasons why many policies in police departments are not implemented correctly.

Part Three: Essay Questions

1. In your opinion, which approach is more effective for achieving the police mission: CompStat or community policing?

2. In your opinion, how realistic is Guyot's idea about switching police departments' management style over to that found in a typical hospital?

3. Is dislike of "the boss" typical to all organizational frameworks?

4. Can a police leader also be a good manager?

13

CHAPTER

Cooperation/Collaboration with Other Police Departments and Criminal Justice Agencies

Introduction

In policing, a refrain that is all too frequently heard is that the administrative units in the law enforcement agency act as silos that rarely communicate with each other. This complaint can also be extended to the interactions within the individual units. Active, important, and timely dialogue is lacking not only between diverse units, but also within individual divisions themselves. Even in small police departments, where there is more interaction among administrators, rank-and-file officers, and support staff than at larger institutions, failure to cooperate and collaborate is often present. Although good contact may exist between officers and agencies, it does not necessarily mean that collaboration takes place. This situation is typically referred to as *fragmentation* (Stevens, 2009). The first published account of police force fragmentation dates to the 1967 President's Crime Commission, which drew attention to the "fragmented crime repression efforts resulting from the large number of uncoordinated local governments and law enforcement agencies" (U.S. Task Force Report, 1967, p. 68).

What are the general characteristics of cooperation or collaboration? In general, these processes refer to situations in which two or more individuals or organizations work together to achieve the same goal or objective. Cooperation is distinct from the activities tied to alignment and networking. Alignment, a term frequently confused with cooperation and collaboration, happens when two or more individuals or organizations have the same goal or objective, but do not engage in cooperative or collaborative activities. Meanwhile, networking is a process of expanding professional contacts in the hopes of improving one's chances for career mobility or meeting other professional goals.

Undoubtedly, some police departments have more contacts and opportunities for cooperation and collaboration than other agencies. For example, the District of Columbia (Washington, DC) police department, because of its strategic location in the nation's capital, must interface with more than 26 police departments, including four neighboring county entities (i.e., Prince George's, Montgomery, Arlington, and Alexandria) along with numerous federal police forces. However, one must keep in mind that that number of contacts and opportunities for collaboration, does not mean they are used efficiently. The New York City Police Department (NYPD), in the aftermath of the 9/11 terrorist attacks and the initiatives of former Police Commissioner Ray Kelly, was a prime actor in increasing and improving municipal police cooperation with the FBI (McArdle, 2006). Just because another police department is geographically close or because an order or policy is legally binding on both parties does not mean that cooperation and collaboration immediately materialize and solve mutual problems.

Police departments, particularly large organizations, have difficulties with communicating both internally and externally with other actors in the community and other police organizations. However, communication is only one aspect of a larger problem related to cooperation and collaboration. The challenges that police officers often have within their communities were reviewed earlier in this book; this chapter will focus specifically at the relationships between police agencies and other criminal justice organizations in terms of cooperation and collaboration. In particular, this chapter is designed to answer the following questions:

- What are cooperation and collaboration?
- In what contexts do police agencies cooperate and collaborate internally, with each other, and with outside participants?
- Should there be more or less cooperation and collaboration in the police force?
- Do you think it is easy or difficult for police agencies to cooperate or collaborate well?
- How can cooperation and collaboration be better fostered?

This chapter will not deal with the issues of written or spoken communication. Although important, these are subcomponents of the wider problem of cooperation.[1]

What Is Collaboration?

Although widely recognized as a major problem, few scholars have actually examined the organizational challenge of cooperation/collaboration in the context of municipal policing. Geller and Morris's study (1992) is, however, one of the primary research projects analyzing this issue. During the course of their investigation, they reviewed the jurisdictional obstacles for collaboration between federal and local law enforcement officers. Geller and Morris argue that the major cause for the lack of communication is: "[the] dynamic interaction between our Constitutional architecture, which allocates power among levels of government, and the operational needs of a nation whose communities and states are highly interdependent" (p. 246). This interaction, they state, is both a blessing and a curse. Their discussion mainly traces the history of federal local collaboration in terms of technical assistance, information sharing, and legal relationships.

Basics of Police Cooperation

Police, by virtue of their role in the criminal justice system, are in contact with different branches such as the courts and occasionally probation and parole. Active duty police officers are frequently asked to testify in court cases. This usually means contact with a prosecutor, and depending on the jurisdiction grand juries too. Police must present the relevant evidence in the criminal case for which they may later be asked to testify.

Over the past two decades this task has evolved into selected partnerships between police and prosecutors, sometimes mandated by state law, that have tackled aggressive driving, prostitution, vagrancy, and drug dealing. Although this kind of relationship historically has been restricted to the judicial branch, some police departments are partnering with correctional agencies (particularly parole) (Parent and Snyder, 1999). These relationships can improve the amount and quality of probation and parole supervision, the arrest of individuals who have violated the conditions of their probation and parole, improved dissemination of intelligence, neighborhood improvement, and helping inmates reenter society. On the other hand, police-corrections partnerships suffer from "mission distortion," the problem of a blurring of the respective roles of criminal justice practitioners (Murphy and Worrall, 2007).

Multijurisdictional Task Forces

Over the past two decades, police departments at local, state, and federal levels have assembled units of officers with expertise in particular types of crimes. In general, they work for limited periods to monitor and collect evidence that can lead to indictments against organized crime groups (e.g., rings) specializing in car-jacking, drug and gun sales, and other such illegal activities. Additionally, the officers may also work occasionally on terrorism-related cases. These units have become highly controversial as they are often expensive to run and their activities are rarely subject to evaluation (Smith, Novak, Frank, and Travis, 2000).[2]

Cooperation in the Post-9/11 Era

With the passage of the PATRIOT Act, the role of many large municipal police forces has expanded significantly (Manning, 2006). In New York City, for example, the NYPD has become more proactive, increasing the number of street stops in neighborhoods and subway stations where illegal immigrants may pass or congregate, at the Port Authority where immigrant taxi cab drivers may pick up and drop off their fares, and at the bridge and tunnel entrances and exits that commuters use to get into and out of Manhattan (McArdle, 2006). The NYPD has also established closer connections with the federal Immigration and Customs Enforcement (ICE). The increased activity of the municipal police forces is somewhat controversial. Some chiefs and commissioners of police have embraced this extra responsibility for their rank and file, while others have indicated that they do not have the resources to be fulfilling what they deem is essentially a federal responsibility.

Dynamics of Cooperation and Collaboration

The issue of collaboration begs several questions, including: What is collaboration, and why is it perceived to be important? Furthermore, there is a widespread belief that collaboration is beneficial in nature; the more collaborative activities exist, the greater the benefits to police departments and the communities they serve. Clearly, there are advantages and disadvantages to collaboration in policing settings. This chapter will present several examples in which collaboration occurs.

The following discussion will examine the advantages and disadvantages of collaboration among and in municipal police departments.

Advantages of Collaboration

On the positive side, collaboration opens up the opportunity for scarce resources to be better shared, utilized, and leveraged. As a result, cost savings can be achieved (Geller and Morris, 1992). In this context, collaboration is perceived as a positive process. Collaboration may help with mentoring, training, and achieving particular unit goals. With respect to the rank-and-file employees, collaboration can provide additional opportunities to help facilitate the exchange of information and to develop and administer new programs. In short, collaboration among the various units is a goal that can help police agencies to achieve their missions.

Drawbacks of Collaboration

There are at least six primary impediments to collaborative activity:

1. Since no widely agreed-upon terminology or definitions exist, it is difficult to operationalize and measure cooperation and collaboration.

2. Police departments are typically evaluated based on crimes solved and/or cases closed. Thus, since there is no measurable system for rewarding collaboration, this issue may not receive much attention from researchers or employees.

3. Everyone, from support staff to police officers to administrators, believes that he or she is working very hard and that it is difficult to balance competing demands. Police staff members often think that their work load is higher than that of other police departments or other criminal justice agencies. In an environment such as this, collaboration is not perceived to be an organizational priority. Although employees may work hard, multiple, competing measures of efficiency countermand the trend toward collaboration.

4. Mandating that units collaborate, and depending on smaller divisions to do this on their own, often does not allow organizations to achieve their discrete sets of objectives.

5. The incentive system does not support collaborative endeavors between unsworn personnel, police officers, and supervisors. At issue is the idea of how to measure individual investment in collaborative activities so that the endeavors can be reflected in each officer's annual performance review and salary determination.

6. There are significant differences in the organizational work expectations and reward structures, among the broad range of work units. It is thus difficult to convince personnel from various departments that collaboration is beneficial to all.

To help promote a cooperative environment, an organizational culture that stresses win-win relationships, rather than competition, should be emphasized and rewarded. Collaboration is dependent on having reliable and experienced frontline personnel, administrators, and support staff in place. Additionally, collaboration often works best among motivated individuals. For example, instead of an order being given, it is most effective when a police officer in one division contacts another about possibly working together on a new project or mutual challenge. And thus in this situation, collaborative initiatives come from the bottom up.

What are the effects of the failure to cooperate? Stevens (2009) cautions that this failure periodically leads to

> duplication in crime labs, investigations and training academies, and it sometimes produces difficulty with prosecution and court proceedings . . . it could also lead to displacement of crime from one jurisdiction to another. . . . The failure to develop consistent standards means that officers are hired, trained, and disciplined in a different manner leading to disparities in policing various communities, and fewer opportunities for detection and control of police corruption." (p. 165)

Organizational Forms of Law Enforcement

As mentioned earlier, police and law enforcement officers are expected to cooperate with colleagues from other units in a variety of situations (e.g., public safety model, consolidation, mutual aid, task force approach). Whether or not the expectation becomes reality is often uncertain. Rarely is the process a smooth one, as there are several impediments to this process. The next section expands on the most common obstacles to cooperation.

Obstacles to the Implementation of Effective Cooperative or Collaborative Endeavors in Police Departments

At least three major factors frustrate the cooperative/collaborative process. First, those wanting to implement joint initiatives often are powerless in the police organizations and thus feel timid about pursuing such a strategy. Also, the policies, practices, and technology that police officers depend on change rapidly. Finally, cooperation requires a large investment of limited resources that most police departments want to protect and not share.

Lack of Seniority

In policing, in order for police officers to rise up through the ranks, they must pass the appropriate tests, take on increasing roles of management and leadership, and move into positions of higher authority as they come open. Recruits and those who are relatively new to the force soon learn that if they are going to survive on the job, they should not take risks or adopt stances that could be viewed negatively by fellow officers and senior administrators; otherwise their superiors will not develop positive opinions about them and possibly frustrate their ability to advance in their careers. Although officers may want to cooperate or collaborate with sister agencies, they often soon learn that such initiatives are often not appreciated and may even inadvertently make their superiors look bad and/or incompetent (Scott, Brock, and Crawford, 2000).

Policies and Technology Evolve Quickly

Not only can there be problems related to organizational delegation, but in many instances, policies, practices, techniques, and technologies evolve so quickly that they cause difficulties. In some cases, new standards are sent to a collaborating agency only to be quickly revised, causing the recipient agency to lag behind. According to Scott, Brock, and Crawford (2000), technology presents another hurdle to collaborative efforts:

> One additional obstacle to the implementation of effective networking in criminal justice has been the fact that the state of technology has been evolving so quickly. . . . It can take years or decades to plan and consummate an

information sharing network. Once implemented, the equipment is effectively obsolete almost as soon as it goes on-line. Agency budgets cannot compete with the relatively cash-rich NCIC which has federal funding. (p. 5)

Costs of Cooperation

Significant financial and staffing resources are necessary for implementing successful cooperative or collaborative projects between police and criminal justice agencies. Even the simplest of projects requires an officer or administrator to spend time working with a sister agency. Much time is spent on explaining an existing or emerging concern or mutual interest. These efforts result in a reduction in the number of hours that can be spent on patrol, supervision, or investigative duties. Instead, the hours must be invested in getting the other agency and its members up to speed on new processes, developments, or intelligence (Scott, Brock, and Crawford, 2000).

Examples of Contemporary Police Interagency Cooperation/Collaboration

Over the past nine decades, numerous programs and institutions encouraging cooperation among international, federal, state, and local policing entities have been established. The following is a brief summary of some of the most important collaborative efforts to date.

International Criminal Police Organization (INTERPOL)

Founded in 1923 and assuming its current name in 1956, this organization is a clearing house for law enforcement agencies when they need information on suspects, crimes, and criminals throughout the world. Interpol has 188 member countries and is headquartered in Lyons, France. As of 2010, its Secretary General is American Ronald Noble, former undersecretary of the U.S. Department of Treasury Bureau of Law Enforcement during the Clinton Administration (www.interpol.int).

National Crime Information Center (NCIC)

Established in 1967 by the FBI, this secure, Internet-accessible national database contains criminal history information and warrants on individuals around the country. Updated information is submitted from police departments in all 50 states. Officers can access the NCIC via computers located in their cars, or they can contact their dispatchers, who can pull up the information on their behalf. Not only is this information accessible by the FBI, but it is also available to U.S. police agencies, the Royal Canadian Mounted Police, and police in the Commonwealth of Puerto Rico. According to Geller and Morris (1992), "NCIC enables law enforcement authorities to make immediate checks for stolen property, wanted persons or warrant information, criminal history data, and missing children" (p. 292).

Regional Information Sharing System (RISS)

Started in 1977 and based in Phoenix, Arizona, this program exists to "enhance the ability of local, state, and federal criminal justice agencies to identify, target, and remove criminal activities and conspiracies spanning jurisdictional boundaries" (Hughes, 1989, p. 6).

Violent Criminal Apprehension Program (VICAP)

In 1985, the FBI started VICAP with a goal to "collect, collate, analyze, and disseminate under appropriate circumstances information about specified categories of violent crime" (Geller and Morris, 1992, p. 294). Some of the more important categories are "solved or unsolved homicides, missing person cases, . . . and cases in which unidentified descendents have been found and homicide is or may be the cause of death" (p. 294). This database is helpful in identifying patterns of serial killings and the evidence needed in the investigations of the same.

Technical Assistance, Technology, and Training (TATT)

Created by the Washington, D.C.-based Police Foundation in 1987, TATT "is meant to help law enforcement departments integrate research into practice. This is especially important given the mindset in some policing agencies that intuition is preferable to anything quantifiable" (Scott, Brock, and Crawford, 2000, p. 4).

Crime Mapping Research Center

Begun during the mid-1990s, and administered by the National Institute of Justice, this unit issues grants, training, and professional seminars and conferences to encourage both researchers and law enforcement agencies to engage in crime mapping as a tool in policing.

Community Safety Information System

Started in 2000 in Winston-Salem, North Carolina, as a joint initiative of five police jurisdictions supported by resources from the National Institute of Justice, this program was intended to "integrate criminal justice and non-criminal justice data and promote data-driven approaches to solving and preventing crime" (Scott, Brock, and Crawford, 2000, p. 4). The program was established to monitor and prevent crime by juvenile offenders.

Problems with Cooperative Efforts

To date, most cooperative initiatives have received little scholarly attention. They also have rarely been evaluated using social scientific methods. Thus, the claims of their success, usually anecdotal in tone and typically issued by their directors and funders, and criticisms of their failures, often expressed by administrators or employees who have been fired, investigative journalists, or members of the public, must be accepted cautiously. Many of these programs can be interpreted as fads or as creative ways to obtain grant funding from different state and federal agencies.

Conclusion

Although cooperation/collaboration among different units inside and outside a police organization is important, often this is wishful thinking rather than accepted reality. This is difficult because policing organizations function in a competitive world in which important information is guarded carefully. Since profit concerns are often key issues in the private sector, collaboration is not a typical normative response in the world of non-profit law enforcement. Other performance measures, such as crime rates, community satisfaction, or fear of crime are stressed, because in part they are more tangible and easy to determine by both insiders and outsiders. Cooperation/collaboration in many respects will for the short term be an elusive goal among police departments.

Notes

1. Those wishing to read a helpful discussion on communication inside police departments are encouraged to read chapter 9 of Swanson, Territo, and Taylor (2008).
2. Other task forces combining law enforcement personnel from different levels of government that have been implemented include: Operation Ceasefire that operated in Boston, MA in 1995; Project Exile, which had its origins in Richmond, VA in 1994; and Project Safe Neighborhoods that started in 2001. Each target a specific type of crime and criminal.

Glossary

Alignment: This occurs when two or more individuals or organizations have the same goal or objective but do not necessarily engage in cooperative or collaborative actions.

Collaboration: This happens when two or more individuals or organizations are working together to achieve the same goal or objective.

Fragmentation: A term used to describe organizations whose component parts either do not make sense or who appear to be dysfunctional.

INTERPOL: International clearing house for law enforcement agencies when they need information on suspects, crimes, and criminals throughout the world.

National Criminal Information Center: A secure national database that contains computer-accessible criminal history information and individual warrants. Information is submitted by agencies throughout the 50 states. Officers can access the NCIC via computers located in their cars, or they can contact their dispatchers to access the database on their behalf.

Networking: The process of expanding one's professional contacts to improve professional chances for career mobility or commercial success.

Violent Criminal Apprehension Program (VICAP): Federal database that stores information about violent crime activities and individuals. Helps in distinguishing patterns of serial killings and the evidence needed in the investigations of the same.

Chapter Questions

Part One: Multiple Choice Questions

1. Which of the following is true about collaboration and cooperation?
   a. only takes place in large police departments
   b. primarily occurs in small police agencies
   c. mainly takes place in municipal rather than state police departments
   d. occurs in all types of police departments
   e. none of the above

2. Among the following options, which is the most important advantage of collaboration among police departments?
   a. serves as a deterrent to criminals
   b. facilitates the teaching of ethics to police officers
   c. keeps criminals off-guard
   d. helps organizations share information
   e. all of the above

3. What is the strongest disadvantage of collaboration among police departments?
   a. increases the possibility of solving crime
   b. provides additional resources
   c. is difficult to coordinate the varying opinions and information sources
   d. enhances communication among organizations
   e. none of the above

4. Which of the following are obstacles to the implementation of effective networking in criminal justice agencies?
   a. Those wanting to implement initiatives have no seniority in the agencies in question.
   b. Technology evolves quickly.
   c. Not all police agencies can afford to support networking opportunities.
   d. all of the above
   e. none of the above

5. Which organization has developed a well-known crime mapping center?
   a. IACP
   b. NICHD
   c. NIJ
   d. ACJS
   e. ASC

6. Which of the following programs and/or institutions is NOT established to encourage cooperation among international, federal, state, and local policing entities?
   a. RESPECT
   b. RISS
   c. NCIC
   d. VICAP
   e. TATT

7. Which cooperative effort has been successfully used to investigate serial killers?
   a. INTERPOL
   b. National Crime Information Center
   c. Regional Information Sharing System
   d. Violent Criminal Apprehension Program
   e. Crime Mapping Research Center

Part Two: Short Answer Questions

1. Define alignment.

2. What is collaboration?

3. What is crime mapping?

4. List two reasons why cooperation is important for police departments.

5. What are five collaborative programs that involve municipal police in the United States?

Part Three: Essay Questions

1. Is there a relationship between cooperation, communication, and an officer's desire for promotion?

2. Which cooperative local, state, and federal law enforcement programs appear to be the most helpful? Which ones do not seem beneficial? Support your responses with concrete reasons.

3. Are there any dangers connected to information sharing among police departments? Clearly outline these and make suggestions for improvement.

14
CHAPTER

Underfunding

Introduction

In addition to enforcing the law, conducting order maintenance, and providing additional essential services, police departments must manage their payrolls, make necessary purchases of goods and services, budget for income and expenses, and provide a functional system for accounting purposes. Lack of adequate resources, particularly money, has long plagued many police departments across the United States. In most municipalities, law enforcement agencies are given a heavy burden and are asked to perform difficult tasks. Without proper financial resources, police forces simply cannot function properly and effectively. All aspects of police work require money: salaries, purchasing of new equipment, training, benefits, bonuses, and maintenance of police vehicles, computers, and communication systems. Additional funds are required to purchase, renovate, and/or improve the departmental infrastructure, such as buildings and offices.

With increased resources, a municipal police department can afford to place additional officers on the streets, to engage in community policing, and to pay its officers for overtime as needed. The problems related to limited financial means have become apparent in many cash-strapped American cities, such as Baltimore, Newark, and Wilmington, where high crime rates strongly motivate voters and politicians to lobby for additional police officers; however, the financial reality is that existing officers cannot even work overtime due to budget limitations.

Police departments often have to work with outdated vehicles, electronic equipment, and communication technology, but they are also regularly asked to make cutbacks. Merely maintaining old technology, including vehicles, is costly.

> Most law enforcement agencies cannot afford to purchase the type of highly technical equipment needed to counter the technology of a criminal enterprise. The needs for sophisticated surveillance equipment, computers, motor vehicles for undercover operations, and other extraordinary purchases can explode a government budget. (Hawkins 1999, p. 26)

Police agencies—in particular, the administration—primarily finance their organizations through local tax dollars. Each year they must manage the affairs of the department within the confines of an annual budget, a document that both predicts the expected costs for operating the organization and helps allocate and track expenditures. This process is accommodated by a budget cycle (i.e., a series of steps through which a police department submits a proposed budget to be approved by the local government body, usually on an annual basis).

Despite all of the planning that goes into a budget, there are always "budget busters." These are unforeseen expenditures that may include: natural disasters (e.g., earthquakes, floods, hurricanes, mudslides, wildfires, winter snows); "steep increases in expenditures" (e.g., gasoline); "prolonged searches for missing persons"; demonstrations, protests, strikes, and riots; "complex investigations seeking to apprehend [certain types of criminals]"; terrorist attacks; protracted union strikes; and industrial disasters (Swanson, Territo, and Taylor, 2008, p. 494). Budget busters are almost always contextual. For example, "In very small departments, the budget may be 'busted' by lesser events, such as having to replace a copier machine or buying a new patrol car because of an accident" (p. 494).

Federal, state, and local police forces in the United States cost about $480 million dollars a year (U.S. Bureau of Justice Statistics, 2005). How is the majority of this money spent? Approximately 85% is allocated to salaries, while the balance is used to maintain the infrastructure (e.g., buildings, communications systems, police vehicles).

Contextual Issues

Police departments have numerous limitations placed on their budgets by other outside parties. One of them is the requirement to implement federal laws and provisions with little or no additional resources to accomplish these goals. In recent years, these unfunded mandates included rules and regulations embedded in various legislative acts, such as the Immigration Reform and Control Act of 1986, Americans with Disabilities Act, Clear Air Act, and Homeland Security Act (Swanson et al., 2008, p. 496).

Moreover, some municipalities have little flexibility in how they manage their financial affairs. Many of these restrictions date back to the stock market crash of 1929, when cities went bankrupt and had to be bailed out or rescued by their states. "As a result, many states passed laws which regulate local finance in such areas as revenue sources, tax collection, level of permissible indebtedness, and budgeting. A system of financial reports was also added which the states monitor carefully" (Swanson et al., 2008, p. 497). A number of other legal guidelines affect how municipal police departments run their financial affairs, including "the city or county charter, ordinances, executive orders, regulations, and customary practices, . . . [and] the form of local government (e.g., mayor versus council dominated, or city-manager run). . . . These generalizations are affected by other factors, such as how much influence a long-serving finance director has accrued and the degree

Exhibit 14.1   **Budget Formats**

In order for police departments and public safety agencies to keep track of the money (and assets) they have, need, and spend, one of five basic types of budget formats is adopted: line item, program, performance, zero-based, and hybrid. Each format has advantages and disadvantages. A line item budget is simple and lists all income and expenses into basic categories. A program budget is organized according to each of the different functions the organization pursues. A performance budget is based on the core functions of the agency organization. With zero-based budgeting, the agency budget is assumed to be zero at the end of the year, and the organization must argue for each individual, prospective expenditure. A hybrid budget usually combines elements of the other budget types and is tailored to the unique circumstances of the organization. Although a municipality may specify the type of budget that a police department or agency must use, a skilled police chief or commissioner can use the budget to lobby for extra resources.

to which a council is more or less proactive in the budget process" (p. 497). (See Exhibit 14.1.)

According to Cordner and Scarborough (2007):

> Many police administrators have little understanding of the budgeting process; their budgets tend to be the same each year, with minor increases or decreases depending on the state of the treasury. This kind of copycat budgeting provides for no evaluation on the actual desirability of various programs and budget categories and leaves no room for innovation. No effort is made to determine what kinds of expenditures might bring the organization closer to achieving its goals and objectives. As a rule, only incremental changes are made. (p. 85)

Solutions

Police administrators are not powerless in the face of the financial burdens that their agencies experience. Through a combination of experience, skill, and creativity, many police departments have thrived and managed to close the gap between needs/wants and available resources. This process includes taking advantage of income from fines and traffic ticket revenue, securing grants, obtaining donations, seizing assets from criminals and their enterprises, assessing user fees, increased use of civilians, consolidation, and subcontracting.

Fines and Traffic Ticket Revenue

Some jurisdictions allow police agencies to add to their budgets through money collected in the context of traffic enforcement (including parking and moving violations). Although many members of the public think that police officers get a commission for this kind of activity they may get overtime for court appearances if those ticketed contest the charge.

Federal and Private Foundation Grants

Periodically many federal departments have funds and equipment that are available for disbursement to state and local law enforcement agencies. Sometimes distribution of this money is considered part of their mandates, while at other times, the funds become available after the passage of special legislation or an act of Congress. Agencies that have made funds available for disbursement include:

- Department of Homeland Security
- National Highway Traffic Safety Administration
- Community Oriented Policing Services (COPS), part of the USDOJ.

The COPS office, established through the *Violent Crime Control Enforcement Act* of 1994, made $9 million available for police departments to hire officers to engage in community policing activities, purchase new technology (especially laptop computers), and pay for civilian salaries as long as it could be demonstrated that it would free up officers time to engage in community policing.

Donation and Fundraising Programs

Occasionally police departments and their allies in the local community establish a fund to raise money on a short term/temporary basis to fund critical police functions and purchase equipment. Fundraising efforts may be used to send police officers to special training, to purchase new communications equipment (e.g., Blackberries), or to send police officers to police games (i.e., an annual event where police departments compete in athletic and work-related competitions) because this has been cut from their budget (Swanson et al., 2008). In addition,

> a number of departments have created non-profit foundations to raise funds. Typically, this has been done in the larger cities to provide unique opportunities for growth, support, and change. The New York City Police Foundation helps support NYCPD detectives who are posted throughout the world to forge relationships and gather information on threats to New York City. (p. 520)

Forfeiture Laws and Practices

Forfeiture laws allow governments to seize the assets of an individual, organization, or business charged and/or convicted of violating the law without requiring the government to compensate the suspected or convicted criminal. These laws are frequently used by law enforcement agencies against entities that engage in racketeering and drug trafficking. Forfeiture prevents the individual or organization in question from continuing to benefit from illegal activities. It may also minimize the ability of individuals and organizations charged with a crime to pay for a vigorous legal defense. Although the law differentiates between civil and criminal forfeiture (Aylesworth, 1992), in civil forfeiture police may seize "vehicles used to transport contraband, equipment used to manufacture illegal drugs, cash used in illegal transactions, computer and technology used to further a crime, and property purchased with the proceeds of a crime" (Hawkins, 1999, p. 24). In general, forfeitures are monitored by the U.S. Department of Justice to prevent abuse of this practice.

There are numerous advantages to forfeiture laws and practices, including deterring the criminal and others engaging in similar illegal activities or considering committing a crime; taking the illegal goods and assets out of circulation; improving the morale of police officers; and sustaining both a forfeiture unit and the police agency in general (Hawkins, 1999).

> Most officers are frustrated by the criminal justice system and its lack of deterrent and remedial effect on crime and criminals. Officers see criminals arrested day after day, with very little, if any, punishment occurring to these criminals in our system of justice. . . . By taking property and the illicit means for criminals to operate, officers can see the immediate effect their actions can have on the offender. (p. 26)

In the context of forfeiture, "the laws serve two purposes: (1) criminals are prevented from profiting from their illegal acts and (2) the seized assets can be used by law enforcement agencies to fund important initiatives" (Swanson et al., 2008, p. 522).

Needless to say, forfeiture laws and practices are controversial. "Some agencies confiscate large sums of property for minor offences without considering the proportionality principle of the law. Other agencies use the incentive of obtaining property and goods as a goal, rather than dismantling and disrupting a criminal enterprise" (Hawkins, 1999, p. 27). In some instances, police and law enforcement agencies specifically target real or alleged criminals and their organizations for investigation because of the assets these targets possess rather than the actual harm they do to the community.

Hawkins advocates five basic ways to prevent forfeiture-related failures: better training for officers doing this kind of work; proper planning to avoid taking the items of innocent individuals and/or specific assets of the accused that will simply be returned to them later; simultaneous arrest of the individual and the seizure of the assets; publicity about law enforcement activities, including informing the public where and how the assets are used; and development of a tracking mechanism for all forfeiture activities. Closely tied to forfeiture practices, many police departments hold sales and auctions of lost property that is not claimed. This added revenue helps agencies in important ways.

User Fees and Police Taxes

In some jurisdictions, after two false alarms at a residence or business, a police department will send the property owners and/or occupants a bill. Another fee-based service involves job clearance issues. If one needs to have one's fingerprints taken in order to apply for a job that requires a security clearance or for immigration-related purposes, some police departments will provide this service for a fee. Finally, in some cities, if one is deemed the at-fault driver in a motor vehicle accident, the police will charge for the investigation.

Use of Civilians/"Civilianization"

Many police departments now recognize the benefits of using both paid and volunteer civilians in the running of police departments. Often civilians can do a job at a fraction of the cost associated having a new police officer do the job. Civilian employees can be utilized in secretarial or clerical functions, in custodial, in training, and in dispatch. "Departments spend a significant amount of money to recruit, train, and outfit sworn police personnel" (White, 2007, p. 152). Most research suggests that many police officers' jobs have little to do with crime-related matters, a fact that encourages the use of civilians in the departmental context, White (2007) suggests:

> There are a number of roles on both the administrative and field services sides of the department that can be sufficiently filled by civilians, rather than the more costly and more hard-to-find sworn officers. These include positions in communications (i.e., dispatch, research and planning, crime analysis, crime scene investigation, traffic, and even calls for service where only reports will be taken (i.e., reports of stolen property). . . . The controversial issue surrounding civilianization is not whether it is a viable option (most agree that it is), but rather, how civilianized should the department become? Although civilians are generally paid less than sworn police, it is necessary to pay more to those with specialized skills such as crime analysts, computer experts, and crime scene investigators. . . . In many places, police unions have become wary of civilianization, viewing civilian personnel as a threat to their livelihood. (pp. 152–153)

As departments become increasingly civilianized, police chiefs must be cautious of the impact of this trend on police officer morale. Police officers may feel that their jobs are in jeopardy. A divided police department with tension between sworn and non-sworn personnel creates an unhealthy and unproductive work environment.

Consolidation

There are numerous small police departments in the United States, and the cost of maintaining them is very high. As early as 1973, the National Advisory Commission on Criminal Justice Standards and Goals recommended that departments with less than 10 officers should be amalgamated. Those who agree with this position have argued that "consolidation should lead to better communication and co-operation among police, better training . . . of the police service, and less duplication of services" (White, 2007, p. 153). Some research has been done on the benefits of consolidation in the United States. One such study looked at this process in Pennsylvania (Grimmel, 1997), and it presented predictable outcomes. Nevertheless, there are downsides to consolidation. For example, police agencies are often reluctant to give up their autonomy, and local residents frequently feel that a larger agency may not be as responsive to their needs as a smaller unit.

Subcontracting

Another method used by police departments and municipalities to minimize costs involves contracting out for services. This approach is especially prominent in smaller jurisdictions. "This strategy is particularly attractive for small towns who can buy police services from larger contiguous towns, county sheriff's departments and state police agencies" (White, 2007, p. 154). There are some drawbacks, though, to contracting out, as White cautions:

> . . . the loss of sense of independence or autonomy, less identification between police and the community, and potential conflicts among communities sharing police service. Also, a community that disbands its police department in favor of contracting for services will be forced to fire their police officers (unless there is an arrangement that they be hired by the other agency). (p. 154)

Among the different criminal justice agencies, police departments have been some of the slowest to subcontract their various job functions.

Conclusion

Although most police departments suffer from underfunding, creative and experienced chiefs, police commissioners, and senior bureaucrats can often develop new and appropriate ways to increase their revenues. From police officers standing at the side of the road to accept donations, to the selling of tickets to police-sponsored raffles and banquets, police officers can be involved in collecting funds. One way to influence local politics is for local police chiefs to frequently explain to city councils and the local media why they need more money for their departments. Unfortunately, this can quickly become a game of smoke and mirrors. As police chiefs gain more experience in budgeting matters, raising additional funds and managing budgets typically becomes easier for them.

Glossary

Budget: A document that both predicts expected operating costs for an organization and helps allocate and track expenditures.

Budget buster: An unexpected occurrence that forces a police department to exceed its original budget (e.g., natural disasters).

Budget cycle: A series of steps through which a police department submits a proposed budget to be approved by the local government body, usually on an annual basis.

Budget format: The organized layout in which a budget is arranged.

Line item budget: A simple budget format that categorizes all income and expenses into basic categories.

Hybrid budget: A budget that typically evolves over time and combines elements of the other budget types. It is tailored to the unique circumstances of each organization.

Performance budget: A budget that is organized along the core functions of the agency organization.

Program budget: A budget that is based on the various functions that an organization pursues.

Zero-based budget: As each budget year ends, the agency budget is assumed to be zero. From this perspective, an organization must argue for each individual, prospective expenditure.

Chapter Questions

Part One: Multiple Choice Questions

1. Which of the following is NOT a common way that police departments can supplement their budget?
   a. federal and private foundation grants
   b. donation and fundraising programs
   c. forfeiture laws
   d. policeman's ball
   e. user fees and police taxes

2. Which of the following is the term used for an unexpected occurrence that may force a police department to spend more money than initially planned?
   a. budget buster
   b. budget cycle
   c. zero-based budgeting
   d. both b and c
   e. none of the above

3. Which of the following is NOT an unfunded federal mandate that has had a financial impact on American police departments?
   a. Americans with Disabilities Act
   b. The Clean Air Act
   c. Homeland Security Act
   d. Prisoner Rape Elimination Act
   e. Immigration Reform and Control Act of 1986

4. Which of the following are federal agencies that have made money available to police departments over the past decade?
   a. Department of Homeland Security
   b. National Highway Traffic Safety Administration
   c. Community Oriented Policing Services (COPS)
   d. all of the above
   e. none of the above

5. When police charge residents for responding to false alarms, this is an example of:
   a. fees
   b. foundation grants
   c. donations
   d. forfeiture laws
   e. none of the above

6. Forfeiture laws are
   a. used by every large police department in the United States
   b. used by very few large police departments in the United States
   c. earn police departments a considerable amount of income
   d. controversial
   e. none of the above

Part Two: Short Answer Questions

1. What are four budget busters for police departments?

2. Beyond yearly appropriations from the municipal or state government, list four basic ways a police department can secure more funding.

3. What is a forfeiture law, as applied within the context of a police department?

4. What is a budget cycle?

5. List four legal guidelines that may affect how municipal police departments manage their financial affairs.

Part Three: Essay Questions

1. Do you see any problems with the mechanisms that police departments use to supplement their budgets?

2. List four basic budget formats used in police departments. Why is a discussion of budget formats important to understanding municipal policing in the United States?

3. Most police academies do not teach recruits the principles of accounting such as budgets. How then do police chiefs/commissioners learn this type of knowledge?

Inadequate Wages and Compensation

Introduction

Police officers, like other criminal justice practitioners, often feel that they are not paid adequately and that their benefits (e.g., education, health, retirement) are not equivalent to their positions. This perspective can be the source of numerous issues, such as the difficulties related to the hiring of appropriate candidates and the retaining of effective officers. On some occasions, perceptions concerning inadequate wages and compensation may lead some police officers to perform their duties at less than adequate levels and/or to succumb to the temptations of corruption in order to boost their salaries.

Although this problem was especially prevalent during the political era of policing (see chapter 2) in the 1960s, this challenge has recently resurfaced. One of the most visible effects of inadequate wages and compensation has been the separation of the rank and file and the higher officer ranks into separate unions (i.e., organizations that are legally entitled to represent their member-workers in contractual matters that involve an employer). The unions have lobbied for increased longevity pay, shift differential pay, better retirement and death benefits for surviving children and spouses, time-and-a-half for overtime, and compensation for court-related absences (Gammage and Sachs, 1972; Hervey and Feuiile, 1973; Levi, 1977).

Overview

One of the most important responses to poor wages and working conditions has involved the creation of police associations and unions by the rank and file. These organizations have both advantages and disadvantages. Most personal opinions about the groups are grounded in the specific kind of police organization in which one is involved or the particular role that one plays in the provision of police services (e.g., consumer, commentator). Several different unions represent the diverse interests of police officers (i.e., the rank and file) and the police professionals at various ranks. At the officer level, the Fraternal Order of Police (FOP), the Patrolmen's Benevolent

Exhibit 15.1   The Boston Police Strike of 1919
In 1919, Boston Police Commissioner E. V. Curtis rejected the rank and file's new union. In response, approximately 1,100 police officers went on strike for four days. As a result, crime increased in the city during this time, including murders, looting, and property damage. In order to re-establish control, Governor Calvin Coolidge (who later politically benefitted from his decisive behavior during this historical event in his platform for the presidency of the United States) called out 5,000 members of the National Guard. All of the officers participating in the strike were fired, and the press vilified the strikers as "Bolsheviks." Adding insult to injury, spokesmen for the American Federation of Labor publicly stated that the officers had acted inappropriately and pulled the AFL chapter out of Boston, frustrating for decades the ability of the police to unionize (Slater, 2009).

Association (PBA), International Union of Police Associations (IUPA), and the International Brotherhood of Teamsters (IBT) are the four most prominent organizations.

Police unions in the United States have a long and tumultuous history, including a number of violent labor actions (see Exhibit 15.1). The first union was formed in 1894 by New York City police officers and was called the Patrolmen's Benevolent Association. In 1915, officers from Pittsburgh formed a similar organization called the Fraternal Order of Police (FOP). Four years later, 33 police associations and unions joined the American Federation of Labor (AFL), one of the largest labor unions at that time. Approximately 73% of all police departments are unionized (Reaves and Hickman. 2004). Almost all of the big city police departments have unions, while smaller police departments are less likely to have them. Unions are typically affiliated with either the Fraternal Order of Police (FOP) or the International Union of Police Associations (IUPA).

The Emergence of Collective Bargaining

During the 1960s and 1970s, a number of factors contributed to increased unionization and public-sector collective bargaining. *Collective bargaining* refers to the process whereby unions negotiate with employers over matters concerning remuneration, benefits, and working conditions. These issues are reflected in a collective agreement (i.e., contract). Swanson, Territo, and Taylor (2008) list the significant forces that motivate collective bargaining:

(1) the needs of labor organizations;
(2) the reduction of legal barriers;

(3) police frustration with the perceived lack of support for their 'war on crime';
(4) personnel practices in police agencies;
(5) salaries and benefits;
(6) an increase in violence directed at police; and
(7) the success of police departments already unionized in making an impact through collective action. (p. 458)

The Needs of Labor Organizations

Labor organizations, like most groups, seek to maintain or increase their power base. In the case of labor unions, this is typically done by expanding their membership. Why do they do this? The goal is to increase the union's sphere of influence and power. Unions have long recognized that there is strength in numbers, a truism that has motivated the growth of many unions over the past century. Up until the 1960s, labor organizations primarily recruited within the private sector. When public employees were granted the right to collective bargaining, labor unions saw new fields from which to garner new members.

The Reduction of Legal Barriers

The passage of the National Labor Relations Act in 1935 gave workers in the private sector the right to collective bargaining. In 1959, the State of Wisconsin became the first state to grant these same rights to public-sector (i.e., government) employees. Thus, "many of the legal barriers that had been erected in the wake of the Boston police strike of 1919 began to" erode (Swanson et al., 2008, p. 258). Other states soon followed Wisconsin's lead. Governors across the country, facing rapidly approaching elections, saw in the public-sector workers potential political supporters, so they extended the field of benefits in a bid to increase their voter base. Then in 1962, "President John F. Kennedy granted limited collective bargaining rights to federal workers" (p. 459). This expansion of public-sector workers' rights was subsequently supported by the courts.

Police Frustration with Support for the "War on Crime"

During the 1960s both the perception that many members of the public disliked the police and the rise of the due process revolution led many police officers to believe that they had few allies in their fight against crime. As a result, they became united in their need for a collective voice to fight for their needs (Swanson et al., 2008). This was typically through the creation, joining and work of unions.

Personnel Practices

In most organizations, whether they are public or private, policies and practices become regularized and eventually formalized. Even though these mechanisms may not make sense in later years, many employees still hang on to the old ways they know best. This phenomenon is generally called *bureaucratic ritualism*. For example, it can be seen in the traditional hiring practices, particularly in the context of the physical requirements of police departments.

In the late 1960s, many traditions of police organizations were called into question by officers who had received undergraduate and post-graduate educations (Swanson et al., 2008). The officers questioned

> the requirement to attend, unpaid, a 30-minute roll call immediately before the 8-hour [shift]; . . . uncompensated court attendance during off-duty time; short notice changes in shift assignments; having to return to the station from home for minor matters, such as signing reports without pay or compensatory time for such periods; favoritism in work assignments and selection for attendance at prestigious police training schools; and arbitrary disciplinary procedures. (p. 459)

Over time, conflicts between the rank and file and their management increased, and police officers turned to their unions to step in and solve these problems.

Salaries and Benefits

Starting in the 1960s, police unions successfully managed to bring about a number of changes in departmental policies: "increasing entry-level salaries, . . . obtaining longevity pay, shift differential pay, and improved retirement benefits for its members, . . . time and a half for all overtime, including court appearances, [and increased] paid holidays" (Swanson et al., 2008, p. 460).

Advantages and Disadvantages of Unions

Advantages

In general, unions provide numerous benefits to their members by engaging in the following activities:

- advocate on behalf of employees
- provide legal representation for employees
- guide/mentor new employees on their rights regarding work-related policies and practices
- maintain and increase salaries and benefits
- address the job-related ethical concerns of employees (especially those concerning fairness and integrity)
- occasionally assist employees in financial matters
- lobby to improve working conditions

- lobby for legislation
- provide a sense of brotherhood
- promote peace of mind

Labor unions seek to include all their members, including officers who are working the streets and may not have a chance, because of rotating shifts, to receive important job-related information. These officers also might not have the time to respond to new work-related developments that affect them; instead, they can rely on their union to represent their interests.

Disadvantages

Despite these positive attributes, there are drawbacks to unions as well. Often these negative impacts depend on the specific job or duties that an individual has in a police organization. The disadvantages include:

- the requirement to pay dues and the continuous need to increase these amounts
- concerns that union dues are sometimes spent in a questionable way
- the potential for unequal distribution of union benefits
- failure to accommodate exceptional service actions or needs among union members
- the potential for corruption or manipulation by members of management
- the inability for employees to act independently
- the political element of electing union leaders, which may result in posturing and dishonesty
- the potential for union leadership to lobby for or against important legislation even if individual members are not in agreement with the union's position

Other Considerations For and Against Unions

Not only have unions worked directly for the benefit of their membership, contend Swanson and colleagues (2008), but they have influenced numerous police policies and practices:

In various cities they have thwarted the use of civilian review boards; advocated the election of "law and order" candidates; resisted the replacement of two-officer cars with one-officer cars; litigated to avoid layoffs; lobbied for increased budgets, especially for raises; caused the removal of chiefs and other high-ranking commanders; advocated the elimination of radar guns from patrol vehicles because of potential adverse health risks associated with their use; and opposed annexation and the firing of union members. (p. 461)

Cities, and the politicians who run them, have the power to mobilize bias against unions (Bacharach and Baratz, 1962). What does this mean? Municipal politicians can create situations to discourage police officers, unions, and average citizens from participating in local politics. This is achieved by structuring meetings and opportunities for meaningful political participation at times and in places that officers have difficulty attending, so that their voices will not be heard and their input considered.

Despite the positive changes that they have brought about, police unions and their representative bodies "have contributed to racial tensions" (Swanson et al., 2008, p. 461). Such was case in 1990 when the president-elect of the Boston Police Patrolmen's Association told a forum on crime and violence that "if black men want to go out and fornicate and don't want to take care of their nests . . . then we have a problem" (p. 461). Some unions have been accused of being racist because they have encouraged their membership to elect "white candidates running against African Americans" (p. 461). Moreover, police unions have consistently opposed the establishment of civilian review boards.

The main reason why the advantages of police unions outweigh the disadvantages is because the union-related problems can easily be remedied through increased membership, participation, and effort. Ideally, each member of a union should do his or her part to help the union achieve its goals. All organizations, including unions, need active, engaged members to achieve success. Having a union allows for more exposure and insight into how the management works and provides support during bargaining.

As mentioned, the advantages and disadvantages of police unions are linked directly with each officer's and administrator's rank and/or role within the police agency. Lower rank-and-file officers receive more advantages from unions than upper-level officers and administrators. In fact, in most police departments officers above the rank of lieutenant are barred from union membership because they are no longer rank and file but managers. Police administrators may view union leaders as adversaries creating disorder among the rank and file. Officers choosing not to participate in unions may be ostracized or secluded, and female and minority officers may be resistant because the unions have traditionally not represented their concerns particularly well. This division may lead to the creation of additional unions or organizations in order to satisfy the needs of various members, thus creating further disunity.

For employees, unions are like an insurance policy. They are created and used by their members in special cases. Most people do not like paying for insurance, but they do so just in case they need the services offered to them.

The General Structure of Laws Governing Collective Bargaining

One of the most important aspects of unions is their power to engage in collective bargaining with management (i.e., police chief/commissioner and the city's elected representatives). According to Swanson and colleagues (2008):

> Under the terms of the federal National Labor Relations Act, state governmental bodies and their political subdivisions, such as cities and countries, are excluded from the definition of "employer" and are not brought within the scope of federal labor laws. As a result, laws regulating collective bargaining for state, country, and city law enforcement officers have developed on a state by state basis and, occasionally on a local basis. (p. 462)

Three models have been developed to date: binding arbitration, meet and confer, and bargaining not required. Let us review the details of each model.

Binding Arbitration

In this model, both parties in the collective bargaining process agree that any disputes will be submitted to a neutral third party for final decision. Both the police and the management agree to heed to the arbitrator's recommendations.

Meet and Confer Model

Some state laws do not permit binding arbitration in labor negotiations, Swanson and colleagues (2008) explain:

> Law enforcement officers have the same rights to organize and select their collective bargaining representative as those in the binding arbitration model. However, in such states, employers are only obligated to "meet and confer" with the collective bargaining representative, with no method of impasse resolution typically specified in the bargaining law. (p. 463)

Bargaining Not Required Model

Swanson and colleagues list yet another model for negotiations between police unions and management. This model is:

> found in states that do not statutorily require or, in some cases, allow collective bargaining for law enforcement officers. In some of these states, bargaining laws have been enacted by the state legislature, only to be declared unconstitutional later by courts. . . . In the majority of states, a statewide collective bargaining statute covering law enforcement officers has never been enacted. In some states where collective bargaining has not been granted on a statewide basis, certain cities and countries within the state have voluntarily chosen to bargain with the law enforcement officers. (p. 464)

Unfair Labor Practices

Although police agencies are required to uphold the law, they have been known to violate the law upon occasion in labor-related issues. There are at least six unfair labor practices in which police departments have engaged:

A refusal to bargain in good faith over subjects that are mandatory for bargaining;

Interference, restraint, or coercion of employees because employees have exercised their collective bargaining rights;

The domination of a labor organization by an employer;

The failure to furnish information relevant to the collective bargaining process;

Inappropriate interference by an employer with the internal activities of a labor organization;

Discrimination against employees who have exercised their collective bargaining rights. (Swanson et al., 2008, p. 466)

When unfair labor practices are detected, members who are so motivated usually complain to their shop steward, union representative, and/or the union headquarters, or they can file a complaint with their state labor relations board or the National Labor Relations Board (NLRB). The NLRB typically investigates each complaint, and if merit for the complaint is found, the agency can legally force the police department's management to comply with the union's demands.

Grievances

When officers have difficulties with the work they are required to perform or believe that they have been treated unfairly in a work situation, they should examine their collective agreement/union contract, which typically explains not only their rights and obligations but also the process whereby they can launch a grievance. In general, a grievance typically refers to a dispute. All term definitions are provided in the collective agreement or contract between management and the union. Officers typically need to follow a number of specified steps to file an effective grievance. If the grievance is not solved to the employee's satisfaction at an early stage, then the grievance typically progresses to the next stage.

Job Actions

Since police officers are not legally allowed to strike and can suffer criminal prosecution if they do, they resort to different tactics to enforce their will. When police officers are unhappy with their managers or the administration, they have an array of options, typically called *job actions*, to press their case. These job actions may include:

- vote of confidence in union leadership
- work slowdowns
- work speed-ups
- work stoppages

One of the most popular job actions is the so-called "blue flu." This occurs when numerous officers from a single police agency do not come to work by feigning sickness. This action forces middle management to perform the duties of the rank and file. The supervisors are not happy about performing this task, and it increasingly forces the management to consider the demands of the union.

Why are police officers not allowed to strike? Like nurses and emergency room doctors, they fulfill what are considered essential services. One major problem that can arise in a union is related to the situation that can develop when two unions are in conflict. For example, this can occur when there is a disagreement between a rank-and-file officer and his sergeant, who may be in another union. "This would not necessarily represent a conflict of interest, except that negotiations sometimes include areas under the control of sergeants and other middle police managers, such as one or two-officer patrol cars, transfers and promotions, and duty assignments" (Stevens, 2009, p. 199).

Conclusion

Beyond the noble goals of helping one's community, or arresting and "putting away the bad guys," few police officers and their administrators can ignore the sensitive issue of wages and compensation. Wages and compensation are political hot buttons in police officers' lives and in municipal politics. Failure to pay adequate wages leads to numerous problems, including a difficulty to attract suitable candidates and retain seasoned police professionals. Additionally, despite the public and the officials' general disdain or apathy about the presence of unions in the workplace, when the arguments for and against the police unions are distilled, there seems to be little source for the fear that is engendered. At the very least, unions contribute to the overall professionalization of the policing vocation.

Glossary

Association: This group provides benefits to its members and, depending on its individual mission, helps arrange necessary job actions.

Binding arbitration: This occurs when parties in a dispute allow a neutral third party to make a decision that both sides agree to follow.

Blue flu: One of several job actions that police officers can engage in against police management. It refers to a specific action when numerous officers from a single police agency do not come to work by feigning sickness. This forces the members of middle management to perform the duties of the rank and file.

Bureaucratic ritualism: A procedure and/or practice that never or no longer makes sense anymore; however, because the process has become regularized, formalized, and/or employees and management do not want to challenge the way things are done, they continue to engage in this procedure or practice.

Collective bargaining: The term given to the process whereby unions negotiate with employers over matters concerning remuneration, benefits, and working conditions.

Grievance: a formal (written-down) dispute between a worker and his or her immediate supervisor. The process is typically outlined in a collective agreement or contract between management and the union. The worker may need to complete a number of steps within a certain time frame for a grievance to be considered valid. If the grievance is not solved to the employee's satisfaction at an early stage, it typically progresses to the next stage.

Job actions: In general, legally permissible tactics police officers use to enforce their wills against police management.

Labor union: An organization that is legally entitled to represent the workers of an organization in contract matters with an employer.

Mobilization of bias: Powerful entities create situations in which it can be difficult for individuals and organizations to participate in political decisions. This is achieved, for example, by structuring meetings and opportunities for meaningful political participation so that the targeted group or individuals cannot be present nor can their voices be heard.

National Labor Relations Act: The federal legislation that governs the relations between unions and their employers.

Chapter Questions

Part One: Multiple Choice Questions

1. In 1935, the National Labor Relations Act allowed which of the following:
   a. unionization of public-sector employees
   b. establishment of a labor law court
   c. unionization within the private sector
   d. a ban on unionization in the private sector
   e. ability of workers to strike

2. Between 1959 and the late 1970s, which of the following combined to foster public-sector collective bargaining?
   a. the needs of labor organizations
   b. police frustration with perceived lack of support for their "war on crime"
   c. salaries and benefits
   d. all of the above
   e. none of the above

3. Which of the following is NOT a model of collective bargaining for police departments?
   a. binding arbitration model
   b. job action method
   c. meet and confer model
   d. bargaining not required model
   e. all are methods of collective bargaining

4. Which of the following is NOT a job action?
   a. vote of confidence
   b. work slowdown
   c. work shortcoming
   d. work speed-ups
   e. work stoppages

5. The police call a press conference to announce that they have reached an agreement with a union to represent them. This can be considered what kind of action?
   a. work stoppage
   b. work slowdown
   c. vote of acceptance
   d. vote of confidence
   e. vote of support

6. What is the term for a situation when numerous officers from a single police agency do not come to work by feigning sickness?
   a. blue wall of silence
   b. blue flu
   c. gleaning
   d. grievance
   e. none of the above

7. Why do states prevent or make it illegal for police to strike?
   a. States consider police officers to provide essential services.
   b. If they went on strike, anarchy would prevail on the streets.
   c. It would only empower them.
   d. some of the above
   e. none of the above

8. Which of the following are mandatory subjects of bargaining?
   a. terms of employment
   b. hours
   c. wages
   d. all of the above
   e. none of the above

Part Two: Short Answer Questions

1. What is arbitration?

2. What is collective bargaining?

3. What are the three models of collective bargaining?

4. What is the National Labor Relations Act?

5. What are two unfair labor practices?

6. What are four reasons why police departments became unionized?

Part Three: Essay Questions

1. Do the advantages of police unions outweigh the disadvantages? Justify your position.

2. Is it fair that police officers are not allowed to strike while other public-sector workers can?

3. Given the risks that police officers take, do you think they are paid sufficiently or not? Justify the position you take.

Ineffective/Insufficient Recruitment, Education, and Training

Introduction

Since the creation of the first police department, law enforcement organizations have struggled to develop appropriate and effective methods to recruit, educate, and train prospective officers. In the early years of modern police history, jobs in police departments were typically given to individuals who were loyal to the local political machine or who had the means to bribe someone to obtain their positions. Thus, the criteria for employment were either low or nonexistent. Although the pay was better than could be earned at a typical factory job, wages were relatively low, and officers often compensated for this deficiency by engaging in corrupt practices. Moreover, police officers typically held their jobs only as long as the political machine that was in power remained in control of the municipal government. When the politicians in power left office (through retirement, death, or election defeat), many police personnel usually found themselves out of work. Thus, there was no such thing as job security. This chapter reviews the history of police recruitment, educational requirements, and police officer training with special attention to the challenges and solutions that have been proposed over the years.

History of Recruitment

Since the turn of the 20th century, the criteria for the recruitment, education, and training of police officers have improved. The ability to adequately recruit appropriate candidates has been difficult from time to time. Although some select hiring practices were reviewed in the earlier chapter on the history of municipal policing, it is important to emphasize that the hiring criteria used by the early police departments were tied to either political connections or to the means to "buy" the job. In addition, "there were no preservice standards as we know them. No background checks were completed. There were no minimum standards for health, physical condition, education, intelligence, eyesight or moral character" (White, 2007, p. 2).

One of the earliest changes that had an effect on recruitment and retention was the passage of the Pendleton Act. This federal legislation, passed in 1883, sought to reduce corruption in the hiring and firing of government employees. With respect to policing, the passage of the act meant that police officers could no longer be fired for political reasons (i.e., supporting an opposing candidate for mayor or alderman).

In the early 1900s, the push for reform was led by prominent and often controversial police chiefs, including August Vollmer, Orlando W. Wilson, and William Parker. Vollmer (1876–1955), originally hired as the town marshal of the Berkeley (California) Police Department, introduced bicycle and later motorized patrol, traffic lights, interrogation techniques, and scientific evidence in crime scene processes. He also increased the number of full-time officers in the department. Among other important accomplishments, Vollmer reduced police corruption and introduced intelligence tests into the hiring process (Carte and Carte, 1975).

Wilson (1900–1972), a student of Vollmer's at the University of California at Berkeley, started as a patrolman in the Berkeley police department and rose up through the ranks to become chief of police in Fullerton, California, and later Wichita, Kansas. In the 1960s, he was appointed Superintendent of the Chicago Police Department. In all the departments he led, Wilson helped minimize corruption, championed professionalism, and advocated the introduction and use of new technology.

Parker (1902–1966) was successively promoted through the ranks of the Los Angeles Police Department (LAPD) to become its chief during the 1950s. During this time, the police department was embroiled in corruption problems, and in the 1960s, the crisis reached its climax when local confidence in the force plummeted as result of accusations of racial intolerance. Parker was able to professionalize the LAPD and minimize corruption in its ranks. Parker served a total of 39 years with the LAPD.

The shifts away from corruption and toward education and training were considered instrumental in the long-term efforts to professionalize the police force. Professionalism involves the acknowledgement that a job possesses a distinct body of knowledge and experience and that the actions of those employed in a certain sector are governed by a set of widely agreed-upon standards.

Starting in the 1960s, as numerous race riots, anti-Vietnam war protests, and student protests rocked the American nation, both the public and the politicians came to believe that police forces were ill prepared to deal with these new kinds of civil unrest. Consequently, a number of national commissions were established to investigate not only the causes of crime and urban disorder, but also the role, hiring, training, and educational requirements of law enforcement officers (e.g., President's Commission on Law Enforcement and Administration, 1967; National Advisory Commission on Civil Disorders, 1968; U.S. National Commission on the Causes of Crime and Disorder, 1968). Of crucial importance in these reports were a series of recommendations on how to best reform the police force at large. The reports made suggestions concerning recruitment, educational requirements, and training. Many of these suggested changes were slowly implemented over the following two decades.

Special Issues in Police Personnel Practices

Traditionally policing has been the purview of white male officers. The early police force was also long composed of a disproportionate number of working-class individuals whose main goal was to elevate their financial status above that of their parents. Since the 1960s, police departments around the country have focused on recruiting officers from middle-class backgrounds, as well as women and individuals from diverse ethnic and racial backgrounds. Furthermore, this era witnessed the rise in competition between various other police agencies for recruits (Stevens, 2009). Over the past two decades, new labor-related legislation has also had an effect on police departments. The new laws impact departments' hiring, promotion, and termination practices.

Officers and Disabilities

One of the most important pieces of legislation in recent decades is the Americans with Disabilities Act (ADA). This federal legislation, passed in 1990, was intended to "eliminate barriers to disabled persons in such areas as public transportation, telecommunications, public accommodations, access to government facilities and services, and employment" (Swanson, Territo, and Taylor, 2008, p. 388). The act "makes it unlawful to discriminate against people with disabilities in all employment practices, including retirement, hiring, promotion, training, layoffs, pay, firing, job assignments, transfers, leave and benefits" (p. 388). In 1994, the ADA was amended to include employers with 15 or more workers. With respect to municipal police departments, compliance with the act is monitored by the federal Equal Employment Opportunity Commission (EEOC).

Difficulty Hiring the Right People

Why would someone want to become a police officer? Individuals are motivated to become law enforcement agents for a wide variety of reasons, including job security, a desire to help people, a motivation to combat crime in their community, and the anticipated excitement they believe is inherent in the job (Lefkowitz, 1977; Meagher and Yentes, 1986; Carpenter and Raza, 1987). On the other hand, some less savory motivations exist as well: "people most interested in law enforcement have historically not been the 'best' students in traditional classrooms. They are probably attracted to police training because they want to hone their skills in driving, shooting, and defensive tactics more than acquire knowledge about crime causation, diversity and the law" (Chappell, Lanza-Kaduce, and Johnston, 2005, p. 75).

Another hiring issue that has been a primary focus in recent years concerns the employment of women, visible minorities, and gay and lesbian members of society. Although successful lawsuits have been filed against various police departments for their failure to properly recruit police officers [e.g., *Board of the County Commissioners of Bryan County, Oklahoma v. Brown* (1997)], there are numerous reasons why hiring practices can be problematic. According to Stevens (2009), the following factors may affect the quality and number of police officers being hired at any given time: the negative opinions that individuals or social groups may have about police (this may be especially true among African-Americans and Hispanics); the perception that those who become police officers are unduly concerned with achieving or maintaining a macho image; repeated scandals; more prestigious and better paying job opportunities; the paramilitary, bureaucratic nature of the police organization; the concern that one's personality may not be suited for the demands of the job; insufficient secondary school education; an inadequate supply of acceptable candidates; and having a close friend, relative, or loved one who was injured or killed in the line of duty.

In recent years, in order to increase the number of suitable police officers being hired, police agencies have engaged in and promoted community outreach activities, mass hirings, and the police corps. Police departments have become more visible by regularly attending community events and job recruitment fairs, setting up tables with brochures, and adopting simplified application forms and hiring procedures. On a less positive note, mass hirings have been controversial since their beginning. In 1989, for example, the District of Columbia police department hired 1,800 new officers. Either background checks were not done, or they were conducted after the fact. "[Almost] 100 of the officers from the 1989 and 1990 recruit classes were subsequently arrested on criminal charges ranging from shoplifting to murder" (White, 2007, p. 21).

Although various permutations of the Police Corps have been around for the past century (Skolnick and Fyfe, 1993), the modern-day version was funded as part of the *Violent Crime and Law Enforcement Act of 1994* (i.e., Crime Bill), through the Office of the Police Corps and Law Enforcement Education.[1] This program, championed for a number of years by Robert Sargent Shriver, Jr. (a well known U.S. politician who is connected by marriage to the powerful and political Kennedy family), was established to help local and state enforcement agencies increase the number of community police officers who have advanced education and training. Cadets live in barracks and go through training similar to that of a boot camp. And "college students who are accepted into the program can receive up to $15,000 to pay for college . . . provided they serve a minimum of four years" (White, 2007, p. 21).

The Police Corps has both its champions and its detractors. On the positive side, "The selection standards . . . are generally more stringent than local requirements, including attendance at a four year accredited college or university" (White, pp. 21–22). Additionally, since the training standards are high, the Police Corps holds the promise that if enough recruits graduate from the program, over time it could increase the overall educational level of police officers. This training practice could also change the organizational culture of the police profession. particularly those who think it is a waste of federal government resources.

Nonetheless, several disadvantages are inherent in the program. With the exception of Pate (2005), few scientific evaluations of the effectiveness of the Police Corps training program have been published. Also, the living conditions and training are antithetical to the community policing movement. Whereas the training emphasizes a military ethic where orders are followed without questioning one's superiors, in community policing, officers must listen to community representatives and often take leadership roles in mobilizing the community to action. Finally, the program is very expensive compared to the number of graduates it produces. In 1997, the Police Corps cost $59 million but only had 246 graduates.

Solutions to Problems with Recruitment

How have police departments attempted to deal with the hiring of appropriate applicants? Through a combination of public relations programs and bonuses to existing officers, police agencies have tried to identify and employ appropriate candidates. Some departments have established mobile recruiting vans, which they use to drive out to college campuses or military bases in search of potential candidates. Some organizations have offered their own officers such perks as extended vacation time if they can personally sign up new recruits. Other departments have offered recruits significant signing bonuses to join the force.

It should come as no surprise that police departments have historically been the purview of white males. Because of this entrenched tradition, police agencies have been reluctant to hire visible minorities, women, and those with homosexual and lesbian sexual orientations. One of reasons for this is the hostility that has long existed between police agencies and the African-American community. This animosity is slowly changing. Not only has Affirmative Action legislation had an effect on hiring practices, but so has the creation of the Commission on Accreditation for Law Enforcement (CALEA). CALEA recommends in its Standards for Law Enforcement Agencies that police departments should reflect the racial and ethnic composition of the communities in which they work. Affirmative Action programs are based on a series of federal laws, the first of which was passed in 1965, that are governed by the Equal Employment Opportunity Act. The legislation seeks to ensure that individuals are not discriminated against in employment-related matters because of their race, age, gender, ethnicity, or national origin.

Recruiting and Retaining Female Police Officers and Minorities in Police Departments

Recruiting and Retaining Female Police Officers

Female police officers represent approximately 15% of sworn law enforcement professionals in large municipal police departments (Langton, 2010). As of the early 21st century, about 200 female police chiefs were employed in the United States (Schultz, 2003), including, at the time of this writing, Cathy L. Lanier, the head of the Washington, D.C., Police Department. Detroit has the largest number of female police officers, accounting for 27% of all sworn personnel.

Female police officers face many dilemmas. Historically they have been subjected to workplace bullying and incivility, including exposure to sexual jokes, innuendo, and harassment by their male colleagues. At the beginning, many male officers felt that the presence of female co-workers would only be a short-lived fad, but time has proven this perception wrong (Bell, 1982). Some men were and continue to be paternalistic toward female police officers, taking special care that they would not get hurt or killed. Police departments accommodated the introduction of female police officers through a series of reforms, including changes to physical agility tests and height and weight requirements (Birzer, 2003). Although they may not be as powerful or large as men, scholarly research suggests that most female police officers are more even-tempered than their male counterparts. This characteristic is of great value in communication with potentially violent offenders (Martin, 1980, 1990).

Numerous legislative steps facilitated the general increase of women and minorities in the police forces. The initial phase started with the passage of Title VII of the Civil Rights Act of 1964. Section 703A of that act forbids discrimination in employment matters (i.e., hiring, pay, benefits, promotion, and firing) based on an employee's race, color, religion, sex, age, pregnancy, or national origin. However, it was not until 1972 when the Equal Employment Opportunity Act (EEOA) was passed that recruitment (especially of minorities and women) significantly changed in police departments. Most importantly, the EEOA sought to reduce discrimination in the hiring process. Police organizations were responsible for employing equal numbers of individuals according to the racial or ethnic percentage breakdown of the existing population. The EEOA also required police organizations to use a different physical agility test for women. In many respects, this exacerbated the problem, by fostering more lawsuits being filed against police agencies for alleged unfair employment practices.

In 1984, Congress passed the Pregnancy Disability Act. Females were now allowed to take off a limited amount of time for paid maternity leave. Women in law enforcement were also given the opportunity, when pregnant, to go on light duty (i.e., work at a desk or other lighter work), instead of continuing their usual street patrols. This legislation, backed up by the positive professional experiences of female coworkers, has led to the continued acceptance of women in law enforcement.

Recruiting and Retaining Minority Police Officers

It has been difficult for municipal police departments to consistently hire and retain qualified minority employees of African-American, Hispanic, American Indian (Ross 2006a), and Asian-American (Ross and Dai, 2011) descent. Once individuals from these backgrounds are hired, they frequently face considerable discrimination. There are numerous incidents involving minority police officers having to call in a white officer to help them when they need to arrest a white individual. In some southern jurisdictions, African-American police officers historically executed their patrols in vehicles labeled "colored." Although the South may have been an extreme case in some instances, most areas in the United States were discriminatory in their hiring and promotion practices. Before the 1970s, few police departments anywhere in the country had African-Americans in their forces beyond the rank of patrol officer (Schmalleger and Worral, 2010, p. 18). Since the passage of civil rights legislation, however, the fate of African-Americans and other minorities in the police has improved.

Quotas

To meet the requirements of the federal equal employment standards, many police agencies use what are generally referred to as quotas (i.e., a designated proportion of their workforce that must be filled by minorities and women). This is a highly controversial practice, but thus far, no viable alternative solution has been developed. Affirmative Action was established to prevent, among other things, discrimination by employers in their hiring, firing, and promotion practices. The relevant legislation ensures that minorities, women, and others who typically experience discrimination are treated fairly in employment-related matters and have access to schools, housing, and other amenities. While quotas can make it easier for minorities and women to find jobs, once hired they may feel like tokens. Moreover, quotas can lead to reverse discrimination in which qualified individuals are passed by solely because of their racial background or gender. Moreover, in some job-related cases, standards have been lowered to meet the work- and educational-related abilities of the applicant pool.

Residency Requirements

By requiring police officers to live in the same communities in which they are employed, police departments hope to improve relations between police officers and the communities they serve. It is commonly believed that police officers make good neighbors, improve trust, and deter crimes from occurring in their neighborhoods. Various arguments against residency requirements also exist. For example, there may be a shortage of qualified applicants for police departments in certain areas. The residency requirement may also be interpreted as an unnecessary and heavy handed infringement on each officer's right to choose where he or she wants to live. Furthermore, the residency requirement may place an unnecessary financial burden on a police officer. Take, for example, a police officer who might be forced to live in New York City where the cost of living is exceedingly high. This policy may cause the officer greater stress and thus lead to burnout and a higher-than-average turnover rate for the police department. One potential unforeseen side effect of residency requirements involves the fact that officers may become too friendly with their neighbors and may become reluctant to enforce the law against them when the need arises. Finally, no empirical evidence has been found to link residency to an improvement in police officer performance, citizen perceptions of the police, or police perceptions of the community.

The Police Personnel Selection Process

The steps in the hiring process are arranged so that the police agency invests increased resources at each stage, from initial application to completion of the probationary period with the police department. The least resource-intensive tests are generally used first in order to weed out inappropriate candidates early in the process. Police departments typically cast their net wide to attract recruits. This process may include attending job fairs held by local colleges and universities; using print, radio, and television advertising, maintaining a Web site with information concerning career prospects and a downloadable application form; approaching retiring members of the military; and occasionally recruiting officers from other law enforcement agencies (White, 2007; Swanson et al., 2008). Some police agencies rely on process engineering techniques. They attempt to discover what motivates particular recruits to become police officers and then use this information to improve their hiring procedures.

Most police departments require candidates to be between the ages of 21 and 35 and to have completed a high school diploma. Some agencies, however, have found that lowering the starting age has helped increase the size of the applicant pool. Others have increased their standards to try to increase the quality of their applicant pools. "An increasing number of police departments are requiring either two-year or four-year college degrees. Many departments will substitute military experience for educational requirements" (White, 2007. p. 271). After a prospective candidate fills out the necessary paperwork, the application sets into motion a series of steps. Keep in mind that no police department relies upon one single test for admittance to the police training academy. Typically, a long period passes before recruits are accepted into the academy and that the sequence of steps varies from one police agency to the next. Guiding these efforts have been the establishment of "Police Officer Standards and Training Commissions (PSOTs) were created, often with the incentive of Law Enforcement Assistance Administration (LEAA) grants to initiate operations and to ensure that uniform minimum standards—including training—were met" (Swanson et al., 2008, pp. 18–19).

Basic Criteria

In the course of their daily work, police officers need to be able to communicate with many different audiences, including fellow workers, supervisors, and members of the community (i.e., those that they stop, question, search, and arrest). Officers spend a good portion of their work day talking with people, filling out numerous forms, and submitting reports to their superiors (i.e., the police bureaucracy), some of which are then used by the courts in legal proceedings. These reports are important for judges, juries, and lawyers (i.e., prosecutors and defense attorneys) to pursue court cases. Good writing helps to create and maintain a professional image.

In general, there are 9 basic minimum requirements used by most police agencies in the initial consideration of an applicant.

1. U.S. citizenship
2. high school diploma/earning a GED
3. minimum age of 18 to 21 (varies based on jurisdiction) and maximum age (usually 35)
4. valid and clean driving record
5. good medical and physical health
6. completion of drug and alcohol testing
7. proportional height and weight
8. no criminal record
9. residency (an officer must live within the jurisdiction in which he or she works)

The following is a discussion of the most important steps that must be taken by an applicant to a police department.

Tests

Once a candidate has met a department's basic requirements, he or she is then subjected to several tests that aid in the selection process. These include an entrance examination, a physical ability/agility test, a polygraph test, a character investigation, interviews and oral boards, and psychological testing. Approximately 10 distinct tests are used to delimit the pool of prospective police academy inductees.

Entrance Examination

Most of the initial tests that prospective police officers take are so-called "paper and pencil" civil service exams. These tests pose basic questions that assess candidates' basic intelligence, and they sometimes probe further into their knowledge of the criminal justice system, criminal law, and the specific police department and municipality in which they would be working. "The purpose of the exam . . . is to assess each candidate's basic skills in reading, writing, comprehension, logic, memory, and perhaps mathematics" (White, 2007, p. 8).

Physical Ability/Agility Test

Police agencies also want to know if the candidates will be able to meet the physical demands of their new jobs. In general, these kinds of tests emphasize a candidate's ability to run fast and upper body strength. The prospective officer might be required to run a distance in a specified period and perform a certain number of push-ups and sit-ups. Other kinds of physical tests include running an "obstacle course, climbing a wall, performing a dummy drag . . . and running" (White, 2007, p. 19). According to Swanson and colleagues (2008), "These kinds of tests have received criticism in recent years. [They are] outdated, are not job-related, and are testing for physical requirements not needed to perform the job of a modern law enforcement officer" (p. 401).

The Polygraph Test

During the 1990s, almost two thirds of all police departments in the United States reported using a polygraph test, also known as a lie detector test, in their selection process (Horvath, 1993). A polygraph test measures the degree to which a subject's heart rate increases or decreases over time when they are subjected to questions. "The Federal Employee Protection Act of 1988 prohibits the use of the polygraph in most private-sector preemployment screening, but all government bodies are exempt from this restriction. . . . Nationally, 56.6 percent of police agencies reported using the polygraph in employment screening" (Swanson et al., 2008, 403). The federal Polygraph Protection Act prohibits employers from using lie detector tests as a pre-employer screener; however law enforcement agencies are considered exempt from this rule (White, 2008, p. 19).

Character Investigation

Police agencies also "review and verify all responses made by the applicant as to his or her education, military service, prior employment history, and related matters to check the references listed and develop other references" (Swanson et al., 2008, p. 405). Usually this research involves a series of background checks: criminal record, driving record, credit history, interviews with previous employers, family and character references, transcripts from educational institutions, and volunteer service.

Alcohol and Drug Testing

Police agencies now require candidates to submit to a urine test to detect the presence of drugs and alcohol in their blood stream. "Some police departments will hire medical staff to conduct the drug testing on site; others will simply require applicants to submit a sample to their own physician as part of a more general physical examination" (White, 2007, p. 13).

Psychological Testing of Police Applicants

A number of psychological tests are used to gain a sense of each candidate's mental health.[2] One or more of the following tests may be administered: Inwald Personality Inventory, California Psychological Inventory (CPI), Minnesota Multiphasic Personality Inventory (MMPI), and Wonderlic Personnel Test (WPT). "Each test has varying degrees of validity and no test has been determined to be foolproof" (Swanson et al., 2008, p. 408).

Interviews and Oral Boards

One of the key steps in the hiring process is a face-to-face interview with one or more police personnel experts. Sometimes this is performed with one individual who has been given the authority to make evaluations, while at other times the prospective police candidate is interviewed by a team of police representatives (Swanson et al., 2008, p. 406). An alternative to this process is an Oral Board Review.

> [This involves] a face-to-face contact between a three-or-more member panel and the police applicant. Panel members may be police officials, representatives of the civil service or merit board, community members, or combinations of these people. A standard set of job-related questions is drawn up ahead of time, and panel members are trained in the use of the written evaluation form, which they incorporate into their consideration of each candidate. (p. 406)

White (2007) adds, "Although the format varies, the oral interview usually involves multiple interviewers (3 to 5) , lasts 30 to 60 minutes, and covers a range of topics" (p. 8).

In addition to these traditional methods, new ones have cropped up as well. One of the most well known is the Assessment Center Approach: "a method of supplemental traditional selection procedures with situational exercises designed to simulate actual officer responsibilities and working conditions" (Stevens, 2009, p. 266). This approach has two major advantages; it helps to weed out prospective candidates and provides a way that the police agency can protect itself from unfair legal challenges by potential recruits who are denied employment (Decisso, 2000; Dayan, Kasten, and Fox, 2002).

Importance of a College Education

Since the 1920s, many police departments and their leadership have advocated college education, if not for their rank and file, then at least for their leadership. The first program in law enforcement was started in 1929 when the University of Southern California founded its program in public administration, which had a specialization in law enforcement. In 1935,

Michigan State University established a Bachelor program in police administration. But it was not until the LEAA operated that college education for police officers became more common. Subsequently, during the 1960s and into the 1970s, several federal commissions (e.g., National Advisory Commission on Criminal Justice Standards) and other organizations advocated the adoption of a minimum of two years of college for police officers.

The impulse toward high education standards led to increased federal funding of post-secondary school programs for police officers. Requiring police officers to have a university degree, however, is a controversial restriction. There are both arguments for and against this kind of standard.

On the one hand, the police occupation is complex and demanding in nature. Thus, if law enforcement wants to be considered a profession by others (especially the public and the politicians that fund them and in whose trust they depend), then the field needs a university degree component to legitimize it. Also, as Americans become increasingly educated, the police need to keep pace with the greater public. College applicants are typically older, more mature, and well rounded. College typically helps students to improve their communication skills. And, college studies can help officers improve their ability to write reports well.

On the other hand, requiring a college degree unnecessarily limits an already thin applicant pool. The necessity of having a college education negatively impacts the recruitment of minorities, as there usually is a lower level of university enrollment among many minorities.[3] It can also be argued that college education does not teach the skill set needed to perform the job of a police officer. Finally, there is no consistent empirical evidence that indicates that college-educated police officers outperform police officers without a college degree.

Academy Training

The training of police officers has changed over time, but improvements have been slow and often lag behind current developments in police practice. In the early days of policing in the United States, rookies learned their jobs directly from senior police personnel through observation and asking questions. Over time, departments introduced classroom instruction prior to recruits entering the field. Naturally, some subjects (e.g., firearms, self-defense techniques) were emphasized more than others (Chappell et al., 2005). Part of the problem in determining an appropriate curriculum lies in the lack of consensus about whether policing should be considered a craft or a profession. As a craft, "the primary skills are learned through on the job training" (p. 72). If law enforcement is to be viewed as a profession, the requisite skills and knowledge are best communicated in an academic setting. And only once the recruits complete their course requirements should they be allowed to pursue their field experience.

A number of different training methods exist for police officers. "Law enforcement agencies will sometimes sponsor their recruits as they go through training at the local community college training center. Other prospective officers pay for their own training in hopes of being recruited after they complete training and become certified" (Chappell et al., 2005, p. 73). Most commonly, officers go through some kind of basic training at a training academy, sometimes called an Institute for Public Safety or a Criminal Justice Training Center. Large departments may even have their own academies. If a department is small, it may send its rookies to a state or regional training academy. These last two types of facilities also offer specialized, continuing education courses for experienced police officers. Each state mandates a certain number of courses and types of training for rookie officers. Some academies offer more than the minimal required courses. There are numerous types of police academies, and each model has its advantages and disadvantages (Haberfield, 2002; Haley, 2003).

When recruits graduate, they usually are put on some sort of probation and are allowed to ride with a more senior officer who is designated as a Field Training Officer (FTO). "Some large law enforcement agencies operate their own academies and pay for the training of their recruits. More often training centers are linked with institutions of higher education, especially those geared toward vocational training like community colleges" (Chappell et al., 2005, pp. 72–73).

In order to improve training opportunities, the states have developed protocols and standards. "In 1959, the New York State Legislature created the first state-mandated police-training program in the United States, requiring that a recruit receive 80 hours of training prior to becoming a police officer anywhere in the state of New York" (White, 2005, p. 36). Other states followed suit. In the 1980s, four organizations (the International Association of Chiefs of Police, the National Organization of Black Law Enforcement Executives, the National Sheriff's Association, and the Police Executive Research Forum) formed the Commission on Accreditation for Law Enforcement which "developed [944] standards designed to professionalize the police and a process for accrediting law enforcement agencies," some of which deal with recruit training (p. 36).

Curriculum

At the police academies, recruits take classes in various subjects that are directly relevant to them becoming effective officers. Some of this information is similar to what all police officers across the United States might learn, whereas other information is specific to a particular jurisdiction or police department. The course offerings typically conform to state-mandated or accreditation standards (see Exhibit 16.1). Improvement in training standards is also due to costly lawsuits by citizens against police departments for previously failing to properly train their officers [e.g., *City of Canton, Ohio v.*

Exhibit 16.1 List of Classes for Recruits in the Police Academy	
Civil Law	Investigation
Constitutional Law	Oral and Written
Criminal Law	Communication
Crowd Control	Patrol
Disaster Response	Physical Training
Diversity Training	Police Department Policies and
Driver Training	Practices
Ethics	Police Powers
Fire Arms Training	Report Writing
First Aid	Technology
Human Relations	Use of Force Training

Harris (489 U.S. 378 1989)]. The awareness that local citizens are watching may encourage police departments to do their jobs better.

Training Challenges

Both general and specific problems have been identified in the context of police officer training practices. Thibault, Lawrence, and McBride (1998) identified a number of problems with the traditional police academy training model:

1. deficiencies in the content of the course offerings, especially in terms of human relations, communications, adult versus juvenile behavior, and other topics

2. inadequate teaching ability by instructors and trainers pulled from the field

3. old and outdated training facilities

4. mainly lectured-based teaching

5. emphasis on part-time instructional personnel

6. a less-than-optimal experience for part-time students in comparison to full-time students

7. the practice of granting police powers to rookies before they graduate

8. inconsistencies in requirements for post-graduation reviews of police officer performance

Curriculum and Delivery Challenges

Police departments must ensure that their academy and in-service training keeps up with recent developments in pedagogy, technology, teaching styles, and the law. Well-run police academies are in a constant state of change and fluctuation based on their ability to meet the demands of the community and their profession.

Occupational Socialization, Recruitment Challenges, and Informal Lessons

It is common knowledge in police circles that both informal and formal curricula exist in police academies. As mentioned in chapter 4, police officers are given a recognized body of information they must learn and a number of skill sets they must master. However, the academy students' fellow and more senior police instructors often maintain that the book may teach something one way, and an alternate set of standards or issues holds sway on the street.

Legal Protection and Failure to Train

Training to be a police officer, as is the case for a rookie firefighter or new recruit in the military, involves a certain set of risks. In the course of training, a candidate may be injured. Over the past few decades, recruits who have been injured or killed (or where applicable, their families) have sued various police organizations. Today candidates are usually required to sign a liability waiver before the training begins and to spend time specifically learning about the potential risks and hazards related to the training period.

Problems Related to the Training Academies

Many policing experts believe that most training academy experiences in and of themselves are insufficient and must be followed up with field training. Some experts argue that the training academies ignore important subjects such as ethics, discretion, and the use of confidential informants (Walker and Katz, 2004). Also, there is a disproportionate emphasis on the lecture model versus one that is interactive and experiential. This approach is not particularly useful for the typical police recruit or the profession at large. Other scholars have suggested that the typical police training academy is too militaristic in its focus (Skolnick and Fyfe, 1993; Ortmeier, 1997; Birzer, 2003) and that this is to be avoided. In addition, the anti-intellectual nature of many academies has been criticized:

> . . . such as understanding of community relations, ethical considerations, and specific critical issues (the underlying issues associated with mental illness and domestic violence, for example), while large blocks of time . . . are devoted [to] danger-related skills. (White, 2007, p. 42)

Field Training Officers

When candidates graduate from an academy, they are typically assigned to a borough or district and put under the supervision of a Field Training Officer

(FTO). The FTO is an experienced, senior police officer who supervises a rookie's performance in the field during a probationary period. In most professional police agencies, this position goes to veteran police officers who compete for the position.

There are many different FTO programs and in order for a police department to be accredited by the CALEA, police departments need to use FTOs in their training process. In general, they are designed to prepare and evaluate the performance of rookies for patrol. FTO programs have been established to supplement the courses taught in the police academies, allowing rookies to actually experience the kinds of things a police officer is likely to encounter in the streets. With some FTO programs, the police department systematically conducts a task analysis of the patrol function in order to capture the breadth of responsibilities involved (Doerner et al., 2003). Recruits are assigned different FTOs over the course of their training periods, so that they can observe and be evaluated by different members of the police organization. Typically, at the end of each shift, the FTO writes a report on the rookie's performance and submits it to his or her commanding officer. Feedback is given to the rookie with instructions about where improvement is needed.

In-Service Training

After police officers have graduated from the academy, passed their field training, and completed their probationary periods, they receive periodic training while on the job. Not only will officers in specialized units and those who are entering or continuing in management typically receive additional training, but most police departments and the states in which they operate require officers to receive in-service training on a periodic basis.

As with field training, CALEA requires police departments to offer in-service training. White (2007) notes that

> traditionally, in-service training has focused on specialized skills such as requalifying at the gun range, pursuit driving, and the usage of other nonlethal weapons. . . . Other areas that have recently been the focus of this type of training include changes in criminal or constitutional law, domestic violence, handling the mentally ill, counterterrorism, youth gangs, and community policing. (p. 46)

During the past 20 years, some in-service training programs have focused on the knowledge and skills related to community policing, especially problem-oriented policing, while others kinds of training have emphasized broader cultural issues, such as diversity, stress management, domestic violence, dealing with the mentally ill, and communication, technology, and counterterrorism.

Conclusion

Recruitment, educational requirements, and the training of police officers to enter the force are fraught with numerous difficulties. Police agencies frequently lag behind the ever-evolving realities of the external environments in which they operate. Although well-known policing experts, like Vollmer, Wilson, and Parker, were important early reformers, the pivotal 1960s recommendations published in various federal government reports (via the National Institute of Justice) increased comparison and competition between jurisdictions, and the establishment of CALEA has greatly improved police practices in recent years. The changing economy and workforce dynamics will continue to have an effect on policing for years to come.

Notes

1. The idea of having police departments train their own police cadets has been around for the past century. The difference today is that the federal government plays a role in the creation and maintenance of the Police Corps. See, for example, Skolnick and Fyfe (1993, pp. 261–266) for the NYPD's proposal.

2. This section builds upon the information related to public relations issues that was presented in chapter 4.

3. This statement does not apply to Asian Americans, who are routinely identified as having higher SAT scores than the average American high school student.

Glossary

Affirmative Action: A series of federal laws, the first of which was passed in 1965, governed by the Equal Employment Opportunity Act. These laws established standards to monitor and ensure that individuals are not discriminated against in employment-related matters because of their race, age, ethnicity, or national origin.

Equal Employment Opportunity Commission (EEOC): The federal body charged with ensuring that employers do not violate the provisions of the Equal Opportunity Act.

Field Training Officer: An experienced, senior police officer who supervises a rookie's performance in the field immediately after he or she graduates from the police academy.

In-service training: Supplemental training that officers receive after completing the training academy and probation period. Typically officers are trained in new policies and practices in specific contexts.

Police academy: An educational and training institution where police rookies who have passed the selection tests are sent and where they learn the basics of policing.

Police Candidate Assessment Center: An alternative screening method for potential candidates. This model involves simulated exercises and improves an agency's ability to select appropriate recruits while minimizing the possibility of legal suits.

Professionalism: The understanding that a job has a distinct body of knowledge and experience and that the actions of those engaged in this field are governed by a set of widely agreed-upon standards.

Chapter Questions

Part One: Multiple Choice Questions

1. Over the history of modern policing, the criteria for hiring police officers has
   a. remained the same
   b. improved
   c. decreased
   d. all the above
   e. none of the above

2. In the history of the Los Angeles Police Department, which former chief is most credited with implementing significant changes in recruitment, training, and promotion?
   a. William Bratton
   b. W. O. Wilson
   c. William Parker
   d. Jack Maple
   e. none of the above

3. Which proposal included in the 1994 Crime Act affected the hiring and recruitment of police officers?
   a. reduced citizenship requirements
   b. requirement that all new recruits have a college education
   c. introduction of the Police Corps
   d. residency requirements
   e. none of the above

4. What does the scholarly literature reveal about the role of college education in hiring in police departments?
   a. College-educated police officers perform better.
   b. College-educated police officers perform poorly.
   c. College-educated police officers report boredom in their jobs.
   d. The college program that was attended makes a difference in the likelihood of hiring.
   e. The evidence is mixed.

5. The number of female municipal police officers is
   a. increasing
   b. decreasing
   c. remaining stable
   d. up and down in a cyclical fashion
   e. none of the above

6. What does a thorough background check involve?
   a. Interviewing former employers
   b. Interviewing family members
   c. Examining employment history
   d. Examining school performance
   e. All of the above

7. Police officers who graduate from the academy are most likely under the supervision of a
   a. Mentor
   b. Sergent
   c. Spiritual advisor
   d. Field Training Officer
   e. Prosecutor

Part Two: Short Answer Questions

1. List three police reformers in the history of modern policing.

2. What is Affirmative Action?

3. List three subjects recruits learn at the police academy.

4. What are five subjects that candidates study while they are in the academy?

5. Why is it important for police candidates to be interviewed by a board?

Part Three: Essay Questions

1. Do quotas have a positive or negative impact on the hiring process of police departments?

2. Does it make sense to invest fewer resources at the front end of the hiring process?

3. Which of these is the most problematic: recruitment, educational requirements, or training?

17

Working Conditions

Introduction

Police officers, like most criminal justice practitioners, labor in unique working conditions. The demands of the job include shift work, the emotions linked to fear and danger, and the stress that must be dealt with on a daily basis. In many respects, police officers share similar working conditions with other first responders, such as emergency services personnel or firefighters. Yet, there are also significant differences. Most importantly, unlike other first responders, very few people, except for most crime victims, are happy when police officers intervene in a situation.

Moreover, working conditions vary according to the types of job that officers perform, the kind of police force for which they work, the neighborhood environment (e.g., sector, district, borough), and rank. Because most of a police officer's daily shift routine does not involve the actual enforcement of the law and has more to do with order maintenance and the provision of services, police are typically delegated the responsibility of solving, at least initially, many of society's ills. They are given the tasks in an urban setting that no other municipal agency wants to pursue (Walker, 1999).

Police officers, especially recruits, encounter a wide variety of citizens and are required to maneuver the criminal justice system, the department, and the seniority system. Most officers realize that the public is not as cooperative as they expected them to be. "Officers encounter some hostility from citizens. This is a shock because officers tend to choose law enforcement as a career because they want to work with people and help the community" (Walker, 1999, p. 323). Officers are also subjected to numerous stereotypes perpetrated by the media, many of which cause the public to view the police with uncertainty:

> Citizens feel discomfort at being around a person with arrest powers. Sometimes citizens will even openly make jokes about breaking the law. To avoid the discomfort of these incidents, police officers tend to socialize primarily with other officers, thereby increasing their isolation from the public . . . Police officers are also expected to solve many of their culture's problems.
>
> [They] perform society's "dirty work" handling unpleasant tasks that no one else wants to perform or is able to handle. The police see humanity at its worst. They are the first people to find the murder victim. . . . Officers

encounter the victims of serious domestic abuse, child abuse, and rape first-hand. These kinds of situations accumulate over time, affecting their attitudes about people in general. (Walker, 1999, pp. 323–324)

As the years pass, many officers become cynical about the criminal justice system. "They see what happens to arrests, how cases are plea bargained, and how judges work. They observe incompetent prosecutors, defense attorneys, and judges every day" (Walker, 1999, p. 324). Police officers also work frequently with the impression that they are little respected by other criminal justice practitioners.

Many officers, particularly rookies, have difficulties understanding the unique organizational culture of police departments, particularly when they see other officers whom they believe to be undeserving be promoted or protected from disciplinary measures. They witness abundant examples of favoritism and work with policies and practices that may have made sense at one point in time but now seem antiquated. Some officers may also come to believe that they will not be rewarded for their efforts and may be little inspired to do more than the absolute minimum to get by (Walker, 1999).

Since the majority of officers are assigned patrol, the following discussion mainly focuses on the working conditions of this aspect of policing.

The Effects of Police Work

The unique working conditions of police officers and the situations to which they are exposed commonly result in a diverse but related series of negative experiences: boredom, cynicism, decreased contact with their significant others and loved ones, fear, intense and increased scrutiny of their actions, continuous fatigue, stress, and burnout.

Boredom: Patrolling and responding to 911 calls can make officers feel like they are glorified taxicab drivers, pizza delivery persons, or factory assembly line workers. Although there are opportunities for creativity, particularly in terms of the types of enquiries officers may ask the individuals they stop, question, or search, police personnel must work within procedural legal guidelines, lest the fruits of their labor (e.g., arrest, conviction) be overturned in court on a technicality.

Cynicism: The frequent hostility, abuse, and distrust officers encounter not only from the citizens they serve and protect, but also occasionally from supervisors, can lead even the most benign officer to become cynical after a while. During the 1960s, as part of a general trend to better understand the nature of police officers, Niederhoffer (1969) brought attention to the widespread problem of police cynicism. He argued that because of the officers' work experiences, particularly their interactions with the public, they can tend to become cynical over time. Since the publication of this study, other researchers have tried to determine the prevalence and preconditions of police cynicism.

Decreased Contact with Significant Others and Loved Ones: Unlike most government services, police departments are active 24 hours a day, seven days a week. This means that officers must periodically work at times when the general population (and often their significant others and loved ones) are sleeping. The necessity to work rotating shifts may also mean that officers miss significant opportunities for bonding with their children and/or taking care of their other loved ones (e.g., aging parents).

Intense and Increased Scrutiny: The availability of cell phones (particularly smart phones) has increased the public's ability to contact the police almost instantaneously. Police must almost respond in an expeditious fashion to reported serious crimes, or they may be accused of real or alleged wrongdoings. Two-way communications, including computer-aided technology, can now track the physical whereabouts of officers. Video monitors in patrol cars are not only used in criminal cases, but they also open officers' actions to greater review and possible sanction. The public's use of cell phones (with audio and video capability) has led some members of the public to record their interactions with the police

Ongoing Fatigue: Unless officers have reached senior positions or have been assigned permanent work shifts, they are typically tired and fatigued because of their ever-changing schedules. The problem is exacerbated if the officer is holding down a part-time job, attending university part-time, or there is a newborn in the house. Officers may also lack appropriate opportunities for pursuing healthy lifestyles, as reflected in poor eating habits, irregular visits to the doctor, and minimal physical exercise.

Stress: Police officers experience a disproportionate amount of stress because of continuously dealing with difficult and sometimes dangerous situations, feelings of ineffectiveness and inadequacy, and possible increased scrutiny of their actions. Sometimes stress is connected to fear of contracting communicable disease (e.g., HIV/AIDS). Stress is an intense physical and mental response to episodic or recurring tough situations or events. If not handled properly, stress can lead to both psychological and physical problems. As reviewed in chapter 3, the contribution of stress to divorce, alcohol use etc. must be treated with caution.

Burnout: This occurs when officers' effectiveness and performance are compromised because of accumulated stress, boredom on the job, and/or constant fatigue combined with cynicism. In such situations, officers may be tempted to take shortcuts that could end up backfiring on them (e.g., corrupt activities, failing to take adequate precautions in dangerous situations). Officers often do not recognize the symptoms and ramifications of burnout.

Despite these drawbacks, officers may suffer from what is called golden handcuffs. In situations like this the officers believe that because of the relative benefits of the job (e.g., pay or ability to meet financial obligations, respect in the community) they cannot (or should not) leave the field of policing to find a different more enjoyable job, even though this is what they truly want to do.

The following sections deal with two of the most prominent problem areas facing officers: dangerousness and stress.

Dangerousness

Although dangerousness coupled with the prevalence of accidents, injuries, and deaths on the job was discussed in chapter 3, it is appropriate to return to this discussion in the context of this chapter. Dangerousness is both embedded in actual rates and inherent to perceptions of the same. As one can well imagine, the issues at hand are not as clear cut as they could be.

Policing is a relatively dangerous job. The word "relatively" is used in this context because some tasks and situations in which the police are involved are more threatening than others. Dangerousness is typically measured through assault and death statistics. This way of measuring dangerousness, however, ignores other dangerous aspects of police work, including accidents (Brandl and Stroshine, 2003).

In order to partially remedy this situation, Brandl (1996) conducted a study of officer-involved accidents that lead to injury or death. After reviewing 2,000 incidents resulting in police officer injuries or death, he found that approximately 10% were caused by assaults, and 54% were a result of accidents. The balance (36%) were the result of an uncooperative suspect. In a follow-up study, Brandl and Stroshine (2003) determined that accidents were the cause of most serious injuries, medical treatment and days lost at work.

Numerous similar studies have been conducted. Violanti, Vena, and Marshall (1996) compared the causes of police officer deaths to those of other municipal workers. They discovered that police officers had a higher rate of death and suicide, but died less often because of accidents. Peek-Asa et al. (1997) "examined assaults across occupations and found that . . . police departments reported the highest rates among the 9 industries that reported any assaults. The police group was calculated to be 73.1 times more likely to be assaulted at work than the overall industry average" (from Brandl and Stroshine, 2003, p. 561).

In 2003, Brandl and Stroshine "explore[d] the absolute dangers associated with police work by broadening the definition of danger typically used by researchers in this area. Specifically, [they] examine[d] injuries that occurred as a result of assaults, resisting subjects, and accidents" (p. 561). The study is a little limited in its applicability because the researchers only pursued the study over one year and in the context of a single city.

Potential versus Actual Dangers

All professions differ between potential and actual dangers. In policing, as in most jobs, there is a risk of confounding the two, in which potentially dangerous situations are mistaken as being actually dangerous.

Improving Safety and Reducing Fatalities

Several issues need to be addressed to significantly improve the working conditions of the rank and file. These changes could lead to a reduction in the fear-related stress linked to dangerous situations; better training; clearer policies and practices surrounding both potential and actual dangerous situations; and better supervision. Indeed, the quality and type of training that police officers receive has improved markedly over the years. Police departments now host frequent in-service training sessions to orient officers to new policies and procedures. Nonetheless, there is always room for improvement. Officers are frequently confused or have difficulty with the numerous policies and practices used in their departments. Most supervisors, particularly at the lower ranks, do not receive adequate training for their jobs; instead, they learn while on the job through trial-and-error experiences. Police departments also need to free up more resources for their officers to receive the appropriate level of training for their supervisory positions. Also, police officers who find the job monotonous and boring can seek or apply for temporary or permanent transfers in their organization or other criminal justice agencies to learn additional skills and make themselves more amenable for promotion. This practice is referred to as cross-training.

Stress and Law Enforcement

The subject and impact of stress among police officers has been well documented and researched. The findings are complicated and somewhat contradictory. Some researchers have focused on analyzing police officers in terms of life expectancy and other quality-of-life measures. The findings, as counterintuitive as they might sound, generally indicate that police officers are no more prone to dying earlier than workers in other professions. It is also important to understand that the sources of stress differ between workers and managers. Many police scholars divide the stress that police officers experience into two types: internal and external. Internal stress is related to pay, benefits, affirmative action, and lack of supportive administration. External stress can be caused by court decisions that have a negative effect on officers, lack of community support, and the work of civilian review boards. (See Exhibit 17.1.)

Sources of Stress

A considerable number of stressors influence a police officer's work environment. In addition to the factors mentioned earlier in the chapter, Selye (1981) and Stotland (1991) identified several issues that can lead to stress: death of a police partner, critical incidents, rotating shifts, isolation, dealing with the criminal element, moving from call to call without getting any closure on an incident, gender, family situation, and certain personality characteristics. Stress can also result from the normal day-to-day activities of a police officer.

Exhibit 17.1   Biography of Hans Selye

Hungarian immigrant and Canadian citizen Hans Seyle (1907–1982) is the most widely recognized researcher on stress. Trained as an endocrinologist and working out of McGill University and later University of Montreal, Seyle conducted some of the first rudimentary research on this type of psychological problem. His original research was conducted with mice, and his prodigious endeavors set the foundation for further research into the stress responses of various organisms and humans. Seyle's widespread, international reputation resulted in him being granted the prestigious Companion of Canada Award.

Not all police departments place the same kinds of demands on their police officers' time. Thus, officers in relatively large cities share many of the same sources of stress. Those in smaller jurisdictions often deal with different sets of issues, unique to their environments. "Over time, the effects of such stressors may spill over into officers personal lives, leading them to distrust even their own family and friends" (Wrobleski and Hess, 2006, p. 426).

Effects of Stress

Stress can be either positive or negative in its impact. If individuals do not experience even a small amount of stress, they may not be motivated to take precautionary steps in their behavior, such as avoiding certain individuals, situations, and places. Too much stress, however, can overload the psyche and can cause all sorts of physical and mental problems. Additionally, stress can be episodic or continuous in nature. In a policeman's job, episodic stress can be caused by a shootout during a bank robbery, which is a rare occurrence. Continuous stress may be brought about by an undercover operation to which an officer has been detailed.

Everybody reacts to stress differently. For some people, the stresses of modern life are often insurmountable. Many households cannot remain financially solvent without both husbands and wives working. Some people live paycheck to paycheck, which often is a constant source of stress. As a result of this kind of stress, some people find it difficult to balance the competing demands made upon their time. Other individuals learn to live with less money and fewer things, but appear to be more content. In other words, there is variability in reactions to stressful situations.

Stress can manifest itself in numerous ways: physical reactions, sleep and health problems, burnout, and diminished job performance. Stevens (2007) reports:

> Stressed officers are 30 percent more likely to experience health problems than other personnel, 3 times more likely to abuse their spouses, 5 times more

likely to abuse alcohol, 5 times more likely to have somatization (multiple, recurrent), 6 times more likely to experience anxiety, and 10 times more likely to be depressed—yet police officers are the least likely of all occupational group members to seek help. (p. 542)

Physical Reactions: Stress causes changes in a person's body, triggering what is often called a "flight or fight" reaction. The body readies itself to do whatever is necessary for survival (either to fight or run away) by increasing the heart rate, tensing the muscles, dilating the pupils, increasing the speed and depth of breathing patterns, and raising blood pressure. Over time, stress takes a toll on physical and mental health. If not addressed, it typically leads to serious medical problems, like heart disease, high blood pressure, strokes, circulatory problems, stomach ulcers, urinary problems, and loss of interest in sexual activity.

Sleep and Health Problems: The nature of police work can lead to sleep and health problems. Changing shift work is stressful on the body because it disrupts the body's natural sleeping pattern, causing a person to always feel tired. In order to deal with this situation, officers may drink copious amounts of coffee or use over-the-counter drugs to keep themselves awake. Neither of which is good for the body.

Burnout: Officers who are stressed much of the time may suffer burnout, which can compromise an officer's effectiveness and performance. Burnout is usually caused by the accumulated impact of stress, job-related boredom, and constant fatigue. "The literature shows that police officers have a high burnout rate, caused in part by their habit of ignoring stress, a lack of coping with family problems, occupational stress, low status, low public trust, and likelihood to become involved in civil litigation" (Stevens, 2008, pp. 542–543).

Job Performance: Stress can manifest itself in recurring tardiness to work or meetings, calling in sick, absenteeism, abuse, irritability, and feelings of hopelessness. If stress is not minimized, not only does it have an effect on the individual employee, but it can also affect the ability of an institution to operate effectively and efficiently.

The Federal Government's Reaction

The problem of officer stress has not gone unnoticed by the federal government. The pervasive nature of job-related stress in law enforcement was highlighted in 1986 when a nationwide assessment of law enforcement training needs found that state and local officers in all types and sizes of agencies ranked the need for training in personal stress management as their highest priority. Reported negative stress-related consequences included high rates of alcohol abuse, marital difficulties, domestic violence, stress-related health problems, disability retirements, and ultimately suicide. An increasing number of police departments, particularly in larger jurisdictions, now operate various forms of stress reduction and employee assistance programs; in some cases, the departments also make the program services available to officers' families. It should be noted that an important aspect of the 2004 "Law Enforcement Family Support" legislation (section 210201 of the *Crime Act*) is the emphasis it places on family well-being and the provision of stress-reduction and support services, not only to law enforcement officers, but also to members of their families. The act stated that the federal government will "assist Federal, State, and local law enforcement agencies to develop and implement policies and programs to reduce stress and promote family well-being through programs of research, training, technical assistance, and financial support."

How to Deal with Officer Stress

Police officers are reluctant to complain about their stress both to co-workers and their superiors for fear that they will be perceived as "weak, untrustworthy, and unlikely to back up an officer during a critical altercation" (Stevens, 2008, p. 540). Moreover, when information such as this is passed on to the police, there is a sort of blaming the victim kind of response. "Typically, management blames the officer for his or her stressed condition, which in turn reduces the officer's chances of promotion (or recovery)" (p. 540).

Often officers avoid talking about their stress to other officers and their loved ones. They keep it bottled in, sometimes with disastrous outcomes.

Police departments need to identify the sources of stress in their agencies and develop effective ways for their rank and file to deal with work-related pressures. Many law enforcement agencies either employ a full-time police psychologist or have them on retainer, and typically, they can effectively and positively implement ways to deal with the stress officers encounter on the job. An early warning indicator program can often prevent negative outcomes both to the officers who are identified by these systems, their families and loved ones, and the public as a whole.

Experts claim that it is not the amount of stress that causes health problems; rather, it is the way that each person deals with stress that really matters. Therefore, police officers need to learn how to manage the stress they have in their lives. They need to find productive, socially acceptable ways of releasing it so that it does not harm them or anyone with whom they come in contact. Stress is an important factor in officer retention

"Treating stress that results from critical incident experiences can enhance the officers' self-esteem, encourage nonabusive behavior toward an officer's own children and life partner, discourage substance abuse, and prevent suicide" (Stevens, 2008, p. 551). One of the best coping strategies is debriefing, which "is a type of short-term psychological intervention used to help officers who experience temporary extreme emotions to recognize, correct, and cope with them as a result of a critical incident" (p. 552). Other coping mechanisms can be cultivated in external and internal programs, ranging from meeting with the police psychologist to engaging in group therapy sessions.

Although superiors or colleagues may recommend to a police officer that he or she seek psychological help or take part in a stress reduction program, the final decision is typically left in the officer's hands. White (2007) identifies six basic programs that can be instituted to help reduce stress issues: stress inoculation, police family stress reduction units, peer support, critical incident stress debriefing units, early warning systems, and a dedicated police stress unit.

Haberfield (2002) recommends another methodology, the Feelings-Inputs-Tactics (FIT) approach, which, White (2007) explains,

> builds on existing department resources but adds this missing component. Participation is the program is mandatory for all officers thereby eliminating the stigma often faced by those who seek out help. . . . FIT sessions occur on a regular basis and each officer takes turns discussing their feelings. . . . Other officers offer suggestions and advice, and the meeting is facilitated by a professional. . . . The program should be introduced at the academy, so officers become familiar with it and are more accepting once on the job. The overall goal of the FIT model is to reduce the stigma of participation in such programs, to create a formal mechanism for all officers to express their emotions, and eventually, to reach the point where officers are admired as much for their psychological self-defense as for their physical. (p. 53)

Unfortunately FIT lacks general acceptance. No officer wants to admit to others that he or she is mentally/psychologically weak. Another way to minimize stress is to ensure that you feel competent in your skill set and to take the necessary safety precautions in potentially dangerous situations.

Conclusion

Every profession presents its workers and their supervisors with certain challenges, and policing is no different. The unique working conditions of being a police officer can lead to high rates of turnover (i.e., police officers leaving the job) and difficulties in retaining police officers. There is hope, though, that since many police departments and the federal government have recognized the debilitating effects of stress, a broad array of programs will help officers to minimize the negative effects of this silent killer.

Glossary

Burnout: This occurs when an officer's effectiveness and performance is diminished because of the accumulated impact of stress, job boredom, and ongoing fatigue.

Cross-training: When officers temporarily work in a police department position that is not their own.

Cynicism: A belief that others are primarily motivated by self-interest; this perspective can cause officers to be skeptical of the intentions and actions of others.

Golden handcuffs: An expression that refers to officers' perception that because of the relative benefit (e.g., pay or financial obligations they have) they cannot (or should not) leave the field of policing to find a different more enjoyable job.

Helping professions: These vocations include nurses, teachers, social workers, social workers, and first responders.

National Institute of Justice (NIJ): The research arm of the United States Department of Justice.

Rotating shift work: The lack of permanent shifts. This practice requires employees to work for changing, short periods of time over day, evening, and night shifts.

Stress: An intense physical and mental response to an episodic or continuing demanding situation or event. If not handled properly, stress can lead to both psychological and physical problems.

Turnover: The frequency with which an institution loses or fires employees.

Chapter Questions

Part One: Multiple Choice Questions

1. What term describes the mental state of police officers who feel they are stuck in their position based on their relative education and the steady pay they receive?
   a. post-traumatic stress disorder
   b. insane workplace syndrome
   c. golden handcuffs
   d. toxic workplace disorder
   e. none of the above

2. Which of the following factors affects burnout?
   a. age
   b. gender
   c. years on the job
   d. marital status
   e. all of the above

3. In what year did the Department of Justice take an active interest in stress among police officers?
   a. 1980
   b. 1994
   c. 2004
   d. 2005
   e. none of the above

4. Which of the following have been recommended to reduce police officer stress?
   a. allow police officers to contribute to their unit's decision-making process.
   b. maintain physical health.
   c. engage in deep relaxation.
   d. all of the above
   e. none of the above

5. Which of the following is NOT a factor affecting the working conditions of police officers?
   a. age
   b. neighborhood in which they are assigned
   c. assigned shift
   d. specialization
   e. personal attitudes

6. In policing what is cross-training?
   a. constantly changing shifts
   b. learning a different skill or job in your organization
   c. improving your ability to run the police marathon
   d. using weights, swimming, and running to improve cardiovascular health
   e. none of the above

7. Stress among police officers is always
   a. bad
   b. good
   c. creates negative physical and psychological problems
   d. leads to divorces
   e. none of the above

Part Two: Short Answer Questions

1. What four things can police officers do to prevent contracting a disease in the workplace?

2. List four factors that mediate police officer burnout.

3. What are four ways that suppressed anger or burnout may be expressed?

4. What is meant by the term "organizational culture" in the context of policing?

5. How can a police officer overcome the golden handcuffs problem?

Part Three: Essay Questions

1. Design a program for your fellow police officers that would reduce their stress within a 10-day period. How would you demonstrate that your proposal is effective?

2. How different are the working conditions of police officers from other first responders? Whose job do you think is more stressful and why?

3. How can police officers improve their working conditions without the agency incurring more expenses?

The Future of
Municipal Policing

Introduction

Since the establishment of urban police forces in London and the United States, municipal policing has experienced numerous changes. Most of these developments have improved law enforcement, making both police officers and the agencies they work for more professional, efficient, accountable, and better able to serve and protect the public. This evolution has not occurred without a considerable amount of research, experimentation, resource expenditure, and political battles. This book has analyzed the most significant current challenges facing municipal police departments, the men and women who work for them, and the solutions that have been marshaled. Each chapter integrated the scholarly literature and historical evidence that bear upon the challenges and responses that have been proposed, those that have been implemented and those that have been effective.

Unfortunately, police forces, like many of our public institutions, fall prey to fads, such as a new technology, whose manufacturers and salespeople guarantee will make policing easier and safer, or a new management technique that simultaneously furthers the accomplishment of policing goals and cultivates happiness and loyalty in all employees from the chief down to the rank-and-file officers. When these innovations fail, as they often do, the outcome leads to the expenditure of limited resources, demoralization, and cynicism. Knowing this, departmental managers should be cautious about quick-fix solutions, particularly ones that so-called experts, consultants, and pundits propose to improve policing or selected aspects of it.

That being said, numerous recent events have changed the landscape of policing for the foreseeable future. Immigrant-related (both legal and illegal) crime and victimization, the 9/11 terrorist attacks and heightened fears of oppositional political terrorism (Ross, 2006a), and increased vigilance and surveillance as a result of the passage of the PATRIOT Act have forced significant changes in policing, particularly in big-city police departments (see Exhibit 18.1). These developments have led experts to call into question the subtle abandonment of community- and problem-oriented policing, the widespread embrace of CompStat, and the deep concerns and alert awareness of terrorism. This process has highlighted the importance of close relationships and partnerships in the communities served by police and the significance of alliances with other governmental entities.

Several central questions remain: Who is going to fund the additional burdens that are now being placed on municipal police departments? Will the resources come from the private or public sector or from a combination of the two? And from which level of government will these monies be provided?

Also important is the necessity for ongoing relevant and essential research on the policing function. Although a considerable amount of insightful, unfunded research can be conducted, some of the important questions facing police departments require large-scale evaluation efforts, and these need to be paid for either by the federal government (Ross, 2000a) or by private foundations. The ongoing availability of federal funds to conduct studies and support evaluations should increase practical knowledge about policing practices. Whether police agencies act upon this information is a different story. With this in mind, this chapter briefly summarizes the most important challenges facing the future of municipal policing in the United States.

The Developments

The Necessity of Studying CompStat

As previous chapters have noted, CompStat is being integrated into the working philosophy and practice of many police departments. Its champions have ascribed considerable importance to the system's accomplishments. Despite being in the field for almost 15 years, few evaluation studies have been conducted. The time is now ripe for a major research endeavor to determine CompStat's relative effectiveness. This could be aided by the federal government, through grants sponsored by the National Institute of Justice, or via private foundations that are willing to support this important review and analysis process.

Police Treatment of Crime Victims

Police treatment of victims of crime continues to be an issue of concern. Many police departments and the state prosecutors offices have responded to this problem by hiring police victim advocates (VAs). Properly trained individuals working in paid or volunteer positions can help victims of crime who may be physically and psychologically traumatized. The restorative justice framework has renewed attention to the need to look at victim

Exhibit 18.1 The 1993 World Trade Center Bombing and 9/11/2001 Attacks

New York City's World Trade Center building was a symbol of American capitalism and progress, which are anathema to fundamentalist Muslims, Osama bin Laden, and his organization al Qaeda (Gunaratna, 2002; Burke, 2003; Glantz and Lipton, 2003). On February 26, 1993, Ramzi Yousef and his accomplice Mohammad Salameh, members of the al Qaeda terrorist organization, drove a rented Ford Econoline van laden with explosives into the basement parking lot of the World Trade Center. It was a primitive bomb with a long fuse, but it managed to ignite and explode at midday, and the explosion was powerful enough to destroy five floors of the building directly above it and short out all electricity in the structure (Reeve, 1999, pp. 11–12).

Initially, many people thought it was simply a fire or an electrical transformer explosion. But when workers exited the building, some were "crushed underfoot as panic began to spread" (Reeve, 1999, p. 13). The New York City Fire Department "sent a total of 750 vehicles to the explosion, and did not leave the scene for the next month. It took hundreds of firefighters two hours to extinguish the blazes and more than five hours to evacuate both towers" (Reeve 1999, p. 14). Six people were killed and 1,042 injured.

Yousef wanted to cause one of the buildings to fall into the other. If he had been successful, he would have ended up killing almost a quarter of a million people working in the buildings that day. According to Yousef, "Only carnage on such a level would be sufficient punishment for supporting Israel, America's friend and ally, and the fundamentalists' sworn enemy because of its treatment of the Palestinians" (quoted in Reeve 1999, p. 24). After the attack, Yousef almost immediately left the country for Karachi, Pakistan. Investigators combing the scene found the van's vehicle identification number relatively quickly and were able to determine that it was rented by Salameh.

Salameh, unlike Yousef, foolishly went back to the rental company to recoup his deposit. There, waiting for him, was an FBI officer posing as a rental agent. After a series of questions, Salameh was arrested. Then, based on this initial investigation, the FBI took into custody a number of co-conspirators. In order to capture Yousef, the authorities disseminated the information worldwide, and he was later captured on February 7, 1995, in Pakistan (while plotting to launch a major offensive against the American presence in the Philippines) and returned to the United States.

On the morning of September 11, 2001, shortly after takeoff, nineteen members of the al Qaeda organization managed to commandeer four large jet airplanes. At approximately the same time, two crashed separately into the twin towers of the World Trade Center in New York City, one into the Pentagon in Washington, DC, and the fourth in a field in rural Pennsylvania. Close to 3,000 people died. Responsibility for this attack was placed squarely on the al Qaeda terrorist organization (Ross, 2006a, pp. 166–167).

involvement in all stages of the criminal justice system process, including how they are perceived and treated, whether special programs or units exist within criminal justice agencies (e.g., police departments) to address victims' issues and needs, whether victims are "revictimized" by system agencies, and what attitudes police display toward victims. Rarely are these issues studied in a broad spectrum of jurisdictions and police agencies, including those serving American Indian communities, as well as rural and metropolitan areas.[1]

Police–Labor Relations Issues

Labor relations and labor organizations are a significant and influential entity within American law enforcement. As discussed earlier in this text, they have the potential to impact the actual and programmatic direction of police departments and the communities they serve. With the implementation of new policies and practices, technology, and laws, police-labor unions and associations are bound to be impacted. Support or resistance from police labor organizations during transition periods may have a significant effect on the success or failure of new policies or measures.

Cooperation and Coordination among Police Departments and with Other Government Departments and Private Security Organizations

In many areas, several police departments co-exist and operate within the same jurisdiction. These entities may include federal, state, and local law enforcement agencies responsible for a variety of functions, such as parks, housing, and transit. Private police officers may also be operating within a specific area as well. One issue of pressing concern is understanding how these disparate agencies cooperate and coordinate with each other and with other government units in pursuit of mutual goals and how this cooperation can be improved. Private security companies are involved in many of the same functions as state and local police departments. In addition, some private security organizations have at their disposal larger revenue sources than state and local law enforcement organizations. On occasion, the private companies employ on a part-time basis some of the same officers who are simultaneously employed by governmental police agencies. Research is needed to analyze the complex relationship between private (e.g., security officers/guards/services) and public police agencies.

Purchase and Integration of New Technology

Understanding the infusion, transfer, and impact of technology on police officers, managers, organizations, and communities is critically important in determining the future directions of technology development and its utilization. Along with salaries and benefits, the purchase and use of new technology requires a large financial outlay for most law enforcement agencies. New federal programs (e.g., Commercial Equipment Direct Assistance Program) seek to facilitate the purchase of Homeland Security-related equipment (e.g., night vision goggles) by municipal police departments. However, this financial support provides only a small amount of relief when compared to most agencies' current and future needs.

Immigrant-Related Crime

Special problems arise for police departments when foreign nationals (legal or illegal immigrants) engage in crimes in the United States and when American citizens flee to other countries to avoid detection, capture, and prosecution. Of additional concern is the lack of local, state, and federal cooperation in policing illegal immigration. Many municipal police departments (e.g., in Arizona) are being asked to assume what is essentially and traditionally a federal role. Some have embraced this task, while others, which are understaffed, have requested increased resources from their state and/or the federal government. Finally, many immigrants are victims of crime. Afraid of being detected, illegal immigrants are reluctant to report these crimes to the police, and thus, local law enforcement agencies may have a truncated perception of the kinds and amount of victimization that are occurring in their jurisdiction.

Oppositional Political Terrorism

Police departments must be vigilant against both domestic and international terrorism. Although numerous definitions of terrorism exist, oppositional political terrorism generally refers to violence in support of a political, religious, or ideological goal in which the amount and type of violence is perceived to be extra-normal by most observers (Ross, 2006a). Although subcomponents of terrorism, such as cyber-terrorism, narco-terrorism, and eco-terrorism, are significant, these types of violence are often the purview of the federal government. They are typically monitored and handled by the Federal Bureau of Investigation, the Drug Enforcement Agency, and in the case of eco-terrorism, the Bureau of Land Management or National Park Service officers. Local law enforcement officers have had a prominent role in almost all of the terrorist incidents in the United States, mainly because the attacks have occurred in large municipalities. Some of the locations that are now the focus of increased police surveillance include transportation hubs (including subways, train stations, airports, and bus stations) and government buildings. With respect to the 9/11 attacks, in addition to the deaths of 343 NYC firefighters, 23 NYPD officers perished on that day. "Departments have been forced to revise training, deployment, and communications strategies and to create counterterrorism units within their departments" (White, 2007, p. 193). These new strategies often mean that police located in larger jurisdictions provide extra patrol and security around critical infrastructures.

Consequently, the NYPD has a special unit, employing approximately 1,000 officers whose sole job is to respond to terrorism-related threats. Schmalleger and Worrall (2010) report that

> the NYPD has assigned detectives to work abroad with law enforcement agencies in Canada, Israel, Southeast Asia, and the Middle East to track terrorists who might target New York City, and it now employs officers with a command of Pahsto, Farsi, and Urdu languages of the Middle East to monitor foreign television, radio, and Internet communications. The department has also invested heavily in new hazardous materials protective suits, gas masks, and portable radiation detectors. (p. 388)

Improvements in Police Scholarship

Every few years, a new English-language scholarly journal focused on policing is launched. This is accompanied by much fanfare from the editors and the publishing company involved in the journal. Overall, this trend has led to an increase in police research that should have an impact on policy and practice. Needless to say, over the past two decades, few policing scholars have performed replication studies (i.e., the repeated execution of the same test or experiment, using the same (or near similar) conditions on a variety of subjects or in an array of locations to more clearly detect similarities and differences). These replications would determine if patterns of policing (e.g., patrol, detective work) are still being performed the way they traditionally were. Moreover, numerous police practices lack a sufficient research base. One of these weaknesses pertains to research on minority recruitment beyond the African-American and Hispanic communities. For example, little research has been done on the recruitment and retention of Native Americans and Asian-Americans. In short, additional scholarship should focus on both traditional and emerging concerns and on contemporary issues that will affect municipal policing. This being said, researchers need to build upon existing studies and not simply assume that no research has been conducted on the subject. In turn, they should push the boundaries of what is known of current police policies and practices.

Evidence-Based Policing

Over the past decade, many knowledgeable and progressive police administrators have seen the value of social scientific research in helping them shape the day-to-day policies and practices of their departments. This trend has been called evidence-based policing (Sherman, 1998). Following the examples in the medical field, Sherman and others argue that if policing is going to improve, it must integrate the methodology of scientific research, particularly that which integrates experimental methods and replication.

Studying the Future of Policing

Since the 1980s, a group of researchers has devoted a portion of their scholarship to identifying future trends in policing. The Society of Police Futurists International is composed of law enforcement professionals, both practitioners and scholars, who meet regularly and provide advice on what they believe will be the future of policing. This group can trace its origins to a course taught by Bill Tafoya at the FBI academy. Since then, the group has grown its membership. Each year it holds a conference where members present papers. Over the years, a number of methods are used to predict possible scenarios, including the Delphi method, trend extrapolation, historical analogies, and scenarios.

Conclusion

Through the combined processes of globalization and development and the use and diffusion of new communications technologies (e.g., Internet, cell phone, smart phone), many new crimes, especially those that are transnational in nature (e.g., identify theft, cybercrime, human trafficking, weapons trafficking), are coming to the attention of municipal police officers. Unfortunately, the ability of urban and local police departments to properly combat these crimes is negligible due to the specialized nature of these kinds of crimes and the lack of resources. Reports on these activities are usually forwarded to state and federal law enforcement agencies that are better able to monitor, track, and combat these more complicated infractions. Over time, however, with increasing sophistication and resources, local police departments may be asked or voluntarily choose to take a greater role in responding to these kinds of crime.

As students who may become police officers one day, you are entrusted with a great responsibility to uphold the law and to remain fair and unbiased when the people you deal with on a daily basis are less than cooperative and even aggressive toward you and others. It takes a special kind of person to be a police officer. For those of you who will assume positions in other parts of the criminal justice system, hopefully this book has sensitized you to the unique features of a sister agency with which you may work in the future. You will have a greater appreciation of the police officer's lot.

Note

1. See, for example, http://hartfordcounty.md.gov/statesattorney/victim Witness.html, the Maryland State Board for Victim Assistance, and the website of the National Center for Victims of Crime.

Glossary

Cybercrime: The use of computers and computer technology (i.e., the Internet and World Wide Web) as tools to commit crimes.

Evaluation research: This research determines whether a new policy or practice has been implemented correctly or if it has a measurable effect on the thing, process, or attitude it was designed to change.

Evidence-based policing: The application of the techniques of social science, especially experimentation, to improve the policies and practices of policing.

Homeland security: This term was popularized following the 9/11 attacks. It refers to the process of monitoring external threats and attacks to the United States. A further component of this program focuses on ensuring that the appropriate federal, state, and local agencies can provide emergency preparedness in the case of natural disasters, such as floods, hurricanes, and earthquakes.

Oppositional political terrorism: Violence in support of a political, religious, or ideological goal in which the amount and type of violence is perceived to be extra-normal by most observers.

Replication: The repeated execution of the same test or experiment, using the same experimental conditions on a variety of subjects or in an array of locations to more clearly detect similarities and differences.

Victim advocate: Individual who helps victims of crime who may be physically and psychologically traumatized by the crime in which they were involved. They may work for police departments or prosecutors' offices.

Chapter Questions

Part One: Multiple Choice Questions

1. Which of the following areas are in need of more research?
   a. traditional
   b. emerging concerns
   c. contemporary areas
   d. both a and b
   e. all of the above

2. In all likelihood, eco-terrorist attacks will be a priority for
   a. municipal police departments
   b. state agencies
   c. FBI
   d. National Park Service
   e. Drug Enforcement Agency

3. Which of the following crimes are enhanced by globalization?
   a. cybercrime
   b. human trafficking
   c. weapons smuggling
   d. drug smuggling
   e. all of the above

4. When was the first terrorist attack on the World Trade Center?
   a. March 10, 1980
   b. February 26, 1993
   c. June 12, 1990
   d. July 20, 1998
   e. September 11, 2001

5. What happens when a police department falls prey to fads?
   a. Officers can become demoralized.
   b. Scarce resources are needlessly consumed.
   c. Cynicism grows among rank and file and citizens.
   d. all of the above
   e. none of the above

6. What is the name of the organization that studies the future of policing?
   a. U.S. Department of Justice
   b. National Institute of Justice
   c. Police Executive Research Forum
   d. Society of Police Futurists International
   e. National Academy of Sciences

Part Two: Short Answer Questions

1. What is a replication?

2. What is homeland security?

3. What is cybercrime?

4. What is a victim advocate?

5. What is evidence-based policing?

Part Three: Essay Questions

1. If you were the chief of police/commissioner of a medium-sized department, what three new programs would you implement to make your department more effective? Explain your reasons.

2. What is the role of research in the future of policing?

3. Given what you have learned in this book, how would you go about determining the most important problems facing municipal policing in the United States?

Answer Key for Multiple Choice Questions

Chapter 1		Chapter 2	
1.	c	1.	e
2.	c	2.	d
3.	d	3.	d
4.	b	4.	c
5.	c	5.	b
6.	c	6.	e
7.	b	7.	b
8.	d	8.	d
9.	c	9.	b
10.	b	10.	e
11.	e	11.	e
12.	d	12.	a
13.	d	13.	d
14.	a	14.	b
15.	e	15.	d
16.	d		
17.	c		
18.	a		

Chapter 3

1. b
2. e
3. d
4. d
5. d
6. b
7. d
8. d
9. e
10. d
11. e
12. a
13. b

Chapter 4

1. a
2. d
3. d
4. e
5. e
6. a
7. a

Chapter 5

1. c
2. a
3. e
4. d
5. c
6. e
7. d

Chapter 6

1. b
2. d
3. d
4. a
5. a
6. c
7. e
8. b

Chapter 7

1. b
2. c
3. a
4. a
5. e
6. d
7. a
8. e

Chapter 8

1. e
2. d
3. b
4. c
5. a
6. c
7. b
8. c
9. d

Chapter 9

1. e
2. c
3. a
4. b
5. b
6. b
7. e
8. a
9. d
10. d
11. b
12. c
13. c
14. c
15. e
16. e
17. c
18. c

Chapter 10

1. e
2. c
3. d
4. b
5. a
6. e
7. d
8. b
9. b
10. d
11. b
12. d
13. d
14. e
15. b
16. d
17. d
18. e
19. a
20. b
21. a

Chapter 11

1. e
2. d
3. c
4. c
5. a
6. a

Chapter 12

1. c
2. e
3. b
4. a
5. d
6. a
7. a

Chapter 13

1. d
2. d
3. c
4. d
5. c
6. a
7. d

Chapter 14

1. d
2. a
3. d
4. d
5. a
6. d

Chapter 15

1. c
2. d
3. e
4. c
5. d
6. b
7. a
8. d

Chapter 16

1. b
2. c
3. c
4. e
5. a
6. e
7. d

Chapter 17

1. c
2. e
3. c
4. d
5. e
6. b
7. e

Chapter 18

1. e
2. d
3. e
4. b
5. d
6. d

Bibliography

Ackroyd, J. W. 1975. "Rejoinder to Grant, Alan, 'The Control of Police Behavior.'" In W. S. Tarnoplsky (ed.), *Some Civil Liberties Issues of the Seventies*. Toronto: Osgoode Hall Law School, pp. 111–116.

Adams, Kenneth. Geoffrey P. Alpert, Roger G. Dunham, Joel H. Garner, Lawrence A. Greenfeld, Mark A. Henriquez, Patrick A. Langan, Christopher D. Maxwell, and Steven K. Smith. 1999. "What We Know about Police Use of Force," *National Institute of Justice Research Report*, October. http://www.ncjrs.gov/txtfiles1/nij/176330.txt (downloaded October 22, 2010).

Adlam, Robert K. C. 1982. "The Police Personality: Psychological Consequences of Being a Police Officer," *Journal of Police Science and Administration*, Vol. 10, No. 3, pp. 334–349.

Adler, Patricia. 2005. *Constructions of Deviance*. Belmont, CA: Wadsworth.

Advisory Commission on Intergovernmental Relations. 1971. *Police Reform*. Washington, DC: U.S. Government Printing Office.

Alderson, J. C. 1979. *Policing Freedom*. Plymouth, England: MacDonald and Evans.

Allen, R. K. 1977. *Organizational Management Through Communication*. New York: Harper and Row.

Alpert, Geoffrey P. and Roger Dunham. 1992. *Policing Urban America* (2nd ed.), Prospect Heights, IL: Waveland Press.

Alpert, Geoffrey P. and Roger Dunham. 1997. *Policing Urban America* (3rd ed.), Prospect Heights, IL: Waveland Press.

Alpert, Geoffrey P. and Lorie Fridell. 1992. *Police Vehicles and Firearms: Instruments of Deadly Force*. Prospect Heights, IL: Waveland Press.

Alpert, Geoffrey P., Dennis J. Kenney, R. G. Dunham, and W. C. Smith. 2000. *Police Pursuits: What We know*. Washington, DC: Police Executive Research Forum.

Angel, John. 1975. "The Democratic Model Needs a Fair Trial," *Criminology*, Vol. 12, No. 4, pp. 379–385.

Arrigo, Bruce (ed.). 1999. *Social Justice/Criminal Justice*. Belmont, CA: Wadsworth.

Aylesworth, G. N. 1992. "Forfeiture of Real Property: An Overview," *Police Executive Research Forum*, Vol. 14, No. 1, pp. 1–64.

Bachrach, Peter and Morton S. Baratz. 1962. "Two Faces of Power," *American Political Science Review*, Vol. 5, No. 4, December, pp. 947–952.

Balagopal, K. 1986. "Deaths in Police Custody: Whom and Why Do the Police Kill?" *Economic and Political Weekly*, Vol. 21, November 22, pp. 2028–2029.

Balch, R. W. 1972. "The Police Personality: Fact or Fiction?" *Journal of Criminal Law, Criminology and Police Science*, Vol. 63, No. 1, pp. 106–119.

Baldwin, John. 1992. "Video-Taping Police Interviews with Suspects—An Evaluation," London: Home Office Police Department, Police Research Series: Paper No. 1.

Banton, Michael. 1964. *The Policeman in the Community* New York: Basic Books.

Barker, Thomas. 1977. "Peer Group Support for Police Occupational Deviance," *Criminology*, Vol. 15, No. 3, pp. 353–366.

Barker, Thomas. 1978. "An Empirical Study of Police Deviance Other Than Corruption," *Journal of Police Science and Administration*, Vol. 6, No. 3, pp. 264–272.

Barker, Thomas. 1983. "Rookie Police Officers' Perceptions of Police Occupational Deviance," *Police Studies: International Review of Police Development*, Vol. 6, No. 2, pp. 30–38.

Bayley, David H. 1971. "The Police and Political Change in Comparative Perspective," *Law and Society Review*, Vol. 6, No. 1, pp. 91–112.

Bayley, David H. 1979. "Police Function, Structure, and Control in Western Europe and North America." In Norval Morris and Michael Tonry (eds.), *Crime and Justice: An Annual Review of Research*, Vol. 1. Chicago: University of Chicago Press, pp. 109–144.

Bayley, David H. 1985 *Patterns of Policing: A Comparative International Analysis*. New Brunswick, NJ: Rutgers University Press.

Bayley, David H. 1988. "Community Policing: A Report from the Devil's Advocate," In Jack R. Greene and Stephen D. Mastrofski (eds.), *Community Policing: Rhetoric or Reality*. New York: Praeger, pp. 225–238.

Bayley, David H. 1990. *Patterns of Policing: A Comparative International Analysis*. Piscataway, NJ: Rutgers University Press.

Bayley, David H. 1994. *Police for the Future*. New York: Oxford University Press.

Bayley, David H. and Harold Mendelsohn. 1969. *Minorities and the Police*. New York: Free Press.

Beare, M. E. 1987. "Selling Policing in Metropolitan Toronto: A Sociological Analysis of Police Rhetoric, 1957–1984," Ph.D. Dissertation, Columbia University.

Becker, Howard. 1963. *The Outsiders: Studies in the Sociology of Deviance.* London: Free Press.

Bell, D. J. 1982. "Policewomen—Myths and Reality," *Journal of Police Science and Administration,* Vol. 10, No. 1, pp. 112–120.

Bennett, Georgette. 1989. *Crimewarps: The Future of Crime in America* (rev. ed.). New York: Doubleday.

Bennett, G. 1990. "Cultural Lag in Law Enforcement: Preparing for the Crimewarps," *American Journal of Police,* Vol. 4, No. 3, pp. 81–126.

Bennett, Wayne W. and Karen Hess. 1996. *Management and Supervision in Law Enforcement.* (2nd Ed.) St. Paul, MN: West Publishers.

Beral, H. and M. Sisk. 1963. "The Administration of Complaints by Civilians Against the Police," *Harvard Law Review,* Vol. 77, pp. 499–519.

Binder, A. and Lorie Fridell. 1984. "Lethal Force as a Police Response," *Criminal Justice Abstracts,* Vol. 16, pp. 256–280.

Binder, A. and Peter Scharf. 1980. "The Violent Police Citizen Encounter," *Annals of The American Political and Social Science,* Vol. 452, No. 1, pp. 111–121.

Birzer, M. L. 2003. "The Theory of Andragogy Applied to Police Training," *Policing: An International Journal of Police Strategies and Management,* Vol. 26, No. 1, pp. 29–42.

Bittner, Egon. 1967a. "The Police on Skid Row: A Study of Peace Keeping," *American Sociological Review,* Vol. 32, No. 5, October, pp. 699–715.

Bittner, Egon. 1967b. "Police Discretion in Emergency Apprehension of Mentally Ill Persons," *Social Problems,* Vol. 14, No. 3, pp. 278–292.

Black, Donald J. 1970. "The Production of Crime Rates," *American Sociological Review,* Vol. 35, No. 4, pp. 733–748.

Black, Donald J. and Albert J. Reiss Jr. 1970. "Police Control of Juveniles," *American Sociological Review,* Vol. 35, No. 1, February, pp. 63–77.

Boyd, David. G. 1995. "On the Cutting Edge: Law Enforcement Technology," *FBI Law Enforcement Bulletin,* Vol. 64, No. 7, July, pp.1–5.

Box, Steven and Ken Russell. 1975. "The Politics of Discreditability: Disarming Complaints against the Police," *Sociological Review,* Vol. 23, No. 2, pp. 315–346.

Braithwaite, John. 1989. *Crime, Shame and Reintegration.* Cambridge, England: Cambridge University Press.

Brandl, Steven G. 1996. "In the Line of Duty: A Descriptive Analysis of Police Assaults and Accidents," *Journal of Criminal Justice,* Vol. 24, No. 3, pp. 255–264.

Brandl, Steven G. and Meghan S. Stroshine. 2003. "Toward an Understanding of the Physical Hazards of Police Work," *Police Quarterly,* Vol. 6, No. 2, pp. 172–191.

Bratton, William. 1997. "Crime Is Down in New York City: Blame the Police," in Norman Dennis (ed.), *Zero Tolerance: Policing in a Free Society*. London: IEA Health and Welfare Unit, pp. 29–42.

Bratton, William. 1998. *The Turnaround: How America's Top Cop Reversed the Crime Epidemic*. New York: Random House.

Brooks, Laure Weber. 1997. "Police Discretionary Behavior: A Study of Style," in Roger G. Dunham and Geoffrey P. Alpert (eds.), *Critical Issues in Policing: Contemporary Readings* (5th ed.). Prospect Heights, IL: Waveland Press, pp. 149–166.

Brown, Michael. 1981. *Working the Street: Police Discretion and the Dilemmas of Reform*. New York: Russell Sage.

Burke, J. 2003. *Al Qaeda: Casting a Shadow of Terror*. London: I. B. Tauris.

Cain, M. 1973. *Society and the Policeman's Role*. London: Routledge and Kegan Paul.

Caplan, Gerald and Patrick V. Murphy. 1991. "Fostering Integrity," in William A. Geller and Darryl W. Stephens (eds.) *Local Government Police Management*, Washington, DC. ICMA Press, pp. 239–271.

Carlson, Robert O. 1968 "Public Relations," in David L. Sills (ed.), *International Encyclopedia of the Social Sciences*, Vol. 13. New York: Macmillan, pp. 208–217.

Carpenter, Bruce N. and Susan M. Raza. 1987. "Personality Characteristics of Police Applicants: Comparisons Across Subgroups and with Other Populations," *Journal of Police Science and Administration*, Vol. 15, No. 1, pp. 10–17.

Carte, G. E. and E. Carte. 1975. *Police Reform in the United States: The Era of August Vollimer 1905–1932*. Berkeley, CA: University of California Press.

Chappell, Allison, T. Chappell, Lonn Lanza-Kaduce, and Daryl H. Johnston. 2005. "Law Enforcement Training: Changes and Challenges," in Roger G. Dunham and Geoffrey P. Alpert (eds.), *Critical Policing: Contemporary Readings*. Long Grove, IL: Waveland Press, pp. 71–88.

Chu, James. 2001. *Law Enforcement Information Technology: A Managerial, Operational, and Practitioner Guide*. Boca Raton, FL: CRC Press.

Chermak, Steven and Alexander Weiss. 2005. "Maintaining Legitimacy Using External Communication Strategies: An Analysis of Police–Media Relations," *Journal of Criminal Justice*, Vol. 33, No. 5, pp. 501–512.

Christensen, Jon, Janet Schmidt, and Joel Henderson. 1982. "The Selling of the Police: Media, Ideology and Crime Control," *Contemporary Crisis*, Vol. 6, No. 3, pp. 227–239.

Clayton, Richard R., Anne Cattarello, and Katherine P. Walden. 1991. "Sensation Seeking as a Potential Mediating Variable for School-Based Prevention Intervention: A Two-Year Follow-Up of D.A.R.E.," *Health Communication*, Vol. 3, No. 4, pp. 229–239.

Conley, John A. 1994. *The 1967 President's Crime Commission Report: Its Impact 25 Years Later*. Cincinnati, OH: Anderson Publishing.

Conyers Commission. 1984. *Hearings in New York City on Police Misconduct*. Washington, DC: U.S. Government Printing Office.

Cooper, L. B. 1974. "Controlling the Police." In E. C. Viano and J. H. Reiman (eds.), *The Police in Society*. Lexington, MA: Lexington Books, pp. 241–248.

Cordner, Gary. 2005. "Community Policing: Elements and Effectiveness," in Roger G. Dunham and Geoffrey Alpert (Eds.), *Critical Issues in Policing*. (5th ed.). Long View, IL: Waveland Press.

Cordner, Gary and E. P. Biebel. 2005. "Problem-Oriented Policing in Practice," *Criminology and Public Policy*, Vol. 42, No. 2, pp. 155–180.

Cordner, Gary and Katheryn Scarborough. 2007. *Police Administration* (6th ed.). Newark, NJ: Lexis-Nexis.

Crawford, Charles. 1999. "Law Enforcement and Popular Movies: Hollywood as a Teaching Tool in the Classroom," *Journal of Criminal Justice and Popular Culture*, Vol. 6, No. 2, pp. 46–57.

Crew, B. Keith, 1990. "Acting Like Cops: The Social Reality of Crime and Law on TV Police Dramas," in Clinton R. Sanders (ed.), *Marginal Conventions: Popular Culture, Mass Media, and Social Deviance*. Bowling Green, OH: Bowling Green State University Popular Press, pp. 131–143.

Cumming Elaine, Ian Cumming, and Laura Edell. 1970. "Policeman as Philosopher, Guide and Friend," in A. Niederhoffer and A. Blumberg (eds.) *The Ambivalent Force*. Waltham, MA: Ginn, pp. 184–192.

Daraki Mallet, M. 1976. *The ESA Men*. Athens, Greece: Kendros.

Daley, Robert. 1972. *Target Blue*. New York: Delacorte Press.

Daley, Robert. 1978. *Prince of the City*. New York: Berkley Press.

Davis, Kenneth C. 1969. *Discretionary Justice: A Preliminary Inquiry*. Baton Rouge: Louisiana State University.

Davis, Kenneth C. 1971. *Discretionary Justice: Preliminary Inquiry*. Urbana, IL: University of Illinois Press.

Davis, Kenneth C. 1974. "An Approach to Legal Control of the Police," *Texas Law Review*, Vol. 52, No. 4, pp. 703–25.

Davis, Kenneth C. 1975. *Police Discretion*. St. Paul, MN: West Publishing.

Dayan, Kobi, Rohen Kasten, and Shaul Fox. 2002. "Entry-Level Police Candidate Assessment Center: An Efficient Tool or a Hammer to Kill a Fly," *Personnel Psychology*, Vol. 55, No. 4, pp. 827–849.

Decisso, David A. 2000. "Police Officer Candidate Assessment and Selection," *FBI Law Enforcement*, http://fbi.gov.publications

Deming, W. Edwards. 1994. *Out of the Crisis*. Cambridge, MA: The MIT Press.

Dennis, Norman (ed.). 1997. *Zero Tolerance: Policing a Free Society*. London: IEA Health and Welfare Unit.

Doerner, William, C. Horton, and J. L. Smith. 2003. "The Field Training Officer Program: A Case Study Approach," In Michael J. Palmiotto (ed.) *Police and Training Issue*. Englewood Cliffs, NJ: Prentice Hall, pp. 207–234.

Downs, Raymond L. 2007. "Less Lethal Weapons: A Technologist's Perspective," *Policing: An International Journal of Police Strategies & Management*, Vol. 30, No. 3, pp. 358–384.

Drucker, Peter F. 1954/2007. *The Practice of Management* (2nd ed.). Burlington, MA: Butterworth-Heinemann.

Dukes, R. L., J. A. Stein, & J. B. Ullman. 1997. "Long-Tern Impact of Drug Abuse Resistance Education (D.A.R.E): Results of a 6-Year Follow-Up," *Evaluation Review*, Vol. 21, No. 4, pp. 483–500.

Dukes, Richard L., J. B. Ullman, and J. A. Stein. 1996. "Three-Year Follow-Up of Drug Abuse Resistance Education (D.A.R.E.)," *Evaluation Review*, Vol. 20, No. 1, pp. 49–69.

Durose, Matthew R., Erica L. Smith, and Patrick A. Langan. 2007. "Contacts Between Police and the Public, 2005," Washington, DC: Bureau of Justice Statistics, April, NCJ 215243.

Eck, John E. 1984. *Solving Crimes: The Investigation of Burglary and Robbery*. Washington, DC: Police Executive Research Forum.

Eck, John and W. Spellman. 1987. "Problem-Solving: Problem-Oriented Policing in Newport News." *Research in Brief*. Washington, DC: National Institute of Justice.

Ekblom, P. and K. Heal. 1982. *The Police Response to Calls from the Public*. Research and Planning Unit Paper 9. London: Home Office.

Ellis, Tom. 1997. "The Citizen Police Academy," *Law Enforcement Technology*, Vol. 45, No. 10, October, pp. 56–60.

Engel, Robin Shepard, Jennifer M. Calnon, and Thomas J. Bernard. 2002. "Theory and Racial Profiling: Shortcomings and Future Directions in Research," *Justice Quarterly*, Vol. 19, No. 2, pp. 249–273.

Ericson, Richard. 1981. *Making Crime: A Study of Detective Work*. Toronto: Butterworths.

Ericson, Richard. 1982. *Reproducing Order: A Study of Police Patrol Work*. Toronto: University of Toronto Press.

Farmer, D. J. 1984. *Crime Control: The Use and Misuse of Police Resources*. New York: Plenum.

Feld, B. C. 1970–1971. "Police Violence and Protest," *Minnesota Law Review*, Vol. 55, pp. 731–778.

Fink, Stephen, Joel Beak, and Kenneth Tadded. 1971. "Organizational Crisis and Change," *Journal of Applied Behavioral Science*, Vol. 7, No. 1, January/February, pp. 15–37.

Fishman, Mark 1978. "Crime Waves as Ideology," *Social Problems*, Vol. 25, No. 5. pp. 531–543.

Fishman, Mark. 1980. *Manufacturing the News*. Austin: University of Texas Press.

Flanagan, Timothy J. and Michael S. Vaughn. 1995. "Public Opinion About Police Abuse of Force." In William A. Geller and Hans Toch (eds.), *And Justice For All: Understanding and Controlling Police Abuse of Force*. Washington, DC: Police Executive Research Forum, pp. 113–126.

Fogelson, Robert M. 1977. *Big City Police*. Cambridge, MA: Harvard University Press.

Foster, Raymond E. 2005. *Police Technology*. Upper Saddle, NJ: Prentice Hall.

Fridell, Lorie. 1985. "Justifiable Use of Measures in Research on Deadly Force," *Journal of Criminal Justice*, Vol. 17, No. 1, pp. 157–165.

Friedrich, Robert. J. 1980. "Police Use of Force: Individuals, Situations, and Organizations," *Annals of the American Academy of Political and Social Science*, Vol. 452, No. 1, November, pp. 82–97.

Fyfe, J. 1979. "Administrative Interventions on Police Shooting Discretion," *Journal of Criminal Justice*, Vol. 1, pp. 309–323.

Fyfe, J. (ed.). 1980. *Readings on Police Use of Deadly Force*. Washington, DC: Police Foundation.

Fyfe, J. 1986. "The Split Second Syndrome and Other Determinants of Police Violence," in Anne T. Campbell and John J. Gibbs (eds.), *Situations of Aggression*. Oxford, England: Basil Blackwell, pp. 207–224.

Fyfe, James J. 1988. "Police use of deadly force: Research and reform," *Justice Quarterly*, Vol. 5, No. 2, pp. 165–205.

Gammage, Allen Z. and Stanley L. Sachs. 1972. *Police Unions*. Springfield, IL: Charles C. Thomas.

Gamson, William A. and James McEvoy. 1970. "Police Violence and Its Support," *The Annals of the American Academy of Political and Social Science*, Vol. 341, No. 1, pp. 97-110.

Gardiner, John A. 1969. *Traffic and the Police, Variations in Law Enforcement Policy*. Cambridge: Harvard University Press

Garner, Gerald. W. 1982. "Meet the Press: Media Relations for Police," *Law and Order*, Vol. 30, No. 2, pp. 28–32.

Garner, Gerald. W. 1984. *Police Meet the Press*. Springfield, IL: Charles C. Thomas.

Garner, Gerald. W. 1987. *"Chief, the Reporters Are Here!": The Police Executive's Personal Guide to Press Relations*. Springfield, IL: Charles C. Thomas.

Garner, Joel and Elizabeth Clemmer. 1986. "Danger to Police in Domestic Disturbances—A New Look." Washington, DC: National Institute of Justice. Research in Brief.

Geller, William A. 1982. "Deadly Force: What we know," *Journal of Police Science and Administration*, Vol. 10, No. 1, pp. 151–177.

Geller, William A. and Norval Morris. 1992. "Relations Between Federal and Local Police," *Crime and Justice*, Vol. 15, *Modern Policing*. Chicago: University of Chicago Press, pp. 231–348.

Gelles, Richard J. 1996. "Constraints Against Family Violence: How Well Do they Work?" In Eve S. Buzawa and Carl G. Buzawa (Eds.) *Do Arrests and Restraining Orders Work?* Thousand Oaks, CA: Sage Publications, pp. 30–42.

Glantz, J. and E. Lipton. 2003. *City in the Sky: The Rise and Fall of the World Trade Center*. New York: Times Books.

Goldschlag, William and Frank Lombardi. 1996. "Compstat's Crime Byte Wins Big," *Daily News*, December 4, p. 61.

Goldstein, Herbert. 1977. *Policing a Free Society*. Cambridge, MA: Ballinger.

Goldstein, Herbert. 1979. "Improving Policing: A Problem-Oriented Approach," *Crime & Delinquency*, Vol. 25, No. 2, pp. 236–243.

Goldstein, Herbert. 1987. "Toward Community Oriented Policing: Potential, Basic Requirements and Threshold Questions," *Crime & Delinquency*, Vol. 33, No. 1, pp. 6–30.

Goldstein, Joseph. 1960. "Police Discretion Not to Invoke the Criminal Justice Process," *Yale Law Journal*, Vol. 69, pp. 543–594.

Grant, Alan. 1980. "The Audio-Visual Taping of Police Interviews with Suspects and Accused Persons by Halton Regional Police Force" (Evaluation Final Report). Ottawa, Canada: Law Reform Commission of Canada.

Greene, Jack A. 1999. "Zero Tolerance: A Case Study of Police Policies and Practices in New York City," *Crime & Delinquency*, Vol. 45, No. 2, pp. 171–187.

Greenfield, Lawrence A., Patrick A. Langan, Steven K. Smith, and Robert J. Kaminski. 1997. "Police Use of Force: Collection of National Data." Washington, DC: U.S. Department of Justice, Office of Justice Programs NCJ-165040.

Green-Mazerolle, Lorraine and William Terrill. 1997. "Problem-oriented policing in public housing: identifying the distribution of problem places", *Policing: An International Journal of Police Strategies & Management*, Vol. 20, No. 2, pp. 235–255.

Greenwood, Peter W., Jan Chaiken, and Joan Petersilia. 1975. *The Criminal Investigation Process*. Santa Monica, CA: The RAND Corporation,

Greenwood, Peter W., Jan Chaiken, and Joan Petersilia. 1977. *The Criminal Investigation Process*. Lexington, MA: D.C. Heath.

Grinc, R. 1994. "'Angels in Marble': Problems in Stimulating Community Involvement in Community Policing," *Crime & Delinquency*, Vol. 40, No. 3, pp. 437–468.

Gunaratna, R. 2002. *Inside al Qaeda: Global Network of Terror*. New York: Columbia University Press.

Guyot, Dorthy. 1979. "Bending Granite: Attempts to Change the Rank Structure of American Police Departments," *Journal of Police Science and Administration*, Vol. 7, No. 3, pp. 253–284.

Guyot, Dorthy. 1985. "Political Interference versus Political Accountability in Municipal Policing." In E. S. Fairchild and V. J. Webb (eds.), *The Politics of Crime and Criminal Justice*. Beverly Hills, CA: Sage Publications, pp. 120–143.

Guyot, Dorthy. 1991. *Policing as Though People Mattered*. Philadelphia: Temple University Press.

Haberfield, Maki. 2002. *Critical Issues in Training*. Upper Saddle River, NJ: Prentice Hall.

Hahn, Harlan. 1971. "Ghetto Assessments of Police Protection and Authority," *Law and Society*, Vol. 6, No. 2, pp. 183–194.

Haley, K. 2003. "Police Academy Management: Procedures, Problems and Issues," in M. J. Palmetto (Ed.), *Police and Training Issues*. Upper Saddle River, NJ: Prentice Hall.

Hanewicz, W. B. 1978. "Police Personality: A Jungian Perspective," *Journal of Crime & Delinquency*, Vol. 24, No. 2, pp. 152–172.

Haritos-Fatouros, M. 1988. "The Official Torturer: A Learning Model for Obedience to the Authority of Violence," *Journal of Applied Social Psychology*, Vol.18, No. 13, pp. 1107–1120.

Hartmann, Francis. X. 1988. *Debating the Evolution of American Policing*. Washington, DC: U.S. Department of Justice.

Hawkins, Carl W. 1999. "An Effective Tool," in James D. Sewell (ed.) *Controversial Issues in Policing*, Boston, MA: Allyn and Bacon, pp. 24–28.

Herbert, Steve. 1998."Police Culture Reconsidered," *Criminology*, Vol. 36, No. 2, pp. 343–370.

Hervey, Juris A. and Peter Feuiile. 1973. *Police Unionism: Power and Impact in Public-Sector Bargaining*. Lexington, MA: Lexington Books.

Hickman, Matthew J. and Brian A. Reaves. 2006. *Local Police Departments 2003*. Washington, DC: US Department of Justice, Bureau of Justice Statistics, NCJ 210118.

Horvath, F. 1987. "The Police Use of Deadly Force: A Description of Selected Characteristics of Intrastate Incidents," *Journal of Police Science and Administration*, Vol. 15, No. 3, pp. 226–238.

Horvath, F. 1993. "Polygraph Screening of Candidates for Police Work in Large Police Agencies in the United States: A Survey of Practices, Policies, and Evaluative Comments," *American Journal of Police*, Vol. 12, No. 1, pp. 67–86.

Hudson, James R. 1972. "Organizational Aspects of Internal and External Review of Police," *Journal of Criminal Law, Criminology and Political Science*, Vol. 63, No. 3, pp. 427–433.

Hughes, William. 1989. "What can be Done to Stop the Crips and Bloods Advance across the United States? National Coordination Needed," *Crime Control Digest*, Vol. 23, No. 49, pp. 3–7.

Hurrell, J. J. and R. Kliesmet. 1984. *Stress Among Police Officers*. Cincinnati, OH: National Institute of Occupational Safety and Health.

Inbau, Fred E., John E. Reid, Joseph P. Buckley, and Brian C. Jane. 2005. *Essentials of the Reid Technique: Criminal Interrogation and Confessions* (4th ed.). Boston: Jones and Bartlett.

Inciardi, J. A. and J. L. Dee. 1987. "From the Keystone Cops to Miami Vice: Images of Policing in American Popular Culture," *Journal of Popular Culture*, Vol. 21, No. 2, pp. 84–102.

Jakubs, D. 1977. "Political Violence in Times of Political Tension: The Case of Brazil." In D. H. Bayley (ed.), *Police and Society*. Beverly Hills, CA: Sage Publications, pp. 85–106.

Jefferis, Eric S., Robert J. Kaminski, Stephen Holmes, and Dena E. Hanley. 1997. "The Effect of a Videotaped Arrest on Public Perceptions of Police Use of Force," *Journal of Criminal Justice*, Vol. 25, No. 5, pp. 381–395.

Johnson, David R. 1981. *The American Law Enforcement: A History*. St. Louis: Forum Press.

Kaminski, Robert J., Steven M. Edwards, and James W. Johnson. 1998. "The Deterrent Effects of Oleoresin Capsicum on Assaults Against Police: Testing the Velcro-Effect Hypothesis," *Police Quarterly*, Vol. 1, No. 2, pp. 1–20.

Kanable, Rebecca. 1999. "An Apple for the Officer: Citizen Police Academies Keep Officers in Touch with Community," *Law Enforcement Technology*, Vol. 26, No. 10, October, pp. 56–58.

Kania, Richard R. E. and Wade C. Mackay. 1977. "Police Violence as a Function of Community Characteristics," *Criminology*, Vol. 15, No. 1, pp. 27–48.

Kappeler, Victor E., Mark Blumberg, and Gary W. Potter. 1996. *The Mythology of Crime and Criminal Justice* (2nd ed.). Prospect Heights, IL: Waveland Press.

Kappeler, Victor E., Richard D. Sluder, and Geoffrey P. Alpert. 1994. *Forces of Deviance: Understanding the Dark Side of Policing*. Prospect Heights, IL: Waveland Press.

Kaskinsky, Rene G. 1994. "Patrolling the Facts: Media, Cops and Crime." In Gregg Barak (ed.), *Media, Process and Social Construction of Crime*. New York: Garland, pp. 203–234.

Kelling, George L. and Mark H. Moore. 1988. *The Evolving Strategy of Policing.* Washington, DC: U.S. Department of Justice, National Institute of Justice.

Kelling, George L., Tony Pate, D. Dieckman, and C. Brown. 1974. *Kansas City Preventive Patrol Experiment: A Summary Report.* Washington, DC: Police Foundation.

Kelling, George and James Q. Wilson. 1982. "The Police and Neighborhood Safety," *Atlantic Monthly*, Vol. 249, No. 2, pp. 29–38.

Kennedy, David. 1997. *Juvenile Gun Violence and Gun Markets in Boston.* Washington, DC: National Institute of Justice.

Klockars, Carl B. 1985. *The Idea of the Police.* Beverly Hills, CA: Sage Publications.

Klockars, Carl B. 1988. "The Rhetoric of Community Policing." In J. R. Greene and S. D. Mastrofski (eds.), *Community Policing: Rhetoric or Reality.* New York: Praeger, pp. 239–258.

Knapp Commission. 1973. *The Knapp Commission Report on Police Corruption.* New York: Braziller.

Koenig, Daniel J. 1975. "Police Perceptions of Public Respect and Extra-legal Use of Force: A Reconsideration of Folk Wisdom and Pluralistic Ignorance," *Canadian Journal of Sociology*, Vol. 1, No. 3, pp. 313–324.

Konstantin, David. 1984. "Homicides of American Law Enforcement Officers, 1978-1980," *Justice Quarterly*, Vol. 1, No. 1, pp. 29–45.

Kramer, Alisa S. 2007. "William H. Parker and the Thin Blue Line: Politics, Public Relations and Policing in Postwar Los Angeles (California)," Ph.D. Dissertation, American University.

Kraska, Peter and Victor Kappeler. 1988. "Police On-Duty Drug Use: A Theoretical and Descriptive Examination," *American Journal of Police*, Vol. 7, No. 1, pp. 1–28.

Kraska, Peter and Victor Kappeler. 1995. "To Serve and Pursue: Exploring Sexual Violence Against Women," *Justice Quarterly*, Vol. 12, No. 1, pp. 85–111.

Krippendorf, Klaus. 1981. *Content Analysis: An Introduction to Its Methodology.* Beverly Hills, CA: Sage Publications.

Labovitz, S. and R. Hagedorn. 1971. "An Analysis of Job Suicide Rates Among Occupational Categories," *Sociological Inquiry*, Vol. 41, No. 1, pp. 67–72.

Langton, Lynn. 2010. *Women in Law Enforcement.* Washington, DC: Bureau of Justice Statistics, NCJ 230521.

Langworthy, Robert H. 1989. "Do Stings Control Crime? An Evaluation of a Police Fencing Operation," *Justice Quarterly*, Vol. 6, No. 1, pp. 27–45.

Lasley, J. R. 1994. "The Impact of the Rodney King Incident on Citizen Attitudes Towards Police," *Policing & Society*, Vol. 3, No. 4, pp. 245–255.

Lefkowitz, Joel. 1977. "Industrial-Organizational Psychology and the Police," *American Psychologist*, Vol. 32, No 5, pp. 346–364.

Leighton, Barry N. 1991. "Visions of Community Policing," *Canadian Journal of Criminology*, Vol. 33, No. 3/4, pp. 485–522.

Leishman, F. and P. Mason. 2003. *Policing and the Media: Facts, Fictions and Factions*. Cullompton, Devon, England: Willan.

Leo, Richard. 2008. *Police Interrogation and American Justice* Cambridge, MA: Harvard University Press.

Lester, D. 1983. "Stress in Police Officers: An American Perspective," *The Police Journal*, Vol. 56, No. 2, pp. 184–193.

Lester, David. 1995. "Officer Attitudes Toward Police Use of Force." In William A. Geller and Hans Toch (eds.), *And Justice for All: Understanding and Controlling Police Use of Force*. Washington, DC: Police Executive Research Forum, pp. 177–185.

Levi, Margaret. 1977. *Police Unionism*. Lexington, MA: Lexington Books.

Lindsay, Vicki, William Banks Taylor, Kyna Shelley, (2008) "Alcohol and the Police: An Empirical Examination of a Widely-held Assumption," *Policing: An International Journal of Police Strategies & Management*, Vol. 31, No. 4, pp. 596–609.

Linn, Edith. 2009. *Arrest Decisions: What Works for the Officer?* New York: Peter Lang.

Lipsky, Michael 1971. "Toward a Theory of Street Level Bureaucracy and the Analysis of Urban Reform," *Urban Affairs Quarterly*, Vol. 6, No. 4, June, pp. 391–409.

Lipsky, Michael. 1980. *Street Level Bureaucracy: Dilemmas of Individual in Public Services*. New York: Russell Sage Foundation.

Loftin, Colin, Brian Wiersema, David McDowall, and Adam Dobrin. 2003. "Underreporting of Justifiable Homicides Committed by Police Officers in the United States, 1976–1998," *American Journal of Public Health*, Vol. 93, No. 7, pp. 1117–1121.

Lundman, Richard. J. 1974a. "Domestic Police Citizen Encounters," *Journal of Police Science and Administration*, Vol. 22, No. 1, pp. 22–27.

Lundman, Richard J. 1974b. "Routine Police Arrest Practices: A Commonweal Perspective," *Social Problems*, Vol. 22, No. 1, October, pp. 127–141.

Lundman, Richard J. 1979. "Origins of Police Misconduct," In R. G. Iacovetta and Dae H. Chang (eds.), *Critical Issues in Criminal Justice*. Durham, NC: Carolina Academic Press, pp. 218-229.

Lynam, Donald R., Richard Milich, Rick Zimmerman, Scott P. Novak, T. K. Logan, Catherine Martin, Carl Leukefeld, and Richard Clayton. 1999. "Project DARE: No Effects at 10-Year Follow-up," *Journal of Consulting and Clinical Psychology*, Vol. 67, No. 4, August, pp. 590–593.

Maas, Peter. 1973. *Serpico*. New York: Viking.

Maffe, Steven R. and Tod W. Burke. 1999. "Citizen Police Academies," *Law and Order* 47, No. 10, October, pp. 77–80.

Manheim, J. B. and R. C. Rich. 1986. *Empirical Political Analysis*. New York: Longman.

Manning, Peter K. 1971. "The Police: Mandate, Strategies, and Appearances." In J. D. Douglas (ed.), *Crime and Justice in American Society*. New York: Bobbs Merrill, pp. 149–194.

Manning, Peter K. 1977. *Police Work*. Cambridge, MA: MIT Press.

Manning, Peter K. 1980a. "Violence and the Police Role," *Annals of the American Academy of Political and Social Science*, Vol. 452, November, pp. 135–144.

Manning, Peter K. 1980b. *The Narcs Game*. Cambridge, MA: MIT Press.

Manning, Peter K. 1983. "Organizational Constraints and Semiotics." In Maurice Punch (ed.), *Control in the Police Organization*. Cambridge, MA: MIT Press, pp. 169–193.

Manning, Peter K. 1984. "Community Policing," *American Journal of Police*, Vol. 3, No. 2, pp. 205–227.

Manning, Peter K. 1985. "The Researcher: An Alien in the Police World." In Arthur Niederhoffer and Abraham Blumberg (eds.), *The Ambivalent Force*. Hinsdale, IL: Dryden Press, pp. 103–121.

Manning, Peter K. 1988. "Community Policing as a Drama of Control." In J. R. Greene and S. D. Mastrofski (eds.), *Community Policing: Rhetoric or Reality*. New York: Praeger, pp. 28–45.

Manning, Peter K. 2006. "Transformation: The Emerging Growth of Cooperation Amongst Police Agencies." In Stacy K. McGoldrick and Andrea McArdle (eds.), *Uniform Behavior: Police Localism and National Politics*. New York: Palgrave Macmillan, pp. 203–229.

Maple, Jack. 2000. *The Crime Fighter: How You Can Make Your Community Crime Free*. New York: Broadway.

Marenin, Otwin. 1990. "The Police and the Coercive Nature of the State." In E. S. Greenberg and T. F. Mayer (eds.), *Changes in the State*. Newbury Park, CA: Sage Publications, pp. 115–130.

Martin, Susan E. 1980. *Breaking and Entering: Policewomen on Patrol*. Berkeley: University of California Press.

Martin, Susan E. 1990. *On the Move: The Status of Women in Policing*. Washington, DC: The Police Foundation.

Marx, Gary T. 1970a. "Issueless Riots," *Annals of the American Academy of Political and Social Science*, Vol. 39, No. 1, pp. 21–33.

Marx, Gary T. 1970b. "Civil Disorder and Agents of Social Control," *Journal of Social Issues*, Vol. 26, No. 1, pp. 19–57.

Marx, Gary T. 1981. "Ironies of Social Control: Authorities as Contributors to Deviance Through Escalation, Nonenforcement and Covert Facilitation," *Social Problems*, Vol. 28, No. 3, pp. 221–246.

Marx, G. T. 1988. *Undercover: Police Surveillance in America*. Berkeley: University of California Press.

Marzulli, John and Gene Mustain. 1995. "Top Cops in 'Lion's Den': Brass Grill Finest on Catching Crooks," *Daily News*, July 16, http://www.nydailynews.com/archives/news/1995/07/16/1995-07-16_top_cops_in__lion_s_den__br.html

Mason, T. David and D. A. Krane. 1989. "The Political Economy of Death Squads: Toward a Theory of Impact of State Sanctioned Terror," *International Studies Quarterly*, Vol. 33, No. 1, pp. 175–198.

Mastrofski, Stephen W. 1986. "Police Agency Accreditation: The Prospects of Reform," *American Journal of Police*, Vol. 5, No. 3, pp. 45–81.

Mawby, Rob C. 2002a. *Policing Images: Policing, Communication and Legitimacy*. Cullompton, Devon, England: Willan.

Mawby, Rob C. 2002b. "Continuity and Change, Convergence and Divergence: The Policy and Practice of Police-Media Relations," *Criminal Justice*, Vol. 2, No. 3, pp. 303–324.

McAlary, Mike. 1987. *Buddy Boys*. New York: Charter Books.

McArdle, Andrea. 2006. "Policing After September 11: Federal–Local Collaboration and the Implications for Police–Community Relations." In Stacy K. McGoldrick and Andrea McArdle (eds.), *Uniform Behavior: Police Localism and National Politics*. New York: Palgrave Macmillan, pp. 177–202.

McCabe, K. A. and R. G. Fajardo (2001). "Law Enforcement Accreditation: A National Comparison of Accredited vs. Nonaccredited Agencies," *Journal of Criminal Justice*, Vol. 29, No. 1, pp. 127–131.

McCabe, S. and F. Sutcliffe. 1978. *Defining Crime: A Study of Police Decisions*. Oxford, England: Basil Blackwell.

McCarthy, Bernard J. 1996. "Keeping an Eye on the Keeper: Prison Corruption and Its Control," in Michael C. Braswell, Belinda R McCarthy, and Bernard J. McCarthy (eds.) *Justice, Crime, and Ethics*. (2nd ed.). Cincinnati, OH: Anderson, pp. 229–241.

McDonald, Phyllis P. 2001. *Managing Police Operations: Implementing the NYPD Crime Control Model Using COMPSTAT*. Belmont, CA: Wadsworth/Cengage.

Meagher, M. Steven and Nancy A. Yentes. 1986. "Choosing a Career in Policing: A Comparison of Male and Female Perceptions," *Journal of Police Science and Administration*, Vol. 14, No. 4, pp. 320–327.

Merton, Robert. 1936. "The Unanticipated Consequences of Purposive Action," *American Sociological Review*, Vol. 1, No. 6, pp. 894–904.

Messig, Robert T., Yung Hyeock Lee and Frank Horvath. 2002. "Criminal Investigation," in Encyclopedia of Crime and Punishment, Thousand Oaks, CA: Sage Publications, Inc. pp. 503–508.

Miligram, S. 1974. *Obedience to Authority*. London: Harper and Row.

Miligram, S. 1977. *The Individual and the Social World*. Boston: Addison Wesley.

Miller, Wilbur. 1977. *Cops and Bobbies*. Chicago: The University of Chicago Press.

Monkkonen, Eric H. 1981. *Police in Urban America, 1860–1920*. Cambridge, England: Cambridge University Press.

Moodie, P. 1972. "The Use and Control of Police." In R. Benewick and T. Smith (eds.), *Direct Action and Democratic Politics*. London: Allen and Unwin, pp. 231–237.

Moose, Charles. 2003. *23 Days in October*. New York: Penguin Books.

Morgan, Rod. 1987. "The Local Determinants of Poling Policy," In P. Willmott (ed.) *Policing and the Community*. London: Policy Studies Institute, pp. 29–53.

Motschall, M and L. Cao. 2002. "An Analysis of the Public Relations Role of the Police Information Officer," *Police Quarterly*, Vol. 5, No. 2, pp. 152–180.

Muir, W. Jr. 1977. *Police: Street Corner Politicians*. Chicago: University of Chicago Press.

Murphy, Dan W. and J. L. Worral. 2007. "The threat of mission distortion in police-corrections partnerships." *Policing: An International Journal of Police Strategies and Management*, Vol. 30, pp. 132–149.

Murphy, Patrick V. 1977. *Commissioner: A View from the Top of American Law Enforcement*. New York: Simon and Schuster.

Nadel, M. 1976. *Corporations and Political Accountability*. Lexington, MA: D.C. Heath and Company.

National Advisory Commission on Civil Disorders. 1968. *Report of the National Advisory Commission on Civil Disorders* (Kerner Report). New York: Dutton.

National Commission on the Causes and Prevention of Violence. 1968. *Rights in Conflict: Convention Week in Chicago, August 25–29*. New York: Dutton.

National Commission on Law Observance and Enforcement (Wickersham Commission). 1931. *Report on Lawlessness in Law Enforcement*. Washington, DC: U.S. Government Printing Office.

National School Resource Network. 1979. "The Officer Friendly Program." *Technical Assistance Bulletin* 9.

Newfield, Jack and Wayne Barret 1988. *City for Sale*. New York: Harper and Row.

Niederhoffer, Arthur. 1967. *Behind the Shield: The Police in Urban Society*. Garden City, NJ: Doubleday.

Nolan, James, T. Nolan and Laurie Solomon. 1977. "An Alternative Approach in Police Patrol: The Wilmington Split-Force Experiment," *The Police Chief*, November, pp. 58–64.

Nowicki, E. 2001. "OC Spray Update," *Law and Order*, pp. 28–29.

Oliver, Willard M. 2000. "The Third Generation of Community Policing: Moving through Innovation, Diffusion, and Institutionalization," *Police Quarterly*, Vol. 3, No. 4, pp. 367–388.

Oliver, Willard M. and Cecil A. Meier. 2001. "The Siren's Song: Federalism and the COPS Grants." *American Journal of Criminal Justice*, Vol. 25, No. 2, pp. 223–238.

Ortmeier, J. P. 1997. "Leadership for community-policing: A study to identify essential Officer Competencies." *Police Chief*. October Vol. LXIV, No. 10, pp. 88–95.

Parent, Dale and B. Snyder. 1999. *Police-Corrections Partnerships*. Washington, DC: National Institute of Justice.

Parks, Roger, B. Parks, Stephen D. Mastrofski, Christina DeJong, and M. Kevin Gray. 1999. "How Officers Spend Their Time with the Community," *Justice Quarterly*, Vol. 16, No. 3, September, pp. 483–518.

Pate, Anthony. 2005 "Police Corps." In Larry Sullivan and M. S. Rosen (eds.), *Encyclopedia of Law Enforcement*, Vol. I State and Local. Thousand Oaks, CA: Sage Publications, pp. 336–337.

Pate, Anthony, R. A. Bowers, A. Ferrara, and J. Lorence. 1976. *Police Response Time: Its Determinants and Effects*. Washington, DC: Police Foundation.

Payne, C. 1973. "A Study of Rural Beats," *Police Research Services Bulletin*, Vol. 12, pp. 23–29.

Peek-Asa, C., Howard, J., Vargas, L., Kraus, J.F. 1997. "Incidence of Nonfatal Workplace Assault Injuries Determined from Employer's Reports in California," *Journal of Occupational and Environmental Medicine*, Vol. 39, No. 1, pp. 44–50.

Pepinsky, H. 1975. "Police Decision Making." In Don Gottfredson (ed.), *Decision Making in the Criminal Justice System: Reviews and Essays*. Rockville, MD: National Institute of Mental Health, pp. 21–52.

Perlmutter, D. 2000. *Policing the Media: Street Cops and Public Perceptions of Law Enforcement*. London: Sage.

Perry, C., K. Komro, S. Veblen-Mortenson, and L. Bosma. 2000. "The Minnesota DARE Plus Project: Creating Community Partnership to Prevent Drug Use and Violence." *Journal of School Health*, Vol. 70, No. 30, pp. 84–88.

Peters, Thomas J. and Waterman, Robert H. Jr. 1982. *In Search of Excellence: Lessons from America's Best-Run Companies.* New York: Harper and Row.

Piquero Nicole Leeper and Alex Piquero. 2001. "Problem-Oriented Policing." In (Eds.) Roger C. Dunham and Geoffrey P. Alpert (Eds.) *Critical Issues in Policing: Contemporary Readings,* Fourth Edition. Waveland Press: Prospect Heights, pp. 531–540.

Pollard, Charles. 1997. "Zero Tolerance: Short-Term Fix, Long-Term Liability." In Norman Dennis (ed.), *Zero Tolerance: Policing a Free Society.* London: IEA Health and Welfare Unit, pp. 43–60.

Poulantzas, Nicos. 1973. *Political Power and Social Class.* Atlantic Fields, NJ: Humanities Press.

President's Commission on Civil Rights. 1947. *To Serve These Rights.* New York: Simon and Schuster.

President's Commission on Law Enforcement and Administration of Justice. 1967. *Task Force Report: The Police.* Washington, DC: U.S. Government Printing Office.

Preston, Frederick W. and Roger Roots. 2004. "Law and Its Unintended Consequences," *American Behavioral Scientist,* Vol. 47, No. 11, pp. 371–375.

Przybylski, Roger. 1995. "Evaluation as an Important Tool in Criminal Justice Planning," *The Compiler,* Summer, pp. 3–17.

Punch, M. 1979. *Policing the Inner City.* London: Macmillan.

Punch, M. and T. Nayloy. 1973. "The Police: A Social Service," *New Society,* Vol. 24, No. 554, pp. 358–361.

Radelet, Louis A. 1977. *The Police and the Community* (2nd ed.). Toronto: Collier Macmillan.

Radelet, Louis A. and David L. Carter. 1994. *The Police and the Community* (5th ed.). New York: MacMillan College Publishing.

Raub, R., 1988. "Staffing a State Police Agency for Service and Patrol." *Journal of Police Science and Administration,* Vol. 16, pp. 255–263.

Reaves, Brian A. and Matthew J. Hickman. 2004. "Law Enforcement Management and Administrative Statistics, 2000: Data for Individual State and Local Agencies with 100 or More Officers." Washington, DC: U.S. Department of Justice, Bureau of Justice Statistics, NCJ 203350.

Reeve, Simon. 1999, *The New Jackals: Ramzi Yousef, Osama bin Laden, and the Future of Terrorism.* Boston, MA: Northeastern University Press.

Regan, David E. 1971. "Complaints Against the Police," *Political Quarterly,* Vol. 4, pp. 402–413.

Regoli, Robert M. 1976. "An Empirical Assessment of Niederhoffer's Police Cynicism Scale," *Journal of Criminal Justice,* Vol. 4, No. 1, pp. 231–241.

Reiner, Robert. 1983. "The Politicization of the Police in Britain," In Maurice Punch (ed.) *Control in the Police Organization*. Cambridge, MA: The MIT Press, pp. 126–148.

Reiss Jr., Albert J. 1968. "Police Brutality Answers to Key Questions," *Trans-Action*, Vol. 5, pp. 10–19.

Reiss, Albert. J. 1971. *The Police and the Public*. New Haven, CT: Yale University Press.

Reitzel, J. D., N. Leeper Piquero, and A. R. Piquero. 2005. "Problem-oriented policing," in Roger G. Dunham and Geoffrey P. Alpert. (eds.) *Critical Issues in policing*. (5th ed.). Long Grove, IL: Waveland Press.

Reuss-Ianni, Elizabeth. 1984. *Two Cultures of Policing: Street Cops and Management Cops*. New Brunswick, NJ: Transaction Publishers.

Richardson, James, F. 1970. *The New York Police*. New York: Oxford University Press.

Richardson, James, F. 1974. *Urban Policing in the United States*. London: Kennikat Press.

Roberg, Roy and John Kuykendall. 1993. *Police & Society*. Belmont, CA: Wadsworth.

Roberg, Roy, Jack Kuykendall, and John Crank. 2000. *Police & Society* (2nd ed.). Belmont, CA: Cengage.

Rosenbaum, Dennis P. and Gordon S. Hanson. 1998. "Assessing the Effects of School-Based Drug Education: A Six-Year Multilevel Analysis of Project D.A.R.E.," *Journal of Research in Crime and Delinquency*, Vol. 35, No. 4, pp. 381–412.

Rosett, Arthur. 1972. "Discretion, Severity and Legality in Criminal Justice," *Southern California Law Review*, Vol. 46, No. 1, pp. 12–50.

Ross, Jeffrey Ian. 1992. "The Outcomes of Public Police Violence: A Neglected Research Agenda," *Police Studies*, Vol. 15, No. 1, Autumn, pp. 163–183.

Ross, Jeffrey Ian. 1993. "The Politics and Control of Police Violence in New York City and Toronto," Dissertation, University of Colorado–Boulder.

Ross, Jeffrey Ian. 1994b. "The Future of Municipal Police Violence in Advanced Industrialized Democracies: Towards a Structural Causal Model," *Police Studies: The International Review of Police Development*, Vol. 17, No. 2, pp. 1–27.

Ross, Jeffrey Ian. 1995a. "A Process Model of Public Police Violence in Advanced Industrialized Democracies," *Criminal Justice Policy Review*, Vol. 7, No. 1, pp. 67–90.

Ross, Jeffrey Ian. 1995b. "Confronting Community Policing: Minimizing Community Policing as Public Relations." In Peter C. Kratcoski and Duane Dukes (eds.), *Issues in Community Policing*. Cincinnati, OH: Anderson/ACJS, pp. 243–260.

Ross, Jeffrey Ian (ed.). 1995/2000. *Controlling State Crime*. New Brunswick, NJ: Transaction Publishers.

Ross, Jeffrey Ian. 1998. "The Role of the Media in the Creation of Public Police Violence." In Frankie Bailey and Donna Hale (eds.), *Popular Culture, Crime and Justice*. Belmont, CA: Wadsworth, pp. 100–110.

Ross, Jeffrey Ian. 2000a. "Grants-R-Us: Inside a Federal Grant Making Research Agency," *American Behavioral Scientist*, Vol. 43, No. 10, August, pp. 1704–1723.

Ross, Jeffrey Ian. 2000b. *Making News of Police Violence: A Comparative Study of Toronto and New York City*. Westport, CT: Praeger.

Ross, Jeffrey Ian (ed.). 2000c. *Varieties of State Crime and Its Control*. Monsey, NY: Criminal Justice Press.

Ross, Jeffrey Ian. 2001. "Police Crime & Democracy: Demystifying the Concept, Taxonomies, and Research," In Stanley Einstein and Menachem Amir (eds.), *Police and Democracy*. Huntsville, TX: Office of International Criminal Justice, Sam Houston State University, pp. 177–200.

Ross, Jeffrey Ian. 2006a. *Political Terrorism: An Interdisciplinary Approach*. New York: Peter Lang.

Ross, Jeffrey Ian. 2006b. "Policing Native Americans off the Rez." In Jeffrey Ian Ross and Larry Gould (eds.), *Native Americans and the Criminal Justice System: Theoretical and Policy Perspectives*. Boulder, CO: Paradigm Publishers, pp. 135–142.

Ross, Jeffrey Ian. 2009. *Cybercrime*. New York: Chelsea House.

Ross, Jeffrey Ian and Mengyan Dai. 2011. "Challenges of Asian-Americans and Municipal Police Departments in the United States: Recruitment and Retention," Paper to be presented at the Academy of Criminal Justice Sciences Annual Meeting, Toronto, March 2011.

Rossmo, D. Kim. 2006. "Criminal Investigative Failures: Avoiding the Pitfalls," *FBI Law Enforcement Bulletin*, Vol. 75, No. 10, pp. 12–19.

Rousseau, Jean Jacques. 1763/1983. *The Social Contract*. Middlesex, England: Penguin.

Russell, K. 1976. *Complaints Against the Police: A Sociological View*. Leicester, England: Oldham & Manton Ltd.

Sanders, N. 1977. *Detective Work*. New York: Free Press.

Scharf, Peter and A. Binder. 1983. *The Badge and the Bullet: Police Use of Deadly Force*. New York: Praeger.

Schmalleger, Frank and John L. Worrall. 2010. *Policing Today*. Upper Saddle River, NJ: Prentice Hall.

Schultz, Dorothy Moses. 2003. "Women Police Chiefs: A Statistical Profile," *Police Quarterly*, Vol. 6, No. 3, pp. 330–345.

Scott, Robert F., Deon Brock, and Chris Crawford. 2000. "Agency Networking and the Use of the Internet and Intranets in the field of Law Enforcement," *Police Forum*, Vol. 10, No. 4, pp. 1–5.

Shearing, Clifford. 1981. *Organizational Police Deviance: Its Structure and Control*. Toronto: Butterworth.

Sherman, Lawrence W. 1974a. "The Sociology and the Social Reform of American Police 1950–1973," *Journal of Police Science and Administration*, Vol. 2, No. 2, pp. 255–262.

Sherman, Lawrence W. 1974b. "Who Polices the Police: New York, London, Paris?" In D. E. J. MacNamara and M. Riedel (eds.), *Police: Perspectives, Problems, Prospects*. New York: Praeger, pp. 13–22.

Sherman, Lawrence W. 1978. *Scandal and Reform: Controlling Police Corruption*. Berkeley: University of California Press.

Sherman, Lawrence W. 1980a. "Perspectives on Police and Violence," *Annals of the American Academy of Political and Social Science*, Vol. 452, No. 1, pp. 1–12.

Sherman, Lawrence W. 1980b. "Causes of Police Behavior: The Current State of Quantitative Research," *Journal of Research in Crime and Delinquency*, Vol. 17, No. 1, pp. 69–100.

Sherman, Lawrence. W. 1998. *Evidence Based Policing*. Washington, DC: Police Foundation.

Sherman, Lawrence W. and David Weisburd. 1995. "General Deterrent Effects of Police Patrol in Crime "Hotspots:" A Randomized, Controlled Trial," *Justice Quarterly*, Vol. 12, No. 4, pp. 625–648.

Skogan, Wesley and Susan M. Harnett. 1997. *Community Policing, Chicago Style*. New York: Oxford University Press.

Skolnick, Jerome H. 1966. *Justice Without Trial* (2nd ed.) New York: John Wiley.

Skolnick, Jerome H. and David H. Bayley. 1986. *The New Blue Line*. New York: Free Press.

Skolnick, Jerome H. and David H. Bayley. 1988. *Community Policing: Issues and Practices Around the World*. Washington, DC: National Institute of Justice.

Skolnick, Jerome H. and James J. Fyfe. 1993. *Above the Law: Police and Excessive Use of Force*. New York: Free Press.

Slater, Joseph. 2009. "Labor and the Boston Police Strike of 1919." In Aaron Brenner, Benjamin Day, and Immanuel Ness (eds.), *The Encyclopedia of Strikes in American History*. Armonk, NY: M.E. Sharpe, pp. 239–251.

Smith, Brad W., Kenneth J. Novak, James Frank, and Lawrence F. Travis. 2000. "Multijurisdictional Drug Task Forces: An Analysis of Impacts," *Journal of Criminal Justice*, Vol. 28, No. 6, pp. 543–556.

Smith, D. 1987. "Research, the Community and the Police." In Peter Willmott (ed.), *Policing and the Community*. London: Policy Studies Institute.

Souryal, Sam. 1995. *Police Organization and Administration* (2nd ed.). Cincinnati, OH: Anderson.

South Africa's Children. 1988. "Children Under Attack in the Townships by the Police and Military," *Human Rights Quarterly*, Vol. 10, No.1, pp. 88–107.

Stamper, Norm. 2006. *Breaking Rank: A Top Cop's Expose of the Dark Side of American Policing*. New York: Nation Books.

Stark, Rodney. 1972. *Police Riots*. Belmont, CA: Wadsworth.

Stevens, Dennis J. 2008. *Police Officer Stress: Sources and Solutions*. Upper Saddle, NJ: Prentice Hall.

Stevens, Dennis J. 2009. *An Introduction to American Policing*. Sudbury, MA: Jones and Bartlett.

Stoddard, Ellwyn R. 1968. "The 'Informal Code' of Police Deviancy: A Group Approach to 'Blue Coat Crime,'" *Journal of Criminal Law, Criminology and Police Science*, Vol. 59, No. 2, pp. 201–213.

Stotland, Ezra. 1991. "The Effects of Police Work and Professional Relationships on Health," *Journal of Criminal Justice*, Vol. 19, No. 4, pp. 371–379.

Swanson, Charles R., Leonard Territo, and Robert W. Taylor. 2008. *Police Administration: Structures, Processes, and Behavior* (7th ed.). Upper Saddle River, NJ: Prentice Hall.

Sykes, Richard E. and Edward E. Brent. 1983. *Policing: A Social Behaviorist Perspective*. New Brunswick, NJ: Rutgers University Press.

Tafoya, William. 1986. "A Delphi Forecast of the Future of Law Enforcement," Ph.D. Dissertation, University of Maryland, College Park.

Thibault, Edward A., Lawrence M. Lynch, and R. Bruce McBride. 1998. *Proactive Police Management*. Upper Saddle River, NJ: Prentice Hall.

Tien, James M. et al. 1977. "An Evaluation Report of an Alternative Approach in Police Patrol: The Wilmington Split-Force Experiment." Cambridge, MA: Public System Evaluation.

Tifft, Larry L. 1974. "The Cop Personality: Reconsidered," *Journal of Police Science and Administration*, Vol. 2, No. 2, pp. 266–278.

Tifft, Larry L. 1975. "Control Systems, Social Bases of Power Exercise in Police Organizations," *Journal of Police Science and Administration*, Vol. 3, No. 1, March, pp. 66–76.

Timoney, John F. 2010. *Beat Cop to Top Cop: A Tale of Three Cities*. Philadelphia: University of Pennsylvania Press.

Torrance, Judy. 1986. *Public Violence in Canada*. Montreal: McGill-Queens University Press.

Trojanowitz, R. and B. Bucqueroux. 1990. *Community Policing: A Contemporary Perspective*. Cincinnati, OH: Anderson.

Trojanowicz, R., M. Steele, and S. Trojanowicz. 1986. *Community Policing: A Taxpayer's Perspective*. East Lansing: National Neighborhood Foot Patrol Center, School of Criminal Justice, Michigan State University.

Tuch, Steven A. and Ronald Weitzer. 1997. "The Polls-Trends: Racial Differences in Attitudes Toward The Police," *Public Opinion Quarterly*, Vol. 61, No. 4, pp. 642–663.

Tulley, Tracey. 1998. "Albany State and Local Cops Will Share Data to Pinpoint Areas Favored by Criminals," *The Times Union*, June 9, p. B2.

Turque, B. et al. 1990. "A New Line Against Crime," *Newsweek*, August 27, pp. 36–38.

Uchida, Craig. D. 2010. "The Development of the American Police: A Historical Overview." In Roger Dunham and Geoffrey Alpert (eds.), *Critical Issues in Policing* (6th ed.). Long Grove, IL: Waveland Press, pp. 17–36.

U.S. Bureau of Justice Statistics. 2005. *Sourcebook of Criminal Justice Statistics 2003*. Albany, NY: U.S. Department of Justice, Table 1.17, http//.www.albany.edu/sourcebook/pdf/t117.pdf

U.S. Commission on Civil Rights. 1981. "Who is guarding the guardians?: A Report on Police Practices," Washington, DC: U.S. Commission on Civil Rights.

U.S. Crime Commission. 1967. *Task Force Report: The Police*. Washington, DC: U.S. Government Printing Office.

Vilke, Gary M. and Theodore C. Chan. 2007. "Less Lethal Technology: Medical issues," *Policing: An International Journal of Police Strategies & Management*, Vol. 30, No. 3, pp. 341–357.

Violanti, John M. and Fred Aron. 1995. "Police Stressors: Variations in Perceptions among Police Personnel," *Journal of Criminal Justice*, Vol. 23, No. 3, pp. 287–294.

Violanti, John M. J. E. Vena, and J. R. Marshall. 1986. "Disease Risk and Mortality among Police Officers: New Evidence and Contributing Factors," *Journal of Police Science and Administration*, Vol. 14, No, 1, pp. 17–23.

Walker, Daniel. 1968. *Rights in Conflict*. New York: Signet Books.

Walker, Samuel. 1976a. "The Urban Police in American History: A Review of the Literature," *Journal of Police Science and Administration*, Vol. 4, No. 3, pp. 252–260.

Walker, Samuel. 1976b. "Police Professionalism: Another Look at the Issues," *Journal of Sociology and Social Welfare*, Vol. 3, July, pp. 701–710.

Walker, Samuel. 1977. *A Critical History of Police Reform*. Lexington, MA: Lexington Books.

Walker, Samuel. 1999. *The Police in America: An Introduction* (3rd ed.). New York: McGraw-Hill.

Walker, Samuel, Geoffrey Alpert, and Dennis J. Kenney. 2000. "Early Warning Systems for Police: Concept, History, and Issues," *Police Quarterly*, Vol. 3, No. 2, pp. 132–152.

Walker, Samuel and Charles M. Katz. 2004. *The Police in America: An Introduction* (5th ed.). New York: McGraw-Hill.

Watchorn, D. J. 1966. "Abuse of Police Powers: Reasons, Effect and Control," *University of Toronto Faculty of Law Review*, Vol. 24, No. 1, pp. 48–69.

Waters, Ethan. 2007. "ShotSpotter," Wired, April, pp. 147–151. http://www.shotspotter.com/news/articles/2007/4%20-%20April/Wired%20Magazine/Wired%20Article%20Eprint%204.10.07.pdf (downloaded October 21, 2010).

Watson, Goodwin. 1967. "Resistance to Change," In Goodwin Watson (Ed.), *Concepts for Social Change*. Washington, DC: National Training Laboratories, pp. 10–25.

Weatheritt, M. 1983. "Community Policing: Does It Work and How Do We Know?" In Trevor Bennett (Ed.), *The Future of Policing*. Cambridge, England: Institute of Criminology, pp. 127–143.

Weatheritt, M. 1988. "Community Policing: Rhetoric or Reality?" In J. R. Greene and S. D. Mastrofski (Eds.), *Community Policing: Rhetoric or Reality*. New York: Praeger, pp. 153–177.

Weiler, P. C. 1969. "'Who Shall Watch the Watchmen?' Reflections on Some Recent Literature About the Police," *Criminal Law Quarterly*, Vol. 11, pp. 420–433.

Weinblatt, Richard B. 1997. "Academies Put Civilians in the Shotgun Seat," *Law and Order*, Vol. 45, No. 9, September, pp. 86–88.

Weisburd, David, Stephen D. Mastrofski, A. M. McNally, R. Greenspan, and J. J. Willis. 2003. "Reforming to Preserve: CompStat and Strategic Problem Solving in American Policing," *Criminology and Public Policy*, Vol. 2, No. 3, pp. 421–456.

Welch, Wayne N. and Philip W. Harris. 2004. *Criminal Justice: Policy and Planning* (2nd ed.). Cincinnati, OH: Anderson/LexisNexis.

Welford, Charles, J. V. Pepper, Carol Petrie and the Committee to Improve Research on Firearms Data. 2004. *Firearms and Violence*. Washington, DC: National Academy of Sciences.

West, S. L., and K. K. O'Neal. 2004. "Project D.A.R.E. Outcome Effectiveness Revisited," *American Journal of Public Health*," Vol. 94, No. 6, pp. 1027–1029.

Westley, William A. 1953. "Violence and the Police," *American Journal of Sociology*, Vol. 59, No.1, pp. 34–41.

Westley, William A. 1970. *Violence and the Police: A Sociological Study of Law, Custom and Morality*. Cambridge, MA: MIT Press.

White, Michael D. 2007. *Current Issues and Controversies in Policing*. New York: Pearson-Allyn and Bacon.

White, Michael D., James Fyfe, S. P. Campbell, and John S. Goldcamp. 2003. "The Police Role in Preventing Homicide: Considering the Impact of Problem-Oriented Policing on the Prevalence of Murder," *Journal of Research in Crime and Delinquency*, Vol. 40, No. 2, pp. 194–225.

White, Susan. O. 1972. "Controlling Police Behavior." In Donal E. J. Mac-Namara and Marc Riedel (eds.), *Police: Perspectives, Problems, and Prospects*. New York: Praeger, pp. 23–34.

Williams, Gregory H. 1984. *The Law and Politics of Police Discretion*. Westport, CT: Greenwood Press.

Williams, J. Sherwood, Charles W. Thomas, and B.K. Singh. 1983. "Situational Use of Police Force: Public Reactions," *American Journal of Police*, Vol. 3, No. 1, pp. 37–49.

Willis, James J., Stephen D. Mastrofski, and David Weisburd. 2006. "The Myth That COMPSTAT Reduces Crime and Transforms Police Organizations." In Robert Bohm and Jeffrey Walker (eds.), *Demystifying Crime and Criminal Justice*, pp. 111–119. Los Angeles: Roxbury.

Willman, Mark T. and John R. Snortum. 1984. "Detective Work: The Criminal Investigation Process in a Medium-Size Police Department," *Criminal Justice Review*, Vol. 9, No. 1, pp. 33–39.

Wilson, James Q. 1968. *Varieties of Police Behavior: The Management of Law and Order in Eight Communities*. Berkeley: University of California Press.

Wilson, James Q. 1978. *The Investigators*. New York: Basic Books.

Wilson, James Q. and George L. Kelling. 1982. "Broken Windows: The Police and Neighborhood Safety," *Atlantic Monthly*, March, http://www.theatlantic.com/magazine/archive/1982/03/broken-windows/4465/

Wilson, Orlando. W. 1943/1977. *Police Administration* (4th ed.). New York: McGraw-Hill.

Wrobleski, Henry W. and Kären M. Hess. 2006. *Introduction to Law Enforcement and Criminal Justice* (8th ed.). Belmont, CA: Thompson Wadsworth.

Subject Index

20/20, 4
60 Minutes, 4
9/11 terrorist attacks, 33, 46, 49, 100, 126, 210, 212, 275, 277, 279

A Man in Uniform, 44
academia, policing study and, 5–7
Academy of Criminal Justice Sciences, 6–7
academy training, 254–257. *See also* training, police
accidents, police deaths and, 266
accreditation, 31, 140, 183
actual danger, vs. potential, 266
Adam 12, 106
administrative/organizational versus legal constraints police controls, 163, 165
Advanced Research Projects Agency (ARPA), 187
advisory boards, as police control, 165
affirmative action, 63, 247, 249
African Americans. *See* minorities; racism
age, personnel selection and, 250
agencies. *See* police departments
agent provocateurs, 83
aggressive policing practices, 203

agility tests, recruitment, 252
al Qaeda, 277
Alaska Crime Laboratory, 185
alcohol abuse, of police officers, 48, 269
alcohol testing, recruitment, 252–253
alignment, 209
American Bar Foundation, 92
American Civil Liberties Union (ACLU), 98, 99
American Federation of Labor (AFL), 232
American Indians. *See* minorities
American Journal of Sociology, 4
American Police Beat Magazine, 4
American Sociological Review, 4
Americans with Disabilities Act, 222, 245
AmeriCorps, 67
Amnesty International, 155, 168
analysis, SARA technique, 120
Andy of Mayberry, 95
anticipatory socialization, 58
Anti-Defamation League of the B'nai Brith, 119
arbitration, binding, 237
Argentina, death squads in, 156

armed attacks, as police control, 163
arrest, mandatory, policies and laws, 95–96
articles, peer-review process, 5
Asian Americans. *See* minorities
assassinations, 156
assaults, police deaths and, 266
assessment, SARA technique, 120
Assessment Center Approach, 253
assets, seizure of, 223, 225–226
attitudinal research, police violence, 153
auditors, as police control, 165
authoritarianism, 59
authority
    vs. leadership, 195
    misuse of, 131, 132
    obedience to, police violence and, 156
autobiographies, 196
autonomy, relative, 7–8, 11
avoider police style (Muir), 94

background checks, 246, 252
"bad apple" explanation of deviance, 135, 162
"bad barrel" explanation of deviance, 135
ballistics, 76

Baltimore Department of Parks
and Recreation, 68
Baltimore Police Department,
68, 125, 203
Baltimore Sun, 184
bargaining not required
model, 237
Barney Miller, 95
bean bag technology, 180, 181
beat, effect on behavior, 60
behavior. *See* police behavior
behavioral theories of
leadership, 196
benefits, 231, 234. *See also*
compensation
Bertillon system, suspect
identification, 28
"beyond a reasonable doubt"
standard, 9
bike patrol, 121
binding arbitration, 237
Biography, 141
blood typing, 76
"blue flu," 66, 239
"blue wall" of silence, 49
*Board of the County
Commissioners of Bryan
County, Oklahoma v.
Brown*, 246
Bobbies, 24
body fluid analysis, 183
boredom, of police officers, 264
Boston, Massachusetts,
Operation Ceasefire, 217
Boston Police Patrolmen's
Association, 236
Bowery Boys gang, 26
Brazil, death squads in, 156
bribery, 57, 134
Bridging the Gap initiative, 198
"Broken Windows" (Wilson
and Kelling), 32
broken windows theory, 32, 97
Brooklyn Grand Jury, 142
brutality, police. *See* excessive
force

Buddy Boys investigation, 142
budget busters, 222
budget cycle, 222
budget format, 223
budgets, 222
types of, 223
bulletproof vests, 46, 182, 183
Bureau of Justice Statistics,
14, 152
Bureau of Labor Statistics, 46
Bureau of Land
Management, 279
bureaucracies, police
departments as, 193
bureaucratic/legalistic/scientific
and reform era of modern
policing, 28–30
bureaucratic ritualism, 234
burnout, 265, 269

California Personality Inventory
(CPI), 60, 253
CAPTURE program, 201–202
Car 54, Where Are You?, 106
career mobility, corruption/
deviance and, 136
cell phones, police scrutiny
and, 265
Census of State and Local
Law Enforcement
Agencies, 14
centralization of policing,
29–30
*Challenge of Crime in a Free
Society, The*, 30
change implementation
strategies, 124
character investigations,
recruitment, 252
chemical irritants, 180
Chicago Alternative Policing
Strategy (CAPS), 122
Chicago Crime
Commission, 29
Chicago Police Department,
122, 244

Child Trends, 68
Chile, death squads in, 156
choke holds, 151, 157, 167
citizen advisory boards, as
police control, 163
citizen cooperation,
investigations, 75
citizen hostility, 263, 264
citizen police academies,
49, 69
Citizen Police Academy
Association, 69
citizen police officers,
11–12, 49
City of Canton, Ohio v. Harris,
255–256
civil law, 8–9, 165
civil litigation
as police control, 167, 170
technology use and, 186
Civil Rights Act, 248
civil rights era, 30–31
civil rights legislation, 165, 170,
248, 249
civil service exams, 251–252
civilian employees, 223, 226
civilian review boards, as police
control, 163
civilianization, 226
class control theory, 25
Clean Air Act, 222
clean-beat policing style
(Brown), 94
clean graft, 134
clearance rates, 81
Closed Circuit Television
(CCTV), 183,
184–185
collaboration, 209–211. *See
also* interagency
cooperation/collaboration
basics of, 211
dynamics of, 212–213
multijurisdictional task
forces, 211
post-9/11, 212

collective agreements, as police control, 165
collective bargaining, 29, 232–233
    bargaining not required model, 237
    binding arbitration, 237
    laws governing, 237
    meet and confer model, 237
college education. *See* education
Commercial Equipment Direct Assistance Program, 279
Commission on Accreditation for Law Enforcement Agencies (CALEA), 85, 140, 185, 247, 255, 258, 259
Commission on Law Enforcement and Criminal Justice, 30
Commission to Investigate Alleged Police Corruption, 137, 140–141, 142
communication problems, 194–195
communications technology, 185
community, political-legal, and occupational culture police controls, 163, 164–165
community controls on police, 163, 164
community involvement, CompStat and, 203
community-oriented policing. *See* community policing
Community Oriented Policing Services (COPS), 224
community participation, 115, 116
community police boards, as police control, 163

community policing, 4, 31–32, 49, 203, 276
    change implementation, 124
    literature review, 122–123
    police–community relations and, 121–126
    projects, 111
    as public relations, overcoming, 123–124
community relations. *See* police–community relations
Community Safety Information Center, 216
community service, 115, 116
community service era of modern policing
    1960s, 30–31
    1970s, 31
    1980s, 31–32
    1990s, 32–33
Companion of Canada award, 268
compensation, 231–232, 239
    collective bargaining, 232–233, 237
    corruption/deviance and, 136, 138
    grievances, 238
    job actions, 238–239
    labor organizations, 233
    legal barrier reduction, 233
    personnel practices and, 233–234
    salaries and benefits, 234
    unfair labor practices, 238
    unions, advantages and disadvantages of, 234–237
    "war on crime" support and, 233
competition, vs. collaboration, 213
complaints bureaus, as police control, 163

Comprehensive Computer Statistics (CompStat). *See* CompStat
CompStat, 31, 32, 49, 97, 107, 126, 200–201, 276
    difficulties with, 202–205
    implementation of, 201–202
computer-aided dispatch (CAD), 108
Computer Analysis of Crime Statistics (CompStat). *See* CompStat
conducted esoteric devices, 188
confessions, 85
congressional committees, as police control, 165
consolidation, as funding source, 223, 227
consolidation/amalgamation model, 13
continual stress, 268
continuum of force, 167, 168–169
contraband smuggling, 131
contract law enforcement/ policing, 14
contracting for services, 227
"Contracts between Police and the Public, 2005" report, 152
control mechanisms, police violence, 159–163
    types of, 163–167
conventional/unconventional controls on police, 163, 164
"cooling out," 79
cooperation, 209–210. *See also* interagency cooperation/ collaboration
    dynamics of, 212–213
"cooping," 66, 133
co-optation, 124, 162
Cop Land, 42, 44
COPLINK network, 185

Cops, 4
cops, origin of term, 4
corrections, police partnerships
    with, 211
corruption, 57, 125, 131–132,
    133–134, 142. *See also*
    deviance
  amount of, 132
  causes of, 135–138, 243
  community policing
    and, 123
  controlling, 138–142,
    164, 244
  vs. deviance, 131
  in early detective work, 76
  investigations/
    commissions, 141
  and police–community
    relations, 118
  in the political era, 27,
    133–134
  as result of cynicism, 60
  in society, 137
  types of, 131, 134
cost-benefit analysis,
    technology, 186
counterterrorism, 279
courts, as police control,
    165, 166
crime
  clearance rates, 81
  cybercrime, 281
  fear of, 122, 123
  hot spots, 97
  media coverage of, 43
  police involved in, 134. *See
    also* corruption; deviance
  state, 156
  victimless, 135–136
  war on, 233
Crime Act, 32, 33
Crime Analysis Partnerships to
    Upgrade Regional
    Enforcement
    (CAPTURE) program,
    201–202

Crime Bill, 121
crime control theory, 25
crime deterrence. *See also*
    crime reduction
  street stops and, 105
  zero-tolerance policing
    and, 97
crime displacement, 111
crime fighter image, 43–45
crime mapping, 200. *See also*
    CompStat
Crime Mapping Research
    Center, 216
crime prevention programs, 121
crime reduction
  community policing and,
    122, 123
  CompStat and, 202–203, 205
  patrol and domestic
    violence problems,
    105–112
  problem-oriented policing
    and, 120
  vs. public relations,
    emphasis on, 57–71
crime scene protection, 75
crime statistics, 202–203. *See
    also* CompStat
criminal databases, 105
criminal investigations, 75,
    183–185. *See also*
    detective function
criminal justice
  cooperation in, 211
  degrees in, 6, 31
  rule of law and, 8–11
Criminal Justice Ethics,
    139, 169
Criminal Justice Training
    Center, 255
criminal law, 8–9, 165
Criminal Minds, 4, 86
Criminology, 4
criminology
  degrees in, 6, 31
  rule of law and, 8–11

crisis of legitimacy, 162
critical incident stress
    debriefing systems, 271
CSI, 4
CSI effect, 87
CSI Miami, 86
Curran investigations, 142
curriculum, police academies,
    255–256
  challenges of, 256–257
custody, deaths in, 151, 157
cybercrime, 281
cyber-terrorism, 279
cynicism, of police, 59–60, 137,
    197, 264, 265

danger
  of police work, 45–48,
    266–267
    potential vs. actual, 266
    ten most dangerous jobs, 47
day-watch system, 23–24
Dead Rabbits gang, 26
deadly force, 45, 63, 151,
    157–158, 180
death benefits, 231
death squad activity, 156
deaths
  in custody, 151, 157
  by police, policing myths, 45
  of police, 266, 267
Deaths by Legal
    Intervention, 45
decision making, vs. discretion,
    91–92
defense technology, 179
delegated discretion, 92
Delphi method, 281
democracy, police and, 7–8
democracy-police conflict, 7
demotion, as police
    control, 163
Department of Defense, 179,
    187, 188, 189
Department of Homeland
    Security, 8, 224

Department of Justice, 6, 14, 30, 32, 33, 86, 98, 109, 112, 121, 149, 152, 186, 187–188, 224, 225

Department of Treasury Bureau of Law Enforcement, 215

departments. *See* police departments

detective function, 75
  cases, amount of attention received, 82
  clearance rates, 81
  the CSI effect, 86–87
  detective organization and evidence collection, 78
  detective rank, 77
  history of, 76–77
  intelligence-driven policing, 86
  interrogations, 85–86
  scholarly research on, 78–81
  squad subdivisions, 78
  technology for, 183–185
  undercover and sting operations, 82–85

deviance, 57, 60, 66, 131–132, 142. *See also* corruption
  amount of, 132
  causes of, 135–137
  controlling, 138–142, 164
  excessive force. *See* excessive force
  types of, 131
  typology of, 132–134

devil's advocate, 124

Die Hard, 44

directed/targeted patrol, 106–107
  New Haven, Connecticut, study of, 109–110

dirty graft, 134

Dirty Harry, 94

Dirty War, Argentina, 156

disabilities, 245, 269

disciplinary codes, as police control, 165

discretion, 10–11, 91, 100–101
  contextual factors and, 92–95
  vs. decision making, 91–92
  delegated vs. unauthorized, 92
  importance of, 91
  mandatory arrest policies and laws and, 95–96
  pervasiveness of, 92
  racial profiling and, 98–100
  variability of among officers, 92
  zero tolerance and full enforcement and, 97–98

discrimination, 131, 245, 247, 249

dismissal, as police control, 163

disorder–control theory, 25

disposition, case, 75, 79

District of Columbia Police Department, 210, 246

diversity, regional, early policing and, 24–25

divorce, of police officers, 48

DNA analysis, 183

dogs, police, bites and, 152

domestic terrorism, 279

domestic violence
  mandatory arrest policies and laws and, 95, 96
  by police officers, 268, 269
  police response to, danger and, 46–47

donation funding, 223, 224

downward communication, 194

Draft Riots, 26

"Driving While Black" (DWB), 98. *See also* racial profiling

drug abuse
  DARE program, 69–70
  of police officers, 48, 269

Drug Awareness and Resistance Education (DARE), 69–70

Drug Enforcement Agency, 279

drug testing, recruitment, 252–253

due process revolution, 30, 77, 92, 233

early warning systems, 167, 168, 270, 271

Eastern Kentucky University, 6

eco-terrorism, 279

education, 243. *See also* training, police
  personnel selection and, 250, 253–254
  as police control, 163

electronic evidence, 78
  types of, 79

embezzlement, 131

enforcer police style (Muir), 94

entitlement, 136

entrance examination, recruitment, 251–252

entrapment, 83, 84

Equal Employment Opportunity Act, 247, 248

Equal Employment Opportunity Commission (EEOC), 245

episodic stress, 268

Escobedo v. Illinois, 30

ethics, 139, 167, 169

ethics committees, as police control, 165

evidence-based policing, 280

evidence collection, 75, 78
  technology and, 183–185

evidence types, 79. *See also* *specific types, e.g., physical evidence*

excessive force, 57, 63, 131, 149
  amount of, 152
  causes of, 154–159
  controlling, 159–163
  definitional issues, 149–150

literature review of, 153–154
police controls on, 163–167
public relations and,
    161–163
solutions for, 167–170
types of, 150–152
executive branches, as police
    control, 166
external controls on police
    violence, 160–161
external hiring, 141–142, 167,
    169–170
external stress, 267

facial recognition
    technology, 185
family problems, policing stress
    and, 48, 268–270
family stress reduction units, 271
fatalities. *See* deaths
fatigue, of police officers, 265
Federal Bureau of Investigation,
    28, 81, 86, 210, 215, 216,
    279, 281
Federal Bureau of Investigation
    Police Academy, 6
Federal Bureau of Prisons, 82
Federal Employee Protection
    Act, 252
federal funding, 276, 279
federal government, response
    to officer stress, 269–270
federal grants, 223, 224, 276
federal law enforcement, vs.
    local and state, 211, 278
Federal Law Enforcement
    Training Center, 6, 86
federal mandates,
    unfunded, 222
Feelings-Inputs-Tactics (FIT)
    approach to stress, 271
fees, as funding source,
    223, 226
felonies
    corruption and, 134
    discretion and, 92

fencing operations, 83
Field Foundation, 119
field officer training, 257–258
Field Training Officers
    (FTOs), 255, 257–258
film portrayals of policing, 26,
    42, 43, 44, 49–50,
    140, 141
fines, revenue from, 223, 224
fingerprint evidence, 76
Fingerprint Visualization
    System, 185
fingerprinting process, 81, 183
first responders, 263
FIT (Feelings-Inputs-Tactics)
    approach to stress, 271
flat organizations, 199
fleeing felon rule, 169
fleeing vehicle tagging system,
    180, 182
Flint, Michigan, foot patrol
    experiment, 110
foot patrol, 105
    as community policing, 121
    experiments, 110
force
    continuum of, 167, 168–169
    excessive. *See* excessive force
    lethal, 45, 63, 151,
        157–158, 180
Ford Foundation, 200
foreign nationals, 279
forensic evidence, 76–77, 78
forensic science, 86–87
forfeiture law and practices,
    223, 225–226
formal/informal police
    controls, 163, 165
formal socialization, 58
Fourth Amendment, 99
Fox National News, 125
fragmentation, 209
Fraternal Order of Police
    (FOP), 7, 231, 232
French Connection, 44
full enforcement, 97–98

funding sources, 223–227. *See
    also* underfunding
    federal, 276, 279
fundraising programs, 224
future directions, policing,
    275–276, 281
    CompStat, 276
    cooperation and
        coordination,
        interorganizational, 278
    crime victim treatment,
        276, 278
    evidence-based policing, 280
    immigrant-related crime, 279
    new technology, 278–279
    oppositional political
        terrorism, 279–280
    police–labor relations, 278
    police scholarship
        improvements, 280
    studying, 280–281

Gangs of New York, 26
Garner v. Tennessee, 45, 180
gay officers, recruitment of,
    246, 247
General Social Survey, 153
genetic theories of
    leadership, 196
Gideon v. Wainwright, 30
Global Positioning System
    (GPS), 182, 183
globalization, 281
"golden handcuffs," 265
government departments,
    police cooperation
    with, 278
government reports, police
    violence, 154
government-sanctioned
    violence, death
    squads, 156
governmental regulation, as
    police control, 165
graft, 131, 134, 136
grants, 223, 224, 276

grapevine communication, 194
"grass eaters," 134
gratuities, acceptance/
    solicitation of, 57,
    133, 134
Great Depression, 29
"great man" theories of
    leadership, 196
grievances, 238
Guantanamo Bay, Cuba, 150
guidelines, as police control,
    163, 165
gun buy-back programs, 68
gunshot detection systems,
    183–184

Harvard University, 200
health problems, stress and,
    268, 269
helping professions, 263
hierarchy, as police control,
    163, 165
high-energy beams, 188
High Intensity Drug Trafficking
    Areas (HIDTAs), 97
high-intensity/low-intensity
    controls on police,
    163, 164
Hill Street Blues, 106
hiring. *See* recruitment
Hispanics. *See* minorities;
    racism
historical analogies, 281
hit squad activity, 156
Hollywood films, policing in,
    26, 42, 43, 44, 49–50,
    140, 141
Homeland Security Act, 222
homosexual officers,
    recruitment of, 246, 247
honey trap, 83
horizontal communication, 194
hospital model of
    organization, 199
hostility, toward police,
    263, 264

hot spots, 97
human relations, 118
Human Rights Watch, 155
human trafficking, 281
hybrid budgets, 223

identity theft, 281
illegal activities, protection
    of, 134
illegal surveillance, 57, 131
immigrants
    in the bureaucratic/
        legalistic/scientific and
        reform era, 28–29
    crime and victimization of,
        275, 279
    in the political era, 27
    undocumented, 32
immigration, illegal, 33, 279
Immigration and Customs
    Enforcement (ICE), 212
Immigration Reform and
    Control Act, 222
improper discretion. *See*
    discretion
"in plain sight," 10
inclusive/exclusive police
    controls, 163, 165
Indianapolis, Indiana, policing
    neighborhoods
    project, 111
informal socialization, 58–59
informants, 75, 76, 84
initial investigation, 75
injuries, police officer, 266
inner cities, bureaucratic/
    legalistic/scientific and
    reform era, 28–29
Innovations in American
    Government award, 200
in-service training, 258, 267
Institute for Public Safety, 255
Integrity Officers, 140–141,
    167, 169
intelligence-driven policing, 86
intelligence tests, 244

interagency competition, as
    police control, 165
interagency cooperation/
    collaboration,
    209–210, 217
    collaboration, 210–213
    examples of, 215–216
    future directions of, 278
    obstacles to, 214–215
    organizational forms of law
        enforcement, 214
    problems with, 216–217
Internal Affairs, 44
Internal Affairs departments/
    bureaus (IAD/IAB), 139
    as police control, 163, 167,
        168, 169
internal controls on police
    violence, 160–161
internal/external police
    controls, 163, 165–166
internal payoffs, 134
internal stress, 267
International Association of
    Chiefs of Police (IACP),
    7, 118, 133, 255
international attention, critical,
    as police control, 163, 165
International Brotherhood of
    Teamsters (IBT), 232
International Criminal Police
    Organization
    (INTERPOL), 215
International Union of Police
    Associations (IUPA),
    7, 232
Internet
    community relations
        and, 125
    cybercrime, 281
    as information source, 4
interrogations, 85–86
interviews, recruitment, 253
intimidation, 131, 134, 150
intra-agency competition, as
    police control, 165

investigation, character, 252
investigation, criminal, 75,
 183–185. *See also*
 detective function
investigation, undercover,
 82–85
investigations/commissions,
 police control and,
 167, 169
investigative effectiveness
 studies, detective
 function, 80–81
Investigative Reports, 4
Inwald Personality Inventory,
 60, 253
iPhones, 185
Irish Republican Army, 184
Islamic Fundamentalism,
 racial profiling and, 100

Jackobson v. United States, 84
job actions, 238–239
job performance, stress and, 269
jobs, ten most dangerous, 47
John Jay School of Criminal
 Justice, 6
*Journal of Police Strategies and
 Management*, 4
journals, scholarly, 4–5
jurisdiction, 13
Justice Quarterly, 4

Kansas City, Missouri
 preventative patrol
 experiment, 109
 response time analysis
 study, 110
Kansas City Police
 Department, 110
Kerner Commission, 30, 154
Kevlar vests, 182, 183
kickbacks, 134
kidnapping, 156
Knapp Commission, 137,
 140–141, 142
kobans, 121

L.A. Confidential, 44
labor negotiations. *See*
 collective bargaining
labor practices, unfair, 238
labor unions. *See* unions
Latinos. *See* minorities; racism
law(s)
 civil rights legislation, 165,
 170, 248, 249
 collective bargaining, 237
 criminal vs. civil, 8–9, 165
 equal employment, 247, 248
 family well-being and stress,
 269–270
 forfeiture, 223, 225–226
 mandatory arrest, 95–96
 morality, 27
 personnel practices and, 245
 as police control, 163,
 165, 166
 rule of, 8–11
 substantive vs. procedural,
 9–11
Law and Order, 4
law enforcement
 community relations and,
 historically, 117–121
 definition of, 4
 federal vs. local and state,
 211, 278
 human relations and, 118
 motivations for joining,
 245–247
 organizational forms of,
 13–14, 214
 organizational structure
 of, 13
 as patrol function, 107
 stress and, 267–271
 underfunding of, 221–227
 unions and. *See* unions
Law Enforcement Assistance
 Administration (LEAA),
 6, 30, 119, 250
Law Enforcement Family
 Support legislation, 270

Law Enforcement
 Management and
 Administrative
 Statistics, 14
law enforcement officers, 4. *See
 also* police (officers)
*Law Enforcement Officers
 Killed and Assaulted*, 46
Law Enforcement Personal
 History Questionnaire, 60
leadership. *See also*
 management, police
 organizations
 vs. authority and
 power, 195
 inadequate, 137, 193,
 195–196, 204
 performance and, 195–196
 theories of, 196
learning organizations,
 198–199
legislation, as police control,
 165, 166
legislative oversight, as police
 control, 165, 166
lesbian officers, recruitment of,
 246, 247
less-than-lethal (LTL) weapons,
 167–168, 180–182
lethal force, 45, 63, 151,
 157–158, 180
letters to elected/appointed
 officials, as police
 control, 163
Lexow Committee, 142
license plate recognition
 technology, 185
lie detector tests, 76, 252
life expectancy, 267
line-item budgets, 223
literature review. *See also*
 research, policing
 community policing,
 122–123
 police violence, 153–154,
 160–163

lobbying, as police control, 163, 165
local law enforcement, vs. federal and state, 211, 278
London, England, 24, 184
London Metropolitan Police, 159
London Metropolitan Police Act, 24
longevity pay, 231
Los Angeles Police Department, 69, 149, 244

magazines
    as information source, 4–5
    as policing myths source, 43
Magic Wand, 185
management, police organizations, 193
    communication problems, 194–195
    CompStat and, 200–205
    leadership failure, 195–196
    learning organizations, 198–199
    Management by Objectives, 197–198
    solutions for, 196–199
    total quality management, 198
Management by Objectives (MBO), 197–198
mandatory arrest policies and laws, 95–96
Mapp v. Ohio, 30
marital problems, stress and, 268, 269–270
Maryland State Board for Victim Assistance, 281
Mazet Committee, 142
McGill University, 268
"meat eaters," 134
media
    case attention, amount of, 82

detective function portrayal in, 86–87
as information source, 4–5
negative attention of, as police control, 163, 165
as policing myths source, 43, 49–50
public relations and, 64
meet and confer model, 237
memos, as police control, 163
Michigan State University, 254
Michigan State University (MSU) School of Police Administration and Public Safety, 118, 119
military unit death squads, 156
Minneapolis Domestic Violence Survey, 96
Minneapolis Hot Spot Patrol Experiment, 110
Minnesota Multiphasic Personality Inventory (MMPI), 60, 253
minorities
    affirmative action and, 63, 247, 249
    in the bureaucratic/ legalistic/scientific and reform era, 28–29
    discrimination and, 131, 245, 247, 249
    in police force, 21, 33, 236, 245, 246, 247, 249, 280
    quotas and, 249
    racial profiling of. See racial profiling
    stereotypes and, 98
Miranda v. Arizona, 30
misconduct, 131, 132. See also corruption; deviance
misdemeanors
    corruption and, 134
    discretion and, 92
mission distortion, 211
mobilization of bias, 236

modern policing
    bureaucratic/legalistic/ scientific and reform era, 28–30
    community service era, 30–33
    eras/periods/stages of, 26–33
    police development theories, 25–26
    political era of, 27–28
    regional diversity, 24–25
Modest Police Department, 82
Mollen Commission, 142
monetary appropriations, as police control, 165
Monnel v. Department of Social Services of the City of New York, 95–96, 165
morality laws, in the political era, 27
mortality, of police officers, 48
motorized patrol, 105
mug shots, 76
multijurisdictional
    policing, 14
    task forces, 211
municipal policing, 23, 33–34
    early history, 23–24
    eras/periods/stages of, 26–33
    future of, 275–281. See also future directions, policing
    modern, 24–26
    mythology of, 41–50. See also mythology of municipal policing
    technology and, 179–188. See also technology
    underfunding of, 221–227
murder, 156
Muslim religion, racial profiling and, 100–101
mutual aid model, 13–14

mythology of municipal
    policing, 41
    crime fighter image, 43–45
    dangers of police work,
        45–46
    deaths by officers, 45
    domestic violence calls and
        danger, 46–47
    drug and alcohol abuse, 48
    myth sources, 43
    police divorces, 48
    police mortality, 48
    police stress, 47
    police suicide, 47–48
    solving the problem of,
        49–50

Naked City, 44
narco-terrorism, 279
National Advisory Commission
    on Civil Disorders, 30,
    154, 245
National Advisory Commission
    on Criminal Justice
    Standards and Goals,
    227, 254
National Association for the
    Advancement of Colored
    People (NAACP), 99, 119
National Association of
    Intergroup Relations
    Officials, 118
National Basketball Association
    Center, 125
"National Census of Fatal
    Occupational Injuries
    2008," 46
National Center on Police
    and Community
    Relations, 119
National Center for Victims of
    Crime, 281
National Commission on the
    Causes and Prevention of
    Violence, 154

National Commission on Law
    Observance and
    Enforcement, 29, 154
National Conference of
    Christians and Jews
    (NCCJ), 118
National Crime Information
    Center (NCIC) database,
    105, 112, 215
National Enquirer, 4
National Guard, 232
National Highway Traffic Safety
    Administration, 224
National Institute of Justice, 31,
    33, 96, 108–109, 183,
    184, 187, 188, 189,
    216, 276
National Institute on Police
    and Community
    Relations (NIPCR),
    118–119
National Institute of Standards
    and Technology, 187
National Labor Relations Act,
    233, 237
National Law Enforcement and
    Corrections Technology
    Center, 151, 186,
    187–188
National Organization of Black
    Law Enforcement
    Executives (NOBLE),
    7, 255
National Park Service, 279
National Sheriff's Association
    (NSA), 7, 255
Native Americans. *See*
    minorities
negative media attention, as
    police control, 163
negative public opinion, as
    police control, 163, 165
neighborhood policing
    project, 111
networking, 209–210

New Haven, Connecticut,
    directed patrol study,
    109–110
New Jersey Attorney
    General, 98
New Jersey State Patrol, 98
New Jersey Turnpike, 98
New York City
    CompStat program, 32, 97,
        200, 201, 205. *See also*
        CompStat
    early crime in, 26
    Integrity Officers,
        140–141, 169
    NYPD Special
        Investigations Unit, 140
    officer training
        requirements, 255
    police corruption in, 134
    terrorism in, 33, 46, 49, 100,
        210, 212, 277, 279, 280
New York City Fire
    Department, 277, 279
New York City Police
    Department, 210, 212,
    279, 280
New York City Police
    Foundation, 224
New York Times, 141
New York Transit Police
    Commissioner, 200
Newark, New Jersey, foot patrol
    experiment, 110
news magazine shows, as
    information source, 4
newspapers, as policing myths
    source, 43
Newsweek, 4
night-watch system, 23–24
non-lethal weapons, 180–182

obedience to authority, police
    violence and, 156
observational studies, detective
    function, 79–80

occupational culture, 58, 264
  police controls, 163,
    164–165
occupational deviance, 132
occupational socialization, 257.
  See also socialization
occupations, ten most
  dangerous, 47
Office of Community-Oriented
  Policing Services
  (COPS), 32, 33, 121, 123
Office of Law Enforcement
  Standards, 187
Officer Friendly program, 70
old-style policing style
  (Brown), 94
oleoresin capsicum (pepper
  spray), 180, 181
ombudsmen, as police
  control, 165
Omnibus Crime Control and
  Safe Streets Act, 30
Operation Ceasefire, 217
opportunity, corruption/
  deviance and, 135–136
oppositional political terrorism,
  275, 279–280
Oral Board Review, 253
oral boards, recruitment, 253
order maintenance, 3, 7, 107
organizational forms, law
  enforcement, 13–14, 214

paper evidence, 78
  types of, 79
papers, publishing as peer-
  reviewed articles, 5
paramilitary organizations,
  police departments as, 193
paramilitary unit death
  squads, 156
patrol, 105. *See also specific
  types, e.g., foot patrol*
  importance of, 106
  research on, 108–111

resource determination and
  allocation issues,
  107–108
technology and, 105
television series
  featuring, 106
types of, 106–107
Patrolmen's Benevolent
  Association (PBA), 7,
  231–232
PATRIOT Act, 212, 275
pay rates. *See* compensation
payoffs, 134
peer review panels, as police
  control, 163
peer-reviewed resources, 4, 5
peer support, stress reduction
  and, 27
Pendleton Act, 27, 244
Pentagon, terrorist attacks
  on, 277
pepper spray, 180, 181
performance, leadership and,
  195–196
performance budget, 223
perjury, 136
personal disposition, discretion
  and, 93
personality tests, 60
personnel monitoring systems,
  182, 183
personnel practices, 233–234,
  245–247
personnel selection, 250. *See
  also* recruitment
  basic criteria, 251
  tests, 251–253
pervasiveness, discretion
  and, 92
phaser, 188
Phoenix, Arizona, RISS
  program, 216
photo radar technology, 180
physical ability tests,
  recruitment, 252

physical effects of stress, 269
physical evidence, 78
  types of, 79
Pinkerton National Detective
  Agency, 76
Pinochet regime, Chile, 156
plain clothes operations. *See*
  undercover investigations
police (officers)
  behavior of. *See* police
    behavior
  boredom of, 264
  burnout and, 265, 269
  citizen, 11–12, 49
  community-oriented, 4
  compensation of. *See*
    compensation
  corruption of. *See*
    corruption
  crime fighter image of, 43–45
  cynicism of, 59–60, 137,
    197, 264, 265
  deaths by, 45, 151, 157
  definition of, 3, 4
  democracy and, 7–8
  development theories, 25–26
  deviance of. *See* deviance
  disabilities and, 245
  discretion of, 10–11, 92. *See
    also* discretion
  divorces of, 48
  drug and alcohol abuse of,
    48, 269
  effects of police work,
    264–266
  employment and
    expenditures, 14
  fatigue of, 265
  mortality of, 48
  motivations for becoming,
    245–247
  origin of term, 7
  private and public
    organized, 12–13
  "problem officers," 168

psychology and, 59–60
rankings, 77
recruitment of. *See*
    recruitment
role of, 60
rule of law and, 8–11
safety of, 182–183, 267
special jurisdiction, 14
stereotypes of, 263–264
stress of, 47, 265, 267–271.
    See also stress
subculture, 58
suicide of, 47–48, 266, 269
training of. *See* training,
    police
types of, 11–13
working conditions of,
    263–271. *See also*
    working conditions
police academies, 254–257
Police & Society, 4
Police Athletic Leagues (PALs),
    67–68, 116, 162
police behavior, 196
    alternative explanation for,
        59–61
    departmental characteristics
        and, 61
    factors influencing, 57–61
    police officer role and, 60
    police psychology and,
        59–60
    predispositional theory, 58
    socialization theory, 58–59
    typologies of, 57
Police Chief, 4
police commissions, as police
    control, 163
police–community relations,
    115, 125–126
    definitional issues, 115–116
    improving, 121–125
    poor, history of, 117–121
    public relations and,
        116–117

Police Corps, 246–247, 259
police departments
    accreditation, 31, 140
    as bureaucracies, 193
    characteristics of, influence
        on police behavior, 61
    cooperation/collaboration,
        interagency, 209–217.
        See also interagency
        cooperation/collaboration
    controls on police violence
        in, 160–167
    corruption and deviance in,
        132, 137. *See also*
        corruption; deviance
    detective organization
        within, 78
    funding of, 221–227
    Internal Affairs departments/
        bureaus, 139
    leadership in, inadequate,
        137. *See also*
        leadership
    management, supervision,
        and leadership in,
        193–205. *See also*
        management, police
    organizations
    outside administrators,
        hiring, 141–142, 167,
        169–170
    as paramilitary
        organizations, 193
    personnel practices in,
        233–234, 245–247
    public relations in, 63–67
    rankings within, 77
    recruitment process. *See*
        recruitment
    resource use within. *See*
        resource use, police
        departments
    rules, discretion and, 93
    screening process, 135
    underfunding, 221–227

unfair labor practices in, 238
unions in. *See* unions
Police Executive Research
    Forum (PERF), 7,
    152, 255
police family stress reduction
    units, 271
Police Foundation, 7, 109,
    110, 216
police monitoring units, as
    police control, 163
Police Officer Standards and
    Training Commissions
    (PSOTs), 250
Police Practice and Research, 4
Police Quarterly, 4
Police: Streetcorner Politicians
    (Muir), 94
police training. *See* training,
    police
police violence. *See* excessive
    force
Policeman in the Community
    (Banton), 60
policing. *See also* law
    enforcement
    academic degrees in, 5–6
    aggressive, 203
    centralization of, 29–30
    community. *See* community
        policing
    contract, 14
    dangerousness of, 45–48,
        266–267
    evidence-based, 280
    future of, 275–281. *See also*
        future directions,
        policing
    intelligence-driven, 86
    media and, 4–6
    modern. *See* modern
        policing
    multijurisdictional, 14
    municipal. *See* municipal
        policing

myths of. *See* mythology of
municipal policing
politicalization of, 123
problem-oriented, 31–32,
120–121, 258, 276
professional organizations
focusing on, 7
professionalization of, 29,
31, 244
research on. *See* research,
policing
saturation, 203
study of, 4–7
styles, discretion and,
94–95
technology and. *See*
technology
types of, 11–13
"zero-tolerance," 11, 31–32,
97–98, 107, 200, 203
Policing by Objectives, 121
policing programs, public
relations and, 67
citizen police academies, 69
community relations
programs, 119–120
Drug Awareness and
Resistance education
(DARE), 69–70
gun buy-back programs, 68
Officer Friendly, 70
Police Athletic League,
67–68
ride-alongs, 68, 69
policy manuals, as police
control, 163, 165, 166
political era of modern
policing, 27–28
political-legal police controls,
163, 164
political machines, 27
politicalization of police, 123
politics, unions and, 235–236
Polygraph Protection Act, 252
polygraph tests, 76, 252

popular conceptions, police
deviance, 135
posse comitatus, 12
Posse Comitatus Act, 12, 24
posturing, 162
potential danger, vs. actual, 266
power, vs. leadership, 195
predispositional theory of
police behavior, 58
Pregnancy Disability
Act, 248
preliminary investigation, 75
premonitory/investigative
controls on police,
163, 164
"preponderance of evidence"
standard, 9
President's Commission on
Law Enforcement and
Administration, 244–245
President's Crime
Commission, 209
preventative patrol
experiment, 109
Pride and Glory, 44
Prince of the City, 44, 140
"Prince of the City"
investigations, 142
private detectives, 76
private grants, 223, 224
private organized police, 12–13
private security organizations,
police cooperation
with, 278
private violence, 150
"problem officers," 168
problem-oriented policing,
31–32, 258, 276
police–community relations
and, 120–121
procedural law, 9–11
professional organizations,
policing, 7
professional police style
(Muir), 94

professional policing style
(Brown), 94–95
professionalization of policing,
29, 31, 244
program budgets, 223
programs, policing. *See*
policing programs, public
relations and
Progressive Era, 27–28
progressives, 27–28
Project Exile, 217
Project Safe
Neighborhoods, 217
promotion, as police
control, 163
propaganda, 61
prosecutors, as police control,
165, 166
protests
1960s era, 30, 244
as police control, 163, 165
psychoanalytical processes,
police violence
and, 156
psychological tests, 60, 253
Public Information Officers
(PIOs), 67
public opinion, as police
control, 163, 165
public organized police,
12–13
public protests, as police
control, 163, 165
public relations, 61–62
community participation
and, 116
community–police relations
and, 116–117
community policing as,
overcoming, 123–125
community service
and, 116
controls on police violence
and, 161–163
police, 63–67

public relations vs. crime reduction, emphasis on, 57, 70–71
police behavior, factors influencing, 57–61
police behavior typologies, 57
police public information officer, 67
police public relations, 63–67
policing programs as public relations efforts, 67–70
public relations, 61–62
public safety model/concept, 13
public violence, 150
publicity, 61–62
pursuits/chases, vehicle, 151–152

Q and A, 44
quality circles, 198
quality-of-life measures, 267
quotas, 249

race riots, 29
in 1960s era, 30, 63, 244
police–community relations and, 119
police control in, 151
Rodney King beating, 149
racial profiling, 98–99
expansion of, 100
terrorism and, 100–101
zero-tolerance policies and, 97
racial stereotyping, 98
racism
in 1960s era, 30, 63, 244
in bureaucratic/legalistic/scientific and reform era, 28–29
discrimination, 131, 245, 247, 249
minority recruitment and, 247
unions and, 236

ranking, police, 77
rape, 156
rationalization, corruption/deviance and, 137
reciprocator police style (Muir), 94
recruitment, 243, 259
education and, 253–254
history of, 243–245
issues in, 245–247
selection/screening process, 163, 166, 250–253
of women and minorities, 248–250, 280
red light running devices, 180
reform era, modern policing, 29–30
regional diversity, early policing and, 24–25
Regional information Sharing System (RISS), 216
Reid interrogation technique, 85
relative autonomy, 7–8, 11
remote-control barrier strips, 180, 182
remuneration. *See* compensation
Reno 911, 106
replication studies, 280
research, policing, 6–7
in 1970s era, 31
in 1980s era, 31–32
to combat policing myths, 49
on community policing, 122–123
on corruption/deviance, 135–137
on deadly force use, 157–158
on death squad activity, 156
on deaths in police custody, 157
on the detective function, 78–81

future directions of, 280
as information source, 4–5
on patrol, 108–111
on police controls, 166–167
on police riots, 157
on police torture, 155–156
on police violence, 153–158, 166–167
on recruitment of women and minorities, 280
residency requirements, 249–250
resistance, controls on police and, 161–163
resource use, police departments. *See also* underfunding
community policing and, 126
controls on police violence and, 161
cooperation/collaboration and, 215
detective function and, 87
future directions, 276
patrol and, 107–108
personnel selection and, 250
problem-oriented policing and, 121
public relations and, 64, 66
technology and, 179, 185–186, 221, 278–279
response, SARA technique, 120
response style, discretion and, 93
response time
analysis study, 110
community policing and, 123
gunshot detection systems and, 184
restorative justice, 276
retirement benefits, 231
retraining, as police control, 163
revenue, from fines and traffic tickets, 223, 224

review boards, as police control, 165, 166
revolutionary warfare, as police control, 163
Richmond, Virginia, Project Exile, 217
ride-alongs, 49, 68, 69
Righteous Kill, 44
"Rights in Conflict" report, 154
riots, urban, 29
  in 1960s era, 30, 63, 244
  Chicago, 1968 Democratic Convention, 154
  police, 151, 157
  police–community relations and, 119
  as police control, 163
  Rodney King beating, 149
Rossmo's interrogation approach, 85–86
rotating shift work, 263
routine transfers, officer, 139
Royal Canadian Mounted Police, 215
rule of law, 8–11

safety of officers, improving, 267
  technology for, 182–183
salaries, 234. *See also* compensation
San Diego Police Department, 121
SARA technique, 120
saturation policing, 203
scanning, SARA technique, 120
scenarios, 281
scholarly research. *See* research, policing
scientific method, 28, 76
screening, applicant, as police control, 166. *See also* recruitment
scrutiny, of police, 265
Seabury Committee, 142
search and seizure, 99
Sears-Roebuck Foundation, 70

selection. *See* recruitment
seniority, cooperation/ collaboration and, 214
September 11, 2001, terrorist attacks, 33, 46, 49, 100, 126, 210, 212, 275, 277, 279
Serpico, 44
service, as patrol function, 107
service style policing style (Brown), 94–95
sexual harassment, 131, 248
sheriffs, in early policing, 243
Shield, The, 94
shift differential pay, 231
shift work, 263
shoot teams, as police control, 163
Shotspotter Corporation, 183
Sikhism, 100
situational theories of leadership, 196
sleep problems, stress and, 269
smart guns, 182–183
snitches, 76
Social Contract, 8
socialization
  anticipatory, 58
  corruption/deviance and, 136–137
  occupational, 257
  police control and, 166
  as training challenge, 257
socialization theory of police behavior, 58–59
Society of Police Futurists International, 280–281
Sorrels v. United States, 84
Southland, 106
special jurisdiction police, 14
Special Weapons and Tactical (SWAT) teams, 151
speed cameras, 180
spies, 83
split-force patrol experiment, 110

St. Petersburg, Florida, policing neighborhoods project, 111
Standards for Law Enforcement Agencies, 247
standing orders, as police control, 163, 166
state law enforcement, vs. federal and local, 211, 278
Statistical Analysis Center (SAC), 81
statistics, crime, 202–203. *See also* CompStat
stereotypes
  of police officers, 263–264
  racial, 98
sticky foam, 188
sting operations, 82–85
stool pigeons, 76
"Stop Snitchin'," 125
strategic intelligence, 86
street stops, 105
stress, of police officers, 47, 265, 267, 271
  coping with, 270–271
  effects of, 268–269
  episodic vs. continual, 268
  federal government and, 269–270
  internal vs. external, 267
  sources of, 267–268
stress inoculation, 271
strikes, 238, 239
strobe-and-goggle technology, 180, 182
stun grenades, 182
subcontracting, 223, 227
subculture, police, 58
suburbs, bureaucratic/ legalistic/scientific and reform era, 28–29
substantive law, 9–11
suicide
  of police officers, 47–48, 266, 269
  of suspects in custody, 157

supervision, 193, 197. *See also* management, police organizations
  as internal control initiative, 160–161
  officer safety and, 267
  as police control, 163, 165, 166
Supplementary Homicide Report (SHR), 45
surveillance, illegal, 57, 131
suspect(s)
  identification, Bertillon system, 28
  interrogation, 85–86
  pursuit of, vehicle chases, 151–152
  uncooperative, and officer injury/death, 266
SWAT teams, 151

tactical intelligence, 86
Tammany Hall, 26
tasers, 167–168, 180, 181
task force approach, 14
task forces, multijurisdictional, 211, 217
taxes, police, as funding source, 226
tear gas, 181
technology, 179, 185–188
  communications, 185
  cooperation/collaboration and, 214–215
  costs, 179, 185–186, 221, 278–279
  for criminal investigations, 183–185
  future directions and, 278–279
  less-than-lethal/non-lethal weapons, 180–182
  for officer safety, 182–183

  for traffic enforcement, 180
  underfunding and, 221
Technology Assessment Program Information Center (TAPIC), 187, 188
Technology Assistance, Technology, and Training (TATT), 216
telephone technology, 185
television
  detective function portrayal in, 86–87
  as information source, 4
  police patrol portrayal in, 106
  as policing myths source, 43, 49–50
Tennessee v. Garner, 168–169, 170, 171
terrorism
  in 1980s era, 31–32
  Irish Republican Army, 184
  in New York City, 33, 46, 49, 100, 210, 212, 277, 279, 280
  oppositional political terrorism, 275, 279–280
  police interagency cooperation and, 212
  racial profiling and, 100–101
  September 11, 2001, attacks, 33, 46, 49, 100, 126, 210, 212, 275, 277, 279
  task forces and, 211
  types of, 279
Terry v. Ohio, 30
tests, police recruitment, 251–253
thieftakers, 76
"thin blue line," 50
threats, 134

Thurman v. Torrington, 96
Time, 4
Times, 43
Title VII, Civil Rights Act, 248
tolerance, corruption/deviance and, 136
torture, 150, 155–156
total quality management (TQM), 198
traditional/random patrol, 106–107
traffic citations, corruption and, 134
traffic collisions, officer deaths and, 46, 266
traffic enforcement technology, 180, 184
traffic ticket revenue, 223, 224
training, police, 243, 259
  academy, 254–257
  challenges of, 256–257
  community relations, 124
  ethics, 139, 167, 169
  field, 257–258
  human relations, 118
  in-service, 258, 267
  interrogation techniques, 86
  officer safety and, 267
  as police control, 163, 165, 166
  Police Corps, 246–247, 259
  in technology use, 186
Training Day, 44
traits approach theory of leadership, 196
transfers, officer, 139
  as police control, 163
trend extrapolation, 281

unauthorized discretion, 92
undercover investigations, 82–83
  sting operations, 83–85

underfunding, 221–222, 227
    contextual issues, 222–223
    future directions, 276
    solutions (sources of
        funding), 223–227
unfair labor practices, 238
Uniform Crime Report (UCR),
    28, 45, 81
unions, 231–232, 235–236
    advantages of, 234–235
    collective bargaining,
        232–233
    disadvantages of, 235
    future directions, 278
    grievances, 238
    job actions, 238–239
    legal barrier reductions
        and, 233
    needs of, 233
    personnel practices and,
        233–234
    salaries and benefits and, 234
    unfair labor practices
        and, 238
United States Commission on
    Civil Rights, 119
United States National
    Commission on the
    Causes of Crime and
    Disorder, 30
United States Public Health
    Service, 45
*United States v. Jimenez
    Recio,* 84
University of Arizona, 185
University of California–
    Berkley, 6, 244
University of Montreal, 268
University of Southern
    California, 253
University of Wisconsin, 7
University of Wisconsin–
    Madison, 32

upward career mobility,
    corruption/deviance
    and, 136
upward communication, 194
urban dispersion theory, 25
urban riots, 29
    in 1960s era, 30, 63, 244
    Chicago, 1968 Democratic
        Convention, 154
    community–police relations
        and, 119
    police, 151, 157
    as police control, 163
    Rodney King beating, 149
U.S. Commission on Civil
    Rights, 168
U.S. Constitution, 99
U.S. Department of Defense,
    179, 187, 188, 189
U.S. Department of Homeland
    Security, 8, 224
U.S. Department of Justice, 6,
    14, 30, 32, 33, 86, 98,
    109, 112, 121, 149, 152,
    186, 187–188, 224, 225
U.S. Department of Treasury
    Bureau of Law
    Enforcement, 215
U.S. National Commission on
    the Causes of Crime and
    Disorder, 245
U.S. News & World Report, 4
user fees, as funding source,
    223, 226

Varieties of Police Behavior
    (Wilson), 61
vehicle chases/pursuits,
    151–152
vehicle collisions, officer
    deaths and, 46, 266
venue, 13
vertical raids, 203

victim advocates, 276
victimless crimes, 135–136
victims
    blaming, 162, 270
    number of, sting operations
        and, 84
    police treatment of,
        276–277
videotaping
    of police, 265
    of suspects, 183
vigilantes, 12, 156
violence
    police. *See* excessive force
    public vs. private, 150
    state, 156
Violent Crime Control and
    Law Enforcement Act,
    32, 33, 152, 224, 246
Violent Criminal
    Apprehension program
    (VICAP), 216
Vital Statistics reports, 45
vote of confidence, 239

wages. *See* compensation
war on crime, 233
Washington, D.C., Police
    Department, 248
weapons
    gunshot detection systems,
        183–184
    less-than-lethal (LTL),
        167–168, 180–182
    non-lethal, 180–182
    restricted, 131
    smart guns, 182–183
    trafficking, 281
Web sites
    community relations and, 125
    as information source, 4
"weed and seed areas," 97
Western Illinois University, 6

Wichita State University, 6
Wickersham Commission,
    29, 154
Wilmington, Delaware, split-
    force experiment, 110
Wilmington Police
    Department, 110
Winston-Salem, North
    Carolina, Community
    Safety Information
    System, 216
women, in police force, 33, 236,
    245, 246, 247, 248, 280

Wonderlic Personnel Test
    (WPT), 253
work slow-downs, 239
work speed-ups, 239
work stoppages, 239
working conditions,
    263–264, 271
    dangerousness, 266–267
    effects of police work,
        264–266
    stress and, 267–271
*Working the Street: Police
    Discretion* (Brown), 94

World Trade Center, bombing
    of. *See* September 11,
    2001, terrorist attacks
World War II, 30, 118

YouTube, 125

zero-based budget, 223
zero-tolerance policing, 11,
    31–32, 97–98, 107,
    200, 203

Author Index

Ackroyd, J. W., 160
Adlam, Robert K. C., 59
Adler, Patricia, 131
Alderson, J. C., 122
Allen, R. K., 194
Alpert, Geoffrey P., 41, 43, 44, 45, 46, 47, 48, 136, 151
Amnesty International, 168
Angel, John, 199
Asbury, Herbert, 26
Aylesworth, G. N., 225

Bacharach, Peter, 236
Balagopal, K., 156
Balch, R. W., 59
Baldwin, John, 183
Banton, Michael, 60
Baratz, Morton S., 236
Barker, Thomas, 48, 131, 132, 133, 135, 136
Barret, Wayne, 137
Bayley, David H., 118, 119, 122, 123, 124, 160, 165
Beak, Joel, 161
Beare M. E., 66, 162
Becker, Howard, 49, 136
Bell, D. J., 248
Bennett, Wayne W., 194
Bernard, Thomas J., 98
Biebel, E. P., 121
bin Laden, Osama, 277
Binder, A., 158
Birzer, M. L., 248
Bittner, Egon, 107
Black, Donald J., 107

Bloomberg, Michael, 205
Bowers, R. A., 110
Brandl, Steven G., 266
Bratton, Bill, 200, 201, 203, 204, 205
Bratton, William, 196
Brent, Edward E., 107
Brock, Deon, 214, 215, 216
Brooks, Laure Weber, 91, 92, 93, 94, 97
Brown, C., 31, 109
Brown, Lee, 6, 31
Brown, Michael, 94
Buckley, Joseph P., 85
Burke, J., 277
Burke, Tod W., 69

Cain, M., 107
Calnon, Jennifer M., 98
Campbell, S. P., 120
Caplan, Gerald, 134
Carlson, Robert O., 62
Carpenter, Bruce N., 245
Carte, E., 29, 244
Carte, G. E., 29, 244
Carter, David L., 62, 66, 115, 116, 118, 119, 120
Cattarello, Anne, 70
Chaiken, Jan, 31, 66, 78, 80, 81
Chan, Theodore C., 181
Chappell, Allison, 246, 254, 255
Chappell, T., 246, 254, 255
Chen, Hsinchun, 185
Chiklis, Michael, 94

Christopher, Warren, 33
Chu, James, 183
Clayton, Richard R., 70
Clemmer, Elizabeth, 46–47
Committee to Improve Research on Firearms Data, 68
Condit, Gary, 82
Conley, John A., 30
Coolidge, Calvin, 232
Cooper, L. B., 165
Cordner, Gary, 115, 121, 223
Crank, John, 75, 76, 77, 80, 92, 94, 95
Crawford, Charles, 43
Crawford, Chris, 214, 215, 216
Crew, B. Keith, 43
Cumming, Elaine, 107
Cumming, Ian, 107
Curtis, E. V., 232
Cutting, Bill "the Butcher," 26

Dai, Mengyan, 249
Daley, Richard, 140
Daraki-Mallet, M., 156
Davis, Kenneth C., 10, 91, 170
Dayan, Kobi, 253
Decisso, David A., 253
Dee, J. L., 43
DeJong, Christina, 111
Deming, W. Edwards, 198
DeNiro, Robert, 42
Dennis, Norman, 11
Diallo, Amadou, 205
Diaz, Cameron, 26

DiCaprio, Leonardo, 26
Dieckman, D., 31, 109
Dobrin, Adam, 45
Downs, Raymond L., 179
Drucker, Peter, 197
Dukes, R. L., 70
Dunham, R. G., 151
Durose, Matthew R., 152

Eastwood, Clint, 94
Eck, John E., 81, 120
Edell, Laura, 107
Edwards, Steven M., 181
Ekblom, P., 107, 123
Ellis, Tom, 69
Engel, Robin Shepard, 98
Ericson, Richard, 66, 78, 80, 107

Fajardo, R. G., 140
Farmer, D. J., 81
Feld, B. C., 154, 155
Ferrara, A., 110
Feuiile, Peter, 231
Fink, Stephen, 161
Fishman, Mark, 66
Flanagan, Timothy J., 153
Fogelson, Robert M., 25, 133
Foster, Raymond E., 179
Fox, Shaul, 253
Frank, James, 211
Fridell, Lorie, 151, 158
Friedrich, Robert J., 107
Fyfe, J., 120, 157, 158, 160,
     246, 257, 259

Gammage, Allen Z., 231
Gamson, William A., 153
Gardiner, John A., 61
Garner, Gerald W., 64, 162
Garner, Joel, 46–47
Gates, Darryl, 69
Geller, William A., 158,
     210–211, 212, 215, 216
Gelles, Richard J., 96
Glantz, J., 277
Goldkamp, John S., 120

Goldman, Ron, 9
Goldschlag, William, 200
Goldstein, Herman, 7, 10, 16,
     32, 91, 120, 122, 168
Grant, Alan, 183
Gray, M. Kevin, 111
Green-Mazerolle, Lorraine, 120
Greenspan, R., 201
Greenwood, Peter W., 31, 66,
     78, 80, 81
Gunaratna, R., 277
Guyot, Dorthy, 199

Haberfield, Maki, 255, 271
Hagedorn, R., 47
Haley, K., 255
Hanewicz, W. B., 59
Hanley, Dena E., 153
Haritos-Fatouros, M., 156
Harnett, Susan M., 122
Hartmann, Francis X., 34
Hawkins, Carl W., 221, 225
Heal, K., 107, 123
Hervey, Juris A., 231
Hess, Kären M., 75, 194, 268
Hickman, Matthew J., 14, 232
Holmes, Stephen, 153
Home Affairs Committee, 157
Hoover, Herbert, 29
Horvath, F., 158, 252
Hudson, James R., 160, 165
Hughes, William, 216

Inbau, Fred E., 85
Inciardi, J. A., 43

Jakubs, D., 156
Jane, Brian C., 85
Jefferis, Eric S., 153
Johnson, David R., 23
Johnson, James W., 181
Johnson, Lyndon, 6
Johnston, Daryl H., 246, 254

Kaminski, Robert J., 153, 181
Kanable, Rebecca, 69

Kania, Richard R. E., 155
Kappeler, Victor E., 41, 43, 44,
     45, 46, 47, 48, 136
Kaskinsky, Rene G., 43
Kasten, Rohen, 253
Katz, Charles M., 44, 197, 257
Keitel, Harvey, 42
Kelling, George, 23, 26, 31, 32,
     34, 35, 109, 110
Kelly, Raymond, 205, 210
Kennedy, David, 120
Kenney, Dennis J., 151
King, Rodney, 32, 149
Klockars, Carl B., 65, 122,
     123, 125
Koenig, Daniel J., 153
Koons, Stacey, 149
Krane, D. A., 156
Kraska, Peter, 48
Kuykendall, Jack, 3, 7, 8, 10,
     11, 12, 13, 14, 16, 24, 25,
     26, 27, 28, 29, 33, 57, 58,
     59, 60, 75, 76, 77, 80, 92,
     94, 95, 106, 107, 108,
     132, 133, 135, 137,
     165, 193

Labovitz, S., 47
Langan, Patrick A., 152
Langton, Lynn, 248
Langworthy, Robert H., 84
Lanza-Kaduce, Lonn, 246,
     254, 255
Lasley, J. R., 153
Lefkowitz, Joel, 245
Leighton, Barry N., 64
Leishman, F., 43
Leo, Richard, 85
Lester, David, 153
Leuci, Robert (Bob), 140
Leukefeld, Carl, 70
Levi, Margaret, 231
Levy, Chandra, 82
Lewis, Daniel Day, 26
Lindsay, Vicki, 48
Linn, Edith, 92

Liotta, Ray, 42
Lipsky, Michael, 159
Lipton, E., 277
Loftin, Colin, 45
Logan, T. K., 70
Lombardi, Frank, 200
Lorence, J., 110
Louima, Abner, 205
Lumet, Sidney, 140
Lundman, Richard J., 107
Lynam, Donald R., 70

Maas, Peter, 141
Mackay, Wade C., 155
Maffe, Steven R., 69
Mangold, James, 42
Manheim, J. B., 41
Manning, Peter K., 63, 78, 122, 123, 124, 154, 164, 212
Maple, Jack, 200, 201, 205
Marenin, Otwin, 7
Marshall, J. R., 266
Martin, Catherine, 70
Martin, Susan E., 248
Martin, William "Billy," 82
Marx, G. T., 83, 157, 160
Marzulli, John, 200, 201
Mason, P., 43
Mason, T. David, 156
Mastrofski, Stephen W., 111, 140, 201
McAlary, Mike, 142
McArdle, Andrea, 210, 212
McCabe, K. A., 140
McCabe, S., 91
McCarthy, Bernard J., 131
McDonald, Phyllis, 200
McDowall, David, 45
McEvoy, James, 153
McNally, A. M., 201
Meagher, M. Steven, 245
Meier, Cecil A., 122
Mendelsohn, Harold, 118, 119
Milich, Richard, 70
Miligram, S., 156
Monkkonen, Eric H., 25

Moodie, P., 165
Moore, Mark H., 23, 26
Moose, Charles, 196
Morgan, Rod, 123
Morris, Norval, 210–211, 212, 215, 216
Muir, W. Jr., 94, 95
Murphy, Dan W., 211
Murphy, Patrick V., 134, 162
Mustain, Gene, 200, 201

National Advisory Commission on Civil Disorders, 6, 154
National Commission on Law Observance and Enforcement, 154
National Commission on the Causes and Prevention of Violence, 154
National Law Enforcement and Corrections Technology Center, 151
Naylor, T., 107
Newfield, Jack, 137
Niederhoffer, Arthur, 59–60, 161, 197
Novak, Kenneth J., 211
Novak, Scott P., 70
Nowicki, E., 181

Oliver, Willard M., 122
Ortmeier, J. P., 257

Parent, Dale, 211
Parker, William, 244
Parks, B., 111
Parks, Roger, 111
Pate, Anthony, 110, 247
Pate, Tony, 31, 109
Payne, C., 107
Peek-Asa, C., 266
Peel, Sir Robert, 11, 24
Pepinsky, H., 107
Pepper, J. V., 68
Perlmutter, D., 43
Peters, Thomas J., 196–197

Petersilia, Joan, 31, 66, 78, 80, 81
Peterson, Laci, 82
Peterson, Scott, 82
Petrie, Carol, 68
Piquero, Alex, 120
Piquero, Nicole Leeper, 120
Pollard, Charles, 202, 203
Poulantzas, Nicos, 11
Powell, Laurence, 149
President's Commission on Law Enforcement and Administration of Justice, 6
Przybylski, Roger, 204
Punch, M., 107

Radalet, Louis A., 62, 66, 115, 116, 118, 119, 120, 162
Raub, R., 48
Raza, Susan M., 245
Reaves, Brian A., 14, 232
Reeve, Simon, 277
Regoli, Robert M., 60
Reid, John E., 85
Reiner, Robert, 162
Reiss, Al, 111
Reiss, Albert J., 48, 107, 154
Reuss-Ianni, Elizabeth, 193
Rich, R. C., 41
Richardson, James F., 23
Roberg, Roy, 3, 7, 8, 10, 11, 12, 13, 14, 16, 24, 25, 26, 27, 28, 29, 33, 57, 58, 59, 60, 75, 76, 77, 80, 92, 94, 95, 106, 107, 108, 132, 133, 135, 137, 165, 193
Rosenbaum, D., 70
Rosett, Arthur, 10, 91
Ross, Jeffrey Ian, 33, 63, 70, 123, 126, 142, 149, 150, 162, 165, 249, 275, 276, 277, 278
Rossmo, D. Kim, 85
Rousseau, Jean Jacques, 7, 8

Sachs, Stanley L., 231
Salameh, Mohammed, 277

Sanders, N., 66, 78
Scarborough, Kathryn, 115, 223
Scharf, Peter, 158
Schmalleger, Frank, 86, 249, 280
Schultz, Dorothy Moses, 248
Scorsese, Martin, 26
Scott, Robert F., 214, 215, 216
Serpico, Frank, 141, 143
Seyle, Hans, 267, 268
Shapiro, Robert, 9
Shelly, Kyna, 48
Sherman, Lawrence W., 110, 138, 157, 160, 164, 165, 170, 280
Shriver, Robert Sargent, 246
Simpson, Nicole Brown, 9
Simpson, O. J., 9
Singh, B. K., 153
Skogan, Wesley, 122
Skolnick, Jerome H., 78, 92, 122, 123, 246, 257, 259
Slater, Joseph, 232
Sluder, Richard D., 41, 43, 44, 45, 46, 47, 48, 136
Smith, Brad W., 211
Smith, D., 123
Smith, Erica L., 152
Smith, W. C., 151
Snortum, John R., 80, 81
Snyder, B., 211
Souryal, Sam, 63
Special Counsel to the Los Angeles Sheriff's Department, 197
Spellman, W., 120
Stallone, Sylvester, 41
Stamper, Norm, 196
Stark, Rodney, 154, 165
Steele, M., 123
Stein, J. A., 70
Stephens, Darryl, 122–123
Stevens, Dennis J., 26, 46, 48, 58, 71, 81, 84, 85, 87, 95, 111, 142, 182, 193, 197, 198, 209, 213, 239, 245, 246, 253, 268, 269, 270

Stotland, Ezra, 267
Stroshine, Meghan S., 266
Sutcliffe, F., 91
Swanson, Charles R., 30, 120, 168, 195, 196, 217, 222, 223, 224, 225, 232, 233, 234, 235, 236, 237, 238, 245, 250, 252, 253
Sykes, Richard E., 107

Tadded, Kenneth, 161
Taylor, Robert W., 30, 120, 168, 195, 196, 217, 222, 223, 224, 225, 232, 233, 234, 235, 236, 237, 238, 245, 250, 252, 253
Taylor, William Banks, 48
Terrill, William, 120
Territo, Leonard, 30, 120, 168, 195, 196, 217, 222, 223, 224, 225, 232, 233, 234, 235, 236, 237, 238, 245, 250, 252, 253
Thibault, Edward A., 256
Thomas, Charles W., 153
Tien, James M., 110
Tifft, Larry L., 59, 160, 165
Torrance, Judy, 150
Travis, Lawrence F., 211
Trojanowicz, R., 123
Trojanowicz, S., 123
Tuch, Steven A., 153
Tulley, Tracey, 202
Turque, B., 64, 66
Tweed, William "Boss," 26

U.S. Bureau of Justice Statistics, 222
U.S. Crime Commission, 6
U.S. Task Force Report, 209
Uchida, Craig D., 24, 25
Ullman, J. B., 70

Vaughn, Michael S., 153
Vena, J. E., 266
Vilke, Gary M., 181

Violanti, John M., 266
Vollmer, August, 29, 244

Walden, Katherine P., 70
Walker, Samuel, 44, 154, 197, 257, 263, 264
Watchorn, D. J., 165
Waterman, Robert H. Jr., 196–197
Waters, Ethan, 184
Watson, Goodwin, 161
Weatheritt, M., 123
Weiler, P. C., 170
Weinblatt, Richard B., 69
Weisburd, David, 110, 201
Weitzer, Ronald, 153
Welford, Charles, 68
Westley, William A., 153, 154
White, Michael D., 77, 78, 86, 87, 95, 96, 98, 106, 112, 120, 121, 122, 135, 136, 139, 152, 181, 197, 199, 201, 202, 205, 226, 227, 244, 246, 247, 250, 252, 253, 255, 257, 258, 271, 279
White, Susan O., 165
Wiersema, Brian, 45
Williams, Gregory H., 91
Williams, J. Sherwood, 153
Williams, Willy, 6, 31
Willis, J. J., 201
Willman, Mark T., 80, 81
Wilson, James Q., 32, 34, 35, 61, 78, 110
Wilson, Orlando W., 6, 29, 244
Worden, Robert, 111
Worral, John L., 86, 211, 249, 280
Wrobleski, Henry W., 75, 268

Yentes, Nancy M., 245
Yousef, Ramzi, 277

Zimmerman, Rick, 70